2
7 50

THE TEACHING OF READING

A Developmental Process

THE TEACHING OF READING

A DEVELOPMENTAL PROCESS

PAUL A. WITTY
Professor of Education, Northwestern University

ALMA MOORE FREELAND
Associate Professor of Elementary Education, University of Texas

EDITH H. GROTBERG
Associate Professor of Education, The American University

D. C. HEATH AND COMPANY   BOSTON

372.414
W788t
1966

Library of Congress Catalog Card Number: 66–18437

COPYRIGHT © 1966 BY D. C. HEATH AND COMPANY

No part of the material covered by this copyright may be reproduced in any form without written permission of the publisher.

Printed in the United States of America.

Printed November 1967

ENGLEWOOD CHICAGO SAN FRANCISCO ATLANTA DALLAS

Preface

THIS BOOK, *The Teaching of Reading—A Developmental Process,* has been planned and written from the developmental point of view. Accordingly, reading instruction is looked upon as continuous, extending throughout the elementary and secondary school and into college and adult life.

In recent years, many developments have transpired in the area of reading instruction. One of these is the increased acceptance of the role of interest as a factor in motivating effective reading. In this book the results of research and study by the senior author and his co-authors are presented and related to classroom instruction in reading. Investigations by other scholars in reading and allied areas are also described and related to the reading process. These studies include the importance of recent innovations, such as television and other mass media which have influenced our culture deeply. The impact of these influences is fully recognized in this book, and suggestions are made for using interests constructively.

Another strong influence on effective reading instruction is found in the current emphasis upon developmental needs or "tasks" in education. Throughout this book ways of meeting needs through reading are suggested. Illustrations of need fulfillment are drawn from the work at the Psycho-Educational Clinic of Northwestern University, under the direction of the senior author, and from related endeavors by the co-authors in other educational projects. At each level, suggestions are made to the teacher for the identification of pupils' needs and provisions for their fulfillment.

Much of the discussion in the chapters treating the teaching of reading from the primary grades throughout college is associated with practices developed and supervised by the authors in Illinois, Texas, and the District of Columbia schools. Throughout the book, emphasis is placed on reading instruction as a sequential process associated with interest and need, and related closely to the other language arts. Stressed also is the significant work of classroom teachers who have experimented with individualized instruction and other innovations.

In chapters 1 through 7, the developmental approach to reading instruction is presented and related to the other language arts — speaking, writing, and listening — through the medium of the pupils' interests and needs. Chapters 8 through 12 include descriptions of developmental reading programs from the primary grade level through the college and adult levels. Remedial instruction is treated in Chapter 13. Chapters 14 and 15 are concerned with the teaching of reading to exceptional children. Special attention is also given to the development of challenging reading programs for superior and gifted pupils. Chapters 16 and 17 are devoted to the role of the teacher in reading instruction and to the nature of a program which evaluates pupil development.

The authors wish to express their appreciation to the writers and publishers of professional books and magazine articles who have permitted them to quote from their works.

The obligations of the authors are great to their colleagues who have contributed to the developmental approach to reading. The authors are especially indebted to Professor A. I. Gates for his leadership and inspiration. They are grateful to the Graduate School of Northwestern University for the support given to a number of research projects described in this book. The authors further wish to acknowledge the generous cooperation of school administrators and teachers who have worked with them.

Finally, appreciation is expressed to Ann Bowman and Robert Fuller of D. C. Heath and Company, and to Ann Coomer, research assistant to Dr. Witty, for help in the preparation of the manuscript.

PAUL A. WITTY
ALMA MOORE FREELAND
EDITH H. GROTBERG

Contents

1. **THE EVOLUTION OF DEVELOPMENTAL READING INSTRUCTION** 1

    The Need for Effective Reading Instruction   2
    The Developmental Reading Program   7
    Concluding Statement   11

2. **READING INSTRUCTION—PAST AND PRESENT**   14

    Development of the Reading Textbook   24
    Characteristics of an Effective Reading Program   29
    Concluding Statement   35

3. **THE ROLE OF INTEREST**   37

    Interests of Children and Adolescents   42
    Application of Pupil Interest in Classroom Practice   52
    Concluding Statement   56

4. **THE ROLE OF DEVELOPMENTAL NEEDS**   59

    The Identification of Developmental Needs   60
    Developmental Needs and the Reading Process   65
    Concluding Statement   72

5. **READINESS FOR EFFECTIVE READING**   75

    Basic Concepts of Reading Readiness   75
    The Factors of Reading Readiness   78
    Determining Reading Readiness   83
    Experiences in a Readiness Program   89
    Readiness Activities for Different Grades   95
    Concluding Statement   95

6. **WORD RECOGNITION AND VOCABULARY DEVELOPMENT**   101

    Word Identification   101
    Word Interpretation   109
    Improving Readability of Printed Materials   118
    Concluding Statement   123

7. **LITERATURE FOR CHILDREN AND YOUNG PEOPLE** 127

    Recommended Literary Materials 132
    Experiences and Activities Associated with Books 145
    Evaluating the Literature Program 149
    Concluding Statement 155

8. **THE ROLE OF LANGUAGE DEVELOPMENT** 158

    Speaking and Reading 162
    Listening and Reading 165
    Writing and Reading 174
    Concluding Statement 176

9. **READING INSTRUCTION IN THE PRIMARY GRADES** 180

    Experience Chart—Basal Reading Approach 181
    New Approaches 200
    Concluding Statement 210

10. **READING INSTRUCTION IN THE INTERMEDIATE GRADES** 213

    Reading Habits and Skills for the Intermediate Grades 215
    Reading in the Content Fields 226
    Materials and Resources for Reading 229
    Evaluative Procedures in the Middle Grades 233
    The Importance of Developmental Needs and Tasks 234
    Concluding Statement 239

11. **READING INSTRUCTION IN JUNIOR AND SENIOR HIGH SCHOOL** 242

    Need for Developmental Reading Programs 243
    The Developmental Program 246
    Determining Pupil Needs 251
    Materials of Instruction 256
    Evaluating Growth in and Through Reading 260
    Concluding Statement 262

12. **READING INSTRUCTION FOR COLLEGE STUDENTS AND ADULTS** 265

    The Changing Role of College and Adult Reading 267
    Developmental Reading for the College Student and Adult 269
    Reading Instruction for the Educationally
       Retarded and the Disadvantaged 275
    Concluding Statement 285

13. REMEDIAL READING   289

   The Retarded Reader   290
   Diagnosis of Reading Disability   300
   Remedial Reading Practices and Programs   313
   Concluding Statement   317

14. READING INSTRUCTION FOR THE SLOW-LEARNING PUPIL   320

   Diagnosis of Each Child's Needs   323
   Factors in Teaching the Slow-Learner   326
   Curriculum Principles   330
   Concluding Statement   334

15. READING PROGRAMS FOR THE GIFTED   337

   The Identification of the Gifted   338
   Guiding the Reading of the Verbally Gifted   341
   A Case Study of a Verbally Gifted Child   349
   Concluding Statement   353

16. THE ROLE OF THE TEACHER   356

   Desirable Personal Assets for Teaching Reading   357
   Professional Qualifications for Teaching   362
   Concluding Statement   370

17. EVALUATION OF DEVELOPMENT IN READING   373

   Essential Factors in Evaluation   373
   Evaluation Procedures   376
   Concluding Statement   395

Index   413

THE TEACHING OF READING

A Developmental Process

I

THE EVOLUTION OF DEVELOPMENTAL READING INSTRUCTION

> Reading is an adventure, when you go with the poets into the realm of fancy and imagination; you see life with the novelist; you go down to the sea in ships and unto the ends of the earth with the great explorers; the scientist takes you into his laboratory; in biography you are let into the mystery of men's lives; the historian reconstructs the past and gives you glimpses of the future, and the philosopher gives you a glimpse of his wisdom.
>
> —From *The Pleasures of Reading*
> by Holbrook Jackson

Reading can indeed be a great pleasure. Many of us are not aware of our debt to reading. And many others seem to be unaware of the fact that there is no substitute for reading—either in the particular joy it gives or in its usefulness in providing the information we need and the facts and ideas that make our lives more effective, rewarding, and secure. Observe the child of seven who has discovered that he can read and is finding undreamed-of rewards in *Katy-No-Pocket* or *Make Way for Ducklings*. His absorption reflects his interest and his joy. One seven-year-old boy commented in this way about the teacher who helped him learn to read: "When I went to school I couldn't read and I didn't have any friends. She is the best teacher in the world. She taught me to read. Now I have real friends at school and imaginary friends in books. I shall never be lonely again."

Let us look also at Bill, aged ten, who has discovered *Homer Price,* and observe the keen pleasure that reading gives him. Looking up from this exciting book, he inquires: "Do you have any more good books like this?" And there is Susan, who at twelve found *Strawberry*

Girl, and at the same time discovered that reading may provide the avenue for an understanding and appreciation of people. "This book helped me to know how people feel and why they act the way they do," she said.

These children may not always be aware of the fascination or value reading holds for them, but their behavior shows how they react to reading. For them, reading offers an irresistible satisfaction. In "Larval Stage of a Bookworm," a chapter in the book *Happy Days,* H. L. Mencken stated that as a boy, eight or nine years of age, his discovery of Huckleberry Finn was "probably the most stupendous event of my whole life." He appreciated then the excitement of reading and realized that from that time on reading would be a vital part of his life.

THE NEED FOR EFFECTIVE READING INSTRUCTION

The satisfactions in books are available to nearly all children and young people. To realize these satisfactions, they must not only be able to read effectively, but they must also have access to suitable materials. A primary goal of effective reading instruction is to help boys and girls enjoy the act of reading and its results. They will enjoy the act of reading when they have acquired flexible skills which enable them to read widely. They will enjoy the results of reading when they encounter materials in various fields that fulfill their interests or meet their needs. It is our hope that this book will help teachers better understand this goal and attain it more successfully.

Some Special Values of Reading

There are some practical reasons for our efforts to help children and youth to learn to read with ease and satisfaction.

1. Effective reading is necessary in order for any person to become well-informed generally and to acquire specific information in many fields. At one time educators stated: first a pupil must learn to read; then he must read to learn. To some degree, this statement is true, but it should be recognized that during the initial stages of learning to read, the pupil should acquire information that makes the process more than merely preparatory for later learning. Learning to read, at all stages, should be regarded as an intelligent act in which meaning is derived from or associated with the printed material. Learning occurs from the beginning, and simultaneously extends and enriches the

experience of boys and girls. Throughout the sequential development of reading skills, there should be a continued acquisition of knowledge. Later the flexible use and application of the fully developed skills should make rapid learning in many areas possible to a greater degree.

2. There is another important value in being able to read proficiently. Through wide reading, one may become a more interesting person; for as Thomas Carlyle stated:

> All that mankind has done, thought, gained, or been; it is lying as in magic preservation in the pages of books.

A person who reads widely has much to say that is interesting to others. He is also able to share his interests and to contribute to discussions and conversations. He is, therefore, likely to be welcomed as a friend, and esteemed as an individual.

3. Another reason for learning to read effectively is that success in school depends to a large degree on rapid, skillful reading. Silent reading skills are required in a high percentage of schoolwork assignments of various kinds. Courses in English, social studies, science, and mathematics, for example, require a student to spend much time applying study skills in reading textbooks, references, and related materials. Hence, skillful reading and academic success tend to go hand in hand. Good students are usually good readers, and good readers are usually good students.

4. Effective reading will help most people prepare for and make progress in their work, for today most jobs require skill in reading. Of course we should recognize the fact that the demands of different jobs vary widely; however, in most of them it is necessary for the worker to read a variety of printed materials in books, magazines, pamphlets, and newspapers. The jobs may require, too, the reading of letters and manuals and the use of specialized sources. Initial and continued success in most jobs depends to a considerable degree upon an individual's ability to read quickly, critically, and with a high degree of understanding.

5. Through reading, a pupil may obtain other benefits, too; for as John Masefield said, "The days that make us happy make us wise." This is indeed the case. By reading, a pupil can share in the progress of a nation, the discovery of planets, the invention of a machine, the development of space travel, the conquering of disease. He can live richly in the present age, and he can project himself into the future —dreaming of a world to come. He can go back into almost forgotten centuries and gain greatly in his understanding of the present through an enhanced appreciation of the past. He can travel throughout his

country and the world, becoming acquainted with all kinds of people in amazingly varied places and situations. In addition, he can find answers to many of his questions and solutions to some of his problems in the varied and wonderful world of books. Fortunately, there are books to satisfy almost every taste, interest, mood, or appetite. Another goal of reading instruction is to help pupils gain access to these wonderful treasures.

Need for Improved Skills in Reading

Although few persons would deny the values of reading cited above, far too many children and adults in America are unprepared to realize them fully. Some are handicapped by inadequate skills, and others by unfavorable attitudes and habits.

There are many boys and girls, in fact, who have not acquired effective reading skills. In the middle grades, studies show the presence of large numbers of very poor readers. For example, the reading test results of 2,212 third-grade pupils in one city were studied.[1] According to grade equivalents, 742 made scores which fell between mid-second and mid-third grade standards. The scores of 801 were above and 669 fell below the norm for mid-third grade. The range extended from first-grade to seventh-grade accomplishment among these pupils, all of whom were in third-grade classes.

A wide range in reading ability and the presence of large numbers of poor readers will be found not only in the elementary school but also in classes throughout both the junior and senior high schools. Reading retardation will vary, of course, from community to community and from school to school. Thus it was found that, in one school located in a section of relatively low socioeconomic status within an industrial city, about half of the eighth-grade pupils made scores which fell one year or more below the norms for their grades. In a more prosperous community it was found that, among 518 eighth-grade pupils, only 89 fell at or below the seventh-grade norms.[2]

The wide variation in reading comprehension of high school pupils is dramatically shown in Figure 1 by the distribution of reading scores of over eighteen thousand junior and senior high school pupils.

---

[1] William H. Waite, "The Improvement of Reading in the Omaha Public Schools," *The Elementary School Journal,* 48:306 (February, 1948).

[2] Glenn Myers Blair, *Diagnostic and Remedial Teaching,* rev. ed. (New York: The Macmillan Co., 1956), pp. 5–7.

Figure 1

Distributions of Pupil Total Scaled Scores in Independent Schools Participating in Achievement Testing Program[3]

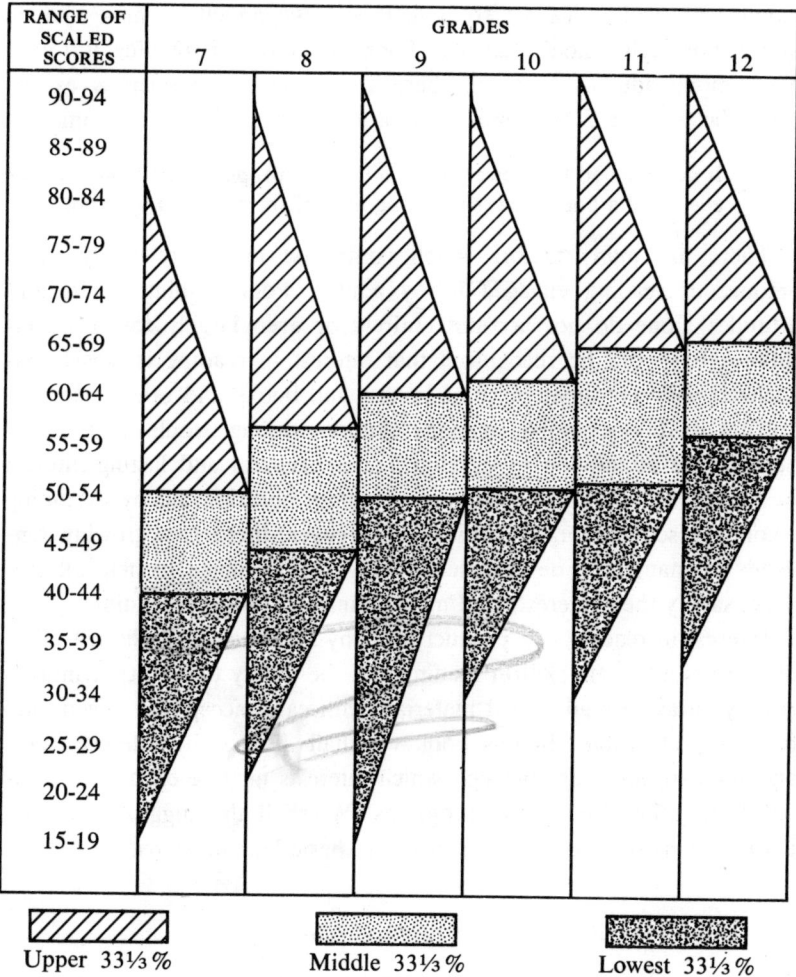

Need for Increased Interest in Reading

Evidence of the need for reading instruction and the encouragement of reading at all school levels is found in the lack of interest displayed by many young people and adults today. It is generally recognized that to cope successfully with occupational and civic demands of

[3] Adapted from Table 4 in *Educational Records Bulletin,* "Achievement Testing Program in Independent Schools and Supplementary Studies," 77:11 (New York: Educational Records Bureau, 1960).

modern life, a tendency to read widely is desirable and necessary. Wide reading is also essential to successful accomplishment in school. Many studies over the past twenty-five years have revealed a relatively small amount of reading (apart from textbook assignments) among junior and senior high school students. Lack of interest in reading is found also among adults. Although there are, of course, numerous exceptions the average adult reads very little. Allan McMahan comments:

> It is estimated that fewer than half of the people in the United States ever read a book; fewer than one fifth of them every buy a book.[4]

There are many factors which contribute to the relatively small amount of reading engaged in by adults. Poor reading habits and attitudes alone do not account entirely or even largely for this condition. It should be recognized that interest in reading is closely associated with the availability of books; and books and other materials are not readily accessible to many children, young people, and adults. Schools are attempting to develop a more general and lasting interest in reading by establishing elementary school libraries and by extending secondary school library facilities. Moreover, there is a growing tendency to inaugurate developmental programs designed to help all students satisfy their interests and meet their needs through reading.

Interest in reading is a product of many factors and conditions. One of these is adequate skill in reading and the ability to adapt techniques readily so as to read varied materials with ease, acceptable speed, and full comprehension. In this book we shall discuss the interest factor and shall suggest ways through which interests may be effectively cultivated and utilized in reading programs. We shall also suggest how reading programs may be designed to satisfy basic human needs.

Need for Effective Reading Programs

Teaching children to read effectively is a major aim of every school system in this country. A continuous, systematic, and balanced reading program is necessary if children and youth are to be taught to read successfully.

A continuous program in reading should begin in the primary grades and continue through the junior and senior high schools. Systematic instruction should occur at each level of a continuous program. In

---

[4] Allan McMahan, "Make Friends with Your Bookseller," in Alfred Stefferud (editor), *The Wonderful World of Books* (New York: New American Library of World Literature, Inc., 1952), p. 226.

discussing reading programs, William S. Gray summarized the research and reflected opinions of most authorities when he stated:

> ... (a) systematic basal instruction makes its greatest contribution in promoting essential understandings, attitudes, and skills in reading; (b) stimulating supplementary reading and activity programs are highly productive in cultivating favorable attitudes toward reading, in deepening reading interest, and in enriching the experiences of children; (c) a sound reading program should make use of the advantages inherent in both systematic instruction in reading and challenging activities in all curriculum fields; (d) the optimum amount of systematic instruction varies with conditions, such as the needs and capacities of children and the skill of the teacher.[5]

Another aspect of reading programs is the provision for aiding the poor reader. There is heartening evidence that, in the case of poor readers, efforts to improve reading ability are often most successful. As early as 1939 there were programs in which the poorest readers in metropolitan elementary and secondary schools made outstanding gains in reading skills during a single semester of remedial instruction.[6]

Despite our recognition of the necessity for corrective work, our chief interest is in the establishment of effective reading programs which will lessen the need for remedial endeavor. In this book we shall describe developmental reading instruction that aims to help all students to make steady progress in the sequential acquisition of reading skills.

THE DEVELOPMENTAL READING PROGRAM

The nature of the reading process requires a systematic and developmental teaching approach. In such a program emphasis should be placed on reading as a meaningful act associated with clearer and more effective communication. This concept of reading is but one among various points of view, as may be readily observed by examining the concepts set forth today by leaders in this field.

What Is Reading?

Definitions of reading ability vary widely. Thus E. A. Betts states:

---

[5] William S. Gray, "Reading," *Encyclopedia of Educational Research* (New York: The Macmillan Co., 1960), p. 1122.

[6] Paul Witty and David Kopel, *Reading and the Educative Process* (Boston: Ginn and Co., 1939).

Reading is a language process rather than a subject. In a psychological sense, reading is a thinking process. In another sense, reading is a "social process" that "relates the reader to his environment, and conditions that relationship." Psychophysiological factors, such as seeing and hearing, also are embraced by an adequate concept of reading as a process.[7]

The many aspects of reading are considered further by Ruth Strang, who concluded:

Reading, broadly speaking, includes several interrelated components. Reading is the visual task of obtaining a clear, unblurred image of the printed words. This visual image must be instantly associated with meaning if a basic sight vocabulary is to be built. Getting the meaning of unfamiliar words requires word-recognition skills, one of which is phonics. Reading for meaning, however, goes far beyond this word-calling stage. Comprehension on several levels requires three abilities: the ability to read the lines and merely repeat what the author says; the ability to read between the lines to interpret and appraise what the author says; and the ability to read beyond the lines to reflect on what the author says, to arrange his ideas into a new pattern, to draw inferences and conclusions. Comprehension is usually accompanied by a feeling response—satisfaction or annoyance, hope or despair, approval or disapproval. . . . The broad view of reading includes recognition of its influence on the reader's point of view, on his attitudes and behavior, and, through these, on his personality and character.[8]

There are, of course, many other definitions and concepts of reading. We shall in this book think of reading as a process involving meaningful reaction to printed symbols. We shall recognize the fact that reading is both silent and oral, that the pupil's response is determined not only by the printed symbol itself, but also by his own nature and needs, which influence his reaction and color his interpretation. With this concept of reading in mind, we shall devote special consideration to reading in accord with different purposes as well as to reading designed to satisfy interests and fulfill needs.

Characteristics of Developmental Programs

The foregoing attitude toward the nature and goals of effective reading instruction is increasingly endorsed by scholars in psychology

---

[7] Emmett A. Betts, *Foundations of Reading Instruction* (New York: American Book Co., 1957), p. 70.

[8] Ruth Strang, "Controversial Programs and Procedures in Reading," *The School Review*, 69:413–414 (Winter, 1961).

and education. Some emphasize the role of semantics; others stress structural linguistics. But there is a greatly increased tendency to accept the developmental approach. As Henry P. Smith and Emerald V. Dechant point out, "Only within the past twenty years has our emphasis been on developmental reading programs." Such programs, according to these authors, have the following characteristics:

> *First,* the developmental program recognizes that reading is an integral part of the much broader educational program. Reading shares the responsibility for communicative development with the other linguistic and artistic activities. It is a program in which parents, teacher, pupils, and administrators have a positive concern. It is flexible, continuous, and comprehensive. It encompasses diagnosis and remediation.
>
> *Second,* the developmental reading program is distinguished from the reading program of the past in that it is concerned with every pupil and continues from elementary through high school years. It is vitally concerned with maintaining maximum progress for the average, the slow, and the gifted learner and with locating and correcting the special problems of the retarded reader. . . .
>
> *Third,* the developmental program focuses on individual needs and individual differences. Reading experiences and pupil progress are not dictated by a calendar. Grade-limits disappear and mass instruction in reading is replaced by an emphasis on pupil needs. It begins at each learner's current level and attempts to lead him at his own success rate to his maximum achievement.
>
> *Fourth,* the developmental program helps the child to fulfill his developmental needs and tasks as they appear. In our reading program we recognize that, because the child is a developing organism, we must adjust our instruction to his developmental needs. We try to identify the most teachable moment for each specific reading skill. A child should not be rushed into walking; neither can we successfully rush him into reading. However, we can help him to become ready.
>
> *Fifth,* the developmental program provides the child with the opportunities to learn skills needed to satisfy his needs for reading, as he advances through school . . . .
>
> *Sixth,* the developmental program satisfies, extends, and enriches the child's interests. Indeed, to be successful, the reading program must be based on pupil interest.[9]

Basic Principles of Developmental Programs

In order to develop any pattern of instruction it is necessary to identify our aims or goals. The general aims of reading common to

---

[9] Henry P. Smith and Emerald V. Dechant, *Psychology in Teaching Reading* (Englewood Cliffs, N.J.: Prentice-Hall, Inc., 1961), pp. 378–379.

all stages are: (1) To develop a permanent interest in reading; (2) to extend and enrich the experience of the reader; (3) to develop standards of appreciation in reading; (4) to provide recreation and pleasure by reading; (5) to develop abilities and skills in reading; and (6) to promote critical thinking on the part of the reader.

The general nature of these goals makes it difficult for teachers to formulate effective programs of instruction. Smith and Dechant stress the following basic principles to help teachers and supervisors make the developmental program effective:

1. The developmental program must be an all-school program directed toward carefully identified educational goals. It must receive the support and cooperation of the entire school staff.
2. The developmental program must be concerned with the social and personal development of each student as well as his growth in the skills, understandings, and attitudes necessary for successful reading.
3. The developmental program coordinates reading with the pupil's other communicative experiences.
4. The developmental program must be a continuous program extending through the elementary and secondary grades and college. It must provide instruction and guidance in basic reading skills, in content-area reading, in study-skills, and in recreational reading.
5. The developmental program must be a flexible program that is adjusted at each level of advancement to the wide variations in student characteristics, abilities, and reading needs.
6. The developmental program must have a stimulating classroom setting in which attitudes, interests and abilities are developed effectively.
7. The developmental program must provide plentiful reading materials that cover a wide range of difficulty and interest.
8. The developmental program must include continuous measurement and evaluation of the effectiveness of the program as a whole and of its more specific aspects.
9. The developmental program must provide for continuous identification and immediate remediation of deficiencies and difficulties encountered by any student.
10. The developmental program must include differentiated instruction to meet the needs of each child, but it cannot ignore the commonality of needs, interests, and abilities among children.
11. The developmental program must look upon reading as a process rather than as a subject. Reading is taught on all levels in all subject areas by all teachers.
12. The developmental program must emphasize reading for understanding and aim to develop flexibility in comprehension and

rate in accordance with the student's abilities and purposes and the difficulty levels of the materials.
13. The developmental program must allow each student to progress at his own success rate to his maximum capacity.
14. The developmental program must seek to develop reading maturity. A mature reader reads all kinds of materials. He perceives words quickly and accurately and reacts with correct meaning. He reads both for information and recreation.[10]

CONCLUDING STATEMENT

The teaching of reading, like education itself, is regarded by many educators as a process in which the maximum development of every boy and girl is sought according to his unique nature and needs. The trend at present is to treat reading as one aspect of a language-arts program and to utilize methods of teaching which are consonant with this objective. Above all else, meaningful reading is accorded primary importance. To be meaningful in a full sense, reading material must not only be understood and assimilated, but its content must also be interpreted and evaluated. The pupil's reaction to the facts and ideas presented is viewed as a significant feature of his reading. Thus meaningful reading stresses not only the pupil's understanding and clear comprehension of different types of material, but also his ability to interpret, select, and apply facts or ideas according to his needs and purposes for reading.

Although the details of a developmental reading program may differ, the following delineation encompasses the main points:

1. A developmental reading program is continuous. It aims to cultivate mastery of skills needed in effective silent and oral reading at different levels. Moreover, it recognizes the significance of the sequential development of skills and attitudes. Accordingly, instruction and guidance in reading are given from the primary grades throughout the junior and senior high schools and in college as well as in adult life, when individual or group acquisitions are found to be inadequate.
2. Developmental reading approaches take into account various needs for reading. Some needs relate to common attainments; others are highly personal but nonetheless significant for individual welfare. Some needs are temporary, whereas others may constitute a basis for long-range planning. In such a program, needs are evaluated and provision is continuously made for their fulfillment. Experi-

---

[10] Henry P. Smith and Emerald V. Dechant, *op. cit.*, pp. 379–380.

ence in reading is recognized as an effective means of need fulfillment.
3. Developmental reading instruction recognizes the importance of the interests of children and youth in the cultivation of reading skills and attitudes.
4. Developmental reading programs utilize experiences and activities operating in association with reading; they do not rely on reading as the sole basis for satisfying needs and interests. Adequate satisfaction implies an effective relationship of reading to other experiences in the individual's total life pattern.
5. A developmental program is geared closely to other aspects of language-arts instruction.[11]

Thus, a developmental program points up the values of continuous, systematic instruction, the utilization of interests, the fulfillment of developmental needs, and the relationship of experience in reading to other types of worthwhile activity. In this way, steady growth in reading skills is made possible, and the attainment of basic human satisfactions is facilitated. At the same time, the maximum growth of the individual, according to his unique nature, is fostered.

Perhaps the greatest problem in offering effective instruction in the modern school grows out of the range of individual abilities within classes, and the varied purposes for which pupils must read. This problem is reflected by the serious reading retardation of many pupils in the middle grades of the elementary school. In the junior and senior high schools, too, reading retardation is frequent and serious. To meet this problem we shall have to provide remedial and corrective reading. But we have an additional obligation, namely, to teach reading to all children and youth so effectively that remedial reading will be unnecessary or rarely needed in future years. We must give every pupil an opportunity to learn to read with ease, effectiveness, and pleasure. In order to take their places as worthy citizens of tomorrow, pupils in our schools today must also be led to comprehend and to evaluate the facts presented in varied printed forms. Moreover, this effort should be looked upon as part of a larger program in communication that leads children and youth to speak clearly, to write effectively, and to listen intelligently. Through such an approach it is possible to equip young people more adequately for responsible citizenship.

---

[11] Adapted from Chapter 1, Paul Witty (chairman), *Development In and Through Reading* (Sixtieth Yearbook of the National Society for the Study of Education, Part I. Chicago: University of Chicago Press, 1961).

Selected References

Anderson, Irving H. and Walter F. Dearborn, *The Psychology of Teaching Reading* (New York: The Ronald Press Company, 1952).

Barbe, Walter B., *Teaching Reading: Selected Materials* (New York: Oxford University Press, 1965).

Betts, Emmett A., *Foundations of Reading Instruction* (New York: American Book Company, 1957).

Bond, Guy L. and Eva B. Wagner, *Teaching the Child to Read,* rev. ed. (New York: The Macmillan Company, 1950).

DeBoer, John J. and Martha Dallmann, *The Teaching of Reading* (New York: Holt, Rinehart & Winston, Inc., 1964).

Gray, Lillian and Dora Reese, *Teaching Children to Read,* 2nd ed. (New York: The Ronald Press Company, 1957).

Gray, William S. (chairman), "Reading in the High School and College," *The Forty-seventh Yearbook of the National Society for the Study of Education,* Part II (Chicago: University of Chicago Press, 1948).

Hester, Kathleen, *Teaching Every Child to Read* (New York: Harper & Row, Publishers, 1964).

Hildreth, Gertrude H., *Teaching Reading* (New York: Holt, Rinehart & Winston, Inc., 1958).

Jennings, Frank G., *This Is Reading* (New York: Bureau of Publications, Teachers College, Columbia University, 1965).

Russell, David H., *Children Learn to Read,* 2nd ed. (Waltham, Mass.: Blaisdell Publishing Company, 1961).

Smith, Henry P. and Emerald V. Dechant, *Psychology in Teaching Reading* (Englewood Cliffs, N. J.: Prentice-Hall, Inc., 1961).

Smith, Nila B., *Reading Instruction for Today's Children* (Englewood Cliffs, N. J.: Prentice-Hall, Inc., 1963).

Strang, Ruth M., *Diagnostic Teaching of Reading* (New York: McGraw-Hill Book Company, Inc., 1964).

Vernon, Magdalon D., *Backwardness in Reading: A Study of Its Nature and Origin* (New York: Cambridge University Press, 1957).

2

READING INSTRUCTION—PAST AND PRESENT

Criticisms of public schools have been widespread since about 1950. Varied factors have prompted critics to compare unfavorably the schools of today with those of the past. Often we have heard generalizations similar to this:

> The schools are no longer teaching the fundamentals. I know a boy thirteen years old in the sixth grade and he cannot read at all. When I was in school, we never had anyone in the sixth grade who could not read.[1]

This type of generalization, based on a single case, is usually unwarranted. Similarly when school surveys of reading attainment have shown a wide range of reading ability within each grade, critics remark that in their own school days all pupils in a certain grade could read at least on that level; they point out, too, that pupils often were not promoted unless they could read the materials of their grade.

When mobilization for a world war occurred and thousands of young men were identified who could not read fourth-grade materials, critics cited this fact as evidence that public schools were failing to do the job they did twenty, thirty, or more years before. Repeatedly since that time, the charge has been voiced.

A strong indictment of reading instruction appeared in two widely discussed books: *Tomorrow's Illiterates,* by Charles C. Walcutt,[2] and *What Ivan Knows That Johnny Doesn't,* by Arthur S. Trace, Jr.[3] These authors deplore the low level of reading attainment among American

---

[1] Cited by Elsa Butcher, "Are Schools Still Teaching Reading?" *Peabody Journal of Education,* 28:99–103 (September, 1950).

[2] Charles C. Walcutt (editor), *Tomorrow's Illiterates: The State of Reading Instruction Today* (Boston: Little, Brown and Company, 1961).

[3] Arthur S. Trace, Jr., *What Ivan Knows That Johnny Doesn't* (New York: Random House, Inc., 1961).

children and youth. In a review of *Tomorrow's Illiterates* which appeared in *Newsweek* of November 13, 1961, it was stated:

> If there's anything guaranteed to rouse the fears of the modern parent, it's an article or book which sweepingly insists that American children are growing up unable to read. . . . Professor Charles C. Walcutt and six associates estimate that three out of four young Americans are not reading as well as they should or could.
> Without citing any statistical sources for this estimate, Walcutt . . . blames the situation on the "word recognition" method of reading instruction.[4]

Perhaps Walcutt's statements have some validity in those few schools that rely solely on word recognition techniques. The majority of children today, however, are being taught to read with a variety of methods and materials.

Studies of Reading Achievement Then and Now

Let us examine comparative studies of reading attainment to determine the validity of the criticisms and the status of reading achievement among pupils today.

In 1948, Judith L. Krugman and J. Wayne Wrightstone reported some results of a city-wide testing program. Tests were administered to pupils in the sixth and eighth grades during the years from 1935 to 1941. After comparing test results, Krugman and Wrightstone conclude:

> Certainly there is no evidence in these results to substantiate the claim that reading has become poorer. Nor can we state that the reading level has improved. Though averages do not by any means give a full picture, they do at least reflect the general trends and the trend here shows that the reading level has remained about the same, that it has fluctuated close to the national norm, tending generally to be slightly above that norm.[5]

To make a more valid comparison of reading attainment at different times it is necessary to employ the same tests. There are several studies in which the same tests have been used for this purpose. Most of these studies reveal superiority for pupils taught in more recent times. For example, in 1949, Ernest W. Tiegs reported a comparison of achievement as shown by the reading scores of approximately 230,000 elementary school pupils on the Stanford and the Progressive Achievement

---

[4] *Newsweek*, 58:90 (No. 20, November 13, 1961).
[5] Judith L. Krugman and J. Wayne Wrightstone, "Reading: Then and Now," *High Points*, 20:59 (April, 1948).

Tests given before and after 1945. These pupils represented sixty communities distributed throughout seven states. Tiegs concluded:

> The achievement of public school pupils is not falling; in fact the data show a slight though probably not statistically significant gain in achievement.[6]

In 1956, George D. Spache[7] reviewed twelve comparative studies in reading achievement that covered a span of over one hundred years. Eleven of the studies indicated that modern-day pupils are superior in many aspects of reading.

It should be pointed out that the above results, although constituting clear refutation of the indictment of some critics, are by no means indicative of a really satisfactory or commendable status in reading attainment today. Most impartial critics would probably concur in stressing the fact that in our schools there are far too many poor readers who from year to year make little progress in reading achievement. We should also recognize the fact that superior pupils are far too often insufficiently challenged by the present reading curriculum, and that the abundant and varied reading materials needed for efficient instruction are unavailable in far too many schools. In short, there is still much to be accomplished in improving reading instruction.

Criticisms of Reading Methods

Criticisms of reading have not been restricted to the teaching of reading in general. Numerous criticisms have been directed toward specific methods and practices. One of the most criticized factors has been phonics. Perhaps the most exaggerated position is represented by Rudolph Flesch, who stated: "Teach the child what each letter stands for and he can read."[8] Moreover, Flesch recognized no limitation in the phonic approach—in teaching children to read or in remedial reading. He declared:

> The reading "experts" of course will say that such a program of remedial reading is much too simple. What about Johnny's emotional troubles, what about such nervous habits as reversals, what about

---

[6] Ernest W. Tiegs, "A Comparison of Pupil Achievement in Basic Skills Before and After 1945," *Growing Points in Educational Research* (Washington, D. C.: American Educational Research Association, 1949), pp. 50–57.

[7] George D. Spache, "Are We Teaching Reading?" in Albert J. Harris (editor), *Readings on Reading Instruction* (New York: David McKay Company, Inc., 1963), pp. 25–28.

[8] Rudolph Flesch, *Why Johnny Can't Read* (New York: Harper & Row, Publishers, 1955), p. 3.

correcting his eye movements? But my answer to all of that is phonics. Phonics is the key.[9]

Two other writers have examined current problems a little more realistically, but have arrived at a similar conclusion concerning the role of phonics. It is stated on the book jacket of *Reading: Chaos and Cure* that the authors, Sibyl Terman and C. C. Walcutt, "advocate an application of the phonics method as opposed to the 'reading readiness' and 'word configuration' program now widely in use."[10] These authors also maintain that the teaching of reading is a simple process and that most American children could learn to read in a few weeks or months at the age of five.

The aforementioned critics appear to be interested mainly in mere pronunciation of words. They seem to have a limited appreciation of reading as an intelligent, meaningful act through which thinking is promoted. Certainly pronunciation without understanding is not the aim of modern reading instruction, nor is meaningless pronunciation regarded as reading. Reading is considered to be a thinking process through which meaning is obtained from printed symbols. It is recognized that we do not get the meaning of a word, invariably or even generally, merely from its spelling or its pronunciation. Failure to obtain meaning is considered by most educators the most significant and unfortunate outcome of faulty or inadequate reading instruction. The child who is not encouraged to find appropriate meanings in various ways, such as by examining the context, is not being taught to read effectively. Rather, he may be engaged merely in a parrotlike routine exercise.

Some critics ignore or ridicule much that experimentation has divulged in the past twenty or thirty years about child growth and development in relation to effective instruction in reading. For example, they categorically deny that there is such a thing as readiness for the various steps in the process of learning to read. They discount, too, the importance of the interest factor and of goals, purposes, and needs in the reading program.

Evidence from research clearly indicates that teaching reading through a heavy phonics program does not always bring about greater reading skill. A significant early study by Arthur I. Gates and David H. Russell[11] was conducted with three groups of pupils. Group D received

---

[9] *Ibid.*, p. 116.

[10] Quote is from the book jacket, Sibyl Terman and C. C. Walcutt, *Reading: Chaos and Cure* (New York: McGraw-Hill Book Company, Inc., 1958).

[11] Arthur I. Gates and David H. Russell, "Types of Materials, Vocabulary Burden, Word Analysis, and Other Factors in Beginning Reading," *Elementary School Journal*, 39:27–35 and 119–28 (September and October, 1938).

a small amount of phonics; Group E was given moderate amounts of informal, newer-type word analysis, comparisons and the like; Group F received a large amount of conventional phonics instruction. Group E, who were given moderate amounts of informal, newer-type word analysis work, exceeded those in the other two groups in all tests of word recognition and comprehension.

Criticisms assume various guises. A few advocates of specific procedures such as phonic instruction also recognize the possibility that other factors may cause or contribute to poor reading. For example, Glenn McCracken has some reservations about the complete adequacy of phonic approaches. He recommends that interest should come first:

> I do not agree with Dr. Flesch, however, that phonics constitutes the only important teaching technique necessary for producing superior readers. The maintenance of interest must always come first. If interest is low, success will be lower. Particularly among slower learners better results will accompany accelerated interest.[12]

We should like to stress the fact that "accelerated interest" also will foster learning among average and rapid learners. It is also important to comment that criticism was in part justified by the neglect of phonics in some schools.

Another criticism that may be somewhat justified concerns oral reading. Henry P. Smith and Emerald V. Dechant state: "Studies have indicated that the young people of today are not as proficient in oral reading as those of thirty years ago."[13] Here again we see the effects of the abandonment of appropriate emphasis on one factor in reading instruction.

At one time oral reading was the sole method of teaching reading. The emphasis on meaning and individualization of the reading process caused a shift to silent reading. The change found many schools abandoning oral reading completely. Somehow, a misinterpretation of principles occurred because few authorities recommended complete reliance upon silent reading. Inconceivable as it may now appear, a group of educators in one city school system at one time sponsored a non-oral reading program.

The amount of oral reading should diminish as one ascends in grades; however, there should still be the teaching of oral reading and the use of oral reading at all grade levels.

---

[12] Glenn McCracken, *The Right to Learn* (Chicago: Henry Regnery & Company, 1959), p. 156.
[13] Henry P. Smith and Emerald V. Dechant, *Psychology in Teaching Reading* (Englewood Cliffs, N.J.: Prentice-Hall, Inc., 1961), p. 185.

Other criticisms have been leveled at the content of basal readers, the use of workbooks, and the preparation of teachers. Instruction in reading must recognize many factors and conditions that prevail throughout the learning and teaching process. As we have pointed out, a developmental reading program recognizes the value of continuous, systematic instruction, utilization of interests, fulfillment of developmental needs, and the articulation of reading experience with instruction in other types of language expression. The chief aim of this reading program is to help pupils become skillful and independent readers. At all stages, reading as a thinking process is emphasized.

It is difficult for many teachers to adopt a consistent approach to reading instruction because of the frequency with which new methods are adopted. Arthur I. Gates states:

> "New" methods of teaching reading are appearing now with unusual frequency. More than a dozen types of phonic training, many varieties of individualized teaching, a host of teaching machines and gadgets, and several augmented alphabets have been recently advocated, some with extraordinary enthusiasm. Several procedures developed in other lands, such as the German "Sprechspur" program, are less well publicized.[14]

We agree with Gates, who stresses the need for welcoming innovations but also the necessity of trying to determine the merits of varied new as well as old approaches. How can we do this? We can of course consider whether an approach conforms with established principles of learning. Again Gates says:

> For example, the practice of providing a substantial amount of individual diagnosis and instruction is grounded in sound psychological principles. The method of beginning reading with an augmented alphabet, on the other hand, is in one respect faulty in principle. One of the soundest principles of psychology is that it is unwise to use a crutch or propaedeutic (that is, to require a person to learn a procedure that must later be unlearned or discarded and replaced by another) if one can avoid it. If such a crutch shows merit, one should find out what its fundamental virtue is (it is often not the one it appears to be), and then exhaust every possibility of securing its advantages in some other way. The merit of the extended alphabet is that it simplifies the phonic problems in beginning reading, and several other ways of doing this without crutches have already been suggested.[15]

---

[14] Arthur I. Gates, "How Can One Tell What New Practices Are Most Promising?" *Improvement of Reading Through Classroom Practice,* Proceedings of the Annual Convention, vol. 9 (Newark, Delaware: International Reading Association, 1964), p. 23.

[15] *Ibid.*

In considering a "new" approach, it is desirable also to examine the evidence given to support it. Gates continues:

> I have never experienced such a flood of propaganda, unsupported by real evidence, as that now descending on us. This makes it all the more important to study such research data as are available. Assistance in carrying out this difficult task has been provided by several recent publications such as Helen M. Robinson's annual "Summary of Investigations Related to Reading," the latest of which is in *The Reading Teacher,* February 1964, pp. 326–392; and in various topical summaries such as Edward Fry, "Programed Instruction in Reading," *The Reading Teacher,* March 1964, pp. 453–459; and Patrick Groff, "Comparisons of Individualized and Ability Grouping Approaches to Teaching Reading: A Supplement," *Elementary English,* March 1964, pp. 238–241. You will note in Groff's report, for example, that comparative studies of "individualized teaching" give different results depending on the grade, the teacher, the locality, and the particular procedure. You will often observe that practices for which the author claimed remarkable results when they were first introduced show no such merit in later tests in other situations. For example, note the results of studies of the New Castle text-film method reported in Robinson's review above.[16]

Individualized Reading and the Improvement of Instruction

Although some critics do not attribute poor reading to single factors, a few stress their belief that a single method such as "individualized reading" will bring about more effective results. "Individualized reading" means many things to the different persons who recommend the practice. Some advocates of the method do not insist that it be depended upon as a single approach. Thus, Leland Jacobs states:

> In the first place, "individualized reading" is not a single method with predetermined steps in procedure to be followed. It is not possible to say that every teacher who would individualize guidance in reading must do this or that. It is not feasible or desirable to present a simple, single methodological formulation of what is right in "individualized reading" which every teacher shall follow.[17]

Other writers have not followed such a moderate approach, but have defined "individualized reading" as a unique program and have emphasized its value as a method of instruction. We would agree with the persons who recommend "individualized reading" as a significant phase

---

[16] *Ibid.*
[17] Leland Jacobs, "Individualized Reading Is Not a Thing," in Alice Miel (editor), *Individualizing Reading Practices* (New York: Bureau of Publications, Teachers College, Columbia University, 1958), pp. 1–17.

of a total developmental approach. But we see little need for calling the program "individualized" and designating this approach as "the method" to be followed, as is suggested by the following statement:

> "Individualized reading is not subordinate to nor an adjunct of the basic reading program—*it is the basic program.*"[18]

Why can we not recognize that neither group nor individual practices alone constitute the reading program? Why can we not grant the importance of both approaches and cease to think of them as mutually exclusive practices? May not agreement be reached so as to utilize the undeniably desirable features of both approaches in a program which encourages thinking, independent choice, and self-directed behavior? Admittedly, such a procedure will necessitate the abandonment of some practices associated with the typical textbook pattern of instruction; it will necessitate, too, the disavowal of belief in a single pattern to be followed by all children in a class. Adaptations, revisions, and extension of current practices will be necessary.

Characteristics of the Individualized Reading Program

Many teachers have made a significant contribution to instruction by the use of a combination of individualized and group approaches. Some of them have described helpfully the distinguishing features of "individualized reading." For example, Dorothy M. Dietrich emphasizes these characteristics as follows:

> Presently, numerous articles have been written concerning the individualized approach to the teaching of reading. Although these reports vary as to the organization and methods used, they do agree that the elements necessary for conducting an individualized reading program include: (1) a large classroom library made up of basal and supplementary readers, books brought from home by the children and/or materials borrowed from the public or school libraries; (2) a free choice by the children of the reading materials depending upon interest and/or readability; (3) a follow-up activity which may be a series of questions devised by the teacher pertaining to each book, a general report of the book read, a visual presentation of the highlights of the book to the class as a whole, or a discussion with other children concerning characters, plots, etc.; (4) a conference between each child and the classroom teacher, the number of conferences depending upon the class size and individual need; (5) a reading skill

---

[18] May Lazar, "Individualized Reading; A Program of Seeking, Self-selection, and Pacing." Chapter 15 in Jeannette Veatch (editor), *Individualizing Your Reading Program* (New York: G. P. Putnam's Sons, 1959), p. 196.

program which may be taught to the class as a whole, or in some cases, on a flexible small group basis depending upon the emerging needs of the individual.[19]

Although teachers differ in their approaches to "individualized reading" there appear to be certain common characteristics. Six common characteristics are:

Planning. Teachers give directions to pupils and discuss plans for the reading period.

Reading period. Children select materials and read them silently.

Conference period. While pupils are reading independently, the teacher meets with individual children.

Teacher's record. Teachers record the strengths and weaknesses of individual pupils as they work with them.

Children's record. Children keep records of their readings and note areas in which they need help.

Culmination. A group evaluation of plans that were made and/or a sharing of books at the end of the reading period.

Professional journals, especially for the period 1958–1962, contain numerous reports of experimental studies dealing with individual versus basal programs. The success of either program could be proved depending upon the particular studies that one wishes to cite. Rather than making it an "either-or" situation, several writers have concluded that the most desirable procedure is to adapt the best features of individualized and of group instruction to the particular conditions and needs existing in different schools. H. W. Sartain reports the results of an experiment "to determine whether second-grade groups would make greater progress in reading skills when taught for three months by the method of individualized self-selection or when taught for an equivalent period by the method of ability grouping using basic readers plus a variety of supplementary books."[20] He concludes:

> In summary, because this study and others that have been carefully controlled show that the individualized method does not produce better reading gains than a strong basal program, there is no reason to forfeit the advantages of a well-planned basic system. Instead the benefits of the individual conferences should be obtained by their addition to the basic reader plan.[21]

[19] Dorothy M. Dietrich, "Experimental Procedures Significant for Future Trends in Reading Instruction: 9. For Reading Supervisors; a. Methods and Materials," in J. Allen Figurel (editor), *Reading in a Changing Society,* International Reading Association Conference Proceedings (New York: Scholastic Magazines, 1959), Part V, vol. 4, p. 233.

[20] Harry W. Sartain, "The Roseville Experiment with Individualized Reading," *The Reading Teacher,* 13:277 (April, 1960).

[21] *Ibid.,* p. 281.

In addition to the benefits derived from individual conferences with pupils there are other strengths inherent in an individualized program. The self-selection feature appears to develop an interest in reading resulting in more extensive reading by children. Motivation for individual improvement and pupil responsiveness to reading materials are increased.

There are, however, some serious weaknesses of the individualized method when sole dependence is placed upon it. An obvious weakness is the lack of a systematic program of word attack and comprehension skills. Certain children at any grade level who cannot work well independently tend to waste time. The individualized method is also inefficient because of the time required to teach skills individually. Moreover, many children progressing at about the same rate often have similar needs in terms of reading skills. Although many teachers have been enthusiastic about children's reactions to reading in an individualized program, some teachers become frustrated in attempting to provide individual conferences for a number of pupils who need them each day. Yet the use of individual conferences is usually a desirable practice.

In view of the limitations we have noted not all of the writers on individualized reading recommend dropping basal textbooks. A number of experimenters and teachers have found that a combination of basal and individualized reading is very efficient and desirable. Thus, Maida Wood Sharpe describes a program in which the teacher worked "one or two days each week with the basal readers for systematic study and instruction in basic reader skills," and used on the other days an individualized reading program.[22] Also Louise G. Carson reports that in her school district the teachers were "not yet convinced that a completely individualized program" was "necessary or advisable," but that they were interested in the idea of individualizing reading. She states that were she able to embark on such a program, she would retain groups in "basal reading" and "would individualize all supplementary reading."[23]

Another distinct innovation is suggested by Margaret Kirby, who described a program in which reading skills are presented and demonstrated to the children. For three days each week the children work independently, and on the other two days they work together. An important feature of this program is its arrangement for books. Six to eight books of like levels are placed on shelves covered with varying

---

[22] Maida Wood Sharpe, "An Individualized Reading Program," *Elementary English*, 35:507–512 (December, 1958).
[23] Louise G. Carson, "Moving Toward Individualization—A Second Grade Program," *Elementary English*, 34:362–366 (October, 1957).

colors of paper. Kirby thus describes the use of these books by the children:

> Each child is told to choose the book he wants from a shelf of a particular color. No book may be put back on the shelf until checked by the teacher. A move to another shelf is determined by the child's own progress. When a new shelf is started, the basic book is required reading. In this way every child is getting the basic vocabulary.
> If a child asks for a book from another shelf, I let him try. In most cases the child has come back and asked to go back to the shelf he had originally been assigned. This gives the child a chance to make an evaluation of his own ability. One child read a book much below his reading level. Together teacher and child evaluated this reading experience and decided that sometimes a book is worthwhile because of the enjoyment it gives or the information it presents. Another child wanted a more advanced level and proved that she was capable of handling this level because she was willing to put forth the extra effort it required.
> During the independent reading period I work with one child at a time at my desk. Theoretically each child has one ten-minute conference each week.[24]

A reasonable conclusion, in view of the criticisms of reading instruction and the pros and cons of individualized and basal reading programs, is that there isn't any *one* approach to efficient instruction. Moreover, we believe that one should continue exploration to determine which combination of approaches is most effective in various situations. We admire greatly the ingenious efforts of teachers to solve this problem and the remarkable results obtained with individualized and personalized approaches.

However, it seems idle to debate whether individualized *or* group approaches are preferable. Common sense as well as many studies support the use of both approaches. It is important, of course, to recognize the need for the abandonment of the routine basal approach and the use of a single textbook; but this would not rule out systematic instruction in which reading textbooks are employed as needed. This type of instruction, best described as developmental, is sometimes admirably developed and designated "personalized" or individualized.

DEVELOPMENT OF THE READING TEXTBOOK

Progress in teaching reading may be best appreciated by tracing the development of the reading textbook, which parallels changing con-

[24] Margaret Kirby, "Tête-à-Tête Lessons Develop Independent Readers," *Elementary English*, 34:302–303 (May, 1957).

cepts in our thought about the nature of reading and ways to offer instruction. Study of the origin and growth of the reading textbook will disclose also significant steps in the progress of educational theory and practice; moreover, it will show the influence of research in child development and of emerging concepts of the learning process.

Development of Elementary School Texts

The beginning device in reading instruction was probably the hornbook—misnamed, since it was not actually a book. It consisted typically of a short-handled paddle made of wood and varying in size from one and a half to six inches in width and from two to nine inches in length. A sheaf of parchment or paper, pasted on the paddle, was inscribed with the following: a cross; the alphabet in both small and capital letters; the vowels and vowel-consonant combinations; the benediction "In the name of the Father and the Son and of the Holy Ghost, Amen"; the Lord's Prayer; and at the end, if space permitted, the Roman numerals. The parchment or paper was covered with a transparent sheet of horn, held in place by strips of brass fastened to the edges of the paddle.

A variation of the hornbook was known as the battledore. This toy paddle was used by children in America while playing battledore and shuttlecock. The letters of the alphabet were either painted on or cut into the paddle. Another ingenious device, designed for girls and found widely in colonial homes, was the sampler. It was made by embroidering upon cloth the alphabet and excerpts from the Bible, the Lord's Prayer, hymns, and sometimes a little of the child's own creative verse. These devices constituted an important phase of learning to read during colonial days.

In tracing the history of reading materials from 1607 to 1934, Nila B. Smith cited *The Protestant Tutor,* which appeared in 1685, as the first American reading textbook.[25] She noted also that the *New England Primer* was advertised in a Boston almanac in 1690 and that the earliest extant copy was printed in Boston in 1721. The *New England Primer,* often referred to as "The Little Bible of New England," was usually oblong-shaped and was covered with thin pieces of oak. The most frequently published edition was about three inches by four and a half inches in size. The print and illustrations were necessarily small. The size, appearance, and physical features offer a striking contrast to modern textbooks.

---

[25] Nila B. Smith, *American Reading Instruction* (Morristown, N.J.: Silver Burdett Co., 1934).

Throughout the many editions of this book, the content remained basically the same. There was usually a frontispiece which, before the Revolutionary War, was an engraved portrait of the reigning monarch of England. During the war the pictures of the monarchs were replaced by engravings of American patriots. After the war the favorite frontispiece portrayed George Washington. The alphabet was then introduced, followed by "Easy Syllables for Children," such as the vowel-consonant combinations. Next came columns of words beginning with one-syllable words and ending with words of five syllables. Following these were little pictures with alphabetically rhymed couplets. For example, the letter *A* was shown with a small picture of Adam, a tree, and a serpent, and was accompanied by the verse:

> In Adam's Fall.
> We sinned All.

The *New England Primer* was not only a textbook; it became also an important cultural force, since during the period 1690–1830 it was found in nearly every New England home. The total sales of the primer during this one-hundred-and-forty-year period have been estimated as varying from three to eight million copies.

Another important contribution to reading instruction was made by Noah Webster, who constructed a series of readers under the title *Grammatical Institute*. This series, published first as a single book, later was divided into three separate texts. One of these, the *American Spelling Book,* better known as *The Blue-Back Speller,* became a most influential factor in American education. This extremely popular book was one of the "best-sellers" of its day, second only to the Bible. It was estimated that nearly 100,000,000 copies of the speller were sold. In this series, reading instruction was associated intimately with the teaching of spelling and grammar.

Other books of this period, usually moralistic in tone, reflected the influence of a growing nationalistic spirit. The orators and statesmen of the period—Thomas Paine, Benjamin Franklin, and others—wrote materials of nationwide significance and interest, a type of literature which was included in textbooks such as the four-book series of John Pierpont. The inclusion of American selections was a departure from the practice of earlier compilers, whose texts had utilized English authors only.

Lyman Cobb was probably the first to compile a carefully graded set of readers in this country. Several other series appearing between 1840 and 1860 reflected a trend toward the establishment of school grades. The best known of these were prepared by William Holmes McGuffey, whose books had far-reaching effects upon American education and life, as is suggested by the following passage:

> It remained for McGuffey to make the exact choice of materials for the West. No one who has not grown up amidst the conditions in the new land could understand the social and religious mind of the new civilization. The textbook writers of New England were still steeped in the spirit of Puritanism. McGuffey knew such of the current of English thought as would appeal to his great audience of youth, the first native-born generation of the Ohio country. This differentiation in the selection of literature and in the original stories of the *McGuffey Readers* was great enough to make this series the chosen texts of the rising millions.[26]

Many factors contributed to the popularity of the *McGuffey Readers* throughout the years from 1836 until 1920. Very important, no doubt, was the emphasis given to commendable traits of character. The selections had meaning for the reader as well as an interesting style.

During the period just prior to the beginning of the twentieth century, textbooks began to show a marked improvement in mechanical makeup. For example, the textbooks constructed by Edward G. Ward and published by Silver Burdett Company in 1894 were set in more readable type than that formerly employed. In some of the earlier books, pupils learned the alphabet and then proceeded to the phonic units, and finally to reading words and larger elements. Ward, however, stressed the significance of the child's acquiring a stock of sight words before phonetic analysis was attempted. The Ward readers, although well liked, did not attain the widespread popularity of the McGuffey series.

Among the widely used textbooks which appeared about 1920, the Buswell and Wheeler *Silent Reading Hour* (published by Wheeler Publishing Company) and the Horn and Shields *Learn to Study Series* (published by Ginn and Company) came into high favor. They employed attractive colored illustrations, varied content, and simplified vocabularies. A unique feature of these readers was the inclusion of a separate teacher's manual, one for each grade. In the manuals, detailed suggestions and directions were given for using the books. About this time, one writer, Emma M. Bolenius, developed a most comprehensive first-grade manual, more than five hundred pages in length.

A simplified vocabulary, gradually introduced, became one of the outstanding features of textbooks published during the period 1930 to the present. The Winston Company offered one of the earlier series which followed this practice. Similarly, the *Elson-Gray Readers,* revised later

---

[26] Harvey C. Minnich, *William Holmes McGuffey and His Readers* (New York: American Book Company, 1936), p. 53.

to become the *Scott-Foresman Curriculum Foundation Series,* employed a controlled vocabulary. This series became the most widely used series in American schools.

In the thirties, another trend was represented by the introduction of textbooks of wide appeal because of the interesting story content and the artistic appearance of the books. Striking among these was the *Alice and Jerry Series* (of Row-Peterson), which introduced the profuse use of color in the illustrations and included stories of literary merit. The trend toward the use of superior art work, attractive story content, and emphasis on the interest factor was represented by D. C. Heath's *Reading for Interest Series.*

Recognition of the wide range of abilities within present-day classes has led to the development of another type of reading textbook, sometimes designated as "multi-level." For example, a series of basal readers, published about 1950 by Lyons and Carnahan, contained the same stories written on two levels for each grade. One level is easy, the other more difficult. Perhaps the most comprehensive development of multi-level materials, designed to help teachers make provisions for individual differences, is found in the *Reading Laboratories* of Science Research Associates. The graded cards of the SRA Laboratories extend from primary to secondary school level in difficulty, with many boxes of cards for varied reading levels.

For years the use of a single textbook series constituted the *basal* reading program in many elementary schools. During the period 1930–1950, some elementary schools began to use two or more series of *basal* books, which were referred to as *co-basal.* Not only are several textbook series now used in many schools, but there is also a tendency to employ supplementary series in association with the basal books. Thus, some school systems adopt a *basal* or *co-basal* series and employ also somewhat comparable books from one or more supplementary series. Another practice involves little or no use of *basal* materials and the substitution instead of appropriate materials from children's literature in *individualized* reading instruction, as differentiated from group practice associated closely with the textbook.

In the early 1960's there was a tendency in many schools to use various combinations of basal, supplementary, and library materials. We shall see in Chapter 9 of this book that a combination of individualized and group approaches to reading instruction has been followed with outstanding success in many schools.

Development of Secondary School Texts

Although basal reading materials are usually designed for grades 1 through 6, textbooks have recently been developed for high school pupils. These series are usually limited to grades 7, 8, and 9. Such a series may serve as a part of a comprehensive developmental program. The introduction of developmental reading at the high school level is based on the conviction that continued group instruction and individual guidance in reading are essential for *all* pupils. It is recognized that there are many poor readers in the high school who should be offered appropriate instruction in reading. And it is recognized also that there are many superior readers in every class whose needs are best met by the opportunities offered through a developmental reading program.

In some high schools teachers are employing varied materials to help each pupil gain not only more effective habits and skills but also to achieve better personal and social adjustment through reading. Novels, short stories, biographies, and other sources are provided for this purpose. In fiction, pupils encounter numerous incidents in which the central characters experience conflict, uncertainty, and anxiety concerning problems which beset most adolescents. Directed reading of this type of literature enlarges the student's understanding of human personality. Under expert guidance he arrives at a better understanding of himself and his own problems, as well as a better understanding of others.

CHARACTERISTICS OF AN EFFECTIVE READING PROGRAM

A review of reading instruction and the implications in the evolution of the textbook lead one to ponder: What shall be done to create better reading programs—programs which will take into account the present-day needs of boys and girls for reading? The following are some principles that may be used to guide our efforts to improve reading instruction:

1. *An effective reading program should be "functional."* In our schools a functional program should be planned to assure every child an opportunity to acquire reading habits and skills which will fulfill his varied and changing needs. Such a functional approach should be employed from the first. The topics about which pupils read in the pre-primers and primers should be real and meaningful in terms of the children's own activities and experiences. The functional approach should be continued as reading ability develops. Moreover, the entire

program should be based on facts of child development and presented in such a way that materials will have meaning and relevance in terms of changing needs. Of course, a functional reading program will utilize a variety of materials covering many topics, and it will clearly differentiate and make provisions for reading experiences to satisfy essential and varied needs.

2. *An effective reading program should be closely associated with worthwhile interests.* The practicability of using children's interests to foster maximum development in reading has been repeatedly demonstrated. The information derived from an investigation of interests will prove to be of inestimable value in giving guidance throughout the school year. But the failure to recognize and utilize interest and motive are so general that extreme methods and suggestions have been advanced as correctives. For example, George Norvell has indicated some inadequacies of high school programs of reading in terms of the interests of secondary school pupils. After analyzing the selections commonly taught in certain high schools of New York, he suggests that "three-fourths of the selections in our current program be replaced with selections of equally high merit that children endorse."[27]

3. *An effective reading program should give increased attention to accurate vocabulary and concept building.* Teachers of primary children generally have become aware of the futility of trying to develop meaningful reading experiences through the use of textbooks which employ too few words to convey ideas that represent children's experience validly. Word order and usage are often inconsistent with the children's natural patterns of speech. Carl A. Lefevre, criticizing the tendency to teach reading from a word unit rather than a structural unit, states:

> Simply by talking, normal children from five to seven years old demonstrate their mastery of the basic structures of American English. Children should learn to read and write the language they already speak and understand.
>
> Efficient reading requires consciousness of the relative equivalency of the graphic counterparts to spoken language structures.[28]

Many studies have shown that boys and girls have fairly large vocabularies; hence the small vocabularies used in pre-primers and primers are considered inappropriate. Moreover, the repetition of words is deemed excessive. Gates, for example, reported two studies conducted in 1958

---

[27] George W. Norvell, "Some Results of a Twelve-Year Study of Children's Reading Interests." *The English Journal,* 35:531–536 (December, 1946).

[28] Carl A. Lefevre, *Linguistics and the Teaching of Reading* (New York: McGraw-Hill, 1962), p. 19.

and 1959 with elementary school pupils in New York City to determine the value of vocabulary control in basal reading material. He reports:

> Third-grade children of average ability in the thirteen classes from four different New York City public schools, as a result of the abilities they have acquired to work out the recognition and meaning of unfamiliar words and the experience they have had in reading by themselves, appear to have little more difficulty with the "new" words in the fourth-grade basal books which had not as yet been used in school than with words already encountered in earlier basal books in the series. For such children the listing and conventional controls of such "new" words in grade four seem to be a waste of time in teaching and a needless expense in book production. . . . Indeed the top quarter of youngsters two-thirds through the second grade have so little trouble with both "new" fourth- and third-grade words as to make conventional vocabulary control of doubtful value to them.[29]

Clearly, first-grade textbooks and related materials should use a sufficiently large vocabulary within the context of the child's experiences to challenge him and foster his growth. We should guard against keeping the primary child too long on a plateau of learning through needless repetition of words already known. On the other hand, we must be zealous to insure that the vocabulary burden of first books is not so great as to block learning. All reading materials should be built in strict accord with known principles of learning and child development and in consideration of the wide range of ability found within every class. Attention must be given to the child's experience, his maturity, and his goals. In such a program, vocabulary development is an important concern but it is not an *end* in itself; it is instead an item of significance in the total array of factors which operate together to promote steady growth in reading power.

4. *An effective reading program should make a judicious use of textbooks and other materials to help insure the acquisition of reading skills by every girl and boy.* The role of the textbook is still debatable. Some teachers suggest an abandonment of textbooks; others prefer the use of a combination of textbooks and supplementary materials; and some depend almost solely on a single textbook. Studies do not support the claim that textbooks are unnecessary or undesirable in many situations. Indeed, some studies have shown that textbooks used in combination with a wide assortment of supplementary materials yield superior results.

Moreover, many teachers assert that textbook materials may aid them substantially in providing systematic instruction in basic skills, and enable

---

[20] Arthur I. Gates, "Vocabulary Control in Basal Reading Material," *The Reading Teacher,* 35:85 (November, 1961).

them to guide and evaluate the students' acquisition of skills. It has been found, too, that the use of a textbook sometimes gives the teacher a measure of security and satisfies the parents' concern that children are being taught to read. Textbooks should constitute only one part of instructional materials. They should be selected and used with discrimination in combination with other materials.

John DeBoer and Martha Dallmann offer the following suggestions for modifying conventional textbook practice:

> Certain general cautions should be observed in the planning of a basal reading program. For example, reliance should not be placed upon a single basal reader for the whole class; indeed it should not be placed upon an entire single series. In any given class, basal readers designed for many levels of reading ability and containing many different kinds of material should be provided. Basal readers should not be labeled according to grade level or difficulty, although the publisher's estimate of difficulty level may be indicated by some code device. All basal readers should be amply supplemented with general reading materials on many subjects and representing many levels of reading difficulty.[30]

A provocative point of view concerning the use of a textbook is expressed by Russell G. Stauffer:

> It is recommended, then, that a modified basic reader approach be used. To do this effectively one must first drop the notion that a basic reader program in and of itself is final and sacred. It is not. Second, one must drop the notion that time can be equated with equality. Not every group must be met every day for the same length of time. Third, the idea that a basic book recommended for a grade level must be "finished" by all pupils in a grade before they can be promoted must be discarded. Fourth, teaching reading as a *memoriter* process by presenting new words in advance of the reading and then having pupils tell back the story must be stopped. If reading is taught as a thinking process, even short basic-reader stories will be read with enthusiasm. . . . Sixth, effective skills of word attack must be taught. Basic reading books do not provide for such skill training; neither do trade books.[31]

The use of textbooks and other materials becomes an important factor in an effective reading program. It has been recognized that misuse of even the best materials renders the materials ineffective. Overdependence upon any one type of material can weaken a program. It is im-

---

[30] John J. DeBoer and Martha Dallmann, *The Teaching of Reading* (New York: Holt, Rinehart & Winston, Inc., 1960), pp. 340–341.

[31] Russell G. Stauffer, "Individualized and Group Type Directed Reading Instruction," *Elementary English,* 37:381 (October, 1960).

portant to emphasize here that a definite skills-development program must accompany any materials a teacher selects. Textbooks and trade books are implements through which the skills are learned and practiced.

5. *An effective reading program should make provision for remedial reading as a temporary expedient.* Most authorities assert that remedial reading programs are necessary as a temporary expedient in some elementary schools and in the junior and senior high schools. One of the most significant aspects of modern remedial programs is the attention they give to individuals and to small groups. In addition, there is a conscientious effort to diagnose carefully the varied reading levels and needs of the pupils, to provide useful and stimulating materials, and to offer systematic instruction for a long enough time to assure improvement. At present, remedial reading is deemed essential in many schools. Criticisms of remedial programs center mainly around the fact that the classroom teacher should ideally provide adequate experiences for every child to learn within a developmental reading program; hence, remedial reading is theoretically unnecessary. However, limitations in materials and teacher training, and such factors as large classes, tend to create problems leading to the need for remedial reading programs.

Proponents of developmental programs sometimes describe their programs as "preventive." The idea that a developmental program will decrease the need for remedial programs is theoretically sound. However, different learning rates of children and the problem of caring for individual differences in large classes creates a need for remedial programs for the less fortunate children in many schools.

6. *An effective reading program should make provision for instructing children at appropriate levels.* An important aspect of teaching children to read is the level of material from which children are instructed. Emmett Betts states:

> When the learner is confronted with materials that have readability beyond his grasp, he is likely to be frustrated in his learning activities. On the other hand, maximum development is not likely to accrue when the learner is given a diet of reading materials dealing with facts and expressed in a language that does not challenge his best intellectual endeavors.[32]

Research workers have identified the instructional level as that level at which a child can identify ninety-five to ninety-eight percent of the running words and comprehend at least seventy percent of the ideas

[32] Emmett Albert Betts, *Foundation of Reading Instruction* (New York: American Book Company, 1957), p. 447.

presented. Children make their greatest growth when instructed at the proper level.

7. *An effective reading program should make wide use of auditory and visual materials.* At this point comment is needed concerning the proper use of visual and auditory materials in a balanced reading program. The unusual wartime success of programs which made wide use of visual and auditory materials has brought a new interest as well as rash predictions concerning their use. The present interest in self-instruction devices, machine teaching, and programmed learning is also indicative of the continuing search for more adequate and effective ways of teaching reading. The specific value of self-instructing devices is not yet established; hence extreme claims concerning their merits cannot be estimated with finality. We have reason to believe that each of these items may prove of value as a part of a total program but should not be regarded as a panacea.

8. *An effective reading program requires the cooperation of parents and librarians.* Parents should be encouraged to foster reading by obtaining good books for the home. Indeed, some teachers provide parents with book lists and suggest that they buy books as presents for their children. A varied assortment of books and magazines made available in and out of school offers children the essential materials for strengthening reading skills and cultivating appreciations.

Because a balanced reading program is developed best when there is a central library in each school, many elementary schools are now employing a full-time librarian, trained in library science and in child psychology. Such an enthusiastic and well-qualified person can make the library one of the most inviting spots in the school. Here a lasting love for books can be cultivated in children. The services of the school library should be correlated with those of the public library in encouraging children to read widely.

Library facilities, both school and public, need to be greatly expanded. Public libraries in the United States have been organized as municipal services, and are dependent on local initiative for their creation and on local tax sources for their support. One result, reported in 1950, is that half of the incorporated places are too small or too poor to have any public library, and two-thirds of the people in the unincorporated areas are equally without direct library service.[33] Ways must be found to extend the services of the public library to every child.

---

[33] Robert D. Leigh, *The Public Library in the United States: The General Report of the Public Library Inquiry* (New York: Columbia University Press, 1950), p. 227.

The public school of America (through its teachers and librarians working in cooperation with parents) has a unique opportunity to bring into children's lives balanced programs in reading. The school, representing "society's most extensive investment for its children," cannot operate effectively without cooperative endeavor on the part of the teachers, parents, and others who serve boys and girls.[34] Better reading habits will result when these adults pool their resources in an effort to understand each child and to guide him to the realization of the inexhaustible wealth of information and enjoyment to be found in good books.

CONCLUDING STATEMENT

Probably no subject of the curriculum has been the target for more persistent attack than has reading. It should be recognized that criticism is sometimes justifiable and may serve to stimulate thinking about procedures designed to improve instruction. Some critics, however, seem to be seeking merely to promote their own convictions and to recommend the use of simple panaceas which have not been validated: they seem to desire to propose a method rather than to test hypotheses. It is true, of course, that much needs to be done to improve reading instruction, but improvement probably will not be associated with proposals based on a single theory of causation or the use of a single device, machine, or method. Instead, improvement will come as we try out different methods and combinations of methods and base our recommendations on the results of careful study and research.

Although the quality of reading instruction has tended to improve over the past thirty years, we are not satisfied with its present status. There is much still to be accomplished in the improvement of instruction in reading as well as in using more generally the excellent materials now available.

An effective reading program will be functional, and will be closely associated with children's interests. Remedial programs will meet the needs of certain children, and differentiation of instruction will insure that children are instructed at their proper levels.

In such an approach the home and the school will aim to coordinate their efforts and work cooperatively in seeking improvement. The challenge is great. It is essential that we utilize our best skill and knowledge

---

[34] Jean Betzner and Annie E. Moore, *Everychild and Books* (Indianapolis: The Bobbs-Merrill Company, Inc., 1940), p. 33.

for the promotion of better reading instruction. Our aim must be to help pupils become skillful, self-reliant, and independent readers who by reading will enrich their understandings and satisfactions throughout their lives.

Selected References

Barbe, Walter B., *Educator's Guide to Personalized Reading Instruction* (Englewood Cliffs, N.J.: Prentice-Hall, Inc., 1961).

Betts, Emmett Albert, "Unsolved Problems in Reading: A Symposium I," *Elementary English,* 31:325–338 (October, 1954).

Darrow, Helen F. and Virgil M. Howes, *Approaches to Individualized Reading* (New York: Appleton-Century-Crofts, 1960), 102 pp.

Davis, Frederick B., "Research in Reading in High School and College." *Review of Educational Research,* 22:76–88 (April, 1952).

Gates, Arthur I., "Vocabulary Control in Basal Reading Material," *The Reading Teacher,* 15:81–88 (November, 1961).

Kandel, I. L., "Some Unsolved Issues in American Education," *Educational Forum,* 20:269–278 (March, 1956).

Keyser, Margaret Lee, "Research in Reading in the Elementary School," *Review of Educational Research,* 22:65–75 (April, 1952).

Smith, Nila Banton, "What Have We Accomplished in Reading?—A Review of the Past Fifty Years," *Elementary English,* 38:141–150 (March, 1961).

Strang, Ruth and Donald M. Lindquist, *The Administrator and the Improvement of Reading* (New York: Appleton-Century-Crofts, 1960).

Traxler, Arthur E., *Eight More Years of Research in Reading: Summary and Bibliography* (Educational Records Bulletin, no. 64, New York: Educational Records Bureau, 1955).

Traxler, Arthur E., and Margaret Seder, *Ten Years of Research in Reading* (Educational Records Bulletin, no. 32, New York: Educational Records Bureau, 1941).

Traxler, Arthur E., and Agatha Townsend, *Another Five Years of Research in Reading* (Educational Records Bulletin, no. 46, New York: Educational Records Bureau, 1946).

Witty, Paul, "Problems in the Improvement and Measurement of Growth in Reading," *School and Society,* 78:69–73 (September, 1953).

Witty, Paul, "Reading Instruction—A Forward Look," *Elementary English,* 38:151–164 (March, 1961).

Witty, Paul, "Some Issues in the Teaching of Reading," *The Packet. A Heath Service Bulletin for Elementary Teachers,* 18:3–15 (Spring, 1963).

Witty, Paul, "Unsolved Problems in Reading: A Symposium II," *Elementary English,* 31:421–427 (November, 1954).

3

THE ROLE OF INTEREST

Hugh was nine years old when we first met—a fine boy, enthusiastic and intelligent. But he had one serious shortcoming: he was unable to read. His secure world was being threatened because his parents, teachers, and friends were causing him increasingly to be disturbed by his limitation.[1]

Standardized tests were given him. Hugh's scores were very low on all reading tests, although his IQ was 124. It was interesting to note some of the ways by which he had learned to adjust. For example, when words were dictated to find his spelling ability, Hugh always wrote something, but in only one case in twenty did he write the word dictated. He had learned to comply in his own way to the demands of an impossible situation.

Later he was asked to read aloud some very simple paragraphs. Here the situation was even more embarrassing for him. He stumbled through the first three paragraphs—mispronouncing, inserting, and omitting words. In desperation, he tried to use phonetic rules. When he met the word *again,* he began pronouncing *ag,* then he noticed the *in,* and finally *ain.* At last he abandoned his efforts to unlock this word. Some words, such as *school,* which he had already encountered many times, he omitted and introduced substitute terms instead. When Hugh met the words *enough* and *through,* he recognized an insurmountable difficulty. The blood rushed to his face; stress was apparent in every action.

---

[1] Some of this chapter is based on materials to be found in Paul A. Witty (chairman), *Development In and Through Reading,* Sixtieth Yearbook of the National Society for the Study of Education (Chicago: University of Chicago Press, 1961), Part I, Chapter 8, "The Role of Interest." See also Paul A. Witty, *et al.,* "Studies of Interest—A Brief Summary," *Elementary English,* 38:469–475 and 540–545 (November and December, 1960), and 39:33–36 (January, 1961).

Finally, he remarked plaintively, "Mr. Witty, I'd like to show you a boat I built."

We examined Hugh's miniature vessel. His excellent craftsmanship enabled the boat to sail jauntily on a nearby pond. He was asked to tell about the construction of the boat; and as he talked, his story was recorded. When it was read back to him, he exclaimed, "Did I really say that?" We put many of the words on cards, and read each word several times. Soon Hugh was able to pronounce all the words correctly and repeatedly. Then we turned to the complete story which had been read aloud to him. He was able to read the story himself with success and little hesitation. At this time we examined the words on our cards again, noticing beginnings and endings as well as other phonetic characteristics. And we compiled lists of words in which pronunciation was unusual and irregular. Hugh acquired a secure "stock" of words which he recognized instantly and pronounced correctly. We composed stories using these words, and added to our list other words he was learning.

Simple books on topics related to boats and sailing were given him; the meaning of many new words was now derived from their context, and Hugh found great satisfaction in pronouncing these words and giving their meanings. The dictionary was introduced and practice given in using it. The process continued in the same way—secure accomplishment developed in association with interest and success. As we proceeded with systematic instruction and application, Hugh's insecurity diminished rapidly and his reading proficiency increased.[2]

The Importance of Interest and Skills

Interest is an elusive, subtle, and sometimes fleeting characteristic. Yet when captured or awakened it can provide unusual impetus for sustained effort and accomplishment, as the foregoing account of Hugh reveals. In it one sees the value of channeling a child's specific interest into related tasks that nurture the interest and simultaneously provide opportunities for learning skills such as reading. One notes also the importance of successful attainment and the significance of systematic instruction.

The significance of orderly systematic instruction is insufficiently stressed in the literature dealing with interests. Yet we find that interest is sometimes engendered by successful mastery of reading skills or by the acquisition of background information in a subject field. It should

---

[2] Paul Witty, "Interest, Effort and Success—Bases for Effective Reading," *Education,* 79:480–487 (April, 1959).

be recognized, too, that in many cases it is intensive effort that really educates. Accordingly, goals should be attainable, but they should require effort as their level is gradually raised. It is clear that we should provide, in the primary grades, a meaningful program that is challenging and that calls forth sustained effort. It does not seem that the use of some of the conventional teaching materials actually accomplishes these objectives for many children. Pre-primers and primers may utilize a far too meager vocabulary, repeatedly employed in almost meaningless situations. As a result not only the bright children but others, too, may become convinced that reading is a profitless or unrewarding pursuit.

The importance of assuring the development of adequate skills that stimulate voluntary reading can scarcely be overemphasized as a goal of primary instruction. Moreover, the acquisition of dependable skills makes possible enjoyable and successful reading throughout the child's school career. Even in the junior and senior high schools, it is often necessary to provide for greater mastery and more successful application of reading skills. To be interested in reading, pupils at every level must be led to enjoy the act of reading as well as the results.

Meaning of Interest and Interests

What do we mean by the term *interest?* As a first approach to an understanding of the term, the reader might look back on his own childhood. For most of us there will be a nostalgic glow as we think about interests that led us to collect birds' eggs or stamps, or marbles or dolls. We think about the model auto, playhouse, or boat we build. And we reflect with great pleasure on the butterflies we mounted, or the animals we hunted and photographed.

Such activities were undoubtedly learned, yet they were "freely" chosen—usually just because we wanted to take part in them. They were often unassociated with work and were not usually the result of home or school pressures. In a way, these interests were the result of a need for expression, although the need was rarely recognized. Elizabeth Hurlock makes the following statement about interest:

> An interest is a learned motive which drives the individual to act in accordance with that interest. It is defined as preoccupation with an activity when the individual is free to choose. When the child finds an activity satisfying, it continues to be an interest.[3]

Jacob W. Getzels gives a short but useful definition:

[3] Elizabeth B. Hurlock, *Child Development* (New York: McGraw-Hill Book Company, Inc., 1956), p. 440.

> An interest is a characteristic disposition, organized through experience, which impels an individual to seek out particular objects, activities, understandings, skills, or goals for attention or acquisition.[4]

For purposes of this chapter we have described interest and interests in this way: Interest is a disposition or tendency which impels an individual to seek out particular goals for persistent attention. The goals may be objects, skills, knowledges, and art activities of various kinds. The behavior patterns in seeking these goals may be regarded as particular interests such as collecting objects or viewing TV. They should be looked upon as acquired, although they are based upon such factors as the constitutional nature of the individual and his personality structure as affected by his unique experiences and his particular environment.

Methods and Values of Studying Interests

Various methods have been used to study or identify children's interests: the questionnaire, the interview, the "log" of activities, the interest inventory, the anecdotal record, and observation under various conditions.

A child-study technique, widely used by teachers, is illustrated by the Northwestern University Interest Inventory.[5] Guided by the inquiries on the inventory, the teacher and the pupil discuss informally such topics as favorite leisure activities, hobbies, play preferences, movie and reading habits, and familiarity with community places of interest. The inventory also contains questions related to the child's personal and social problems. Some of the questions which may elicit responses relating to deeper concerns and interests are these:

1. If you could have three wishes which might come true, what would be your
    first wish?
    second wish?
    third wish?
2. Do you often wonder about some things? Yes ...... No ......
   If yes, what?
3. Do you have any strong fears? Yes ...... No ...... If yes, what?

---

[4] Jacob W. Getzels, "The Nature of Reading Interests," in Helen M. Robinson (editor), *Developing Permanent Interest in Reading,* Supplementary Educational Monographs no. 84 (Chicago: University of Chicago Press, 1956), p. 7.

[5] Developed from the Witty-Kopel *Diagnostic Child Study Record* described in Paul Witty and David Kopel, *Reading and the Educative Process* (Boston: Ginn and Company, 1939). See also footnote 6 *infra.*

4. What was the happiest event in your life?

From children's answers to such questions teachers may determine areas of deep concern and interest and use such information for selecting reading materials.

Recently at Northwestern University a series of questionnaires was devised to be employed in studying interests.[6] The items, assembled from diverse sources, were listed in four questionnaires which deal with the following areas: reading pursuits; TV, radio, and movie preferences; play and recreational activities; and vocational and educational interests. For example, in the area of *Reading Interests* these questions illustrate the kinds of information sought to determine pupil interests:

1. Do you enjoy reading?
2. Do you like to have someone read to you?
3. About how much time each day do you spend reading outside school?
4. Do your parents encourage you to read?

Samples of questions relating to interests in *Television, Radio,* and *Movies* are these:

1. How much time do you spend viewing TV?
2. What are your favorite TV programs? Why do you like these programs?
3. List some TV programs you do not like. Why do you dislike these programs?

(Similar questions occur for radio and movies.)

In the area of *Play* and *Recreation* these questions are illustrative:

1. What do you usually do
   after school?
   in the evening?
   on Saturdays?
   on Sundays?
2. What activity do you like best:
   in the summer?
   in the spring?
   in the winter?
   in the fall?

---

[6] *A Study of the Interests of Children and Youth.* A cooperative research project performed (1958–59) in accord with a contract between Northwestern University and the Office of Education, U. S. Department of Health, Education and Welfare. Paul A. Witty, Director of Project (Northwestern University); Robert A. Sizemore, Assistant Director (University of Toledo); Paul Kinsella (Skokie Public Schools); Ann Coomer (Chicago Public Schools); Stanley Krippner (Northwestern University). Report was submitted to the Office of Education, U. S. Department of Health, Education and Welfare in February, 1960. (For the full Interest Inventory records see Appendix C.)

Typical questions providing answers of significance for the teacher of reading concerning pupil interest in *Vocation* and *Education* are these:
1. What kind of work do you want to do when you finish school?
2. When did you decide on the kind of work you want to do?
3. What kind of work does your father want you to do? Why? Your mother? Why?

A first step in the study of interests perhaps involves an examination of the findings of studies in various interest areas. Another step implies consideration of the ways interests can be used to promote growth in and through reading for individuals and for groups. We shall, in this chapter, summarize studies of activities, interests, and preferences of pupils: in play and recreation; in television, radio, and the movies; in reading; and in vocations and education. Then we shall discuss and illustrate some effective applications of pupil interest in classroom practice.

INTERESTS OF CHILDREN AND ADOLESCENTS

Research has indicated that children and adolescents have broad and varied interests in play and recreation; television, radio, and movies; reading; and vocations and education. The following pages will reveal the interests of boys and girls from the ages of six to eighteen in the aforementioned areas.

Play and Recreational Interests

Numerous studies of play and recreational interests are now available. The results vary widely depending on the techniques used, the time the studies were made, and the type of groups employed. In a widely quoted study, published in 1927, Lehman and Witty considered play to be primarily those activities in which children engaged "just because they wanted to."[7] The researchers employed a play quiz which was submitted to thousands of children and youth. Comparable results were reported for boys and girls studied in 1946.[8] In the latter study one may note a persistence of many play activities previously cited. It was

---

[7] H. C. Lehman and Paul A. Witty, *Psychology of Play Activities* (New York: A. S. Barnes and Company, Inc., 1927).

[8] Paul Witty, *Reading in Modern Education* (Boston: D. C. Heath and Company, 1949). See also *A Study of the Interests of Children and Youth, op. cit.*

found that by the time boys and girls were six years old, they began to show differences in their favored pursuits. The six-year-old girl liked to play with dolls and miniature furniture. She enjoyed "playing house" and making things to use in a playhouse. She participated in some group games such as "drop the handkerchief," but often took part in individual activities like jumping rope and playing jacks. When boys were six years of age, they liked best to participate in more active but relatively unorganized games such as tag and hide-and-seek. Most boys eight or nine years of age found pleasure in spinning tops, flying kites, playing marbles, and building houses. They found satisfaction also in playing cowboy and similar games in which they pretended to be aviators, soldiers, sailors, or marines. Other group activities, such as playing catch or games the boys referred to as baseball or football, were popular; but these pursuits were unlike the more formal competitive sports enjoyed by older boys.

By the time the boys were twelve years of age, they turned to more highly organized games, such as tennis and baseball. From twelve to fifteen there appeared to be a sharp decrease in the amount of active, spontaneous play, and a tendency developed on the part of both boys and girls to take part to a greater extent in sedentary pursuits. Going to the movies, listening to the radio, riding in an automobile, and watching contests gained favor during this period.

Another study undertaken prior to the advent of television showed a downward trend in participation in games with increase in age. Approximately three hundred children in grades five through eight in a Midwestern community were asked by Inez Mauck and Esther Swenson to rank six activities (sports, games, radio, reading, movies, and hobbies) according to the way "they used their spare time." The investigators reported in 1949:

> Reading was clearly overshadowed by sports, radio-listening, games, and movie attendance. The pattern of other activities did not vary greatly from grade to grade. Sports were consistently first; hobbies consistently last. Radio-listening stayed near the top, in second or third place for all the grades. Movies seemed to go up somewhat among older children, as might be expected. Games showed the only consistent downward trend with increased age.[9]

After the advent of television, the pattern of favored activities was influenced by televiewing, which was almost invariably given first rank among children's preferred activities. This fact was clearly revealed by

[9] Inez L. Mauck and Esther J. Swenson, "A Study of Children's Recreational Reading," *Elementary School Journal,* 50:147 (November, 1949).

Constance M. McCullough, who in 1957 reported the use of "logs" to ascertain children's out-of-school activities.[10] Her study was made in nine Oakland, California, schools, located in three distinctly different socioeconomic localities. The "waterfront" district was composed "largely of racial minority groups living in low-cost housing and employed as unskilled labor. . . ." The "central group" included three schools located in a district of native-born, skilled laborers of average income. And the third group, the "hill" schools, were situated in a district representing upper-middle-class prosperity. During one week 391 fifth-grade pupils kept a "log" of their out-of-school activities, including before-school, after-school, and after-dinner pursuits. Twenty-six "recreational" activities were cited 6,217 times; fourteen "work" activities, 2,922 times. Televiewing was by far the favorite activity of both boys and girls. Next in popularity for the boys were active sports, followed by caring for pets, games, doing homework, straightening own room, and visiting friends. The girls mentioned televiewing, preparing meals, straightening own room, washing dishes, active sports, doing homework, and games. Book reading was low on the list except in the "hill" schools, where nearly half the children reported reading books.

In the recent Northwestern University–Office of Education study referred to above, participation in sedentary pursuits was indeed frequent.[11] The influence of the mass media—with television first—was evident throughout the study. Other passive activities in addition to televiewing were noted frequently in this study at all grade levels. However, boys and girls still found time to participate in a number of outdoor activities. Boys played baseball and football, swam, and rode bicycles; girls enjoyed skating, jumping rope, building snowmen, and riding on sleds. But both boys and girls reported less frequently activities such as playing marbles, fishing, hunting, hiking, flying kites, and picnicking, which formerly enjoyed greater popularity. Table I presents data concerning favored play pursuits.

In these studies of play and recreation we find a wide range of activities and marked individual differences at every level. Although it is true that some play pursuits are characteristic of younger children while others are favored by older pupils, it is clear too that differences in play activities appear to depend upon many factors, such as the location of the school or group and the time or season of the year. Hence it seems that to ascertain play interests to be employed in motivating instruction,

---

[10] Constance M. McCullough, "A Log of Children's Out-of-School Activities," *Elementary School Journal,* 58:157–165 (December, 1957).

[11] *A Study of the Interests of Children and Youth.* Northwestern University and the Office of Education, U. S. Department of Health, Education and Welfare, *op. cit.*

TABLE I

FREE-TIME ACTIVITY PREFERENCES OF PUPILS IN GRADES 3 THROUGH 9[12]

GROUPS	BOYS	PERCENT	GIRLS	PERCENT
Grades 3–6				
	Watching TV	29.4	Watching TV	24.8
	Playing indoors	21.7	Reading	24.8
	Reading	20.8	Playing indoors	15.9
	Playing outside	13.5	Playing outside	7.0
	Playing baseball	4.0	Ice skating	2.9
	Playing football	4.0		
Grades 7–8				
	Watching TV	31.0	Reading	31.2
	Reading	24.7	Watching TV	23.6
	Playing indoors	9.6	Listening to records	7.4
	Listening to radio	5.3	Listening to radio	6.6
	Playing football	3.0	Visiting with friends	3.8
	Playing outside	3.0	Dancing	3.8
Grade 9				
	Watching TV	31.8	Watching TV	28.9
	Reading	17.4	Reading	26.4
	Playing basketball	7.5	Listening to radio	11.1
	Other sports	7.5	Visiting with friends	8.1
	Visiting with friends	3.5	Listening to records	5.1

a teacher should investigate the interests of each new group or class he is to instruct. Each pupil, moreover, must be studied individually, to ascertain his particular pattern of interests and preferences.

Television—Children's Most Time-Consuming Activity

Diverse opinions have been expressed about the effects of television upon children. Some writers emphasize its potentialities as a positive force; others minimize its significance; still others stress its undesirable results. Parents have asserted that television affects adversely their children's interest in reading and in other academic pursuits. Some teachers, too, have pointed to certain unfortunate features of TV insofar as children's interest and effort in school are concerned. Some have described television as a "time trap for children" and have argued that

---

[12] This table is adapted from Table 23 on page 58 in *A Study of the Interests of Children and Youth,* Northwestern University and Office of Education, U. S. Department of Health, Education and Welfare, *op. cit.*

"TV produces not only idlers, but also bad taste and bad manners." To evaluate the charges made against television, one may profitably examine the results of investigations made since its first appearance.

In 1949, television came to the Chicago area and the nation on a fairly broad scale. By May, 1950, 43 percent of the school children reported that they had access to it. The percentages increased to 68 in 1951, 88 in 1952, and 92 in 1953. In 1955 and 1956, 97 percent of the pupils reported that they had TV sets in their homes.[13]

With the knowledge that there is a TV set in almost every American home, three important questions may be asked: How much time do children and youth spend viewing television? What programs do most of them watch? What is the effect of televiewing on school achievement, other interests, and attitudes?

Children and youth spend a considerable amount of time viewing television. Elementary school children, in 1951, spent an average of 19 hours televiewing per week; this increased to an average of 21 hours in 1959. High school students, from the first, were found to give less time to watching TV than did younger pupils. Their average for 1951 was 14 hours per week and in 1959 it decreased to 12 hours.

Tastes in the type of program viewed on television are different between age groups and between boys and girls of similar ages. Changes in favorite programs occurred over a period of years within each age and sex group. Table II presents the favorite TV programs of elementary and junior high school pupils.

A few studies have been designed to disclose the relationship between the amount of televiewing and attainment in specific school subjects. For example, in San Leandro, California, sixth- and seventh-grade pupils who watched television the most (22 to 69 hours a week) were compared with those who watched very little (0 to 10 hours a week). Some differences favoring those who watched very little appeared in arithmetic and reading, while little difference was found in the language and spelling attainment of the two groups.[14] In the studies of television made in the Chicago area, excessive televiewing seemed to be associated with somewhat lower academic attainment.[15] The Chicago study points out that some pupils were led to do better work in school because of interests

---

[13] Paul A. Witty and Paul Kinsella, "Children and TV—A Ninth Report," *Elementary English*, 35:450–456 (November, 1958). Other studies have been published in *Elementary English*.

[14] Lloyd F. Scott, "Television and School Achievement," *Phi Delta Kappan*, 38:25–28 (October, 1956).

[15] Paul Witty, "What Children Watch on TV," *The Packet*, vol. XIV, no. 2 (Boston: D. C. Heath and Company, Winter 1959–60).

TABLE II
FAVORITE TV PROGRAMS OF ELEMENTARY AND JUNIOR HIGH SCHOOL PUPILS[16]

GROUP	1958	1959	1960
Grades 1–3	Zorro	Huckleberry Hound	Dennis the Menace
	Bugs Bunny	Bugs Bunny	Dobie Gillis
	Mickey Mouse	Disneyland	Huckleberry Hound
	Blue Fairy	Lassie	Bugs Bunny
	Disneyland	Zorro	Danny Thomas
Grades 4–6	Zorro	77 Sunset Strip	Dobie Gillis
	Shock Theatre	Shock Theatre	77 Sunset Strip
	Father Knows Best	Maverick	Dennis the Menace
	Disneyland	Rifleman	Danny Thomas
	Maverick	Father Knows Best	Father Knows Best
Junior high school — girls	American Bandstand	American Bandstand	Twilight Zone
	Dick Clark Show	Dick Clark Show	American Bandstand and 77 Sunset Strip
	Father Knows Best	Father Knows Best	Hawaiian Eye
	Shock Theatre	Maverick	Danny Thomas and Dobie Gillis
	Playhouse 90	Donna Reed Show	Dick Clark Show
Junior high school — boys	Shock Theatre	Maverick	Twilight Zone
	Maverick	Shock Theatre	The Untouchables
	Gunsmoke	Gunsmoke	Baseball
	Zorro	Sea Hunt	Wrestling
	American Bandstand	Rifleman	Alcoa Presents

[16] This table adapted from Table III and Table IV in "Televiewing by Children and Youth," by Paul Witty, *Elementary English,* 38:108 (February, 1961).

awakened by TV. Moreover, in the case of an association between television and poor academic attainment, other undesirable facts in addition to excessive televiewing were found.

Writers have asserted that children today tend to spend less time in outdoor play, hobbies, sports, and creative activities than they did in former years, a condition sometimes attributed to the influence of television. Recent studies have shown a persistence of old hobbies and the appearance of new ones since TV arrived. For example, T. C. Battin found that 57 percent of the boys and 59 percent of the girls followed the same hobbies as before TV. Moreover, 38 percent of the boys and 34 percent of the girls reported the cultivation of new hobbies, while only 5 percent of the boys and 7 percent of the girls indicated fewer hobbies.[17]

[17] T. C. Battin, *Television and Youth,* report published by TV Information Committee, National Association of Radio and TV Broadcasters, Washington, D. C., 1954.

The research indicates that television does not necessarily discourage children from pursuing hobbies, from reading, or from studying. For some children televiewing has replaced many other activities in which they might engage, but television has also opened many new avenues that children explore through hobbies and books. Our studies also indicate that many problems which teachers and parents reported during the advent of television have been more recently reported as decreasing.

Radio and Movie Interests

In the Northwestern University–Office of Education Study it was shown that the radio still has a strong hold upon children and youth.[18] The average amount of time spent weekly in radio listening was about 8 hours by pupils in grades 3 through 9. Although in some of our earlier studies, radio had equaled the popularity of television among high-school students, in this study television was rated first among favored pursuits at all levels. Not only was TV more popular according to pupils' statements, but it also offered, they said, greater possibilities than did radio or movies for fruitful association with schoolwork.

Movies outside the home were found also to attract many boys and girls, who most often attended them once each week or once in every two weeks. Although it is clear that movie attendance outside the home has been curtailed, as compared with the years prior to 1950, pupils continue to be attracted by, and to find satisfaction in, movies.

Boys and girls appear to be attracted to the radio and movies by the same elements—action, adventure, and excitement. Studies of the preferred movies showed generally that elementary school children liked the Disney productions. Films about cowboys and pilots also proved popular. Less favored were pictures of current events, biography and travel, news shorts and commentaries. As Jersild pointed out:

> Children's movie interests roughly parallel their reading and radio interests . . . although there are exceptions. For example, "comedy" seems to figure more in movie than in reading interests (unless comic strips are so classed). Reports of movie interests at any given time must be taken with a good deal of reservation, just as in the case of radio programs, for the choices depend to a large degree upon what happens to have been available recently and upon the tastes that have been cultivated by the kind of fare offered in the past.[19]

---

[18] *A Study of the Interests of Children and Youth.* Northwestern University and the Office of Education, U. S. Department of Health, Education and Welfare, *op. cit.*

[19] Arthur T. Jersild, *Child Psychology,* 5th ed. (Englewood Cliffs, N. J. Prentice-Hall, Inc., 1960), p. 508.

The marked influence of the mass media upon the lives of children and youth is quite apparent. A problem of primary significance in teaching reading is the recognition of this force as well as the importance of efforts to utilize interests awakened through the mass media. Another problem involves the encouragement of pupils to pursue balanced programs of activities in which reading and play interests, as well as response to the mass media, may find expression.

Reading Activities and Preferences

More than two hundred studies of the reading interests of children and youth have been made. From 1893, when M. B. C. True reported "What My Pupils Read," to the present time, studies have been undertaken to determine the amount and nature of voluntary reading and the factors affecting reading preferences and activities.

L. M. Terman and Margaret Lima identified a number of factors inherent in the development of reading interests, such as age, health and physical development, school environment, home training, and differences in mental ability. Although "at every age girls read more than boys," few differences in reading choices appeared until age nine, "when the divergence is very marked and the breach continues to widen up to adult life. . ."[20]

Results of earlier studies, showing sex differences in reading interests and the significance of certain elements in determining the popularity of reading materials, were largely corroborated by George Norvell's extensive investigations of reading interests, published in 1958.[21] Data were assembled from the expressions of opinion by more than 24,000 children in grades 3 to 6. Elements favorable to reading for boys included: adventurous action, physical struggle, human character, animals, humor, courage, heroism, and patriotism. The following unfavorable elements were cited: description, didacticism, fairies, romantic love, sentiment, girls or women as leading characters, and physical weakness in male characters.

Favorable items for girls were: lively adventure, home and school life, human characters, domestic animals and pets, romantic love, sentiment, mystery, the supernatural, and patriotism. Violent action, description, didacticism, boys and girls younger than the reader (except babies), and fierce animals were disapproved elements.

---

[20] Lewis M. Terman and Margaret Lima, *Children's Reading: A Guide for Parents and Teachers*, 2nd ed. (New York: Appleton-Century-Crofts, 1931), p. 131.
[21] George W. Norvell, *What Boys and Girls Like to Read* (Morristown, N. J.: Silver Burdett Company, 1958).

It was found that many selections classified as juvenile increased in appeal to a high point and then declined. Moreover, many rhymes from Mother Goose were enjoyed as late as in grade 6; many others were rejected as early as in grade 3. It was pointed out that *Aesop's Fables* and fairy tales were especially popular in grades 3 to 5; and myths, legends, and hero and folk tales were most popular in grades 5 to 7. Sex differences in children's choices in reading appeared early, and girls were found to enjoy many boys' books, but boys rejected almost all girls' books. Some adult magazines proved popular with both boys and girls.

The results of the recent Northwestern University–U. S. Office of Education investigation in the field of reading are provocative. The kinds of reading and the kinds of stories liked by pupils in grades 3 through 9 are presented in Tables III and IV.

TABLE III
KINDS OF READING LIKED BY PUPILS[22]

GRADES	BOYS — PERCENT	GIRLS — PERCENT
3–6		
Fiction	29.5	28.7
Articles in newspapers and magazines	20.9	16.8
Biography	16.4	11.8
Poetry	13.5	20.8
Plays	13.4	19.5
Essays	6.3	2.4
7–8		
Fiction	33.0	33.7
Articles in newspapers and magazines	30.6	27.0
Biography	27.5	22.3
Essays	3.9	4.2
Plays	2.8	6.9
Poetry	2.1	5.9
9		
Articles in newpspapers and magazines	32.2	26.0
Fiction	31.8	30.6
Biography	20.9	18.1
Plays	5.5	13.2
Essays	5.3	6.7
Poetry	4.3	5.4

[22] Table III is adapted from Table 40, and Table IV from Table 41 on page 70 in *A Study of the Interests of Children and Youth,* Northwestern University and the Office of Education, U. S. Department of Health, Education and Welfare, *op. cit.*

TABLE IV
KINDS OF STORIES LIKED BY PUPILS

GRADES	BOYS — PERCENT	GIRLS — PERCENT
3–6		
Adventure	20.3	16.1
Westerns	17.1	10.3
Mystery	17.0	18.3
Science fiction	12.9	—
Humor	9.3	10.8
Animal	—	14.3
7–8		
Adventure	19.8	7.4
Science fiction	17.2	—
Mystery	16.4	25.4
Humor	15.1	16.6
Animal	6.0	7.6
Romance	—	25.4
9		
Adventure	22.5	10.3
Mystery	19.6	19.8
Science fiction	15.3	—
Humor	13.3	16.0
Westerns	7.9	—
Romance	—	27.0

Most of the books reported by these pupils were in the category of fiction. Poetry, essays, and drama were less often read. Stories of famous people were the best-liked nonfiction group. The most popular books fell in the areas of adventure, mystery, and westerns, though many boys were attracted to science fiction too. Girls turned more frequently to stories involving romance.

The average amount of time devoted to reading voluntarily by the pupils in grades 3 through 9 was 1.1 hours daily.[23] Moreover, the ninth-grade pupil appears to read little more than the middle-grade child. Compared with television, reading has relatively small appeal, except perhaps for gifted children.

The results of this study were not reassuring insofar as reading is concerned. This investigation revealed that relatively little time is spent on books outside the school. Even magazine reading of the older pupils was limited largely to *Life, Look, The Saturday Evening Post,* and news periodicals.

[23] *Ibid.*

A determined effort should be made to improve the status of reading among children and youth today. Certainly, a disproportionate amount of time seems to be given to the mass media as compared with that accorded worthwhile reading. We shall suggest later in this chapter some ways by which this condition may be alleviated through cooperative efforts by parents and teachers.

Vocational and Educational Interests

Numerous early studies have indicated that vocational choices of elementary and secondary school pupils were largely unrealistic. Because vocational interests change markedly prior to adolescence, the choices of senior high school pupils tend to be more realistic than the selections of younger boys and girls.

The pupils in the recent Northwestern University–Office of Education investigation appear to be more realistic in their choices of occupations than pupils in studies made a decade or more ago.[24] This trend was shown in the selection of a relatively small number of occupations by most of the boys and girls—occupations which hold possibilities of absorbing many people today. Girls mentioned more frequently than in earlier studies such occupations as teacher, nurse, and secretary; the boys chose engineer, scientist, and pilot. The choices reflected the impact of the modern world with its growing demand for airline stewardesses, engineers, and pilots. Table V presents the vocational choices of the boys and girls in the three groups: grades 3 through 6, grades 7 and 8, and grade 9. The choices, while not so unrealistic as those in some earlier studies, were, nevertheless, impractical in many cases. Obviously, guidance is a crucial need. It should begin early and should lead to more realistic *individual* choices.

APPLICATION OF PUPIL INTEREST IN CLASSROOM PRACTICE

Many teachers can give abundant examples of the effective use of interests in the classroom. Thus, in September, one second-grade teacher studied the interests of her group with an inventory, and found that in these children at this time an interest in pets and animals was second only to their interest in TV. One child told about the chickens and ducks he had seen on his uncle's farm, and another talked about a visit to a zoo. Other children recounted their interests in animals and

[24] *Ibid.*

TABLE V
VOCATIONAL PREFERENCES OF PUPILS IN GRADES 3 THROUGH 9[25]

GROUPS	BOYS	PERCENT	GIRLS	PERCENT
Grades 3–6				
	Doctor	13.2	Teacher	22.7
	Scientist	8.6	Nurse	18.7
	Baseball player	7.0	Secretary	10.9
	Engineer	5.4	Mother and housewife	6.4
	Soldier	4.9	Airline hostess	6.2
Grades 7–8				
	Engineer	13.2	Teacher	22.0
	Lawyer	9.1	Secretary	13.9
	Scientist	8.7	Nurse	11.8
	Pilot	7.0	Airline hostess	7.5
	Doctor	5.9	Model	5.7
Grade 9				
	Engineer	12.7	Nurse	15.6
	Enlist in Navy	7.0	Teacher	11.4
	Scientist	5.6	Secretary	9.4
	Architect	4.9	Airline hostess	5.2
	Baseball player	3.5	Model	4.2

pets in their own homes. Soon they were reading such books as *One Morning in Maine* and *Make Way for Ducklings*, by Robert McCloskey; *The Valentine Cat*, by Clyde Bulla; and *The Grocery Kitty*, by Helen Hoke.

Three girls with a strong interest in kittens and cats presented to the class pictures of their own animals as well as beautiful pictures in the book by Ylla. Later the teacher brought in Ylla's *Two Little Bears*, and the children shared her enthusiasm for the photographs. These children discussed their favorite cat and bear books. Among the popular books were two in Esther Averill's series, *Jenny's First Party* and *Jenny Goes to Sea*.

One boy whose enjoyment of horse stories began with his discovery of Marguerite Henry's *Little Fellow* reported enthusiastically on Grace Skaar's *A Boy and His Horse*. Another boy read aloud from Louise Fatio's *The Happy Lion*. A humorous dramatization of *The Happy Lion Roars* was later prepared by other class members.

On a dreary November day, arrangements were made for the showing of some *Disney Classics* filmstrips. Part of the book *The Little House*,

[25] *Ibid.*

by Virginia Burton, was first read aloud. Then the filmstrip was shown. A few days later another Disney classic, *Johnny Appleseed*, was presented. The filmstrips seemed to awaken in some children a desire to read.

One day a boy called Sandy came to school greatly excited over his new shepherd dog. The film *Shep, the Farm Dog* was shown, and the accompanying film reader was read by the entire class. *Friendly Little Jonathan,* by Dorothy and Marguerite Bryan, was reviewed by another pupil, Joan, who told about her own puppy. *Finder's Keepers,* by Will and Nicolas, and *The First Book of Dogs,* by Gladys Taber, proved popular with many other pupils at this time.

The children's responses to the question "What do you want to do when you get out of school?" were discussed. Mary wanted to be a ballet dancer; Bill, a carpenter; and John, a cook or baker. Mary found Carla Greene's *I Want to Be a Ballet Dancer* the best book she had ever read; Bill read with great satisfaction Greene's *I Want to Be a Carpenter;* and John found similar pleasure in reading *I Want to Be a Baker.*

Skills in oral reading were fostered by having children read aloud from time to time, an activity which was related to story-telling. Again interests revealed by the inventory were used to guide the selections of stories. The books by Dr. Seuss provided an occasion for oral reading that delighted the boys and girls. Poetry too was enjoyed by these pupils.

During individual interviews the children were asked to make three wishes. Although some of the responses were simply requests for toys or pets—typical reactions of second-grade pupils—in several instances significant individual reactions were obtained. These responses, sympathetically interpreted, enabled this teacher to understand the pupils better and to provide the kind of school atmosphere in which happiness, successful achievement, and steady growth became possible for every child in the group. Books such as *So'm I,* by Theodore Key, were often read with appreciation and value by insecure children.

This teacher studied the varied individual and group interests of her pupils, selected topics of worth, and provided appropriate opportunities for the expression of these interests and for their extension through reading. In addition, she recognized the importance of skill in reading in order to gain from it the greatest pleasure. The basal texts and supplementary materials she used provided the central core around which skills were built and experiences in reading were articulated. The effectiveness of this approach was shown by the unusually efficient progress of her pupils in the mastery of habits and skills and by their development of desirable attitudes toward reading.

In recent educational periodicals and books there are a number of such accounts in which successful endeavor is reported in programs based on a study of pupil interests. Several are found in the monograph entitled *Developing Permanent Interest in Reading*.[26] For example, an analysis of the role of the teacher in the primary grades is presented by Claribel M. Nayder, who stresses the responsibility of the teacher for ascertaining and utilizing interests as well as the necessity of teachers working cooperatively with parents and librarians.[27]

The use of an interest in television to foster improvement in attitudes toward reading and to promote skill in reading among seventh- and eighth-grade boys in a vocational school is reported in a stimulating article by Charles Spiegler, who concludes:

> Beyond a doubt, Johnny reads if his interest is stirred, and, beyond a doubt too, Johnny can best be taught *reading* if interest is the keynote. . . Even with the slowest readers, the skillful teacher makes interest the bridge.[28]

It should be indicated that interests associated with television programs can and often do provide the stimulus for reading. Thus, in the Northwestern University–Office of Education study, it was found that television programs such as the *Story-teller, Shirley Temple, Walt Disney, Bold Journey,* and *Lassie* were indicated as stimulators of reading among elementary pupils, just as the *Bell Science Series, Playhouse 90,* and *Disney* programs were said to stimulate reading among older students. Books cited by the participants as read because of television included *Heidi, Lassie, Little Women, The Yearling, Old Yeller,* and *Kon-Tiki*.[29]

---

[26] Helen M. Robinson (editor), *Developing Permanent Interest in Reading*, Supplementary Educational Monographs No. 84 (Chicago: The University of Chicago Press, December, 1956).

[27] Claribel M. Nayder, "Using Radio and Television to Incite Interest in Reading in Kindergarten Through Grade Three," in Helen M. Robinson (editor), *Developing Permanent Interest in Reading, op. cit.,* pp. 95–98.

[28] Charles G. Spiegler, "Johnny Will Read What He Likes to Read," *Developing Permanent Interest in Reading* (Chicago: The University of Chicago Press, 1956), p. 185.

[29] *A Study of the Interests of Children and Youth.* Northwestern University and the Office of Education, U. S. Department of Health, Education and Welfare, *op. cit.*

CONCLUDING STATEMENT

To offset the threat of television to reading, both parents and teachers can make positive contributions. If parents turn frequently to books for information and pleasure, if they read children's stories aloud and show a liking for books, their children will probably conclude that it is worthwhile to read and will in turn enjoy reading. If parents plan family recreation that includes reading, televiewing and other activities, children will be led increasingly to assimilate TV in balanced and individually suitable programs of leisure activity. And if parents and children together plan and build home libraries and go to the public library frequently, the possible ill effects of television will be further offset.

The teacher has a similar responsibility. A primary task is to ascertain interests and to guide or redirect them into worthwhile channels. The teacher has the added responsibility of possessing knowledge of books that would further the interests of her pupils. The knack of presenting the proper books at the most opportune time must be learned by the teacher. Moreover, each classroom should have a reading corner, neat and attractive; and time should be provided each day to share books, to read, to discuss ideas gained from reading. The teacher must love books and show this love as in the examples offered in this chapter.

Accordingly, existing interests should be ascertained, evaluated, and utilized as avenues for engendering stronger motivation and satisfaction in productive educational effort. Such endeavor recognizes also the necessity for the cultivation of more effective habits and skills which may in themselves lead to a greater interest and zeal for reading. But the role of interest must not be minimized. This combined emphasis on interest and on skill will undoubtedly result in more efficient and successful learning. As George Norvell says:

> ... to increase reading skill, promote the reading habit, and produce a generation of book lovers, there is no factor so powerful as interest.[30]

---

[30] George W. Norvell, "Some Results of a Twelve Year Study of Children's Reading Interests," *The English Journal,* 37:536 (December, 1948).

Selected References

Anderson, Harold A., "Reading Interests and Tastes," in W. S. Gray, *Reading in General Education* (Washington, D. C.: American Council on Education, 1940), pp. 217–271.

Betzner, Jean and R. L. Lyman, "The Development of Reading Interests and Tastes," in W. S. Gray (chairman), *The Teaching of Reading: A Second Report*, 36th Yearbook, Part I, National Society for the Study of Education (Bloomington, Ill.: Public School Publishing Co., 1937), pp. 185–205.

Byers, Loretta, "Pupils' Interests and the Content of Primary Reading Texts," *Reading Teacher*, 17:227–233 (January, 1964).

Celestine, Sister M., "A Survey of the Literature on the Reading Interests of Children of the Elementary Grades," Catholic University of America Educational Research Bulletin, V, nos. 2 and 3 (Washington, D.C.: Catholic Educational Press, 1930).

Dees, Margaret, "Easy to Read: For Beginning Independent Readers," *Elementary English*, 39:418–420 (May, 1962).

"Developing Lifetime Habits in Reading," *Reading Teacher* (theme of the issue), 12 (April, 1959).

Friedman, Kopple C. and Claude L. Nemzek, "A Survey of Reading Interest Studies," *Education*, 57:51–56 (September, 1936).

Gates, Arthur I. and Frank G. Jennings, "The Role of Motivation," in Paul A. Witty (chairman), *Development In and Through Reading*, 60th Yearbook, Part I, National Society for the Study of Education (Chicago: University of Chicago Press, 1961), pp. 109–126.

Getzels, Jacob W., "The Nature of Reading Interests: Psychological Aspects," in Helen M. Robinson (editor), *Developing Permanent Interest in Reading*, Supplementary Educational Monographs, no. 84 (Chicago: University of Chicago Press), pp. 5–9.

Hofer, Louise B., "What Do Sixth Graders Really Like in Poetry?" *Elementary English*, 33:433–438 (November, 1956).

Huus, Helen, "How a TV Program Can Be Used as a Springboard to Further Reading," *Elementary English*, 34:81–88 (February, 1957).

Jersild, Arthur T. and Ruth J. Tasch, *Children's Interests and What They Suggest for Education* (New York: Teachers College, Columbia University, Bureau of Publications, 1949).

Jordan, Arthur M., "Children's Interests in Reading," *The High School Journal*, 25:323–330 (November-December, 1942).

Kuder, G. Frederick and Blanche B. Paulson, *Exploring Children's Interests*, Better Living Booklets (Chicago: Science Research Associates, Inc., 1951).

Martin, Marvin, "Fifty Books They Can't Resist," *Elementary English*, 39:415–417 (May, 1962).

McCarty, Pearl S., "Reading Interests Shown by Choice of Books in School Libraries," *School Review*, 58:90–96 (February, 1956).

McCullough, Constance M., "A Log of Children's Out-of-School Activities," *The Elementary School Journal*, 58:157–165 (December, 1957).

Norvell, George W., *The Reading Interests of Young People* (Boston: D. C. Heath and Company, 1950).

Norvell, George W., *What Boys and Girls Like to Read* (Morristown, N. J.: Silver Burdett Company, 1958).

Robinson, Helen (compiling editor), *Developing Permanent Interest in Reading,* Supplementary Educational Monograph, number 83. (Chicago: The University of Chicago Press, Dec., 1956).

Schramm, Wilbur, Jack Lyle, and Edwin B. Parker, *Television in the Lives of Our Children* (Stanford, California: Stanford University Press, 1961).

Smith, Nila B. (editor), *Developing Taste in Literature,* Research Bulletin of the National Conference on Research in English (Champaign, Ill.: The National Council of Teachers of English, 1963).

Super, Donald E., *The Psychology of Careers* (New York: Harper & Row, Publishers, 1957).

Witty, Paul A., *Reading in Modern Education* (Boston: D. C. Heath and Company, 1949).

Witty, Paul, "Studies in Televiewings 1949–1964," *Science Education,* 49:310–316 (October, 1965).

Witty, Paul A., "What Children Watch on TV," *The Packet. A Heath Service Bulletin for Elementary Teachers,* published by D. C. Heath and Company, Boston, Massachusetts, 14:3–15 (Winter, 1959–60).

Witty, Paul A. and Paul J. Kinsella, "Children and TV—A Ninth Report," *Elementary English,* 35:450–456 (November, 1958).

Witty, Paul A. and David Kopel, *Reading and the Educative Process* (Boston: Ginn and Company, 1939).

Witty, Paul A. and Robert A. Sizemore, "Reading the Comics: A Summary of Studies and an Evaluation," *Elementary English,* 31:501–507 (December, 1954); 32:43–49, 109–114 (January and February, 1955).

Witty, Paul A. (guest editor), "Interests of Children and Youth: Research and Application," *Education,* 83:450–506 (April, 1963).

Witty, Paul A. (assisted by Paul Kinsella and Anne Coomer), "A Summary of Yearly Studies of Televiewing—1949–1963," *Elementary English,* 40:590–597 (October, 1963).

4

THE ROLE OF DEVELOPMENTAL NEEDS

Workers in the field of mental health have long emphasized the importance of basic needs. As early as 1941 one of the authors of this book stressed the responsibility of the home to offer children an atmosphere in which sturdy physical and mental health is nourished. He pointed out that in addition to assuming responsibility for providing the young child with food, clothing, and the other necessities for wholesome physical development, parents should recognize their duty also to foster mental health. In fact, children need affection, security, and sympathetic guidance under consistently stable, reassuring conditions quite as much as they need an adequate physical environment and proper care. Many parents were recognizing these needs, and some were already trying to develop a comprehensive program to insure the continuous wholesome growth of their children. Increasingly they were following the recommendations set forth in books such as *Babies Are Human Beings*.[1] In this book the necessity for careful study and systematic observation to ascertain the unique nature and needs of each child is convincingly presented. Such intelligent and wholesome advice has resulted in widespread appreciation on the part of many parents of the needs of the infant and young child.

These needs are no less important when the child starts to school than they are during the preschool period. Proper food and rest, good vision and hearing, and general vitality are real aids to learning. Mental health is necessary also if the child is to make rapid progress in his school work. Many teachers recognize that it is essential for the child

---

[1] C. A. Aldrich and M. M. Aldrich, *Babies Are Human Beings* (New York: The Macmillan Company, 1938). See also Arnold Gesell and Frances L. Ilg, *Infant and Child in the Culture of Today* (New York: Harper & Row, Publishers, 1943).

to maintain or develop self-confidence, independence, and resourcefulness in thought and action. They understand that these traits are nourished by the judicious use of recognition and praise. Some psychologists have referred to the status attained by the child through his appreciation of his own success as the fulfillment of an integrative need; they know that a harmonious, balanced life-design is rarely achieved unless the child regards himself as competent and successful. As this appreciation grows in the child, it should be balanced by the development of a parallel respect for the needs and worth of others.

The wide range of ability within the typical classroom makes difficult the provision of conditions through which every child may gain recognition. Nevertheless, a classroom rich in opportunities for varied experience and individual expression is likely to be one in which every child has a chance to achieve success. Under such conditions boys and girls learn to respect the achievement of their classmates and to accept with appreciation different levels of competency and understanding.

THE IDENTIFICATION OF DEVELOPMENTAL NEEDS

Because the word *developmental* is used extensively and in varied ways in the educational and psychological literature, it is important to consider the use of the word as it applies to "developmental reading." Marian E. Breckenridge and H. Lee Vincent provide a definition consistent with the point of view of the present book:

> Development can be defined as the emerging and expanding of capacities of the individual to provide progressively greater facility in functioning. . . . Thus the child increases in motor skills from his uncertain first steps to a high proficiency in skilled games at adolescence; from physiologic instability to stability; from the first babbling in infancy to manipulation of language in abstract thinking; from confusion of self with inanimate objects to a clear realization of himself as a person; from the immature child to the man or woman who is able to reproduce.
> This development is made possible by a dynamic relationship between the individual and his environment. The continuous interaction of child and environment provides for the many and complicated changes which characterize development.[2]

Since it is impossible to understand conduct and behavior at any age

---

[2] M. E. Breckenridge and E. L. Vincent, *Child Development. Physical and Psychological Growth Through Adolescence.* 5th ed. (Philadelphia: W. B. Saunders Co., 1965), p. 8.

level without consideration of antecedents, it is desirable for teachers to obtain a comprehensive picture of the growth of infants and young children.

Developmental Needs

Needs may be broad, basic, and universal drives or they may be specific, cultural, and acquired. Abraham Maslow, who has discussed their relative strength and ranged them in order of potency, says: "Human needs arrange themselves in hierarchies of prepotency. That is to say, the appearance of one need usually rests on the prior satisfaction of another, more prepotent need."[3] The hierarchy begins with the most potent needs and builds progressively to the least potent. Maslow has arranged them in this order:

1. *Physiological needs*—The encompassing physiological needs are hunger and thirst, sex, rest, homeostasis, and life. If these needs are not satisfied, subsequent needs in the hierarchy will not appear. When these needs are met, however, subsequent higher needs emerge.
2. *Safety needs*—The safety need expresses itself in childhood by a child's preference "for some kind of undisrupted routine or rhythm. He seems to want a predictable, orderly world. . . . The child needs an organized world rather than an unorganized or unstructured one."[4]
3. *Love needs*—These needs include affection and belonging. Not only in childhood, but also at later times, they continue to be significant. "Now the person will feel keenly, as never before, the absence of friends, or a sweetheart, or a wife, or children. He will hunger for affectionate relations with people in general, namely, for a place in his group, and he will strive with great intensity to achieve this goal."[5] With a satisfactory meeting of the love needs, esteem needs appear.
4. *Esteem needs*—Each individual needs to think well of himself and to receive recognition from others. "Satisfaction of the self-esteem need leads to feelings of self-confidence, worth, strength, capability, and adequacy of being useful and necessary in the world. But thwarting of these needs produces feelings of inferiority, of weakness and of helplessness."[6]
5. *The need for self-actualization*—This need does not always appear, but when it does it creates a new restlessness and motivates

---

[3] Abraham M. Maslow, "A Theory of Human Motivation," in Jerome M. Seidman (editor), *The Child: A Book of Readings* (New York: Holt, Rinehart & Winston, Inc., 1958), p. 418.
[4] *Ibid.*, p. 423.
[5] *Ibid.*, p. 425.
[6] *Ibid.*, p. 426.

the individual to be the best of what he can be. "It refers to the desire of self-fulfillment, namely, to the tendency for him to become actualized in what he is potentially. This tendency might be phrased as the desire to become more and more what one is, to become everything that one is capable of becoming."[7]

The developmental needs encompass the biological and psychological motives of individuals. Applying the knowledge of individual needs is an essential element in a teaching situation. Another factor in a learning situation is a determination of the expectancies of the culture. Another concept that would enhance our knowledge of the individual in terms of biological, psychological, and societal needs is that of "developmental tasks."

Developmental Tasks

Each individual, if he is to make a satisfactory adjustment to society, must learn certain developmental tasks. According to Robert Havighurst, a "developmental task arises . . . at or about a certain period in the life of the individual, successful achievement of which leads to his happiness and to success with later tasks, while failure leads to unhappiness in the individual, disapproval by the society, and difficulty with later tasks."[8]

The following tasks are considered by Havighurst and others to be significant in infancy and early childhood, middle childhood, and adolescence:

Infancy and Early Childhood

1. Learning to walk
2. Learning to take solid foods
3. Learning to talk
4. Learning to control the elimination of bodily wastes
5. Learning sex differences and sexual modesty
6. Forming simple concepts of social and physical reality
7. Learning to relate oneself emotionally to parents, siblings, and other people
8. Learning to distinguish right and wrong and developing a conscience

[7] *Ibid.,* p. 427.
[8] Robert J. Havighurst, *Developmental Tasks and Education* (Chicago: University of Chicago Press, 1948), p. 6. "The Scope of Persistent Life Situations and Ways in Which Learners Face Them," Florence B. Stratemeyer, Hamden L. Forkner, Margaret G. McKim. *See also* A. Harry Passow, *Developing Curriculum for Modern Living,* 2nd ed. (New York: Teachers College, Columbia University, 1957), Chap. 6, pp. 146–332.

Middle Childhood

1. Learning physical skills necessary for ordinary games
2. Building wholesome attitudes toward oneself as a growing organism
3. Learning to get along with age-mates
4. Learning an appropriate masculine or feminine role
5. Developing fundamental skills in reading, writing, and calculating
6. Developing concepts necessary for everyday living
7. Developing conscience, morality, and a scale of values
8. Achieving personal independence
9. Developing attitudes toward social groups and institutions

Adolescence

1. Achieving new and more mature relations with age-mates of both sexes
2. Achieving a masculine or feminine social role
3. Accepting one's physique and using the body effectively
4. Achieving emotional independence of parents and other adults
5. Achieving assurance of economic independence
6. Selecting and preparing for an occupation
7. Preparing for marriage and family life
8. Developing intellectual skills and concepts necessary for civic competence
9. Desiring and achieving socially responsible behavior
10. Acquiring a set of values and an ethical system as a guide to behavior

It may be noted that some developmental tasks stem from physical maturation while others arise from society. Learning to walk is a physical task whereas learning to read is a demand of society. A third source is the personal motive and value which grows out of the interaction of physical and cultural demands.

The concepts of needs and developmental tasks help us to understand the child physically, emotionally, and culturally. These, in addition to interest discussed in the last chapter, should form the basis for learning. Later in this chapter we shall show how these concepts were applied to certain learning situations at the Northwestern University Clinic.

Determining the Needs of Children and Youth

To ascertain the needs of students, good rapport must be established. When students feel comfortable with each other and with the teacher, they will usually be free to express their varied feelings and personal reactions. Sympathetic understanding on the part of the teacher, knowledge of children's needs, and provision of opportunities for pupils to express their difficulties are necessary elements in the establishment of rapport.

Once rapport has been established, the subtle process of discovering student needs will involve the use of various techniques and approaches such as the following:

1. *Interviews guided by interest inventories*—In case studies throughout this book we have pointed to pupils' responses to specific items which have suggested pupil needs, for example, inquiries about fears and anxieties, ambitions, peer and home relations, and failures and successes.

2. *Examination of creative writing of pupils*—The writings of pupils, particularly on topics related to personal feelings and ideas, can prove to be very informative. When creative writing is sincerely motivated, the pupil will often relate freely and accurately those feelings and attitudes which are indicative of his needs.

3. *Observations of pupils in various situations*—The teacher will find it profitable to record items from his observations of pupils' responses in varied types of play and recreation. Observations of play and recreational activities afford the teacher excellent insight into the relationship between a certain child and a group of his peers.

4. *Attitudes expressed by pupils during discussions*—Group and teacher-pupil discussions of characters in stories, biographies, and plays afford the teacher an opportunity to discover the pupils' problems and needs. Children can be at ease identifying with a character in a book because that character does not represent a real threat to the individual.

5. *Open-ended compositions*—Compositions written on topics related to worries, fears, and wishes can be dramatic illustrations of children's needs. Some teachers have found it profitable to ask pupils to respond to inquiries such as: If you could have three wishes that might come true, what would you wish?

6. *Entries in diaries and logs by pupils*—Entries in diaries and logs may be indicative of pupil needs as well as interests. Autobiographies may also be used effectively.

7. *Standardized inventories*—Responses to formal inventories such as the *Detroit Adjustment Inventory* and the *Mooney Check List* yield data which may supplement and extend information derived from more informal approaches.

Thus we see that the discovery of students' needs may involve the use of formal and informal methods. Regardless of the evaluative criteria some children may openly voice their needs, while others may be reluctant to do so or may even not have consciously recognized them.

DEVELOPMENTAL NEEDS AND THE READING PROCESS

Although various goals of reading instruction have been emphasized from time to time in our schools, the assumption has always been made that reading experience would affect not only children's behavior but also their attitudes. For some time, psychologists and teachers have stressed the importance of using reading to help pupils satisfy personal and social needs. They believe that carefully selected books do foster desirable attitudes and behavior by helping boys and girls meet their personal and social needs. Many would grant the significance of interest and the value of certain books, sometimes regarded as classics, in the lives of many persons. But writers on psychology stress the significance also of reading as a way of helping students achieve mental health. Such a goal, they think, is particularly important in the present era of insecurity and anxiety.

If we accept the fact that reading is more than a routine skill, we will concede that it also involves emotional responses and overtones. Reading has come to be recognized increasingly as an aid in developing self-insight as well as a means of promoting security and adjustment.[9]

The teacher may serve as an effective guide, helping the student discover for himself an answer to his personal and social problems. To do this effectively, he must gain an understanding of each pupil and his background. He must also be acquainted with many kinds of reading matter—fiction, biography, drama, essays, poetry, informative prose, etc.[10]

Books to Meet Developmental Needs

Every teacher of primary and middle-grade children has probably discovered certain books that have served admirably to satisfy

[9] This point of view received recognition as early as 1941 in a chapter by Paul Witty, "Children's Needs—The Basis for a Language Program," in Nellie Appy (Chairman), *Pupils Are People,* National Council of Teachers of English (New York: Appleton-Century-Crofts, 1941), pp. 37–58.

[10] Dwight L. Burton and Nancy Larrick, "Literature for Children and Youth," in Paul A. Witty (chairman), *Development In and Through Reading,* Sixtieth Yearbook of the National Society for the Study of Education (Chicago: University of Chicago Press, 1961), Part I, pp. 189–209.

pupils' needs. Thus the primary teacher may have suggested Ted Key's *So'm I* to a boy whose physical condition had led him to doubt his capacity for successful competition. In this remarkable story a colt that is an unlikely race winner develops extraordinary strengths from seeming weaknesses. At the end, this colt demonstrates that all of us can be winners. Similarly, older boys have been able to identify themselves with the courageous hero of *Amos Fortune, Free Man,* by Elizabeth Yates, and to gain help in the building of their ideals of self from this association. Eleanor Estes' *The Hundred Dresses* has been a source of inspiration to many girls, who find in the heroine's use of her meager opportunities a challenge for them to overcome seemingly insurmountable obstacles. Reading of this kind will often help pupils not only in meeting personal problems but also in understanding other people better. Thus Lois Lenski's *Strawberry Girl* offers the basis for a pupil's acquiring an understanding of certain people in Southern states; and *Blue Ridge Billy* and other books by the same author may similarly afford the basis for the appreciation of people who live in other sections of our country.

If, as we have indicated, books may alleviate problems for elementary school pupils, this approach is no less effective at the secondary school level. For example, a group of ninth-grade students who were having serious difficulties in meeting both their personal and social needs found help from such books as Barber's *The Trembling Years,* Tarkington's *Alice Adams,* Felsen's *Street Rod,* and Cavanna's *Paintbox Summer.*

Teachers will find the following bibliographies especially helpful in seeking books to satisfy developmental needs and tasks:

> *A Teacher's Guide to Children's Books* (Columbus, Ohio, Charles E. Merrill Books, Inc., 1960).
> *Best Books for Children* (New York: R. R. Bowker Company, 1960)
> *Bibliography of Books for Children* (Washington, D. C.: Association for Childhood Education International, revised annually)
> *Character Formation Through Books: A Bibliography,* rev. ed. (Washington, D. C.: The Catholic University of America Press, 1952)
> *Treasure for the Taking,* rev. ed. (New York: The Viking Press, 1957).

In order to engage successfully in a developmental program, the teacher must be acquainted with many books as well as with reliable sources for other information. Manifestly, a broad reading program geared to individual needs takes account of a wide variety of reading purposes and utilizes many types of reading matter. Moreover, the approach presupposes the use of various kinds of printed matter, including books, magazines, pamphlets, and newspapers.

Bibliotherapy

Many children present evidence of poor mental health in varying degrees of seriousness. Such children usually display unfulfilled developmental needs which sometimes may be met through reading. They may also display inappropriate attitudes or feelings which need to be reexamined, understood, and reshaped. This may be accomplished through a process sometimes referred to as *bibliotherapy*.

David Russell and Caroline Shrodes define this term as:

> . . . a process of dynamic interaction between the personality of the reader and literature . . . interaction which may be utilized for personal assessment, adjustment and growth. This definition suggests that bibliotherapy is not a strange esoteric activity but one that lies within the province of every teacher of literature in working with every child in a group. It does not assume that the teacher must be a skilled therapist, nor the child a seriously maladjusted individual needing clinical treatment. Rather, it conveys the idea that all teachers must be aware of the effects of reading upon children and must realize that, through literature, most children can be helped to solve the developmental problems of adjustment which they face.[11]

Many writers, according to Russell and Shrodes, "agree that bibliotherapy provides opportunity for catharsis and greater insight into one's own motivation and the behavior of others. They agree that in bibliotherapy some sort of integration of intellectual perception and emotional drive must take place."[12]

A number of classroom teachers have attempted to use books to help pupils face and solve personal problems. Deborah Elkins employed a sociometric scale to find children rejected by their peers, as well as to discover the acknowledged leaders.[13] She requested, too, that the children write about their worries and their wishes. In this way she found that they expressed concern over other people's opinions of them, over their appearance, and over the financial status of their families. Broken homes were also a source of worry. Having concluded that the worries of the children fell into two large areas—"family" and "peer"

---

[11] David H. Russell and Caroline Shrodes, "Contributions of Research in Bibliotherapy to the Language Arts Program, I," *The School Review*, 58:335 (September, 1950).
[12] *Ibid.*, p. 339.
[13] Deborah Elkins, "Students Face Their Problems," *The English Journal*, 38:498–503 (November, 1949).

relationships—she selected books and short stories in these two areas for the pupils to read and discuss. The results of this study appeared to indicate the value of this approach in helping children attain improved mental health.

Another classroom teacher conducted an experiment to determine the effectiveness of bibliotherapy in fostering the personal-social adjustment of ninth-grade students.[14] Two groups were matched according to reading ability. Each student was given the *SRA Youth Inventory* at the beginning of the experiment to determine areas of individual need in personal adjustment and again at the end to note changes in adjustment scores. The experimental group consisted of those students in each class whose scores indicated an area or areas of need in personal-social adjustment. Books were suggested for these pupils to read, the selections being made with the aid of the librarian according to the "area or areas in which students were having difficulty." In the control group all students were free to select whatever books they wished to read. Books that related to specific problems were available but not suggested.

The findings of the experiment indicated that students who are guided in their reading to books related to personal-social adjustment may obtain significant help in solving their problems. The adjustment scores of the experimental group were superior to those of the control group on the *SRA Youth Inventory*.

Teachers are increasingly recognizing the value of guiding children to read books which are related to specific areas of conflict. To aid such teachers, some writers have assembled lists of books which contain episodes related to various emotional problems.[15] Under the supervision of Edith Grotberg, a group of teachers utilized reading material of this type with children whose emotional problems and needs had been diagnosed. The books included Marie Hall Ets' *Mr. T. W. Anthony Woo,* which presents the theme of sibling rivalry, as does Margaret Sweet Johnson's *Joey and Patches.* It was thought that Dorothy Lathrop's *The Littlest Mouse* might appeal to children who felt rejected because of their size. And for the child who showed symptoms of aggression, books such as Clyde Robert Bulla's *Riding the Pony Express* were suggested. In fact, a number of books were assembled which seemed appropriate in offering solutions to each pupil's problems. The children examined and discussed these volumes with the teachers, who

---

[14] Mary Louise Brinkman, "The Value of Directed Reading for Personal-Social Adjustment on the Ninth Grade Level; unpublished Master's Thesis, Northern Illinois University, De Kalb, Illinois, July, 1954.

[15] Henry P. Smith and Emerald V. Dechant, *Psychology in Teaching Reading* (Englewood Cliffs, N. J.: Prentice-Hall Inc., 1961), pp. 316–320.

made sure that the books selected were of appropriate difficulty and content. Scores on tests as well as observation of the behavior and attitudes of the students suggested the value of the approach in ameliorating problems and in changing the attitudes of the students.

Other studies also suggest that bibliotherapy may be advantageously employed in the classroom. The success of such efforts depends in part, as we have indicated, on the teacher's knowledge of developmental needs of children and youth and on his acquaintance with the literature for children of such ages.

The Impact of Reading on Behavior

A basic assumption of those who recommend bibliotherapy is that changes in behavior or attitude result from the practice. This assumption may, however, be questioned. Can children resolve conflicts? Can they gain insights into their motivations? Can they improve their personalities through reading? David Russell, after evaluating research in this area, finds he must conclude:

> From the research point of view, however, the effects of reading are an uncharted wasteland in an otherwise well-mapped territory. We have discovered many facts about eye-movements in reading, reading interests and tastes, and methods of reading instruction—but we don't know much about what reading does to people.[16]

Russell suggests further that effects may vary with (a) the situation in which the reading takes place, (b) the content of materials read, (c) the attitudes, personality, and needs of the reader, and (d) opportunities for using the reading and connecting it to other activities. He adds:

> Evidence about the effects of reading comes largely from introspective reports and case-study data, and it seems that the effects of reading may be largely an individual matter. A biography of conquest over difficulties may be an account of archaeological expeditions to one boy and a description of deserts to another.[17]

It is true, of course, that pupils do not always display the attitudes expected from reading suggested books. Their acceptance of the ideas presented in books and their responses to those ideas are influenced by many factors—their background of experience, their prejudices, and

---

[16] David H. Russell, "Some Research on the Impact of Reading," *The English Journal*, 47:398 (October, 1958).

[17] David H. Russell, "Continuity in the Reading Program," in Paul A. Witty (chairman), *Development In and Through Reading, op. cit.*, p. 252.

their preconceived ideas on different topics.[18] Hence, varied responses and unpredicted attitudes sometimes result, but anticipated changes in attitude and behavior can be noted in many instances.

At the Northwestern Psycho-Educational Clinic it has been demonstrated on numerous occasions that a knowledge of the developmental needs has proved particularly helpful in guiding the reading of elementary and secondary pupil referrals. The following is a case study of a pupil whose rehabilitation is traceable in part to the judicious use of books to satisfy developmental needs[19]:

> Ten-year-old Bill was brought to the Psycho-Educational Clinic by his mother. With Bill was his younger sister, Sue, who in the mother's words, "was the apple of her father's eye." Sue was self-centered, uncontrolled and impulsive. Mrs. X explained that Sue gave her little trouble.
> But Bill, she said, was always in difficulties. The scores against Bill were recounted in detail. In concluding, she remarked: "I couldn't stand it any longer so I brought him to you. When I came home last night and found the neighbors and the police at my home, I knew something must be done."
> It appeared that on getting home from school, Bill had simulated a robbery. He had disarranged the furniture in the bedroom, pulled out dresser drawers, and opened the windows. Then he had announced to the neighbors the departure of the thief. In turn, they had called the police.
> When I asked Bill why he had done this, he said, "Oh, I had nothing to do when I got home. It seemed to me a good idea at the time."
> Mental tests revealed that Bill's IQ was above 160 and standard educational tests showed his attainment to equal the norms for grade VIII. The interest inventory disclosed strong interests in government, science, aviation, and exploration.
> Bill was a good-looking boy whose lack of cleanliness, disheveled hair and general carelessness reflected his aggression toward parental control. I asked him to tell me how he had acquired a scratch on his forehead. "There was that fight yesterday," he explained. Bill had been sitting in the principal's office, when, he said, a classmate went by and shook his fist at him and made fun of him by gestures. The two boys met on the school grounds after school. In the scuffle, Bill fell and scratched his forehead.
> As Bill walked down the hall with me, I noticed that he limped. I asked him about this. He told me that he had been in an automobile accident during the previous summer and was not entirely recovered

---

[18] Douglas Waples, Bernard Berelson, and Franklyn R. Bradshaw, *What Reading Does to People* (Chicago: University of Chicago Press, 1940).

[19] One of the first case studies in which developmental needs and reading were effectively combined was a Clinic case described by Paul Witty in *Pupils Are People, op. cit.*

from the injury. When he discussed his wishes with me, he pointed out that at the present time he was unable to take part in his best liked sports.

Bill's responses during the interview revealed his antagonism toward his father and his home. His father never carried out his promises, he said, and he didn't care what his father thought about him.

When I asked Bill whether he liked school, he answered, "I hate it."

"Have you ever liked school?" I continued.

"When I was in second grade," he responded.

Bill had attended four schools, but his experience in the second grade was the only one he recalled with any pleasure. In this school he had read widely, had participated in group activities, and had been generally happy. School at the present time was impossible, he explained. He spent much of his time in the hall or in the principal's office.

"If I were teaching a fifth grade," I said, "I'd rather have you in my class than any boy I've seen recently."

"Why?" he asked bluntly.

"Because," I answered, "you know so many things and have such fine ability."

I showed him his educational test results, which he examined carefully. I invited him to stay to help me demonstrate later that afternoon such tests before a class of college students.

"Do you really want me to help?" he asked.

I assured him that I did and he agreed to stay. Then he went downstairs "to clean up a little."

Bill returned, not a changed boy, but somewhat improved in appearance. He was extremely thoughtful and cooperative throughout the testing. Before he left, I gave him the book *You and the Constitution of the United States.* I suggested that he might also like to read Lewellen's *You and Atomic Energy* and Hartman's *The Making of a Democracy.* We examined Reynolds' *The Wright Brothers* as well as several other books about planes which interested him.

Bill telephoned the next day to say he liked *You and the Constitution.* "Will you autograph it if I bring it to you?" he asked. I agreed and in a few days Bill came to the Clinic again.

On this visit I suggested that he read *Thicker Than Water,* a collection of stories about family life. Later we discussed the problems presented in several of these short stories. On subsequent visits we talked about other books, such as Evans' *Tim's Place,* a story of an Austrian boy's adjustment in an American family, and R. Considine's *The Panama Canal,* a thrilling account of the courageous acts of five splendid men.

Bill read rapidly and included a variety of books in his growing list —books on science, biographies, short stories, and poetry. He read too such textbooks as *You and Others* and *Life and Growth.*

He was placed in a private school, where he found a wholesome competition with other children of superior ability and accomplishment.

Attention to his needs was given by a sympathetic instructor in a small class.

The extent of change in Bill during these months was remarkable. His appearance improved, and his attitude toward his family and his peers became cooperative. Most important of all, Bill developed an ideal of self that was consistent with his nature and his needs.

CONCLUDING STATEMENT

Because most teachers today recognize the importance of reading in promoting desirable growth in boys and girls, few would insist on reading exclusively for reading's sake. Reading has an impact on children, and although we do not know the exact nature or extent of this influence, we have experimental evidence that it occurs. Studies suggest that desirable traits of character may be developed or fostered through reading. Moreover, reading may help students to resolve particular individual problems. Any book which encourages a pupil to undertake to satisfy the developmental tasks of a given age may make a major contribution to his growth. Developmental needs or the hierarchy of needs suggested by Maslow will be met by children in this way. Teachers who understand child development and who also know children's literature can encourage and assist boys and girls in discovering the values of good books and in building desirable personalities.

The problem of identifying student needs is a difficult one. Some help comes from a recognition of broad general needs common to the total population and from lists of developmental tasks characteristic of a certain age in a specific culture. In addition to these sources the teacher must determine specific needs of individual students. He may rely on interest inventories, observations, interviews, personality inventories, or discussions.

Selecting books to meet either specific or general needs is not a simple task. Fortunately, however, there are excellent book lists which will guide the teacher in his selection. It is advisable that the teacher become familiar with many books so that he can provide a child at a given time with a book to meet some immediate need. The librarian is a most important aid in recommending and locating books related to specific personal and social needs of children and youth.

The responsibility of the teacher is great when he accepts as part of his task the guidance of pupils in social and personal growth. His knowledge both of people and of books must be expanded and his skills in human relations increased.

Selected References

Anderson, Paul S., "McGuffey vs. the Moderns in Character Training," *Phi Delta Kappan,* 38:53–58 (November, 1956).

Baldwin, Alfred L., *Behavior and Development in Childhood* (New York: Holt, Rinehart & Winston, Inc., 1955).

Boyd, Nancy A. and George Mandler, "Children's Responses to Human and Animal Stories and Pictures," *Journal of Consulting Psychology,* 19:367–371 (October, 1955).

Breckenridge, Marian E. and E. Lee Vincent, *Child Development,* 5th ed. (Philadelphia: W. B. Saunders Company, 1965).

Brooks, Alice R., "Books That Contribute to Personal Well-Being," in *Promoting Personal and Social Development Through Reading,* Supplementary Educational Monographs, no. 64 (Chicago: The University of Chicago Press, 1947).

Grace, Harry A. and Joan J. Lohmann, "Children's Reactions to Stories Depicting Parent-Child Conflict Situations," *Child Development,* 23:61–74 (March, 1952).

Hanna, Geneva R. and Mariana K. McAllister, *Books, Young People and Reading Guidance* (New York: Harper & Row, Publishers, 1960).

Havighurst, Robert J., *Developmental Tasks and Education* (New York: David McKay Co., Inc., 1952).

Holmes, J. A., "Emotional Factors and Reading Disabilities," *Reading Teacher,* 9:11–17 (October, 1955).

Kircher, Clara J. (editor), *Character Formation Through Books: A Bibliography* (Washington: The Catholic University of America Press, 1954).

Lane, Howard A. and Mary Beauchamp, *Human Relations in Teaching* (Englewood Cliffs, N.J.: Prentice-Hall, Inc., 1955).

Lodge, Helen C., "The Influence of the Study of Biography on the Moral Ideology of the Adolescent at the Eighth Grade Level," *Journal of Educational Research,* 50:241–255 (December, 1956).

Mussen, Paul H. and John J. Conger, *Child Development and Personality* (New York: Harper & Row, Publishers, 1956).

Osburn, Worth J., "Emotional Blocks in Reading," *Elementary School Journal,* 52:23–30 (September, 1951).

Raths, Louis E., *An Application to Education of the Needs Theory* (Bronxville, N. Y.: Modern Education Service, 1949).

Rudman, Herbert C., "The Informational Needs and Reading Interests of Children in Grades IV Through VIII," *Elementary School Journal,* 50:502–512 (May, 1955).

Russell, David H. and Caroline Shrodes, "Contributions of Research in Bibliotherapy to the Language-Arts Program," *The School Review,* 58:335–342 (September, 1950), and 411–420 (October, 1950).

Shrodes, Caroline, "Bibliotherapy," *The Reading Teacher,* 9:24–29 (October, 1955).

Waples, Douglass, Bernard Berelson, and Franklyn R. Bradshaw, *What Reading Does to People* (Chicago: University of Chicago Press, 1940).

Weingarten, Samuel, "Developmental Values in Voluntary Reading," *School Review,* 62:222–230 (April, 1954).

Weingarten, Samuel, "Reading as a Source of the Ideal Self," *The Reading Teacher,* 8:159–164 (February, 1955).

Witty, Paul, "Meeting Developmental Needs Through Reading," *Education,* 84:451–458 (April, 1964).

Witty, Paul A. (chairman), *Mental Health in Modern Education,* Fifty-fourth Yearbook of the National Society for the Study of Education, Part II (Chicago: University of Chicago Press, 1955).

Witty, Paul, "Promoting Growth and Development Through Reading," *Elementary English,* 27:493–500 (December, 1950).

Witty, Paul, "Reading Success and Emotional Adjustment," *Elementary English,* 27:281–296 (May, 1950).

Witty, Paul, "Reading to Meet Emotional Needs," *Elementary English,* 29:75–84 (February, 1952).

Witty, Paul (guest editor), "Satisfying Needs Through Reading," *Education,* 84:451–490 (April, 1964).

Zolkos, Helena H., "What Research Says About Emotional Factors in Retardation in Reading," *Elementary School Journal,* 51:512–518 (May, 1951).

5

READINESS FOR EFFECTIVE READING

In any teaching-learning situation the most important element is the learner's *readiness* for the experience. This factor is critical in learning to read, since the child's readiness for the initial experience in reading may, to a considerable degree, determine his attitude toward and his success in this significant aspect of his education.[1] An examination of the literature indicates that there is rather general agreement among writers in regard to the basic concepts, the factors involved, the techniques of diagnosis, and the procedures necessary to engender readiness.

BASIC CONCEPTS OF READING READINESS

Readiness at All Levels

Reading readiness should be looked upon not merely as a preparation for successful initial reading. It is important at every stage as boys and girls develop reading habits and skills sequentially; indeed, the high school student will benefit by a readiness program as does the first-grade child.

Readiness for reading is related to the child's development physically, intellectually, socially, and emotionally. Since each child's developmental pattern is unique, readiness must be determined individually. Helen Heffernan expresses the implication of this view in the following way:

> Readiness for any learning means that the child is able to bring to the task abilities equal to the demand of the specific situation. Every child is ready to take *his* next developmental step—whatever that

75

may be . . . it has become axiomatic in American education to begin where the child is.[1]

Unquestionably the ever-increasing amounts of information about children and how they grow and learn have contributed to our understanding of the needs of the learner and the relationship of these needs to the readiness program. From this basic knowledge, concepts relating to reading readiness have gradually evolved. Guy Bond and Eva Bond Wagner point out that these "basic readiness concepts are quite similar at every point in the educational continuum." The differences, they say, "are matters of emphasis rather than of pedagogical practice." Their list of concepts is given below:

1. All children need to learn to read.
2. Reading growth is continuous.
3. Reading growth starts early in the child's intellectual career and continues as long as he reads.
4. Reading readiness is the concern of all teachers at all levels of instruction.
5. Readiness is complex, since it is made up of many highly interrelated attributes.
6. Children develop at all times and in all characteristics at varying rates.
7. At any level in the school, the child must be taken from where he is and developed from that point forward.
8. Each new learning depends upon previous learnings.
9. Development should be neither unduly hurried nor allowed to lag.
10. For the most part, readiness factors are amenable to training.
11. Physiological, mental, emotional, and social capabilities must be taken into consideration in formulating an instructional program.[2]

In the developmental program, growth in reading is viewed as a continuous process; the teacher tries to help each child make the necessary acquisitions for successful experiences, not only in beginning to read but also in each succeeding step throughout the course of learning.

Readiness Is a Composite of Many Factors

Modern thought and practice discount the validity of early research findings which suggested that reading readiness or lack of it could be attributed to a single factor such as mental ability, which was

---

[1] Helen Heffernan, "Pressures to Start Formal School Early," *Childhood Education,* 37:59 (October, 1960).
[2] Guy L. Bond and Eva Bond Wagner, *Teaching the Child to Read,* 3rd ed. (New York: The Macmillan Company, 1960), p. 94.

widely regarded as a guarantee of successful reading. According to Russell:

> The modern concept of readiness is that it is based on a combination of physical, mental, social, and psychological factors. General and specific maturation are important, but so are information, attitudes, and abilities gained through experiences.[3]

Other writers in the field of reading concur in this position and it is now generally conceded that readiness is a developmental condition depending upon the combined operation of a number of related factors. For example, in 1960 Arthur E. Traxler and Ann Jungeblut reported:

> Evidence continues to accumulate that a child's readiness to read does not depend simply upon his chronological age or mental age but that many elements enter into reading readiness and that it is important for children to have kindergarten training to assure the development of these elements before they enter grade I.[4]

In Donald Durrell's opinion, the four basic elements which stand out above all others in reading readiness are: visual and auditory discrimination of word elements, interest in books and printed words, and the "ability to maintain attention in the reading task."[5] Ruth Strickland interprets this to mean that "these four elements are the absolute essentials without which a child cannot succeed while all the other elements of readiness listed form a highly desirable background for the task of learning to read."[6] Although some factors are undoubtedly more important than others, most authorities agree that readiness involves the child's total development at any given level and a combination of factors that determine his behavior. Children who do learn to read before starting to school have been found to have certain acquisitions in common. Dolores Durkin

> identified forty-nine children who read before they entered school. Their IQ's ranged from 91 to 161, and these children came from varied socio-economic levels. In common, these children had excep-

---

[3] David H. Russell, *Children Learn to Read,* 2nd ed. (Waltham, Mass.: Blaisdell Publishing Company, 1961), pp. 168–169.

[4] Arthur E. Traxler and Ann Jungeblut, *Research in Reading During Another Four Years,* Summary and Bibliography, July 1, 1953–December 31, 1957, Educational Records Bulletin No. 75 (New York: Educational Records Bureau, 1960), p. 5. See also: Sister Mary Nila, O.S.F., "Foundations of a Successful Reading Program," *Education,* 73:543–555 (May, 1953); Rachel S. Sutton, "A Study of Certain Factors Associated with Reading Readiness in the Kindergarten," *Journal of Educational Research,* 48:531–538 (March, 1955).

[5] Donald D. Durrell, *Improving Reading Instruction* (New York: Harcourt, Brace & World, Inc., 1956), pp. 42–43.

[6] Ruth Strickland, *The Language Arts in the Elementary School,* 2nd ed. (Boston: D. C. Heath and Company, 1957), p. 246.

tionally good memories, the ability to concentrate, curiosity, persistence, and self-reliance. She hypothesized that current intelligence tests are not measuring "what it takes" to learn to read and that certain personality characteristics and the child's notion of what reading means are important factors.[7]

The Importance of Readiness

Learning to read is a growth process; hence it cannot be sharply delimited as to time or grade. Since the first grade is the period when most children receive their initial formal instruction, it is imperative that they have the preparation and background necessary for success at this time. A child's attitude toward reading may be colored throughout his life by these first experiences. Knowing this, modern first-grade teachers attempt to see that conditions are assured for successful reading from experience charts, pre-primers, primers, and first readers. Readiness for reading is regarded by them as a condition which applies to learning not only from textbooks, but also from every kind of printed material presented throughout the first grade. Obviously, a concern for reading readiness should not terminate at the end of first grade. Since the first grade, however, is the period when most children begin to read, the problem is then of greater importance than at any other time.

There seems at present to be general agreement on two points: first, that readiness can be fostered or developed; and second, that readiness should not be left to chance. Russell expresses this point of view when he says, "The teacher cannot just wait for readiness to be achieved. General maturation is important, but the teacher must also provide experiences which contribute to the growth of reading readiness."[8]

THE FACTORS OF READING READINESS

Reading readiness involves the physical, intellectual, emotional, and social development of children. Let us now examine readiness in terms of these conditions.

[7] Dolores Durkin, "Children Who Read Before Grade One," *The Reading Teacher,* 14:163–166 (January, 1961). Reviewed by Helen M. Robinson in "Summary of Investigations Relating to Reading, July 1, 1960 to June 30, 1961," *The Reading Teacher,* 15:304 (January, 1962).

[8] David H. Russell, *op. cit.,* p. 169.

Physical Factors

A major physical factor in reading is vision. The two aspects of vision that are important to the act of reading are visual acuity, the ability to see at a distance and at near point; and visual discrimination, the ability to differentiate among words and letters. Defects in vision may be noted by the teacher. The use of the Snellen chart may provide a quick screening for visual defects at far point. Teacher observations are also important in noting visual problems. If the teacher notes repeatedly such behavior as rubbing the eyes, squinting, or other signs of discomfort or inattention in a child, it is well to suggest to the parents or school authorities the advisability of a thorough eye examination.

DeBoer and Dallmann comment:

> Some investigators believe that the eyes of the average child are not sufficiently mature for near point reading until the age of eight. This estimate coincides with other estimates which place the ideal age for beginning reading at later than six. Indeed, the phenomenal success claimed for such programs in beginning reading as the one at New Castle, Pennsylvania, may be attributable in part to the fact that the major reliance was placed upon filmstrips, charts, and other large-type material to be read at far point.[9]

Another major physical factor in reading is hearing. In learning to read, a child needs also to hear sounds correctly as well as to reproduce them accurately. If a child's hearing is defective, he receives wrong impressions or merely hears confusing sounds. The teacher needs to know the condition of each child's hearing, including the extent of impairment when it is found. A whisper test will enable the teacher to make a crude evaluation of the pupil's hearing. Observation will also help; thus, cocking the head, straining to hear, or general inattention may prove to be indicators of hearing deficiencies. Adjustments should be made in the classroom to care for minor difficulties, and serious cases should be referred to specialists.

Modern dietary habits, the use of vitamins, and knowledge of good health habits by parents and children have alleviated, to a great extent, the problem of poor general health in children. Of course, children still contract the usual childhood illnesses which tend to affect the child's health for only short periods of time. By and large, today's children are alert, healthy individuals.

---

[9] John J. DeBoer and Martha Dallmann, *The Teaching of Reading,* rev. ed. (New York: Holt, Rinehart & Winston, Inc., 1964), p. 48.

Sex differences have been observed as a factor in reading. Numerous studies support the observation that boys have more difficulty than girls in learning to read. But the fact is that each child's readiness must be determined on an individual basis.

Mental Maturity

Knowledge of each child's mental age is of value in helping the teacher appreciate the range of ability in each class so as to make appropriate adaptations of methods and materials. Only a few years ago some writers stressed the mental maturity of each child as the indicator of reading readiness; a mental age of six years and six months was regarded as the single criterion for reading readiness. Educators urged that reading instruction be postponed until a child attained this level. Repeated studies, however, have demonstrated the fallacy of this position. Delaying reading instruction until the child's mental age is six years and six months will not always insure successful reading and may indeed cause some children to lose their enthusiasm for learning to read.[10]

A review of the research concerning mental age and learning to read caused Henry P. Smith and Emerald V. Dechant to conclude:

> Although there is a high relationship between mental age scores and readiness test scores, it is also true that a high correlation is quite different from a perfect correlation. So long as the interrelation between two factors is imperfect, we expect to find that other factors are operating. Clearly, we cannot expect to predict reading readiness on the basis of intellectual development alone.[11]

In recent years the concept of "organismic age," as developed by Willard Olson and his associates, has caused some educators to attempt to determine reading readiness on the basis of a composite known as "organismic age," which embraces various physical aspects of growth combined with other factors.[12] These factors include height age, dental age, weight age, carpal age, reading age, and mental age. Without question many factors contribute to readiness, but the concept of "or-

---

[10] Guy L. Bond and Eva Bond Wagner, *op. cit.*,
[11] Henry P. Smith and Emerald V. Dechant, *Psychology in Teaching Reading* (Englewood Cliffs, N.J.: Prentice-Hall, Inc., 1961), p. 89.
[12] Willard Olson, *Child Development,* 2nd ed. (Boston: D. C. Heath and Company, 1959).

ganismic age" is seriously questioned by some scholars.[13] Thus Harris states:

> The concept of *organismic age,* developed by Olson, attempts to provide a quantitative base for measuring a child's total development. In computing organismic age, Olson averages together the child's mental age, reading age, and several measures of physical growth such as dental age, height age, weight age, grip age, and metacarpal age (maturity of the small bones of the wrist). The organismic age is heavily weighted in the direction of physical development. Olson believes that children's progress in reading is more closely related to organismic age than to mental age and that retardation in learning to read is simply one aspect of a general retardation in organismic development.
>
> The organismic-age concept has been subjected to severe criticism. Anderson has questioned the propriety of averaging together various dissimilar measures with differing reliabilities into a single scale with equal weights.[14] Stroud and his associates have challenged the basic validity of the concept.[15]
>
> They have pointed out that all growth processes require time, and this relationship to time in itself makes necessary a certain relatedness in various growth functions. They have brought together the results of several research studies in which correlations were found between reading and the various measures that are included in organismic age. The practically uniform conclusion of these studies is that there is a substantial correlation between reading and mental age, and the addition of a variety of measures of physical growth, singly or in combination, increases the correlation by only a negligible amount.[16]

Of all the measures associated with readiness, mental age has perhaps the greatest relevance and highest relationship. Hence, mental test ratings will help the teacher determine the status attained by the child in *one* type of development correlated with successful reading. This information, when combined with other data, may provide a fairly reliable picture of each child's total development. From this knowledge

[13] Paul Blommers, Lotus M. Knief, and J. B. Stroud, "The Organismic Age Concept," *Journal of Educational Psychology,* 46:142–150 (March, 1955); Fred T. Tyler, "Concepts of Organismic Growth: A Critique," *Journal of Educational Psychology,* 44:321–342 (October, 1953).

[14] John E. Anderson, "Methods of Child Psychology," in Leonard Carmichael (editor), *Manual of Child Psychology,* 2nd ed. (New York: John Wiley & Sons, Inc., 1954), p. 8.

[15] Paul Blommers *et al.* See footnote 13 *supra.*

[16] Albert J. Harris, "Reading and Human Development," Chapter 2 in Paul A. Witty (chairman), *Development In and Through Reading,* Sixtieth Yearbook of the National Society for the Study of Education (Chicago: University of Chicago Press, 1961), p. 19.

the teacher may plan instruction and offer readiness experience as needed. In this endeavor individual intelligence tests are, of course, the most reliable type of test to employ. Group tests, however, can be effectively used to obtain ratings of considerable value. When teachers note a sharp discrepancy between a child's classroom performance and his group test results, the giving of an individual intelligence test should be recommended. Information concerning widely used mental tests is given in Table VI on page 96.

Emotional and Social Factors

Emotional and social readiness are so closely related that it is difficult to discuss either one separately. In fact, the social behavior of a child can be interpreted as "an expression or repression of his emotions in situations in which there is interaction with other personalities."[17]

The child who is emotionally disturbed is not usually ready for reading. While most teachers are aware that some children turn to their school work with greater intensity during emotional crises, the weight of evidence is probably on the side of the interference in learning occasioned by emotional disturbances. Children who are socially adjusted are usually in a better state of mental health to do their best work. The child who feels socially rejected has been frequently found to do poor academic work.[18]

The child who is prepared best for reading is able to work well with other children. He knows how to express his own ideas clearly, and he can follow with sustained attention and interest what is transpiring about him. He responds to stories read to him and is able to derive pleasure from listening. He approaches new learning situations with feelings of self-confidence and security. Contributions to the development of these abilities and attitudes are made by a stable home environment and by a good classroom atmosphere. According to Nancy Larrick:

> Reading aloud at home is one of the most effective ways by which a parent can help with his child's reading. This is an activity that should begin in the play-pen days if the child is to grow up with the conviction that reading is a pleasure worth his time and effort. Reading aloud should continue when the child begins to read and even as he becomes an independent reader. At this advanced stage, he still needs the warm reassuring experience of talking over what

[17] Nila Banton Smith, "Readiness for Reading II," *Elementary English*, 27:95–98 (February, 1950).
[18] *Ibid.*

he has read and of meeting new stories under favorable circumstances.[19]

Use of those parts of an interest inventory which relate to personal and social adjustment of children will provide information helpful to the teacher in determining a child's social and emotional readiness (see Appendix).

Attitudes toward reading and learning may be shown in the classroom both by children's verbal expression and by their behavior. The child who pays little attention to reading readiness activities may not necessarily be immature; he may have an unfortunate attitude toward the experiences. The teacher must try to determine the cause of the attitude and attempt to provide experiences which will alter it.

DETERMINING READING READINESS

Determining a child's readiness for initial as well as later reading experiences implies an evaluation of the child's total development. Since the total development of a child must be evaluated the reliance upon a single instrument is not recommended. Three evaluative instruments will be discussed here: teacher-observation form, standardized intelligence tests, and standardized reading readiness tests.

Teacher-Observation Forms

Reading readiness, like all learning, must be continuously evaluated in order to guide the teacher in designing curricular activities for future growth and readiness experiences for future learning. Mildred Dawson and Henry Bamman suggest the following check list to aid the teacher in studying each pupil's readiness for learning to read.[20] The teacher may find it a helpful guide in determining the readiness of each pupil in his class.

PHYSICAL READINESS
Motor development
    1. Are his bodily movements well coordinated?
    2. Does he hold a book and turn pages well?

---

[19] Nancy Larrick, "How to Enlist Parents in the Reading Program," in J. Allen Figurel (editor), *Reading in a Changing Society,* International Reading Association Conference Proceedings, vol. 4 (New York: Scholastic Magazines, 1959), Part IV, no. 12, p. 165.

[20] Mildred A. Dawson and Henry A. Bamman, *Fundamentals of Basic Reading Instruction,* 2nd ed. (New York: David McKay Company, Inc., 1963), pp. 57–59.

3. Is his eye-hand coordination sufficiently developed to enable him to pick up articles accurately, cut, and follow a line?

Auditory development
1. Does he seem to hear what you read and say to the group?
2. Does he listen attentively? What are the audiometer results?
3. Can he pass the 20-foot low-voice test and the 15-inch whisper test?
4. Does he hear and enunciate words accurately?

Visual development
1. Are there signs of eyestrain (blink, squint, watery eyes)?
   a. At a distance
   b. Near eyes
2. Does he tend to hold the book too close or too far from his eyes?
3. Does he see likenesses and differences in objects, letters, words?
4. What does any available clinical or oculist's test show about vision?

Speech
1. Does he use baby talk or other immature speech patterns?
2. Which sounds does he not yet enunciate accurately?

General health
1. Does he tire too easily?
2. Are there evident physical handicaps (eyes, ears, nose-throat, coordination)?
3. Are there signs of poor health and malnutrition?

SOCIAL DEVELOPMENT
1. Does he like to work and play with his fellows?
2. Does he show leadership?
3. Does he cooperate and follow decisions of the group?
4. Does he like to hear his peers express their ideas?
5. Is he learning to be polite?

WAYS OF WORKING
1. Does he stick to a task or a voluntary activity?
2. In taking directions, does he listen attentively and respond promptly?
3. Is he a neat, systematic, careful worker?

MENTAL DEVELOPMENT
1. Can he pay careful attention for several minutes?
2. Does he have a good memory?
3. Is he resourceful in solving his problems?

EMOTIONAL DEVELOPMENT
1. Is he withdrawn, shy, or overly aggressive?

2. Is he at ease in the school situation?
3. Is he self-reliant and confident?
4. Is he a happy, alert child?

Background of Experience
1. Does his family customarily speak English?
2. Is the child included in family planning and conversation?
3. Do both parents work?
4. Do they take the child on trips?
5. Do they discuss pictures and read to him?
6. Does he have playmates, pets, toys, books, tools?

Language Development
1. Does he enunciate and pronounce words clearly and correctly?
2. Does he have a reasonably wide vocabulary?
3. Is it based on well-understood concepts?
4. Does he speak in full sentences?
5. Does he tell a story in good order?

Prereading Interests and Skills
1. Does he pretend to be reading when by himself?
2. Does he voluntarily go to books and look through them?
3. Can he read the story that a picture tells?
4. Does he notice and recognize common signs and labels?
5. Does he know numerous stories and rhymes?
6. Is he curious about new notices that the teacher has put up?

Standardized Intelligence Tests

In recent years the use of group intelligence tests has been widely recommended for the kindergarten and the early months of first grade. The practice today is still rather limited. In order to gain insight into children's intellectual abilities it seems that the administration of intelligence tests is desirable and practical. It is important to observe, however, that the child should display a good adjustment to the classroom situation, whether it be in the kindergarten or first grade, before tests are given. It also seems important to mention that the tests at this level should be given to small groups of children at a time so that a teacher can be reasonably sure that directions are understood and followed.

The *Otis Quick-Scoring Mental Ability Test,* Alpha Short Form, is an example of an intelligence test used at the first-grade level. The content of the test is entirely pictorial and geometric. There are two sets of directions, each referring to the same set of pictures. One set of directions calls for the marking of the one picture in a row of pictures which is different from the others in the row. In Figure 2, the child puts a mark on the picture in each row that is different. The other set of directions requires the marking of one picture in each row, in accordance with specific directions. In Figure 2, the directions for row 9 are: mark the thing used by girls and women and not by boys or men. The first set of directions constitutes what is referred to as the "nonverbal" part of the test, since after the initial instructions the pupil proceeds without any further dependence on either oral or written directions. The second set of directions comprises what is called the "verbal" part of the test since the pupil must comprehend and follow certain oral directions.[21]

The nonverbal section of the test has a twelve-minute time limit, and the verbal part requires about ten minutes. The test yields a mental age score and an intelligence quotient.

Another intelligence test that may be administered to children who have not learned to read is the SRA Mental Ability Test. The K-1 battery may be administered to children in kindergarten or first grade. The test is given in two half-hour sessions and measures verbal meaning, space, perceptual, motor, and quantitative factors. A quotient score is found for each subtest and a total intelligence quotient is also indicated. The results also indicate degree of reading readiness.

Standardized Reading Readiness Tests

Although there is controversy about the value of reading readiness tests, it is usually granted that these tests do serve the purpose of measuring some skills valuable in beginning reading as well as for planning certain types of instruction.[22] The contents of the tests vary, but the "factors frequently measured are ability to interpret pictures, to follow directions, to work in small groups, linguistic maturity, information about common objects, auditory and visual discriminations, and motor control."[23] These tests as a rule are easily administered and interpreted by

[21] Arthur S. Otis, *Manual of Directions,* Otis Quick-Scoring Mental Ability Tests, new edition, Alpha Short Form (New York: Harcourt, Brace & World, Inc., 1954), pp. 1–2.

[22] Robert Karlin, "Research in Reading," *Elementary English,* 37:177–178 (March, 1960). See also: Marvin Powell and Kenneth M. Parsely, Jr., "The Relationship Between First Grade Reading Readiness and Second Grade Reading Achievement," *Journal of Educational Research,* 54:229–233 (February, 1961); Agatha Townsend, "What Research Says to the Reading Teacher—Readiness for Beginning Reading," *The Reading Teacher,* 15:269 (January, 1962).

[23] Guy L. Bond and Eva Bond Wagner, *op. cit.,* p. 130.

Figure 2[24]

[24] Otis Quick-Scoring Mental Ability Tests: New Edition: Alpha Test. Short Form As Copyright 1936, 1952 by Harcourt, Brace & World, Inc. Copyright renewed 1964. Copyright in Great Britain. All rights reserved. Reproduced by special permission, p. 3.

classroom teachers. An important point to remember is that the tests should not be administered until the children have sound orientation in the classroom. For children without kindergarten experience, this may require two or three weeks. The teacher will use his own judgment when he feels that children are ready for the testing experience.

Following are descriptions of some widely used readiness tests:

The *Gates Reading Readiness Test* is an example of a test based on the assumption that it is possible to analyze the components of initial "reading readiness."[25] Five subtests are used. The first, *Picture Directions,* requires the child to listen to directions, to look at and interpret illustrations of farm life and city life, and to follow directions. A second test, *Word Matching,* necessitates the identification of two like words in a series of four-word units. In the third test, *Word Card Matching,* words are displayed on cards and the child is asked to locate like words in a series of four different combinations. In the fourth test, *Rhyming,* the child is asked to examine pictures and to put a cross on the picture which a word "sounds like." Subtest five, an individual test, requires the child to identify as many as he can of the capital and the small letters of the alphabet. He is asked also to read the numbers from zero to nine. The author of this test presents critical scores to assist the teacher in ascertaining the child's readiness for reading.

The authors of the *Metropolitan Readiness Test* recommend the use of these tests either at the end of kindergarten or at the beginning of first grade. Not more than fifteen pupils should be tested in one group, and "even smaller groups are desirable if pupils are known to be immature or retarded."[26] There are six subtests: Word Meaning, Sentences, Information, Matching, Numbers, and Copying. Each test consists of pictures which the child is requested to mark or copy according to instructions given orally by the examiner.

A supplementary test is also included. The child is given ten minutes in which to "make a picture of a man." His drawing is to be rated according to categories listed and described in the *Key for Scoring,* but the result is not to be included in his total score. Provision is made for translating the sum of the scores on the first four tests into a Reading Readiness Status Score. The raw score on Test 5 may be translated into a Number Readiness Status Score. The authors state, however,

---

[25] Paul Witty, "A Modern Interpretation of Readiness for Reading," *Educational Administration and Supervision,* 32:257–270 (May, 1946).

[26] *Metropolitan Readiness Tests,* Directions for Administering and Key for Scoring, p. 2.

that "classification on the basis of the tests should be tentative until the teacher has had sufficient opportunity to verify the test findings by means of her own evaluation of the child's abilities," and that "she should give considerable attention to this matter during the first month of school."[27]

Table VII lists representative readiness tests and gives data concerning each test. These tests have only limited value in an effective developmental reading program. The skillful teacher usually is alert to the terms which are found in most readiness tests and evaluates children's readiness through informal procedures in a well-rounded first-grade program. Thus readiness is appraised continuously in the normal activities of the classroom. But in some situations it is impossible to make informal appraisals, and teachers may wish to obtain a fairly reliable estimate of the child's development in the areas included in readiness tests. In such situations, the results of readiness tests will prove of value.

EXPERIENCES IN A READINESS PROGRAM

The need for a rich background of first-hand experiences applies at all levels in the reading program. The symbols on the printed page can only mean as much as the reader's experiences will allow. What factors are important in gaining experiences?

Experiences That Contribute to Total Readiness

In an effective readiness program five general areas of development are given attention. They are: language, vocabulary, writing, visual and auditory discrimination, and motor skills.

1. *The development of language readiness.*—Since there is a positive relationship between reading and the other aspects of the language arts, much should be done at both the pre-reading and later levels to stimulate interest and growth in listening, speaking, and writing.

Language activities include discussing, conversing, reporting, explaining, giving directions, telling stories, dramatizing, reading aloud, and listening. One of the best times in the day for primary children to use and develop language skills is in the "sharing" or "show-and-tell" period.

[27] *Ibid.*, p. 29.

Gains may also be made through effective use of group discussion periods.[28] The "sharing-time" period provides "an opportunity to improve the understanding vocabulary, the children can grow in self-confidence, in power to relate events in sequence, in ability to predict outcomes, in attentiveness when listening."[29] Since the development of the ability to communicate effectively is one of the principal goals of a readiness program, teachers will need to plan varied experiences through which children may share their language acquisitions.

Good speech development depends upon a number of factors. The teacher should set a good model in his own speech. Further, he should recognize the fact that emotional difficulties may cause insecure feelings that lead to speech problems in children. He needs to make certain that the daily program provides ample opportunities for the improvement of oral expression under conditions that foster mental health. Special provisions are needed by children who have serious speech defects as well as by those who come from non-English-speaking homes or homes where sub-standard English is habitual.

The environment itself must be such that children will not feel rewarded for silence; the emotional and intellectual climate of the classroom must lead to desire not only to communicate, but to do so as effectively as possible. Skill in listening should also be taught. As some children are discussing an event, the others should be encouraged to listen critically in preparation for later discussion. Listening requires attentiveness and critical evaluation.'

Indeed, the improvement of listening is an essential phase of the readiness program. Listening has been seriously neglected, probably bcause its nature and purposes are often misunderstood. Many still hold the erroneous idea that listening is synonymous with "paying attention." But a child who is quiet, passive, and seemingly attentive is not necessarily *listening* in a desirable sense of the term. Effective listening involves not only the physical process of attending, but, what is more important, critical reaction and thinking.

The development of good listening habits should be sought as a part of daily activities throughout the school day. Time should be devoted systematically to listening during story-telling, dramatization, and related activities. It is desirable for children to help in setting up standards for good speaking and listening.

2. *The development of a reading vocabulary.*—The ability to read

---

[28] Lois V. Johnson, "Group Discussion and the Development of Oral Language," *Elementary English,* 33:496–499 (December, 1956).
[29] John J. DeBoer and Martha Dallmann, *op. cit.,* p. 65.

labels, picture-word cards, charts, simple directions, and similar materials will give a good background for meeting later needs. Firsthand experiences too will help in the development of a background for clear concepts. The reading of charts, telling stories, and dramatizing will contribute further to the acquisition of vocabularies essential in meaningful reading.

3. *The development of the skill of writing.*—Skill in writing should be sought to various degrees in preparing children to read. In writing their names and copying materials from the chalkboard and in preparing daily memoranda, the foundation is laid for later progress in writing. Writing brief letters to parents and putting labels or a few words on original drawings illustrate some writing activities of the beginner. It should be recognized that these activities are accompanied by concomitant learnings in the form of observing the shapes of words and noting differences and likenesses in words which facilitate readiness for reading. For excellent materials to encourage these abilities, see the monthly issues of *Highlights for Children*.

4. *Promoting auditory and visual discrimination.*—An important objective of the readiness period is to cultivate skills related to auditory and visual discrimination. These skills include the ability to differentiate between sounds of words and letters, and the ability to see differences and likenesses between words and letters. Since there are great differences in children's abilities to detect such differences and likenesses, instruction must be given according to the needs of individuals within each class. As far as possible instruction should be an integral part of the regular classroom activities. Isolated drill is usually uninteresting and lacking in appeal for children. In Chapter 9, these skills are dealt with in detail and suggestions are made for their acquisition.

Another technique to be acquired is the habit of looking at words, phrases, and sentences from left to right. There are many ways the teacher may proceed to establish this habit. It is important to encourage children to practice the left-to-right eye-sweep in all their reading, including at first the "reading of pictures." Games may help, as well as the repeated reference to the terms "left" and "right" in discussions and in giving directions of various kinds. The acquisition of "top" to "bottom" concept of the page should also be developed and associated with "left" to "right" habits.

5. *Promoting motor skill development.*—Children should be encouraged to play on school apparatus, take part in games, participate in folk dances and rhythms, and engage in fingerpainting. In addition to "large-muscle" activities the children should have many experiences in handling

blocks, cutting out pictures, tracing, and working with clay. Learning to handle equipment and to enjoy books and use them profitably are important as one seeks to develop skills, habits, and attitudes required in good reading.

Contributions of the Home and School

A major responsibility of both the home and the school is to provide opportunities for children to participate in experiences that will help them acquire the basic concepts and understandings that are essential for effective reading. Since a wide variation in children's experiences, interests, and needs will be found in every classroom, it is essential for teachers to provide many types of activities and experiences to compensate for lack of readiness in some pupils and to enrich the levels of readiness in others. Following are suggested activities to promote reading readiness, a number of which the home may provide as effectively as the school.

1. *Field trips and excursions* offer opportunities for children to learn more about their immediate environment within the community. Since the instructional program generally centers around home, school, and community, firsthand experience in observing buildings, objects, animals, trees, gardens, transportation facilities, and people at work contributes to the development of concepts and vocabulary. Teacher-pupil planning and evaluation of discussions offer excellent opportunities for fostering language development.

2. *Looking at pictures and other visual aids* provides a means for meeting children's needs and interests and for building readiness. Attractive arrangements of children's work on the bulletin board or pictures for the teacher's file stimulate discussion and other language experiences. (See pp. 403–404 for list of films, filmstrips, and other aids.)

3. *Story-telling* offers one of the best means of meeting children's needs and interests, giving as it does an opportunity to foster habits of effective listening, including the enlargement of the attention span, and the creation of a taste for good literature. (See pp. 146–147 for recommendations.)

4. *Dramatic play* and other forms of dramatization are much-enjoyed activities which provide children with opportunities to react personally to situations and ideas. Puppet shows and pantomime may also contribute greatly to getting children ready to read.

5. *Observing demonstrations and experiments* can be a source of information and a means of developing concepts. Following directions,

lengthening attention span, and stimulating a desire to read are possible outcomes of this activity.

6. *Play activities,* both supervised and undirected, are essential for children's all-around physical, emotional, and social development. Play activities provide the setting and stimulus for developing adequate self-concepts and should be encouraged as part of a readiness program.

7. *Music and rhythmic expression* provide opportunities for building a needed aesthetic background for reading. Listening to records may also stimulate creative expression in art, music, construction, and dramatics. (See p. 404 for a list of recordings.)

8. *Construction activities, drawing, and painting* also present opportunities for cultivating reading readiness. Children need to move about, and the use of big blocks and certain tools in the constructing of playhouses, bridges, stores, and other unit activities offers appropriate opportunities for this type of development. Painting at an easel or drawing also may provide enrichment. Cooking, sewing, and weaving contribute similarly.

9. *Playing host and hostess to visitors* is another type of enrichment recommended for the promotion of readiness. Such activity gives children a chance not only to acquire information and use a pattern of speech, but also to grow in the acquisition of social amenities.

10. *Library experiences* are extremely valuable in helping to establish readiness for reading, as well as in developing desirable attitudes toward reading and an appreciation of good literature. Many classrooms have a book corner or library table which makes books readily available to pupils. But children must have also the opportunity to learn to use a library for their own development and enjoyment. Of course, the school library should serve kindergarten and first-grade children as well as other pupils. Regular trips should be scheduled to both the school library and the community library whenever possible. One of the most worthy goals of the entire reading program is to help establish the library habit. (See pp. 132–145 for lists of books.)

11. *Making experience charts* involves the recording of individual or group-dictated compositions.[30] Not only do they serve a most useful purpose in the transition to "book reading," but they can have a very desirable influence on children's attitude toward reading. Certainly they offer a way to make reading practical and personally appealing to young readers. They also may be used to foster the development of sentence

---

[30] The making of an experience chart is described fully in Chapter 9.

sense, left-to-right sequence in eye movement, visual discrimination, and perceptual ability.[31]

Another of the values of charts is in helping the child to acquire a basic stock of sight words. It is a common practice for the teacher to place the key words from a chart on cards which are rapidly exposed. When a child is able to pronounce readily and correctly fifty to eighty such words and to give their meanings, he is judged to have fulfilled one requirement of a formal reading readiness program.

12. *Using readiness books* designed to prepare the child for reading may be a pleasant and rewarding experience. In these books, items such as the recognition of similarities and differences in words, discrimination of sounds, and attention to the sequence of ideas are emphasized.

Readiness materials have been severely criticized as undesirable or unnecessary, one of the most provocative critics being Donald Durrell, who, in collaboration with Alice K. Nicholson, makes the following statements:

> Although the lessons of the reading readiness books may develop desirable abilities such as language fluency, motor skills and attention to nonword forms and sounds, it is doubtful that they contribute greatly to reading readiness. Since it has long been demonstrated that children bring to first grade oral vocabularies much larger than will be required for reading, it is unlikely that additional language development will improve the child's chances for reading success. . . . It is not necessary to force children to learn letters or sounds within spoken words. There are many opportunities for awakening interest in letters, such as putting signs on buildings children construct, using pictures which have simple identifying words in them, putting labels on pictures or drawings, answering questions about words and letters, assisting children with their early attempts at writing letters and words, providing games in which letters are used. . . .
> Attention to word sounds may also be taught informally. Rhyming words are always enjoyed, and this is one of the beginnings of interest in word sounds. Pictures of objects whose names begin with the same sound may be displayed and named, with attention being called to the similarity of the initial sounds. The same may be done with objects and with children's names. Children enjoy these discoveries, and the activities may be done in the spirit of play. . . .
> The beginnings of reading and writing need not be a chore for children. It is not necessary for them to work solely with formal reading readiness workbooks hour after hour. In every aspect of the pro-

---

[31] Paul C. Burns, "A Re-examination of the Role of Experience Charts," *Elementary English,* 36:481 (November, 1959).

gram, interest should be kept high, meaning emphasized, and delight in learning encouraged.[32]

READINESS ACTIVITIES FOR DIFFERENT GRADES

At different levels the experiences and activities designed to promote readiness will vary. Some experiences, such as field trips and excursions, observing demonstrations and experiments, and library activities will be found at all levels. Other experiences—looking at pictures, for example, or telling simple stories, and learning to "read pictures"—will be introduced only at the beginning stage. Activities which involve discovering implications and reading critically will receive their emphasis at later stages.

CONCLUDING STATEMENT

The term *reading readiness* is no longer used to refer primarily to readiness for first-grade reading; it has been enlarged to encompass all grade levels. This attitude is consistent with the developmental reading philosophy and is at present endorsed by most authorities in the reading field.

The determination of reading readiness is not confined to single factors such as mental maturity, nor is it gauged through "organismic" age. It includes many factors and considerations related to the physiological, intellectual, emotional, and social development in children. In fact, the total development of the child is evaluated to determine his readiness.

As children grow in reading, their needs for continued development change. Hence, it is imperative that teachers ascertain readiness in successive grades to determine each pupil's preparation for successful endeavor in learning to read. Chapters 9 and 12 of this book provide further information on readiness as it relates to various stages of development in reading.

---

[32] Donald D. Durrell and Alice K. Nicholson, "Preschool and Kindergarten Experience," in Paul Witty (chairman), *Development In and Through Reading*, *op. cit.*, pp. 267–269.

TABLE VI
INTELLIGENCE TESTS FOR KINDERGARTEN AND FIRST-GRADE CHILDREN

Individual Tests

NAME	PUBLISHER	TIME	TYPES OF SCORES	NUMBER OF FORMS
Arthur Point Scale of Performance Tests (1943) ages: 4.5 years and over	C. H. Stoelting Co.	35–40 minutes	Point Score M.A., I.Q.	2
Stanford-Binet Intelligence Scale, Third Revision, Form L-M (1960) ages: 2 years to adult	Houghton Mifflin Co.	30–90 minutes	M.A., I.Q.	1
Wechsler Intelligence Scale for Children (1949) ages: 5–15	The Psychological Corporation	approx. 60 min.	M.A., I.Q.	1

Group Tests

NAME	PUBLISHER	TIME	TYPES OF SCORES	NUMBER OF FORMS
California Test of Mental Maturity, Pre-primary Battery (kdg. and beg. 1)	California Test Bureau	Approx. 50 min.	Non-language M.A., I.Q. Language M.A., I.Q.	1
Detroit First Grade Intelligence Test, rev. ed. (beg. 1)	Harcourt, Brace and World	Approx. 35 min.	Point Score, M.A., I.Q.	1
Kuhlmann-Anderson Intelligence Test, 6th ed. (beg. 1)	Educational Test Bureau	Approx. 45 min.	Median, mental growth units, M.A., I.Q.	1
Lorge-Thorndike Intelligence Test (kdg. and beg. 1)	Houghton Mifflin Co.	Approx. 20 min.	I.Q., grade equiv., age equiv.	2
Otis Quick-Scoring Mental Ability Tests Alpha Form (beg. 1)	Harcourt, Brace and World, Inc.	Approx. 40 min.	M.A., I.Q.	1
SRA Primary Abilities K-1 Form (kdg. and beg. 1)	Science Research Associates, Inc.	Approx. 60 min.	I.Q. score for each factor and total I.Q.	1
Pintner General Ability Tests: Verbal Series Primary Battery (kdg. and beg. 1)	Harcourt, Brace and World, Inc.	Approx. 25 min.	Point Score, M.A., I.Q.	3

TABLE VII
READING READINESS TESTS FOR KINDERGARTEN AND BEGINNING FIRST GRADE

NAME OF TEST	PUBLISHER	GROUP OR INDIVIDUAL	APPROXIMATE TIME	TYPE OF SCORE	NUMBER OF FORMS	SUBTESTS
American School Reading Readiness Test (1955)	Public School Publishing Co.	Group	45 min.	Weighted score and predicted reading grade	1	Vocabulary; visual discrimination of letter forms, letter combinations, geometric forms; recognition of words; following directions; memory of geometric forms
Gates Reading Readiness Test (1942 rev.)	Teachers College, Columbia University	Group and Individual	40 min. and 5 min.	Percentile score and prediction of reading success	1	Picture directions; word matching; word card matching; rhyming; reading letters and numbers
Harrison-Stroud Reading Readiness Profiles	Houghton Mifflin Co.	Group	75 min.	Percentile score and prediction of reading success	1	Using symbols; visual discrimination of words; using context; auditory discrimination; using context and auditory clues; names of letters

TABLE VII (continued)

READING READINESS TESTS FOR KINDERGARTEN AND BEGINNING FIRST GRADE

NAME OF TEST	PUBLISHER	GROUP OR INDIVIDUAL	APPROXIMATE TIME	TYPE OF SCORE	NUMBER OF FORMS	SUBTESTS
Lee-Clark Reading Readiness Test (1962 rev.)	California Test Bureau	Group	15 min.	Percentile score and grade placement equivalents	1	Letter symbols, matching and crossing out; concepts, vocabulary and following directions; word symbols, identification of letters and words
Metropolitan Readiness Test (1949)	Harcourt, Brace and World, Inc.	Group	60 min.	Point score, percentile rank, letter rating, and readiness status	2	Word meaning; sentences; information; matching; numbers; copying
Murphy-Durrell Diagnostic Reading Readiness Test (1949)	Harcourt, Brace and World, Inc.	Group and Individual	60 min. and 20 min.	Point scores and percentile rating	1	Auditory discrimination; visual discrimination; learning rate
Van Wagnen Reading Readiness Scales (1954 rev.)	Educational Test Bureau	Individual	45 min.	Mid-C score (translated into readiness status)	1	Range of information; perception of relations; vocabulary (opposites); memory span for ideas; word discrimination; word learning

Selected References

Almy, Millie Corinne, *Children's Experiences Prior to First Grade and Success in Beginning Reading,* Contributions to Education, No. 954 (New York: Bureau of Publications, Teachers College, Columbia University, 1949).

Anderson, Irving H., Byron O. Hughes, and W. Robert Dixon, "Age of Learning to Read and Its Relation to Sex, Intelligence, and Reading Achievement in the Sixth Grade," *Journal of Educational Research,* 49: 447–453 (February, 1956).

Baker, Emily V., "Reading Readiness Is Still Important," *Elementary English,* 32:17–23 (January, 1955).

Betts, Emmett A., *Foundations of Reading Instruction,* rev. ed. (New York: American Book Company, 1957).

Bond, Guy L. and Eva Bond Wagner, *Teaching the Child to Read,* 3rd ed. (New York: Macmillan Co., 1960).

Bremer, Neville, "Do Readiness Tests Predict Success in Reading?" *Elementary School Journal,* 59:222–224 (January, 1959).

Carroll, Marjorie W., "Sex Differences in Reading Readiness at the First Grade Level," *Elementary English,* 25:370–375 (October, 1948).

Dawson, Mildred A. and Henry A. Bamman, *Fundamentals of Basic Reading Instruction* (New York: David McKay Co., Inc., 1959).

Dean, Charles D., "Predicting First-Grade Reading Achievement," *Elementary School Journal,* 39:609–616 (April, 1939).

DeBoer, John J. and Martha Dallmann, *The Teaching of Reading,* rev. ed. (New York: Holt, Rinehart & Winston, Inc., 1964).

Durrell, Donald D., "First-Grade Reading Success Study: A Summary," *Journal of Education,* Boston University, 140:2–6 (February, 1958).

Durrell, Donald D. and Helen A. Murphy, "The Auditory Discrimination Factor in Reading Readiness and Reading Disability," *Education,* 73:556–560 (May, 1953).

Edmiston, R. W., and Bessie Peyton, "Improving First-Grade Achievement by Readiness Instruction," *School and Society,* 71:230–232 (April 15, 1950).

Fast, Irene, "Kindergarten Training and Grade I Reading," *Journal of Educational Psychology,* 48:52–57 (January, 1957).

Gates, Arthur I., "The Necessary Mental Age for Beginning Reading," *Elementary School Journal,* 37:497–508 (March, 1937).

Gavel, Sylvia R., "June Reading Achievements of First-Grade Children," *Journal of Education,* Boston University, 140:37–43 (February, 1958).

Harris, Albert J., *How to Increase Reading Ability,* 4th ed., (New York: David McKay Company, Inc., 1961).

Hildreth, Gertrude H., *Readiness for School Beginners* (New York: Harcourt, Brace & World, Inc., 1950).

Karlin, Robert, "The Prediction of Reading Success and Reading-Readiness Tests," *Elementary English,* 34:320–322 (May, 1957).

Keister, B. V., "Reading Skills Acquired by Five-Year-Old Children," *Elementary School Journal,* 41:587–596 (April, 1941).

King, Inez B., "Effect of Age of Entrance into Grade I upon Achievement in Elementary School," *Elementary School Journal,* 55:331–336 (February, 1955).

Linehan, Eleanor B., "Early Instruction in Letter Names and Sounds as Related to Success in Beginning Reading," *Journal of Education,* 140:44–48 (February, 1958).

McKim, Margaret G., and Helen Caskey, *Guiding Growth in Reading,* 2nd ed. (New York: The Macmillan Co., 1963).

Milner, Esther, "A Study of the Relationship Between Reading Readiness in Grade One School Children and Patterns of Parent-Child Interaction," *Child Development,* 22:95–112 (June, 1951).

Monroe, Marion, *Growing into Reading* (Chicago: Scott, Foresman and Company, 1951).

Nicholson, Alice, "Background Abilities Related to Reading Success in First Grade," *Journal of Education,* Boston University, 140:7–24 (February, 1958).

Nila, Sister Mary, O. S. F., "Foundations of a Successful Reading Program," *Education,* 73:543–555 (May, 1953).

Olson, Arthur V., "Growth in Word Perception Abilities as It Relates to Success in Beginning Reading," *Journal of Education,* 140:25–36 (February, 1958).

Olson, Willard C. and Byron O. Hughes, "The Concept of Organismic Age," *Journal of Educational Research,* 35:525–527 (March, 1942).

Parke, Margaret B., "'Picture Dictionaries," *Elementary English,* 32:519 (December, 1955).

Russell, David H., *Children Learn to Read,* 2nd ed. (Waltham, Mass.: Blaisdell Publishing Company, 1961).

Smith, Henry P. and Emerald V. Dechant, *Psychology in Teaching Reading* (Englewood Cliffs, N.J.: Prentice-Hall, Inc., 1961).

Smith, Nila Banton, *Reading Instruction for Today's Children* (Englewood Cliffs, New Jersey: Prentice-Hall, Inc., 1963).

Smith, Nila Banton, "Readiness for Reading II," *Elementary English,* 27: 91–106 (February, 1950).

Sutton, Rachel S., "A Study of Certain Factors Associated with Reading Readiness in the Kindergarten," *Journal of Educational Research,* 48:531–538 (March, 1955).

Tyler, Fred T., "Concepts of Organismic Growth: A Critique," *Journal of Educational Psychology,* 44:321–342 (October, 1953).

Wepman, Joseph M., "Auditory Discrimination, Speech, and Reading," *Elementary School Journal,* 60:325–333 (March, 1960).

Williams, Gertrude H., "What Does Research Tell Us About Readiness for Beginning Reading?" *The Reading Teacher,* 6:34–40 (May, 1953).

6

WORD RECOGNITION AND VOCABULARY DEVELOPMENT

Word recognition consists of two basic elements, word identification and word interpretation. A factor related to word recognition is that of readability, that is, the level of difficulty of printed matter.

Word identification has to do with the differentiation of one symbol from another and identifying each symbol correctly. For example, if a child sees the word *cat,* correct identification would tell him the symbol is "cat" and not "house," "moon," or some other thing. As soon as the symbol is identified, the meaning or interpretation of the symbol occurs. In this case the child might think of his own pet "cat" or of "cats" that he has seen. The symbol *cat,* however, has only as much meaning as the child's previous experiences allow.

Readability has to do with the amount of difficulty a child might have with printed matter. For instance, a second-grade child who is reading a fourth-grade science text would probably encounter a great deal of difficulty in identification of words and interpretation of them. If a typical fourth-grade child, however, experiences only slight difficulty with the same material it would appear that the text has fourth-grade readability. This chapter will discuss important factors in word identification, word interpretation, and readability.

WORD IDENTIFICATION

The modern concept of reading employs the teaching of many methods of word identification. The analytic, or whole-word, approach; the synthetic, or phonics, approach; and the analytic-synthetic approach are methods used in word identification. Within each approach various techniques may be followed. For example, the analytic method utilizes the configuration of a word and the word in context, and may also use picture clues. A synthetic method may include structural analysis as well as the sounds of letters.

Phonics, however, has been and still is considered the core of word identification by many writers.

The History of Phonic Study and Word Analysis

Examination of materials related to the teaching of reading shows that phonic instruction in American schools has long been a controversial issue. In 1783 Noah Webster advocated stressing the sounds as well as the names of letters. From time to time other phonic approaches were recommended by American educators, and in 1850 a special method, developed by Edwin Leigh, was introduced in the Boston Phonetic School.[1]

Several phonic systems appeared in the 19th century, and combinations of phonic approaches were in general use throughout the first quarter of the 20th century.

About 1925 a strong reaction set in against phonic systems of instruction. The whole-word methods, which had, of course, appeared earlier, were recommended by some educators. Other writers endorsed an approach known as the analytic-synthetic method. According to one interpretation of this method entire stories composed by the pupils were first presented on experience charts; then words from these charts were selected for drill with flash cards. With a basic stock of sight words thus acquired, word analysis and phonetic study followed. There are, of course, variations in this approach. In some interpretations the story is prescribed, while in others it is the result of firsthand experience. In all versions, however, the story is first presented, then analyzed into its parts, and finally the parts reassembled to make the story again.

The analytic-synthetic method, as well as related approaches widely used, makes phonics a secondary concern and avoids introducing it as the first step in learning to read. Some educators object to this method and advocate phonics as the essential first step in learning to read. It is desirable for teachers to use the most defensible and efficient approach; therefore it will be of interest to examine experimental data and attempt to formulate a tentative decision concerning the role of phonics.

[1] Edwin Leigh, *Pronouncing Orthography* (St. Louis, 1864), p. 8.

Research on the Value of Phonics

In 1938 Arthur Gates and David Russell reported a study of the relative effectiveness of different methods of instruction. One group of children was trained by an "intrinsic" method which stressed words as units of perception. This training was given by the use of various exercises, such as the selection of correct words from groups similar in form or in pronunciation. Instead of instruction through such exercises, a second group of children was given drill in phonics. When it was found that the first group made a greater gain in reading skills, Gates and Russell concluded that excessive amounts of phonics should be avoided.[2]

Many authorities share the above position and assert that overemphasis on phonics may not only block the acquisition of desirable reading skills but also may lead to lack of interest in reading. Not all students of reading, however, accept these inferences. For example, a somewhat different conclusion was reached by Donald Agnew, who also made a comprehensive study of phonics. After testing two groups of children who had received greatly different amounts of training, he found the following advantages associated with the larger amounts of phonetic training:

(a) increases independence in recognizing words previously learned;
(b) aids in "unlocking" new words by giving the pupil a method of sound analysis;
(c) encourages correct pronunciation; and
(d) improves the quality of oral reading.

Agnew's investigations, however, as he states, "provided no evidence on the other arguments in favor of phonetic training."[3]

More recent studies, such as the one by Rose Sabaroff, reveal some interesting uses of phonics. In her study a group of children was given functional phonics, a second group was given systematic instruction in phonics, and a third group did independent reading at their respective levels. The writer concluded that functional phonics is superior for average and above-average achievers while systematic phonic instruction is superior for low achievers.[4]

---

[2] Arthur I. Gates and David H. Russell, "Types of Materials, Vocabulary Burden, Word Analysis and Other Factors in Beginning Reading," *Elementary School Journal*, 39:27–36 and 119–128 (September 1938 and October, 1938).

[3] Donald C. Agnew, "The Effect of Varied Amounts of Phonetic Training on Primary Reading," Duke University Research Studies in Education, no. 5 (Durham, N.C.: Duke University Press, 1939), p. 44.

[4] Rose Sabaroff, "A Comparative Investigation of Two Methods of Teaching Phonics in a Modern Reading Program: A Pilot Study," *Journal of Experimental Education*, 31:249–256 (March, 1963).

Research has also yielded provocative results concerning the time when phonics instruction should be initiated. Edward Dolch and Maurine Bloomster studied the relationship of success under phonic instruction to mental maturity. It was noted that children of mental ages lower than seven years were not successful on the phonics test used in this study. These writers concluded that a higher degree of mental maturity is required to apply phonics principles than is required to learn sight words.[5]

A more recent study by J. B. McDowell[6] reemphasized the findings of an earlier study by Elmer Sexton and John Herron—namely, that the teaching of phonics was of little or no value in the first five months of grade 1.[7]

Nila Banton Smith, in summarizing the research concerning the value of phonics and the time when phonics instruction should occur, concluded:

1. It cannot be assumed that all children need phonics.
2. Phonics is effective with children who need word-recognition help, but its greatest effectiveness is attained when it is taught functionally and is related to children's reading needs.
3. It is advisable to delay intensive phonic instruction until a child has attained a mental age of seven years.
4. Phonics instruction is most valuable at the second- and third-grade levels.
5. The use of configuration clues and context clues should be supplemented with phonics.
6. It would be well to give more attention to both visual and auditory discrimination in teaching all types of word recognition.[8]

Perspectives on Phonics Instruction

The value of phonics appears to have been established. Research has also indicated that a large amount of phonics and phonic instruction begun too early will have little value and possibly will adversely affect the reading habits of children.

In spite of this evidence numerous teachers feel beginning reading instruction could be enhanced by some type of readiness for phonic

---

[5] Edward W. Dolch and Maurine Bloomster, "Phonic Readiness," *Elementary School Journal*, 38:201–205 (November, 1937).

[6] J. B. McDowell, "A Report on the Phonetic Method of Teaching Children to Read," *Catholic Educational Review*, 50:506–519 (October, 1953).

[7] Elmer K. Sexton and John S. Herron, "The Newark Phonics Experiment," *Elementary School Journal*, 28:690–701 (May, 1928).

[8] Nila Banton Smith, "What Research Tells Us about Word Recognition," *Elementary School Journal*, 55:440–446 (April, 1955).

instruction. It has been pointed out that reading readiness implies readiness for reading at all levels. Therefore, the authors feel that definite readiness experiences should precede formal phonic instruction.

In considering "readiness" for phonics, writers have sought criteria to insure the child's ability to profit from phonetic training when it is introduced. Although research data are meager on this topic, it is generally agreed that the most important prerequisites for successful reading are the auditory ability to differentiate between letter sounds and names and the visual ability to differentiate between written words and letters.

Stated more specifically, the child who is ready for phonic instruction will demonstrate these attainments:

> (1) The child should be able to hear that there is a difference between words that sound somewhat alike, such as *man* and *men* or *had* and *hat*. (2) He should be able to detect whether two words begin with the same sound or not. To test this ability, one can ask the child to pick out the one word that begins differently in a spoken list such as: *moon, many, soon, make, mother*. He should also be able to listen to a word and supply two or three other words that begin with the same sound. (3) He should be sensitive to rhymes, should be able to pick out words that rhyme, and should be able to supply words to rhyme with a given word. This ability is fundamental to the construction of "word families." (4) He should be able to hear similarities and differences in word endings. (5) He should be able to hear similarities and differences in middle vowels; e.g., he should be able to tell whether *rub* and *rob* or *hill* and *pit* have the same middle sound. (6) He should be able to listen to the pronunciation of a word sound by sound and fuse or blend the sounds mentally so as to be able to recognize the word intended.[9]

Some of these abilities can be cultivated during the preschool period; for example, speaking distinctly and correctly and listening to and reciting rhymes and poetry. Others might well be delayed until children have acquired a basic stock of sight words.

Although several investigations indicate the need for phonic readiness, few studies have sought to disclose the optimum time to introduce the various phonic elements. Table VIII represents a suggested plan for the introduction of phonic elements in a word-identification program.

In the foregoing discussion we have presented some research and expert opinion concerning phonic instruction, together with the positions of several leaders regarding the place and value of phonic instruction.

---

[9] Albert J. Harris, *How to Increase Reading Ability*, 4th ed. (New York: David McKay Co., Inc., 1961), pp. 330–331.

TABLE VIII
A PLANNED SEQUENCE OF WORD IDENTIFICATION GOALS[10]

READER LEVEL	SIGHT RECOGNITION	VISUAL AND AUDITORY READINESS	PHONICS AND STRUCTURAL ANALYSIS
Preprimer	40–75 words	Matches objects, pictures, letters, words, phrases, sentences. Notes similarity in the sounds of rhyming words. Notes similarities and differences in initial consonant sounds.	Relies mainly on general configuration, picture cues, and context cues. Recognizes same word beginning with capital or lower-case letter. Recognizes plural made with *s*. Learns names of most alphabet letters. Begins to use initial consonants in combination with context.
Primer	80–150 new words	Compares words for similarities and differences in beginning sounds. Compares rhyming words; completes and composes simple rhymes. Compares final consonants in words; notes similarities and differences. Blends and recognizes words spoken in two or three parts.	Continues use of configuration, context, and picture cues. Uses common initial consonants in combination with context cues. Structural analysis: recognizes familiar words with endings *s, es, d, ed, ing*. Recognizes known whole words in compound words (e.g., *into*). Some common word families with initial consonant substitution. Use of some common final consonants.
First Reader	115–200 new words	Review of previous ear training. Listens to and identifies all initial	Review of previously learned phonic and structural skills. Use of all initial consonants and common

[10] Albert J. Harris, *op. cit.*, pp. 351–353.

TABLE VIII (continued)

READER LEVEL	SIGHT RECOGNITION	VISUAL AND AUDITORY READINESS	PHONICS AND STRUCTURAL ANALYSIS
		consonants and common consonant digraphs. Continued use of rhymes. Listens and compares additional final consonants. Notes similarities and differences in middle vowels: *man-men, bill-bell, hat-hot,* etc.	consonant digraphs, *ch, sh, st, th, wh.* Additional word families with initial consonant substitution. Learns endings *-er, -est, -ly.* Changes known words by substituting final consonants. Introduction of short vowel sounds, *a, o, i, u, e.*
Second Reader	300–650 new words	Review of previous ear training. Listens to and compares words with single and double initial consonants: *fight-fright, seal-steal,* etc. Listens to and compares words with long and short vowels: *can-cane, bit-bite, hop-hope, cut-cute,* etc.	Review of previously learned word-attack skills. Learns common initial two-consonant blends, *br, cr, dr, fr, gr, pr, tr, bl, cl, fl, pl, sl, sp, st, sw,* and final consonant blends, *-ng, -nk, -nt, -st.* Reviews short vowels and learns long vowel sounds, *a, e, i, o, u, y,* and rule of final silent *e.* Learns common vowel digraphs, *ai, ay, ea, ee, ie, oa, oo.* Learns effect of following *r* on vowels: *-ar, -er, -ir, -or, -ur.* Learns the change of *y* to *i* before *s* and *d.*
Third Reader	500–1000 new words	Review of previous ear training. Listens to and compares words containing new phonic elements.	Review of all previously learned word-attack skills. Learns less common two-consonant blends, *gl, sc, sm, sn, sw, tw,*

TABLE VIII (continued)

READER LEVEL	SIGHT RECOGNITION	VISUAL AND AUDITORY READINESS	PHONICS AND STRUCTURAL ANALYSIS
		Listens to divide spoken words into syllable units.	*dw, ph;* and three-consonant blends, *scr, str, spl, spr, squ,* and *thr*.
			Learns silent consonants, *wr, kn, gn, qu*.
			Learns vowel diphthongs, *au, aw, ou, ow, ew, ue, oi, oy.* Variant sounds of *ea, ou, ow*.
			Learns hard and soft *c* and *g*.
			Prefixes: *re-, be-, de-, pre-*.
			Endings: *-le, -ble, -tle, -ful, -tion, -sion, -ation, -al, -ity*.
			Recognizes root word in words with these endings.
			Learns to divide easy two- and three-syllable words into syllables.

Emmett Betts, for example, in a review of 199 articles, bulletins, and research reports related to phonics and phonic instruction, deplored what he considered an unjustifiable tendency of some writers to advocate a single system as a basic or corrective method.[11]

Betts cited four important contributions of research to the understanding of the use and methodology of teaching phonics in a balanced and differentiated program:

1. The whole-word, or analytic, method of teaching phonics appears to be more effective than a blending, or synthetic, method.
2. When the attention of the learner is focused on the word form itself in reading and spelling, his needs are served best by analyzing the whole word—undistorted by syllabic divisions, the use of

[11] Emmett A. Betts, "Phonics: Practical Considerations Based on Research," *Elementary English*, 33:357–371 (October, 1956).

colored lettering of parts, or the use of special typographical devices to call attention to "hard spots" and other elements.
3. Certain types of phonic programs tend to make children too "word-conscious," causing them to stop to sound out words they can identify easily.
4. Systematic instruction in auditory perception and speech production appears to make a significant contribution to reading achievement.[12]

Although studies point to the desirability of associating phonic instruction with other phases of the reading program, there are some persons who advocate the use of systems independently and in isolation from the regular program. It is well to remember that many basal reading programs and courses of study devote considerable attention to phonics. If pupils fail to acquire competency under such a program, then it is desirable to offer special help. Such work should, however, always be articulated closely with the basal program, and the entire approach should be made individually appropriate and meaningful. Moreover, selection of the phonic materials to be employed should be made in full consideration of the objectives of the reading program and the needs of the pupils in each class.

One may conclude then that the nature and amount of phonic instruction to be given is still a debatable question. Adherents of any one of a number of positions may find a justification for their views in published sources—from the devotees of the doctrine of "no phonics" to the advocates of highly artificial approaches. Despite the controversy, certain facts do appear clear. There seems to be a phonic readiness which should be ascertained before instruction is offered; phonic study should begin with known words; and an auditory-visual emphasis should be employed.

Many children do need help in the mastery of phonic skills, although some appear to make satisfactory progress in reading without formal phonic instruction. Therefore, careful diagnosis should precede this type of instruction at all levels. Moreover, many workers agree that phonic instruction is particularly effective with disabled or very retarded readers.

WORD INTERPRETATION

As was pointed out at the beginning of this chapter, word identification consists of the recognition of the printed symbol and the inter-

---

[12] *Ibid.*, p. 365.

pretation of that symbol. The student of reading should be aware that these two processes occur almost simultaneously in the reading process. The term "word interpretation" is synonymous with the term "vocabulary" in that the printed symbol, once identified, depends on the child's concept of the symbol's meaning.

The importance of a good vocabulary has been repeatedly stressed as a means to better silent and oral reading and to many significant values associated with everyday life. A good vocabulary enables one to communicate clearly. In almost every phase of life it appears to be a distinct asset.

Although most people will agree upon the worth of a good vocabulary and will approve of continuous attention to its development, there are some who question the importance of specific efforts aimed at improvement. Inasmuch as a good vocabulary, they say, is largely the result of good or superior intelligence, attempts to enhance its development will not usually affect intelligence, which is the primary determiner of vocabulary. But the improvement of a student's vocabulary, others believe, influences his marks in school or his success in learning. In the March, 1955, issue of *College English,* Wilfred Funk is quoted as follows:

> There are those of us who say that building the vocabulary of boys and girls helps to raise their marks in all their studies. There is the other camp that claims that this is putting the cart before the horse. This group asserts that intelligent boys and girls have good vocabularies by virtue of their intelligence and that lower grade mentalities cannot be improved by "vocabulary stuffing."[13]

There is a need for comprehensive experiments to test the conflicting claims that have persisted for many years. There are, however, already available some pertinent data and many convincing statements which attest to the value of efforts to foster vocabulary improvement. William D. Templeman, for example, has reported the confirmation of his observations in extensive investigations at the University of Illinois which indicate that vocabulary-building exercises have value. From his first investigation, conducted during the first semester of 1938–39 with 2,430 freshmen at the University of Illinois and designed to test whether vocabulary training is worthwhile, Templeman concluded:

> If a high-school student is to achieve scholastic success when he goes to college, he should have a larger and better vocabulary than the vocabularies of most of the students who will be his classmates

---

[13] Wilfred Funk, in a letter to William Darby Templeman. Quoted by Templeman in "Does Vocabulary Building Have Value?" *College English,* 16:366 (March, 1955).

in his college. . . . The present investigation may be said to point also toward a conclusion that if at *any* time during his educational career (even after he has entered college or graduate school) a person possesses or builds up a vocabulary greater than the vocabularies of his classmates, his grades in the immediate future will be higher than theirs.[14]

Some studies seem to suggest that a good general vocabulary has widespread transfer value and is likely to be associated also with good special vocabularies. It is frequently pointed out that there is a great need to stimulate children and young people to improve and extend their general vocabularies as well as to master an ever-increasing number of words essential in understanding special areas of interest or endeavor. In this respect the importance of intelligence should be recognized, but the significance of this factor should not be overemphasized. Although it will be found that most students with high IQ's have large vocabularies it should be kept in mind that even these students may benefit from exercises in vocabulary development. Students who take reading improvement classes in college, for example, are sometimes from the high IQ range who express a need to improve their vocabularies. Requirements of highly specialized courses demand unusual proficiencies which these students believe they lack. Investigations reveal that marked improvement may be made by such students. Indeed, studies show that under favorable conditions students generally may make great gains in vocabulary development at all levels in their education.

Accordingly, planning for steady growth in vocabulary is one of the obligations of teachers, and various methods for doing this have been put forward. Some writers have tended to believe that early vocabulary development can be most effectively accomplished through phonetic training. Others have emphasized the importance of word-analysis techniques. Still others have stressed learning through repetition of words, or various other procedures such as attention to context, wide reading, and related activities.

Size of Vocabularies and Word Lists

Another debatable topic pertaining to vocabulary development relates to the size of the children's vocabularies. In the December, 1953, issue of the *Elementary School Journal,* Fred E. Bryan reviewed the literature on this topic and reported the results of his own study. The

---

[14] William Darby Templeman, "Vocabulary and Success in College," *School and Society,* 51:224 (February 17, 1940).

question of the size of children's vocabularies, he said, "seemed fairly well settled until Robert H. Seashore . . . came up with his bombshell."[15] Seashore asserted that common estimates of children's vocabularies as made by "teachers, research specialists and textbook writers" are frequently less than 10 percent of the true size as estimated from written definitions of representative sample lists taken from unabridged dictionaries.[16] Seashore's findings differed markedly from the results of studies by Horn,[17] Thorndike,[18] Buckingham and Dolch,[19] and Rinsland.[20]

Seashore reported that the average first-grader knows 24,000 different words, and the average eighth-grader 49,500 words.[21]

In his article Bryan reported the results of a study to "test the hypothesis that children's vocabularies have been underestimated because they have been developed from (1) single-time situations, (2) limited geographical areas, (3) single-response situations."[22] He devised a plan for periodically checking the vocabularies of children under different geographical conditions, at different seasons of the year, and with common areas of experience used as response stimuli, such as the areas of home, school, farm, and travel. The following table compares his results with those of Seashore:[23]

	MEDIAN VOCABULARY	
GRADE	SEASHORE	BRYAN
II	21,900	4,080
III	25,600	11,615
IV	28,400	13,130
V	25,600	21,543
VI	34,000	25,573

[15] Fred E. Bryan, "How Large Are Children's Vocabularies?" *Elementary School Journal,* 54:210–216 (December, 1953).

[16] J. C. Seegers and R. H. Seashore, "How Large Are Children's Vocabularies?" *Elementary English,* 26:181–194 (April, 1949).

[17] Ernest A. Horn, *A Basic Writing Vocabulary,* Monographs in Education, Series No. 4 (Iowa City, Iowa: University of Iowa, 1926).

[18] Edward L. Thorndike, *A Teacher's Word Book of the Twenty Thousand Words Found Most Frequently and Widely in General Reading for Children and Young People* (New York: Teachers College, Columbia University, 1932).

[19] B. R. Buckingham and E. W. Dolch, *A Combined Word List* (Boston: Ginn and Co., 1936).

[20] F. W. Rinsland, *A Basic Vocabulary of Elementary School Children* (New York: Macmillan Company, 1945).

[21] Fred E. Bryan, *op. cit.,* p. 210.

[22] *Ibid.,* pp. 210–211.

[23] *Ibid.,* p. 213.

Bryan concluded:

> In the present study, Seashore's test was administered to a large number of children in various parts of the United States at three different seasons of the year. The writer did not find that the children know as many words as Seashore estimates; but, based on the sampling of the dictionary, it can be theoretically assumed that children know more words than have been revealed by the free-association studies, the counting of words found in children's written work and other forms of expression, or any combination of these methods used in the past.[24]

It would appear, then, that children's vocabularies are larger than the estimates given in early studies and that they are influenced greatly by experience and opportunity in early childhood. There seems to be a great opportunity for vocabulary enrichment in special interest areas, as well as in all curriculum areas.

Vocabulary and Concept Building in a Developmental Program

Consistent with the developmental reading concept is recognition of the desirability of encouraging continuous growth in vocabulary, for the understanding of new words and concepts is an ever-present task. One important way to foster the development of vocabulary is by emphasizing the ability to obtain the meaning of words from their context. DeBoer and Whipple point out that "a *mature* reader is able through his reading to develop new meanings and concepts that will yield new insight in the field. . . . But most pupils even at the secondary level are *immature* readers."[25] Thus it is singularly important for teachers to guide pupils in the acquisition of new and important words and conceptual terms. DeBoer and Whipple suggest:

> First, such words must be identified by the teacher. The materials for each unit ought to be examined and word lists made up. Second, these words should be taught as needed, always in context and not too many at a time. Experience shows that in introducing each significant new concept, reliance should be placed upon oral communication instead of written communication. . . . Such an informal, developmental and experiential kind of instruction prepares students for their reading.[26]

---

[24] *Ibid.,* p. 215.
[25] John J. DeBoer and Gertrude Whipple, "Reading Development in Other Curriculum Areas," in Paul Witty (chairman), *Development In and Through Reading,* Sixtieth Yearbook of the National Society for the Study of Education, Part I (Chicago: University of Chicago Press, 1961), p. 67.
[26] *Ibid.,* p. 68.

At the primary level word meanings often center around experiences with concrete objects and with associations built between words and objects. As the child proceeds to the middle grades, he broadens his source of word meanings by increased firsthand experiences and, as Grace Boyd says, "The most desirable and dependable method of developing meanings is through *firsthand experience.*" To provide such experiences she recommends field trips, the use of audio-visual aids, and the provision of opportunities for creative expression "in speaking, in writing, in drawing, and in the use of a great variety of art media."[27] These experiences may provide the background for understanding many words and their related concepts.

Some words, it is clear, cannot be learned through a direct sensory approach. Words such as *honesty, charity,* and *democracy* illustrate one group of such words. Since words of this sort are extremely numerous and important in the social studies, failure to comprehend their meanings frequently precludes communication, creates confusion, and leads to misunderstanding or to actual emotional disturbance. Some teachers have developed effective ways of dealing with these words. Here, for example, is a method one teacher employs. The pupils in her class make each week a list of new or difficult words which they encounter in the social studies text. Several words are singled out as being most important for the understanding of the passages under consideration, and these words are discussed by the class and definitions are formulated. The definitions, at the end of a period of discussion, frequently fall into two groups. In the first group are those words whose meanings, the pupils agree, are reasonably clear, although there are sometimes several equally acceptable definitions for each of them. But in the second group are words the meanings of which are vague. Committees are appointed to investigate these words and to submit the results at a forthcoming class meeting. When the words are subsequently presented and their various possible meanings cited, discussion follows and the meanings of the terms as used in the text are identified and clarified. Sometimes several definitions are found to be acceptable for a word as it appears in different contexts. These definitions are placed in *Our Social Studies Work Book,* prepared by the children, with examples from the text of the use of each word.

---

[27] Grace Boyd, "Developing Word Recognition and Meaning Vocabulary in Grades Four through Eight," in Helen M. Robinson (editor), *Corrective Reading in Classroom and Clinic,* Supplementary Educational Monographs no. 79 (Chicago: University of Chicago Press, 1953), pp. 131–135.

The use of films and filmstrips often proves an effective means of improving vocabulary. In the reading program developed in the U.S. Army during World War II, filmstrips and films were widely used. Following World War II, filmstrips were gradually introduced in schools and employed successfully in certain phases of reading instruction. Films, too, were used with outstanding success in association with reading materials; for example, in an experiment conducted by Paul Witty and James Fitzwater, films were employed to present simple narratives of strong appeal to second-grade children.[28] After the children had seen each film and had listened to the commentary, they read the story in a film-reader. Then they developed their own story, which was reproduced and heard by them via the magnetic sound track. This experiment, combining reading with listening and discussion, was demonstrably successful. Under these conditions the acquisition of concepts and of skill in interpreting presentations was greatly enhanced. Although the film played an important role in this program, it was recognized that its use was one factor only in its success. Similarly, the use of filmstrips has been found to foster the development of vocabulary and reading skills.

By the time the pupil enters high school he is capable of abstract thinking and of acquiring broad concepts. He relies less on firsthand experiences and depends more upon gaining the meaning of unfamiliar words by examining their context. One of his main problems now involves the acquisition of specialized vocabularies and the need to discriminate between subtle differences in the meanings of words in order to understand inferences and to read critically. Many high school students will profit from a review of the skills needed for building and extending vocabulary. One recent publication, *Developing Your Vocabulary,* provides systematic review and attempts to guide the high school student in vocabulary development in accord with his changing and varied needs.[29]

The college student is faced with even more complex vocabulary problems. Sometimes he needs to review vocabulary skills he has forgotten or has never learned to apply readily. As in the case of the high school student, he must acquire unfamiliar words and concepts and must increase his vocabulary to meet the demands of new or advanced subject matter. At this level, planning to foster or motivate vocabulary devel-

[28] Paul Witty and James P. Fitzwater, "An Experiment with Films, Film-Readers, and the Magnetic Sound Track Projector," *Elementary English,* 30:232–241 (April, 1953).
[29] Paul Witty and Edith Grotberg, *Developing Your Vocabulary* (Chicago: Science Research Associates, Inc., 1960).

opment is desirable and often necessary. According to the developmental reading philosophy, vocabulary building is a continuous, sequential process. It cannot be assumed that there is a final level of development, for the capable adult also continues to expand his vocabulary.

Contributions from Structural Linguistics

For years important contributions to the teaching of reading were associated with the science of semantics. It is true, of course, that most of the principles were already familiar to students of the reading process and were being practiced by some teachers. But the renewed emphasis, coming from students of semantics, tended to reinforce the work of these superior teachers.

Within the past few years the emphasis has shifted to structural linguistics, about which much has been said and written. Some significant implications may be derived from this approach. We believe that the chief contributions of structural linguistics relate to the type of materials recommended for beginning instruction in reading and to the importance attached to the roles of oral reading and of listening.

These emphases are significant and timely. Their antecedents are clearly evident in the work of semanticists, who stressed increasing the clarity of communication through the use of printed material prepared in the natural form associated with effective speech. This point of view, reiterated by the linguists, has long been recognized by educators. Witty and Lou LaBrant pointed out in 1946 that children on starting to school employ about 2,500 different words.[30] These words are, of course, spoken, and their meanings are usually unmistakably clear, since they have been acquired in asking for things, in putting on clothes, and in other concrete situations. Early investigations showed that by the time the average child is two years of age, he has acquired about 250 different words which appear in his speaking vocabulary. To this list he adds about 600 each year. On entering school at six, he will already have acquired a very large vocabulary, which he will have employed in various forms in almost every type of sentence. It was proposed that the child should be introduced at first to printed materials for silent reading which employ these familiar words and expressions. Suitable presentations, they asserted, will contain words, phrases, and sentences used in a form similar to or identical with children's speech. What then is more natural or more appropriate than to have the child read silently, from

[30] Paul Witty and Lou LaBrant, *Teaching the People's Language* (New York: Barnes & Noble, Inc., 1946).

experience charts, expressions with which he is already familiar through his speech?

The child will first read silently, then later orally. Oral reading will continue to have an important place in the program, maintaining relationship between speech and reading. Robert Pooley stresses that relationship as follows:

> Reading readiness depends to a considerable degree upon acquaintance with the fundamentals of what is to be read. Every adult recalls the experience of laying a book or article aside because of lack of interest or significance in the content, only to return to it later with avidity because of a conversation, a lecture, a radio talk, or a TV-viewing. It is accepted practice in beginning reading to talk about what is to be read, to draw inferences from pictures, and to discuss personal experiences which might bear upon the material about to be read. Somehow, the value of this interrelation between speaking and reading is lost sight of in the upper grades and high school. As children grow older, they are increasingly assigned reading to be undertaken without discussional preview. The significance of preparatory discussion cannot be overstressed: both study reading and the teaching of reading would be almost impossible without it. But with a supply of words, his learning consists, in part, of associating visual symbols with sounds and relating these sounds to his known stock of words. By ear he will also be learning new words, whose visual symbols he will learn in time.[31]

Such a basic practice as that recommended by Pooley and other linguists requires the use in reading instruction of natural and meaningful forms of expression. The procedure differs essentially from the familiar word approach, in which a very limited vocabulary is used and repeated excessively. The emphasis of linguists will be endorsed by many educators. Thus, Jeannette Veatch:

> It is heartening to see such strong support come from a science [linguistics] not generally thought of as being connected to elementary education. And again, those educators who have also felt that reading begins best with experience charts, records, and stories can be encouraged. Those who have argued against asking children to look at, drill upon and mouth words that were not their own can find great and comforting support from the linguists.[32]

Several of the writers in this field of linguistics, however, tend to oversimplify the problem or to complicate teaching unduly by the intro-

---

[31] Robert C. Pooley, "Reading and the Language Arts," in Paul Witty (editor), *Development In and Through Reading, op. cit.,* p. 46.
[32] Jeannette Veatch, "Linguistic Instruction in the Teaching of Reading Kill or Cure?" *Elementary English,* 39:232 (March, 1962).

duction of a very involved system. Veatch comments on an article by John Dawkins, who asserts that "as long as language is 'an oral act' and words are made up of different sounds or vocal responses, children will learn to read *if presented* with systematic patterns of letter sounds in words." Veatch points out that "Dawkins' children can be taught to read by means of their own words."[33]

Children's own words do constitute part but not *all* of the content of suitable reading materials. Moreover, the statement of some linguists to the effect that

"sentences make words rather than words make sentences"[34]

is only partly true, since some words have sentence connotations; other words have many meanings; and still others have conceptual importance which merits consideration. Thus, we see that some writers in the field of linguistics tend to oversimplify the problem of reading instruction in a way similar to that found when strict adherence to a particular word or phonic method is proposed as a panacea. The complexity of effective reading instruction necessitates the use of varied approaches. Within the confines of developmental reading instruction the values of phonic instruction, linguistic approaches, and other methods are fully acknowledged and utilized as parts of a teaching process in which clear communication is an important goal.

IMPROVING READABILITY OF PRINTED MATERIALS

For many years educators have been concerned over the reading difficulty of many publications. Even for many adults much published material is too difficult. Although some of these adults have had little formal education, there are in addition large numbers of individuals who, having attended school eight or nine years, have used reading skills little after leaving. Accordingly, their reading ability appears to have decreased to such an extent that many publications are too difficult for them to read with ease.

Hence, there is a need for simpler materials prepared for these adults. There is a need, too, for a reliable measure of difficulty to use in gauging the suitability of materials, not only for adults but also for children. To help children learn to read, we must make sure that the materials we

---

[33] *Ibid.*
[34] John Dawkins, "Reading Theory—An Important Distinction," *Elementary English,* 38:389–392 (October, 1961).

offer them are neither too difficult nor too easy. Accordingly, readability is a concept of general significance and practicality.

The Concept of Readability

The term *readability* has several meanings. Research workers in the field of typography sometimes regard readability and legibility as interchangeable terms, but a broader concept has been advocated by other students. For example, William S. Gray and Bernice Leary interpreted the term to include such factors as the style of writing and the nature of the subject matter.[35] Perhaps the most comprehensive definition of readability has been suggested by Edgar Dale and Jeanne Chall: "In the broadest sense . . . readability is the sum total (including the interactions) of all those elements within a given piece of printed material that affects the success that a group of readers have with it. The success is the extent to which they understand it, read it at an optimum speed, and find it interesting." These authors include the reader in their definition: ". . . success depends upon other things besides the printed material itself. It depends upon the reader—his skill in reading, his intelligence, his experience, his maturity, his interest and purpose in reading."[36]

Formulae for Readability

In most formulae for determining readability, vocabulary difficulty is an important element. Of course, other factors are also included in determining readability. Table IX presents an overview of the criteria related to the various formulae.

The readability formulae employed most widely are perhaps those developed by Flesch, Dale and Chall, and Spache. Flesch states that his original purpose was to provide a tool for the selection of reading materials for adults, and the American Library Association used the Flesch formula in making a list of very easy books for adults. The formula, however, has been used not only for book selection and grading of books, but also to aid in the preparation of readable materials. It has proved practical too as a guide in editing newspaper reports, advertising copy,

[35] William S. Gray and Bernice E. Leary, *What Makes a Book Readable* (Chicago: University of Chicago Press, 1935).
[36] Edgar Dale and Jeanne S. Chall, "The Concept of Readability," *Elementary English*, 26:23 (January, 1949).

TABLE IX
CRITERIA OF READABILITY FORMULAE

DATE	AUTHOR	CRITERIA
1929	Alfred Lewerenz	Words beginning with *w, h, b* are easier to read than words beginning with *e* and *i*.
1930	George Johnson	Use of relative number of polysyllabic words.
1931	W. W. Patty and W. I. Painter	Average word-weight value derived from Thorndike word list.
1934	Edgar Dale and Ralph Tyler	Number of technical words, number of hard words, number of indeterminate clauses. (Restricted to materials on the topic of health.)
1935	William S. Gray and Bernice Leary	Number of different hard words; number of first-, second-, and third-person pronouns; average sentence length in words; percentage of different words; number of prepositional phrases.
1939	Irving Lorge	Average sentence length, number of different hard words, number of prepositional phrases.
1939	Gerald Yoakam	Different words used on the basis of Thorndike's 20,000 words.
1943	Rudolph Flesch	Average sentence length, affixed morphemes, and number of personal references.
1948	Rudolph Flesch	Average sentence length. (Restricted to determine "reading ease.") Personal words and personal sentences. (Restricted to determine "human interest.")
1948	Edgar Dale and Jeanne S. Chall	Word count and average sentence length based on Dale list of 3,000 words.
1953	George Spache	Vocabulary and sentence length. (Suitable for material below fourth-grade level.)

government publications, and bulletins and leaflets for special groups such as farmers.[37]

Margaret Kerr predicts increased use of readability formulae by schools. She approves the growing tendency of school administrators to appoint committees of teachers to select textbooks and believes that

[37] Rudolph Flesch, "A Readability Formula in Practice," *Elementary English*, 25:344–351 (October, 1948).

classroom teachers, with the aid of such formulae, can make more desirable and efficient choices.[38] Chall has prepared a provocative summary, in which some advantages and disadvantages of the various formulae are suggested.[39]

Evaluation of Readability Formulae

Inconsistencies in the use of different formulae have been reported from time to time. The inconsistencies may be traceable to variation in the criteria employed for estimating readability.

The variability in the elements considered important in different formulae is suggested by the fact that vocabulary difficulty is estimated by authors in various ways such as checking against standard word lists or by counting syllables. Some formulae include a measure of some phase of sentence structure; others introduce the element of human interest. It is apparent that research is needed to determine more fully the value of each of these different factors in determining and appraising readability.

Flesch calls for "a refinement of the available measurement techniques and the utilization of work in related fields, particularly the psychology of personality." A broadened formula should make, he believes, provision for the measurement of other language elements, such as participles, verbs, adjectives, and particles. Above all, the problem should be approached as a study in linguistics.[40]

Margaret Kerr believes that the formulae have practical value in spite of their limitations; however, she warns that the results of their use should serve merely as a departure for a more detailed analysis of printed materials.[41] W. S. Gray also noted that "research should aid in developing more effective ways of identifying the kinds of material that are most readable for given individuals. The fact is widely recognized that comprehension varies with numerous factors, such as intelligence, background of experience, motives, and cultural status."[42]

[38] Margaret Kerr, "Use of Readability Formulas in Selecting Textbooks," *Elementary School Journal*, 49:411–414 (March, 1949).

[39] Jeanne S. Chall, *Readability: An Appraisal of Research and Application*, Bureau of Educational Research Monographs no. 34 (Columbus, Ohio: The Ohio State University, 1958).

[40] Rudolph Flesch, *op. cit.*

[41] Margaret Kerr, *op. cit.*

[42] William S. Gray, "Progress in the Study of Readability," *Elementary School Journal*, 47:491–499 (May, 1947).

Jeanne Chall has suggested that formulae be employed with concern for the following considerations:

> *First,* readability formulas should be critically used. Too often the grade-placement indexes are accepted as true measures of difficulty when they should be considered only as first approximations of difficulty.
>
> *Second,* readability formulas as prescriptions for writing should be approached with extreme caution. The formulas were not devised as rules for writing. They consider only limited aspects of difficulty.
>
> *Third,* validation studies are needed to show the differences in actual reading comprehension as a result of changes effected by typical readability campaigns in journalism and industry.
>
> *Fourth,* validation studies on textbooks are needed to throw light on the degree of confidence that can be placed in the grade-level indexes of the various formulas and the extent of agreement among them.
>
> *Fifth,* there is a need for better exchange of results of readability appraisals, especially in education. Since the time and effort involved in appraising a book is considerable, some provision should be made for exchange of information among publishers, teachers, school systems, and librarians.[43]

The foregoing discussion raises serious questions as to the desirability of placing too much emphasis upon formulae in constructing readable materials or estimating their suitability for students or classes. At best, formulae afford only a rough check on the ease of reading various presentations. The first responsibility is the author's, keeping in mind the group for whom his materials are being developed. He should attempt to present his ideas and concepts clearly, and relate his presentation clearly to the experience of the group. He should bear in mind that interest and motives will affect readability. In addition, if his materials are to be used by persons of limited reading ability, he must avoid run-on or involved sentences, excessive use of affixes, high frequency of prepositional phrases, and unusual words.

Even after materials have been prepared with the foregoing precautions, the manner in which they are used will affect their readability. Of course, formulae do not take into account various teaching procedures and the varied ways in which new words and concepts are introduced.

---

[43] Jeanne S. Chall, "This Business of Readability: A Second Look," *Educational Research Bulletin,* 35:93 (1956). See also C. W. Hunnicutt and William J. Iverson (editors), *Research in the Three R's* (New York: Harper & Row, Publishers, 1958), pp. 176–213.

CONCLUDING STATEMENT

This chapter has presented a view of the interrelationship of word-recognition elements, namely, word identification and vocabulary. The factor of readability was considered, since it has a bearing upon the word-recognition factor.

Robert Pooley emphasized the relationship of phonics and word study:

> The study of phonetics has obvious relationships to the teaching of reading and, by the same token, to the development of the pupil's readiness in word recognition. Because there are thousands of words in the speaking and comprehension vocabulary of a beginning pupil, he already has a resource that may be tapped by learning to convert visual symbols into sounds. One of the principal learning procedures at the early stage is the association of printed letters, singly and in combination, with the typical sounds they represent and the synthesis of these sounds into patterns which the child can recognize as the words he already knows. Some words he will learn as wholes, without the need for analysis; but, increasingly as he meets new words, the power to deal with them analytically in terms of sound related to symbols is a valuable asset.[44]

In addition to word-identification factors, especially phonics, certain principles of vocabulary development which are widely followed by good teachers were presented. In the evolution of these principles, interest centered at one time in the compilation of lists of words and in the restriction of the vocabulary of textbooks to these lists. Gradually the emphasis shifted, until at the present time attention is concentrated on concept building and the development of vocabularies designed to enable pupils to read according to their varied purposes and needs.

Since there are approximately 700,000 or more words in the English language, teachers cannot, of course, present all of them. Nor can they provide the necessary experience to clarify the meanings of all words in the specialized vocabularies of the subject fields. But there are significant steps that they can take in an effort to help pupils acquire functionally useful vocabularies. They can encourage varied firsthand experience which will afford the basis for meaningful vocabulary development. They can lead children to appreciate the fact that words have different meanings and that context affects or determines meaning. Al-

---

[44] Robert C. Pooley, "Reading and the Language Arts," in Paul Witty (editor), *Development In and Through Reading, op. cit.,* p. 41.

though teachers should stress the different meanings of certain words, they should not confuse children by introducing too many meanings, or meanings that are too far removed from the children's own experience.

Teachers can do much to promote vocabulary growth by introducing pupils to profitable forms of word study and word analysis. These efforts should be initiated after a basic stock of sight words has been acquired. Teachers can offer assistance to pupils by stressing the use of picture dictionaries and other standard sources for obtaining information. Pupils should be encouraged to study the different meanings found in the dictionary and to select quickly the most appropriate definition. Discussion of the definitions will help the pupils to acquire clear concepts.

Wide reading will also enable the student to extend his experience vicariously and, as a result, to increase his vocabulary. Teachers can offer further assistance by encouraging pupils to master the specialized vocabularies of various subject areas. If vocabulary development is looked upon as a part of a larger language arts program that aims to foster clear communication, additional gains will be made.

Teachers should recognize the potential value of forces outside the classroom, such as television, the radio, and the motion picture. Through the use, direction, and correlation of these varied forces and activities, the teacher can help children acquire both a functionally useful vocabulary and a positive attitude toward vocabulary building.

Selected References

Ammons, R. B., "Experiential Factors in Visual Form Perception: I. Review and Formulation of Problems," *Journal of Genetic Psychology,* 84:3–25 (March, 1954).

Austin, Mary C. and others, *The First R: The Harvard Report on Reading in Elementary Schools* (New York: The Macmillan Company, 1963), pp. 27–35.

Berry, Althea, "Development of Reading Vocabulary and Word Recognition," in Arthur I. Gates (chairman), *Reading in the Elementary School,* Forty-eighth Yearbook of the National Society for the Study of Education, Part II (Chicago: University of Chicago Press, 1949), pp. 172–192.

Betts, Emmett A., "Phonics: Practical Considerations Based on Research," *Elementary English,* 33:357–371 (October, 1956).

Bond, Guy L. and Eva Bond Wagner, *Teaching the Child to Read* (New York: The Macmillan Company, 1960), pp. 149–199.

Cordts, Anna D., "And It's All Known as Phonics," *Elementary English,* 32:376–378 (October, 1955).

Dale, Edgar and Ralph W. Tyler, "A Study of Factors Influencing the Difficulty of Reading Materials for Adults of Limited Reading Ability," *Library Quarterly,* 4:384–412 (July, 1934).

Dolch, E. W., "Am I Teaching Phonics Right?" *Elementary School Journal,* 34:227–234 (April, 1957).

Dolch, E. W. and Maurine Bloomster, "Phonics Readiness," *Elementary School Journal,* 38:201–205 (November, 1937).

Durkin, Dolores, "Phonics and the Teaching of Reading," in Alice Miel (editor), *Practical Suggestions for Teaching,* No. 22 (New York: Bureau of Publications, Teachers College, Columbia University, 1962).

Francis, W. Nelson, *The Structure of American English* (New York: The Ronald Press Co., 1958).

Fries, Charles C., *Linguistics and Reading* (New York: Holt, Rinehart & Winston, Inc., 1963).

Gates, Arthur I., "Vocabulary Control in Basal Reading Material," *Reading Teacher,* 14:80–85 (November, 1961).

Gray, William S., *On Their Own in Reading* (Chicago: Scott, Foresman and Co., 1960).

Harris, Albert J., *How to Increase Reading Ability,* 4th ed. (New York: David McKay Co., Inc., 1961).

Hildreth, Gertrude, "New Methods for Old in Teaching Phonics," *Elementary School Journal,* 57:436–441 (May, 1957).

Hildreth, Gertrude, "Some Misconceptions Concerning Phonics," *Elementary English,* 34:26–29 (January, 1957).

Johnson, George R., "An Objective Method of Determining Reading Difficulty," *Journal of Educational Research,* 21:283–287 (April, 1930).

Johnson, Wendell, *People in Quandaries: The Semantics of Personal Adjustment* (New York: Harper & Row, Publishers, 1946).

Lewerenz, Alfred S., "Measurement of the Difficulty of Reading Materials," *Los Angeles Educational Research Bulletin,* 8:283–287 (March, 1929).

Lorge, Irving, "Predicting Reading Difficulty of Selections for Children," *Elementary English Review,* 16:229–233 (October, 1939).

McCarthy, Dorothea, "Language Development in Children," in L. Carmichael (ed.), *Manual of Child Psychology* (New York: John Wiley & Sons, Inc., 1946), pp. 476–581.

McCullough, Constance, "An Inductive Approach to Word Analysis," *Education,* 74:583–587 (January, 1954).

McKim, Margaret G. and Helen Caskey, *Guiding Growth in Reading in the Modern Elementary School* (New York: The Macmillan Co., 1963).

Pei, Mario A., *The Story of Language* (Philadelphia: J. B. Lippincott Co., 1949).

Pooley, Robert C., *Teaching English Usage* (New York: Appleton-Century-Crofts, 1946).

Serra, Mary C., "How to Develop Concepts and Their Verbal Representations," *Elementary School Journal,* 53:275–285 (January, 1953).

Smith, Henry P. and Emerald V. Dechant, *Psychology in Teaching Reading* (Englewood Cliffs, N. J.: Prentice-Hall, Inc., 1961).

Smith, Nila B., "What Research Says About Phonics Instruction," *Journal of Educational Research,* 51:1–9 (September, 1957).

Spache, George D., "A New Readability Formula for Primary Grade Materials," *Elementary School Journal,* 53:410–413 (March, 1953).

Spache, George D., *Good Reading for Poor Readers* (Champaign, Illinois: Garrard Publishing Company, 1962, rev.)

Strang, Ruth, Constance M. McCullough, and Arthur E. Traxler, *The Improvement of Reading*, 3rd ed. (New York: McGraw-Hill Book Co., 1961).

Thorndike, Edward L. and Irving Lorge, *The Teacher's Word Book of 30,000 Words* (New York: Bureau of Publications, Teachers College, Columbia University, 1944).

Witty, Paul, "Improving Readability of Printed Materials," *Elementary English*, 28:392–401 (November, 1951).

Witty, Paul, "Phonic Study and Word Analysis," *Elementary English*, 30:296–305 (May, 1953) and 373–379 (October, 1953).

Witty, Paul and Edith Grotberg, *Developing Your Vocabulary* (Chicago: Science Research Associates, Inc., 1960).

Witty, Paul and Robert A. Sizemore, "Phonics in the Reading Program: A Review and an Evaluation," *Elementary English*, 32:355–371 (October, 1955).

7

LITERATURE FOR CHILDREN AND YOUNG PEOPLE

A large number of children are introduced to literature before they are able to read. The parents of these boys and girls select books to read aloud to them. After the children have entered school their parents will continue to aid them in the selection of books from such varied sources as fairy tales, adventure stories, nursery rhymes, and animal stories. In making selections, parents may find help in books such as *Treasure for the Taking* by Anne Eaton, *Your Child's Reading Today* by Josette Frank, *A Parent's Guide to Children's Reading* by Nancy Larrick, *Storytelling* by Ruth Tooze, *Proof of the Pudding* by Phyllis Fenner, and *Family Reading and Storytelling* by Marguerite Martignoni. As a result of these experiences with books at home, many children will have developed a favorable attitude toward reading before they enter school or before they are taught to read. Some children, however, will not have been so fortunate. A major responsibility of the school, then, will be to provide situations that will maintain or engender favorable attitudes toward reading.

Children's Literature and the Reading Program

Children's literature includes a wide variety of subject matter and literary forms. It comes from folklore of the past as well as from recently created stories. As Pooley says,

> "The term 'literature' is difficult to define but easy to understand. We may call literature the oral and written heritage of a culture.... The fruits of this culture come to us in the form of books, legend, and folklore."[1]

[1] Robert C. Pooley, "Reading and the Language Arts," in Paul Witty (chairman), *Development In and Through Reading,* Sixtieth Yearbook of the National Society for the Study of Education, Part I (Chicago: University of Chicago Press, 1961), pp. 50–51.

Thus, the scope of literature will include classics and books that are contemporary. Accordingly, adults who are interested in cultivating in children and youth an understanding and appreciation of literature will not be bound by a restriction that limits selections to particular periods.

There is today general agreement on the idea that the instructional program in reading should not only help children to read but also should encourage them to apply and extend skills by wide reading. Such a program seeks also to develop and heighten appreciation and tastes. This emphasis is timely in terms of the fascination television and other mass media hold for children and the threat they offer to the development of permanent interest in reading.

Although there are diverse opinions regarding the effects of television and other mass media upon the reading interests and habits of individuals, research data are definite in disproving some of the most adverse comments. Indeed, as we pointed out previously, the amount of reading children do appears to be increasing somewhat since the advent of television. There need be no conflict between TV and reading; on the contrary, under supervision television may be used to stimulate interest in reading. The motivation offered through an association of reading with favorite television programs is similar to that afforded by the use of films and filmstrips in relation to books. These approaches constitute essential parts of a developmental program in which the interest factor is recognized as having the utmost significance.

Today the number of books available to satisfy the individual's interests is very great, especially since the advent of low-cost paperback editions. Good literature sometimes attracts readers on its own merits, and it is usually widely read when many worthwhile books on varied topics are made readily available to pupils. Under these conditions, children and youth soon realize that books offer adventure, recreation, inspiration, and challenge.

The guidance of reading will necessitate the use of varied approaches as well as the use of a variety of books. Since each teaching situation is unique, it is neither desirable nor practical to recommend a uniform procedure. However, because a number of characteristics are usually found in good instructional practice, certain suggestions of general applicability can be made. One series of such suggestions may be included as goals of an effective literature program, described by David Russell as follows:

1. The extension and enrichment of the child's experience of the complex ways of man's living
2. Giving opportunity to relive and re-experience the adventures and ideas of others

3. Gaining insight into one's own personality and problems
4. Providing materials which help to create an appreciation and understanding of the problems of others
5. The development of love of country and democratic ideals
6. The discovery of ethical values which are common to different creeds and which form a foundation of good character in the modern world
7. Providing opportunities for fun and for escape
8. The development of worthwhile tastes and permanent interests in good literature[2]

Such goals are clearly consistent with the objectives of a developmental reading program. The aim in encouraging the reading of literature is not merely to preserve and transmit our heritage, although this is of course one important purpose; reading has additional values, both immediate and long-range, in the lives of children and youth. We have already treated fully some of the values of reading in meeting the needs and contributing to the well-rounded development of elementary school pupils. To be similarly effective, Dwight Burton and Nancy Larrick suggest that literature programs in the high school should be based on the following principles:

1. Objectives in teaching literature must be fashioned from an amalgamation of research information about student interests, student motives, and the nature of literature and literary experience.
2. Books written expressly for adolescents will play an important role in the literature program *along with* great works from the literary tradition—there is little reason for an either-or conflict involving "classics" versus contemporary or juvenile selections.
3. Teachers of literature—and of other subjects—must be willing to go beyond the available anthology textbooks and canonized selections if the literature program is to be at all vital.
4. Both intensive and extensive experiences with literature are needed if all youth are to be brought into the closest possible consonance with the literary experience.[3]

The secondary school reading program which follows the preceding principles should contribute broadly to the development of the high school pupil helping him to read the content of the various subject fields effectively and to meet personal and social problems with increasing success. It should serve also to enhance and make more enjoyable his recreation. In such a program, the role of the teacher is of utmost

[2] David H. Russell, *Children Learn to Read,* 2nd ed. (Waltham, Mass.: Blaisdell Publishing Company, 1961), pp. 415–417.
[3] Dwight L. Burton and Nancy Larrick, "Literature for Children and Youth," in Paul Witty (chairman), *Development In and Through Reading, op. cit.,* pp. 197–198.

significance. To function effectively in this role the teacher must both obtain a knowledge of the nature and needs of each pupil, and be informed concerning reading materials of the past as well as of the present.

Children's Literature and the Role of the Teacher

Despite the capability of some pupils to choose books effectively, teachers, parents, and librarians agree that children and youth generally need guidance and encouragement in order to make the most suitable selections. Through the story hour the librarian may augment the work of the teacher and offer stimulation and guidance by discussing books and by introducing them through recordings or filmstrips. Parents may make a significant contribution by encouraging wide and varied use of the library and by sharing books with their children at home.

This is not to suggest that there are no problems to be met in guiding the reading of children and youth. Quite the opposite is true. Bringing children and books together is, and will no doubt continue to be, a challenging and often perplexing task for teachers and parents. As Burton and Larrick state the problem:

> But one thing we can be sure of. Children and youth are not what they were in our day. Not what they were even ten or fifteen years ago. Our changing culture and changing language are affecting their interests and their tastes as well as their response to language, both oral and written. *Moby Dick* was written in another language for another society than ours. We must recognize this if we are to bring it to young readers who have been conditioned to the screen version. Indeed, we may well ask to what extent we should attempt to introduce the literary works which have now become period pieces of another century. Certainly we must re-examine our concept of both reading and literature in the kaleidoscope of the current scene.[4]

One of the most troublesome problems related to literature involves the selection of books that will interest today's children and help them in meeting their problems and in enriching their lives. Such a selection will of course include books of the past as well as of the present, for no period has had a monopoly on books suitable for children.

Although traditionally it has been the function of the librarian to extend reading and to recommend and encourage the use of books not specifically associated with scheduled curriculum areas, this situation is changing, and in today's schools a sharing of these responsibilities is taking place. Now the teacher often assumes leadership in planning for

---

[4] Dwight L. Burton and Nancy Larrick, *op. cit.*, pp. 189–190.

the wide use of books, working closely of course with the librarian in order to give maximum help to pupils. One classroom teacher described the teacher-librarian relationship in this way, "I realize that technically I am responsible for my students' overall literary development, but I could never dream of meeting pupils' needs with any real measure of success without our librarian's assistance. Often my chief contribution to helping a student find the right book is my awareness of *what he needs to read;* Miss X knows which books are available. Together we solve many problems."

Bernice Wiese, in an article "A Dozen Library Do's for Teachers," has suggested some aspects of the teacher's role. In substance they are as follows:

1. *Read children's books yourself.* With a good reading background, a teacher will be more enthusiastic in transmitting to children around her a desire to read.
2. *Use your school and community library.* The teacher must browse, read, and become familiar with a wide variety of materials. In turn, she will be in a position to encourage children to find interesting books and to read widely.
3. *Know the reading interests of your students and their reading abilities and achievement levels.* A knowledge of children's interests is of fundamental importance, too. A teacher can not expect to get the right book for the right child unless she also knows the learner's status with regard to his ability to read.
4. *Plan the literature program.* The results of the "hit or miss" type of literature program are often quite undesirable. A good program must be carefully planned to insure quality, variety, sequence, and happy participation on the part of all learners.
5. *Make books available.* Have books in the classroom to lure children to read in their free time.
6. *Allow time for reading.* The teacher needs to set aside certain times in the day or week for independent reading in order to establish the reading habit.
7. *Share reading interests and show enthusiasm for children's discoveries in books.* Sharing periods should be natural, not forced experiences. A variety of means of expression should be provided. Go far beyond the conventional book reports; find individual ways of sharing enthusiasm for a book or books.
8. *Read a few outstanding books aloud to children.* There are some books that all children should hear and the listening and discussing activities in a class situation enhance the memory of the reading experience. It provides a good sharing experience for a class.
9. *Enjoy reading for pleasure and for information.* A good program will encourage reading for pleasure and joyful discovery.

10. *Encourage challenging reading and the development of reading appreciation.* Challenging the individual with good books is part of a good program; it is an especially desirable technique to use with gifted children.
11. *Develop reading appreciation.* One of the essential aims of good literature is to help the individual grow in an awareness of the full value of reading and in the ability to appraise literature for its quality.
12. *Takes advantage of many ways to stimulate reading.* Pictures, bulletin boards, children's recommendations, book lists, story telling, book talks, and other activities are means of bringing children and books together.[5]

RECOMMENDED LITERARY MATERIALS

The role of the teacher centers around the task of bringing books and children together. In order to accomplish this a teacher must know the needs of children and must be aware of suitable materials in a literary program. A well-rounded program in literature should include material in the categories of folk and fairy tales, animal stories, American folklore, modern fanciful tales, realistic literature, regional stories of the United States, biographies, historical fiction, stories of other lands, and poetry. Each category will be briefly described, and selected material for each category will be presented.

Folk and Fairy Tales

Folk and fairy tales are indispensable for their ability to bring the heritage of the past to young readers and to satisfy children's pleasure in exaggeration, absurdity, cleverness, and amusement. These tales provide a play on words; the foolish and funny folk stories are often presented with broad, bold humor; the animal tales with the talking beasts penetrate deeply into children's consciousness and may reappear years later as treasured memories. Added to these are the stories of the supernatural and the romantic which bring pleasure, wonder, wisdom, and escape to many pupils.

Nearly all young children still derive satisfaction from *Cinderella, The Three Little Pigs, The Old Woman and Her Pigs, The Pancake,* and the *Three Billy Goats Gruff.* Intermediate-grade boys and girls, as well as pupils in junior and senior high school, find pleasure and stimulation

---

[5] Adapted from M. Bernice Wiese, "A Dozen Library Do's for Teachers," *Education,* 75:150–154 (November, 1954).

in folklore. A number of new books are currently appearing that satisfy the older pupil's interest in legend and folklore. Following is a list of some books which appeal to pupils at various grade levels:

PRIMARY GRADES
Chanticleer and the Fox, illustrated by Barbara Cooney (Crowell, 1958).
Once a Mouse, a Fable Cut in Wood, by Marcia Brown (Scribner, 1961).
The Shoemaker and the Elves, told by Grimm brothers (Scribner, 1960).
Sleeping Beauty, told by Grimm brothers, illustrated by Felix Hoffman (Harcourt, 1960).
Tall Book of Fairy Tales, illustrated by William Sharp (Harper, 1947).
Three Billy Goats Gruff, by P. C. Asbjornsen and J. E. Moe (Harcourt, 1957).

INTERMEDIATE GRADES
Arthur Rackham Fairy Book, compiled by Arthur Rackham (Lippincott, 1950).
Castles and Dragons, compiled by William P. duBois (Crowell, 1958).
Emperor's New Clothes, by Hans Christian Andersen, translated and illustrated by Erik Blegvad (Harcourt, 1959).
India's Tales and Legends, by John E. B. Gray (Walck, 1961).
Norwegian Folk Tales, compiled by P. C. Asbjornsen and J. E. Moe (Viking, 1961).
Which Was Witch? by Eleanore M. Jewett (Viking, 1953).

JUNIOR AND SENIOR HIGH SCHOOL
The Beginning: Creation Myths Around the World, compiled by Maria Leach (Funk, 1956).
Beowulf the Warrior, adapted by Ian Serraillier (Walck, 1961).
Greek Gods and Heroes, by Robert Graves (Doubleday, 1960).
Hawaiian Wonder Tales, by Post Wheeler (Yoseloff, 1953).
Heroes of the Kalevala, by Babette Deutsch (Messner, 1956).
Legends of the North, by Olivia E. Coolidge (Houghton, 1951).
Ten Thousand Desert Swords, by Russell Davis and Brent Ashabranner (Little, 1960).
The Trojan War, by Olivia E. Coolidge (Houghton, 1952).

Animal Stories

Stories of animals have had for many decades a strong appeal for readers both young and old. Fortunately the supply of fresh, new stories about animals is constantly expanding and adding to the old favorites which have stirred the imagination and feelings of children for many years. Young readers do not seem to care whether the tales present animals realistically or as talking creatures. Marguerite Henry, Jim Kjelgaard, Glen Rounds, C. W. Anderson, and others offer excitement through animal stories for middle-grade children, while Marjorie Flack, Dorothy Lathrop, Louise Fatio, and others set the younger readers' hearts aglow with the antics of favorite animals. E. B. White's *Charlotte's Web*, is a timeless tale which appeals widely to both children and adults. Following are a few animal stories which attract pupils at different grade levels:

PRIMARY GRADES

Animals Everywhere, by Ingri and Edgar d'Aulaire (Doubleday, 1954).
The Bears on Hemlock Mountain, by Alice Dalgliesh (Scribner, 1962).
Curious George, by Hans A. Rey (Houghton, 1941).
The Fox Went Out on a Chilly Night, by Peter Spier (Doubleday, 1961).
The Happy Lion, by Louise Fatio (Whittlesey, 1954).
In the Forest, by Marie H. Ets (Viking, 1944).
Make Way for Ducklings, by Robert McCloskey (Viking, 1941).
Monkeys Are Funny That Way, by Dorothy Koch (Holiday, 1962).
No Roses for Harry! by Gene Zion (Harper, 1958).
Serafina the Giraffe, by Laurent de Brunhoff (World, 1961).

INTERMEDIATE GRADES

The Blind Colt, by Glen Rounds (Holiday, 1960).
Brighty of the Grand Canyon, by Marguerite Henry (Rand, 1953).
Charlotte's Web, by E. B. White (Harper, 1952).
Harry, the Wild West Horse, by Eleanor Clymer (Atheneum, 1963).
Honk, the Moose, by Phil Stong (Dodd, 1935).
Junket, by Anne H. White (Viking, 1955).
Kildee House, by Rutherford Montgomery (Doubleday, 1949).
Lassie Come Home, by Eric Knight (Holt, 1940).
Mr. Popper's Penguins, by Richard and Florence Atwater (Little, 1938).
Rusty, by Roy S. March (Macrae, 1961).

JUNIOR AND SENIOR HIGH SCHOOL

Big Red, by James A. Kjelgaard (Holiday, 1956).
Call of the Wild, by Jack London (Macmillan, 1903).
Gift Horse, by James L. Summers (Westminster, 1961).
Island of Horses, by Eilis Dillon (Funk, 1957).
Keepers of the Bell, by Beulah Karney (John Day, 1961).
Nacar, the White Deer, by Elizabeth de Trevino (Farrar, 1963).
Old Yeller, by Frederick B. Gipson (Harper, 1956).

The White Falcon, by Charlton Ogburn, Jr. (Houghton, 1955).
The Yearling, by Marjorie K. Rawlings (Scribner, 1939).

American Folklore

Tales centering around clever and humorous American heroes such as Paul Bunyan and Pecos Bill are popular and appealing to children and youth. There are perhaps many reasons for their appeal, not the least of which is the fact that they reflect our American temperament and free spirit. The heroes of our folk literature are symbolic of the traits we so highly regard, namely, courage, an adventurous spirit, shrewdness, and ingenuity. The humor growing out of the characterizations in such books is quite appealing. No library is complete without a supply of books dealing with these heroes. Stories about the American Indian have also found a place in our folklore. Following are some books which interest pupils on an intermediate-grade level and junior and senior high school students:

The Dancing Horses of Acoma, by Helen Rushmore (World, 1963).
The Long-Tailed Bear and Other Indian Legends, by Natalie M. Belting (Bobbs, 1961).
Paul Bunyan, by Esther Shephard (Harcourt, 1941).
Pecos Bill: The Greatest Cowboy of All Times, by James C. Bowman (Whitman, 1937).
Rip Van Winkle and the Legend of Sleepy Hollow, by Washington Irving (Macmillan, 1951).
Yankee Doodle's Cousins, by Anne Malcolmson (Houghton, 1941).

Modern Fanciful Tales

A balance of realistic and fanciful thinking is considered by many to be an essential for the minds of individuals. Reasonable escapes from the realistic life are afforded by fanciful literature. This type of literature includes subject matter that is varied, including talking animals, marvelous machines, and fascinating stories about space. After children have enjoyed Beatrix Potter's *Peter Rabbit,* they are often ready to fall under the spell of Kenneth Grahame's *Wind in the Willows.* Water Rat, Mole, and Toad are memorable characters of many young readers.

The delight shown in the face of a five-year-old child as he huffs and puffs when his toy train runs over the sandbox hill is good evidence of his acquaintance with *The Little Engine That Could.* His older brother's absorption as he reads his coveted copy of *Mike Mulligan and His Steam Shovel* also reveals the appeal of fanciful tales to the young. The question is not whether such books will be included in the literature program, but which books are most appropriate for a particular child or class.

Realistic Literature

Stories about the world around us and the world that preceded modern cultures have a strong appeal for boys and girls, especially those in the intermediate and upper grades, whose need for books of this type is great. Such books help them understand themselves and their immediate environment more adequately. They satisfy curiosity about the real-life activities and patterns of living among people of various geographic, economic, and cultural backgrounds, as well as in different periods of this country's history. Through these books pupils gain an appreciation of the dreams and goals of their own people today, and compare them with the aspirations of their forefathers.

A balanced program of realistic reading will include such books as the following:

PRIMARY GRADES
Adventures of a Letter, by G. Warren Schloat (Scribner, 1949).
At the Harbor. At the Library. At the Post Office, by Lillian Colonius and Glenn Schroeder (Children's Press, 1953).
Boy at Bat, by Marion Renick (Scribner, 1961).
The Day We Saw the Sun Come Up, by Alice E. Goudey (Scribner, 1961).
Heat All Around, by Tillie S. Pine and Joseph Levine (McGraw, 1963).
I Want to Be a Scientist, by Charles Greene (Children's Press, 1961).
Mike's House, by Julia L. Sauer (Viking, 1954).
Papa Small, by Lois Lenski (Walck, 1951).
Three Boys and Space, by Nan H. Agle and Ellen Wilson (Scribner, 1962).
White Snow, Bright Snow, by Alvin Tresselt (Lothrop, 1956).
Who Built the Bridge? by Norman Bate (Scribner, 1954).

INTERMEDIATE GRADES
Ellen Tebbitts, by Beverly Cleary (Morrow, 1951).
Exploring the Weather, by Roy A. Gallant (Doubleday, 1957).
Hurricanes and Twisters, by Robert Irving (Knopf, 1955).
Onion John, by Joseph Krumgold (Crowell, 1959).
Plants That Feed Us, by Carroll L. Fenton and Herminie B. Kitchen (John Day, 1956).
Science in Your Own Back Yard, by Elizabeth K. Cooper (Harcourt, 1958).
When You Go to the Zoo, by Glenn O. Blough and Marjorie H. Campbell (McGraw, 1955).

Junior and Senior High School
>   *The Beginning Gardener,* by Katherine N. Cutler (Barrows, 1960).
>   *Blueprint for Teen-age Living,* by William C. Menninger and others (Sterling, 1958).
>   *Choosing a Career in a Changing World,* by V. V. Westervelt (Putnam, 1959).
>   *Driving Today and Tomorrow,* by Margaret Hyde (McGraw, 1954).
>   *Gemini and Apollo,* by Gardner Soule (Duell, 1964).
>   *How You Grow Up,* by William C. Menninger and others (Sterling, 1957).
>   *It's Like This, Cat,* by Emily Cheney (Harper, 1963).
>   *Manners Made Easy,* by Mary Beery (McGraw, 1954).
>   *So You Were Elected!* by Virginia Bailard and Harry C. McKown (McGraw, 1961).
>   *That Freshman Feeling,* by Judith V. Scott (Macrae, 1960).

Regional Stories of the United States

Children need to understand other persons and their behavior. Regional stories offer excellent opportunities for pupils to become acquainted with, and often understand better, people in various parts of our country. Through reading the books of Lois Lenski, such as *Blue Ridge Billy, Strawberry Girl,* and *Cotton in My Sack,* for example, they come to know real children in different regions of the United States. Many other writers of similar stories have also contributed to our rich heritage. Following are some regional stories which teachers may use in their efforts to help children and youth understand people in different parts of the United States:

Primary Grades
>   *Bluebonnets for Lucinda,* by Frances C. Sayers (Viking, 1934).
>   *Come Again, Pelican,* by Don Freeman (Viking, 1961).
>   *Fly High, Fly Low,* by Don Freeman (Viking, 1957).
>   *Moy Moy,* by Leo Politi (Scribner, 1960).
>   *The Secret River,* by Marjorie K. Rawlings (Scribner, 1955).
>   *Time of Wonder,* by Robert McCloskey (Viking, 1957).
>   *Wonderful Nice!* by Irma Selz (Lothrop, 1960).

Intermediate Grades
>   *Alaska Harvest,* by Elsa Pedersen (Abingdon, 1961).
>   *All-of-a-Kind Family,* by Sidney Taylor (Follett, 1951).
>   *And Now Miguel,* by Joseph Krumgold (Crowell, 1953).
>   *The Bells of Bleecker Street,* by Valenti Angelo (Viking, 1949).
>   *Blue Willow,* by Doris Gates (Viking, 1940).
>   *Millie,* by Bessie H. Heck (World, 1961).
>   *Strawberry Girl,* by Lois Lenski (Lippincott, 1945).

JUNIOR AND SENIOR HIGH SCHOOL
Antelope Singer, by Ruth M. Underhill (Coward, 1961).
The Bearcat, by Annabel and Edgar Johnson (Harper, 1960).
The Buckboard Stranger, by Stephen Meader (Harcourt, 1954).
The Hawaiians, an Island People, by Helen Gay Pratt (Charles E. Tuttle, 1963).
Henry Reed, Inc., by Keith Robertson (Viking, 1959).
High Road Home, by William Corbin (Coward, 1954).
The Horse Catcher, by Mari Sandoz (Westminster, 1957).
The Iron Doctor, by Agnes D. Hewes (Houghton, 1946).
The Long Wharf, by Howard Pease (Doubleday, 1947).
Mama's Bank Account, by Kathryn Forbes (Harcourt, 1943).
Tree House Island, by Scott Corbett (Little, 1959).

Biographies

Biography offers a way to become acquainted with unusual men and women who have played important roles in our national life or in the cultural development of other countries. Moreover, one of the best ways to appreciate the greatness of our country and the significant events which shaped it is to get to know its leaders, past and present. Genevieve Foster in her biographies has brought clearly into focus the relationship between the environment, the times, and the life and contributions of famous men such as George Washington, Abraham Lincoln, and Andrew Jackson. *America's Own Mark Twain,* by Jeannette Eaton, also contains rich background material. Excellent biographies are available in abundance and at every level; in fact, superior biographies may now be obtained in series such as the "Landmark" and "World Landmark" publications. Authentic biographies of world heroes are plentiful and provide the basis for understanding the role of international leaders in all fields of endeavor. The biographies appearing monthly in *Highlights for Children* are providing a source of inspiration to countless boys and girls. Following are the titles of some biographies that have strong appeal for boys and girls today:

PRIMARY GRADES
Abe Lincoln's Hobby, by W. M. Hutchinson (Regnery, 1961).
Abraham Lincoln, by Ingri and Edgar d'Aulaire (Doubleday, 1957).
Ben Franklin, by Estelle Friedman (Putnam, 1961).
The Columbus Story, by Alice Dalgliesh (Scribner, 1955).
Daniel Boone, by Katherine E. Wilkie (Garrard, 1960).
The First Book of Presidents, by Harold Coy (Watts, 1960).
George Washington, by Ingri and Edgar d'Aulaire (Doubleday, 1936).

INTERMEDIATE GRADES
> *Adventure in Courage, the Story of Theodore Roosevelt,* by Frances Cavanah (Rand, 1961).
> *America's Abraham Lincoln,* by May McNeer (Houghton, 1957).
> *America's Paul Revere,* by Esther Forbes (Houghton, 1946).
> *Ben and Me,* by Robert Lawson (Little, 1939).
> *City Neighbor: The Story of Jane Addams,* by Clara I. Judson (Scribner, 1951).
> *Clara Barton,* by Mildred M. Pace (Scribner, 1941).
> *Columbus, Founder of the New World,* by Ronald Syme (Morrow, 1952).
> *Dan Beard: Boy Scout,* by Miriam E. Mason (Bobbs, 1953).
> *Eli Whitney and the Machine Age,* by Wilma P. Hays (Watts, 1959).
> *Helen Keller Story,* by Catherine O. Peare (Crowell, 1959).
> *Jenny Lind and Her Listening Cat,* by Frances Cavanah (Vanguard, 1961).
> *Samuel Morse and the Telegraph,* by Wilma P. Hays (Watts, 1960).

JUNIOR AND SENIOR HIGH SCHOOL
> *Abe Lincoln Grows Up,* by Carl Sandburg (Harcourt, 1928).
> *America's Own Mark Twain,* by Jeanette Eaton (Morrow, 1958).
> *America's Robert E. Lee,* by Henry Commager (Houghton, 1951).
> *Amerigo Vespucci,* by Nina Brown Baker (Knopf, 1956).
> *Amos Fortune: Free Man,* by Elizabeth Yates (Dutton, 1950).
> *Anne Frank: Diary of a Young Girl,* by Anne Frank (Doubleday, 1952).
> *Champlain of the St. Lawrence,* by Ronald Syme (Morrow, 1952).
> *Famous Men of Science,* by Sarah K. Bolton, rev. ed. (Crowell, 1961).
> *Gandhi: Fighter Without a Sword,* by Jeanette Eaton (Morrow, 1950).
> *John F. Kennedy and PT-109,* by Richard Tregaskis (Random, 1962).
> *Lonely Crusader: The Life of Florence Nightingale,* by Cecil Woodham-Smith (McGraw, 1951).
> *Louis Braille, Windows for the Blind,* by J. Alvin Kugelmass (Messner, 1951).
> *Mary McLeod Bethune,* by Emma Gelders Sterne (Knopf, 1957).
> *Profiles in Courage,* by John F. Kennedy (Harper, 1961).
> *Ralph J. Bunche: Fighter for Peace,* by Alvin Kugelmass (Messner, 1952).
> *Silversmith of Old New York: Myer Myers,* by William Wise (Farrar, 1957).
> *Teenagers Who Made History,* by Russell Freedman (Holiday, 1961).

Historical Fiction

One of the most effective ways to appreciate American history is to read good historical fiction. Such books not only provide much authentic information, but also offer strong motivation for the development of an interest in history. Some boys have been led to explore deeply the revolutionary period in American history because of an interest awakened by such a book as Esther Forbes' *Johnny Tremain*. And girls are sometimes similarly influenced by Marguerite de Angeli's *Thee Hannah!*, an appealing story of a little Quaker girl in old Philadelphia. The list of titles which follows includes a number of books which may stimulate an interest in the historical background of our country.

INTERMEDIATE GRADES
  Across from Indian Shore, by Barbara Robinson (Lothrop, 1962).
  Away Goes Sally, by Elizabeth Coatsworth (Macmillan, 1934).
  The Calico Ball, by Margaret Crary (Prentice, 1961).
  Courage of Sarah Noble, by Alice Dalgliesh (Scribner, 1954).
  The Door in the Wall, by Marguerite de Angeli (Doubleday, 1949).
  Down the Mississippi, by Clyde Robert Bulla (Crowell, 1954).
  Fifer for the Union, by Lorenzo Allen (Morrow, 1964).
  Fire in the Wind, by Elizabeth Baker (Houghton, 1961).
  Hitty: Her First Hundred Years, by Rachel Field (Macmillan, 1930).
  Little House on the Prairie, by Laura Ingalls Wilder (Harper, 1953).
  The Lone Hunt, by William O. Steele (Harcourt, 1956).
  Matchlock Gun, by Walter D. Edmonds (Dodd, 1941).
  The Perilous Road, by William O. Steele (Harcourt, 1958).
  Pilgrim Courage, adapted and edited by E. Brooks Smith and Robert Meredith (Little, 1962).
  The Pumpkin Flood at Harpers Ferry, by Lila Gravatt Scrimsher (Reilly, 1962).
  Rasmus and the Vagabond, by Astrid Lindgren (Viking, 1960).
  Steve Marches with the General, by Marion Renick (Scribner, 1962).
  Thee, Hannah!, by Marguerite de Angeli (Doubleday, 1949).
  They Peopled the Pacific, by A. Grove Day (Meredith, 1964).
  The Time of Wolves, by Verne T. Davis (Morrow, 1962).
  To Be a Pioneer, by Paul C. Burns and Ruth Hines (Abingdon, 1962).
JUNIOR AND SENIOR HIGH SCHOOL
  The Beggar's Penny, by Catherine Cate Coblentz (McKay, 1943).
  Daughter of Delaware, by Josephine Savage (John Day, 1964).

Deerslayer, by James Fenimore Cooper (Scribner, 1841).
Drums Along the Mohawk, by Walter D. Edmonds (Little, 1936).
Gone With the Wind, by Margaret Mitchell (Macmillan, 1961).
Indian Captive: The Story of Mary Jemison, by Lois Lenski (Lippincott, 1941).
I, Varina, by Ruth Painter Randall (Little, 1962).
Johnny Tremain, by Esther Forbes (Houghton, 1943).
The Light in the Forest, by Conrad Richter (Knopf, 1953).
The Time of the Tomahawk, by Robert Alter (Putnam, 1964).
The White House Saga, by Nanette Kutner (Atheneum, 1962).

Stories of Other Lands

With our whole world coming so close together through rapid transportation, it is fitting that our children be offered accurate information about the people of other lands. The advent of mass communicative media on an international level will in all probability stimulate individuals to learn more of their neighbors around the world. One of the most effective ways to do this is to encourage pupils to read widely from such engrossing books as Meindert DeJong's *Wheel on the School* and Kate Seredy's *The Good Master.* Below are some titles of books about other lands and other people which are generally liked by children and youth.

PRIMARY GRADES

Boy of the Masai, by Natalie Donna (Dodd, 1964).
The Cow Who Fell in the Canal, by Phyllis Krasilovsky (Doubleday, 1957).
Crow Boy, by Taro Yashima (Viking, 1955).
The Fabulous Firework Family, by James Flora (Harcourt, 1955).
Felice, by Marcia Brown (Scribner, 1958).
Five Chinese Brothers, by Claire H. Bishop (Coward, 1938).
The Forever Christmas Trees, by Yoshiko Uchida (Scribner, 1963).
Great Day in Spain: José's Own Fiesta, by Patrick Pringle (Abelard, 1962).
Happy New Year, by Yen Liang (Lippincott, 1961).
Madeline's Rescue, by Ludwig Bemelmans (Viking, 1953).
My Mother Is the Most Beautiful Woman in the World, by Becky Rayher (Lothrop, 1945).
Ola, by Ingri and Edgar d'Aulaire (Doubleday, 1939).
The Painted Pig, by Elizabeth Morrow (Knopf, 1949).
Pantaloni, by Bettina (Harper, 1957).
Pelle's New Suit, by Elsa Beskow (Harper, 1929).
Pepito's Story, by Eugene Fern (Farrar, 1960).

Piccolina and the Easter Bells, by Pauline Priolo (Little, 1962).
Rain in the Winds, by Claire and George Louden (Scribner, 1953).
The Story About Ping, by Marjorie Flack (Viking, 1933).
Tamarindo!, by Marcia Brown (Scribner, 1960).
Tekla's Easter, by Lillian Budd (Rand, 1962).

INTERMEDIATE GRADES

All Alone, by Claire Huchet Bishop (Viking, 1953).
At the Palace Gates, by Helen Rand Parish (Viking, 1949).
Crystal Mountain, by Belle Dorman Rugh (Houghton, 1955).
Daughter of the Mountains, by Louise Rankin (Viking, 1948).
The First Book of Pakistan, by Jean Bothwell (Watts, 1962).
The Good Master, by Kate Seredy (Viking, 1935).
The Happy Orpheline, by Natalie S. Carlson (Harper, 1957).
House of Sixty Fathers, by Meindert DeJong (Harper, 1956).
I Give You My Colt, by Alice G. Kelsey (McKay, 1956).
Lakhmi, Girl of India, by Dominique Darbois (Follett, 1964).
Lawrence of Arabia, by Alistair MacLean (Random, 1962).
Li Lun, Lad of Courage, by Carolyn Treffinger (Abingdon, 1947).
Lo Chau of Hong Kong, by Betty Cavanna (Watts, 1963).
Miss Happiness and Miss Flower, by Rumer Godden (Viking, 1961).
A Picture History of Italy, by T. L. Jarman (Watts, 1962).
Secret of the Andes, by Ann Nolan Clark (Viking, 1952).
Siti's Summer, by Betty M. Kalish (Macmillan, 1963).
A Stork for the Bell Tower, by Dale Fife (Coward, 1964).
The Two Uncles of Pablo, by Harry Behn (Harcourt, 1959).
Wheel on the School, by Meindert DeJong (Harper, 1954).

JUNIOR AND SENIOR HIGH SCHOOL

Black Forest Summer, by Mabel Esther (Vanguard, 1959).
Continent in a Hurry: The Challenge of Africa Today, by Ella Griffin (Coward, 1962).
The Dalai Lama, by Lowell Thomas, Jr. (Duell, 1961).
India, by Walter A. Fairservis (World, 1961).
Inside Europe Today, by John Gunther (Harper, 1961).
Kon-Tiki, by Thor Heyerdahl (Rand, 1950).
The Land and People of South Africa, by Alan Paton, "Portraits of a Nation" Series (Lippincott, 1955).
Made in China, by Cornelia Spencer (Knopf, 1952).
Meet the Congo and Its Neighbors, by John Gunther (Harper, 1959).
Persia Is My Heart, by Najmeh Najafi; edited by Helen Hinckley (Harper, 1953).
Profile of Kenya, by Leonard S. Kenworthy (Doubleday, 1963).
Summer in Ville-Marie, by Paul Daveluy (Holt, 1962).
Young People of East and South Africa, by Charles R. Joy (Duell, 1962).

Poetry

Many characteristics of poetry appeal to children and youth. Word and sound patterns, rhythm, and probably most of all imagery, are elements that attract children to poetry. The teaching of poetry is further enhanced by our modern culture, for as Paul Anderson points out:

> We teach at a time when rhyme and verse are almost as commonplace as the air we breathe. Singing commercials and jingles are heard too frequently on radio and TV. . . . We also teach at a time when people wish to express sentiments in verse. A major industry has developed around the production of greeting cards for every possible occasion.[6]

A feeling expressed by many teachers, however, is that large numbers of people dislike or are indifferent to poetry. In a recent survey, Freeland[7] discovered that one group of prospective teachers attributed its dislike for poetry to a number of factors, the most important of which was their being required to memorize certain poems. They have been "forced" as children to memorize a particular number of lines of poetry each week to recite in class. The modern school recognizes this situation and attempts to offer children an opportunity to choose poems to read which appeal to the individual. Some years ago Carl Sandburg wrote:

> "Poetry for any given individual depends on the individual and what his personality requires as poetry. Beauty depends on personal taste."[8]

Moreover, poetry today is presented in a meaningful, enjoyable manner and not as a rote memory type of exercise. Poetry, then, in the modern school is introduced so as to develop a sensitivity that will enhance future growth in the appreciation of verse.

The teacher who possesses a broad knowledge of poetry and finds personal satisfaction in it is often able to share his well-loved poems with his students and thus elicit their interest. Although definite plans should be made for introducing poetry, there should be opportunities for children to choose freely and to share their discoveries informally in the situation in which the right poem makes a notable contribution.

The skillful teacher will lead pupils to enjoy the sound and rhythm of poetry, the beauty of word choices and word order. He will read poetry

---

[6] Paul S. Anderson, *Language Skills in Elementary Education* (New York: The Macmillan Co., 1964), p. 303.
[7] Alma Freeland, "A Study of Future Teachers' Background in Children's Literature," unpublished study (Austin, Texas: The University of Texas).
[8] Carl Sandburg, *Early Moon* (New York: Harcourt, Brace & World, 1930), p. 20.

aloud to his pupils and encourage them to select poems they like and also to read them aloud. He will introduce poetry from collections such as Helen Ferris' excellent assembly of well-liked poetry, choosing poetry to match various occasions such as birthdays, holidays, and seasonal celebrations.

Teachers are further motivating the enjoyment of poetry by encouraging children to write poetry. Such poetry read and appreciated by members of a class is sure to elicit interest. A book by Nina W. Walter, entitled *Let Them Write Poetry*,[9] contains excellent suggestions for the stimulation of interest in poetry and its appreciation. It presents also criteria for judging poetry of various kinds. The examples of children's poetry are really remarkable and may serve as an incentive to other children to write and enjoy poetry. Below are three poems chosen from the children's writing.

MUSIC

Music
Is something inside
    of you
That sings.

TIMOTHY HAWKINS
(*age 7*)

POEM

When a poem
Is in my head
It is like God talking
Just to me.

ANITA RUIZ
(*age 6*)

THE TURTLE

The poor little turtle
Walks so slow,
But he gets everywhere
He wants to go.

ROBERT TINSLEY
(*age 10*)

The teacher will find a treasury of good poetry in the following sources:

[9] Nina W. Walter, *Let Them Write Poetry* (New York: Holt, Rinehart & Winston, Inc., 1962).

Aldis, Dorothy, *All Together* (New York: G. P. Putnam's Sons, 1952).

Arbuthnot, May Hill, *Time for Poetry* (Chicago: Scott, Foresman and Co., 1961).

Brown, Margaret Wise, *Nibble, Nibble* (New York: W. R. Scott, Inc., 1959).

Cole, William (editor), *I Went to the Animal Fair* (Cleveland: World Publishing Co., 1958).

Cole, William (editor), *Poems of Magic and Spells* (Cleveland: World Publishing Co., 1960).

De la Mare, Walter, *Rhymes and Verses* (New York: Holt, Rinehart and Winston, Inc., 1947).

Dickinson, Emily, *Poems for Youth* (Boston: Little, Brown & Co., 1934).

Ferris, Helen (editor), *Favorite Poems, Old and New* (Garden City: Doubleday and Co., Inc., 1957).

Frost, Robert, *You Come Too* (New York: Holt, Rinehart and Winston, Inc., 1959).

Graves, Robert, *The Penny Fiddle: Poems for Children* (Garden City: Doubleday and Co., Inc., 1961).

McDonald, Gerald D. (editor), *A Way of Knowing* (New York: Thomas Y. Crowell Co., 1959).

Millay, Edna St. Vincent, *Poems Selected for Young People* (New York: Harper & Row, 1929).

Milne, A. A., *Pooh's Library: A New Collection* (New York: E. P. Dutton & Co., Inc., 1963).

Nash, Ogden, *A Boy Is a Boy* (New York: Franklin Watts, Inc., 1960).

Peterson, Isabel J. (editor), *The First Book of Poetry* (New York: Franklin Watts, Inc., 1954).

Sechrist, Elizabeth H. (editor), *One Thousand Poems for Children* (Philadelphia: MacCrae Smith Co., 1946).

Stevenson, Robert L., *A Child's Garden of Verses* (New York: Grosset and Dunlap, Inc., 1957).

Untermeyer, Louis (editor), *The Golden Treasury of Poetry* (New York: Golden Press, Inc., 1959).

EXPERIENCES AND ACTIVITIES ASSOCIATED WITH BOOKS

The classroom environment undoubtedly has a strong influence on children's voluntary reading. There must be quiet, and space, and comfortable places where the child may enjoy adventures with books. There must be freedom to choose, so that each individual may grow through books, and learn to be independent in reading. Within this setting, then, there must also be varied experiences and activities with books which stimulate or fulfill interests—experiences including storytelling, oral reading, audience reading, dramatization, and sharing experiences.

Storytelling

Storytelling is an effective method of creating interest in good literature, particularly with young children. One of the storyteller's best sources of material is the field of folklore, for these stories often were designed to be told. The elemental nature of their content, their simplicity and directness, and their brevity make them particularly appropriate.

Contrary to popular opinion, the art of storytelling is not simple to acquire. Some persons who appear to charm their listeners with apparent ease have spent many years acquiring this skill. Teachers will want to practice storytelling to reach a proficiency which will enable them to bring stories to life. They will find some of the techniques described in *Art of the Story-Teller* by Marie Shedlock.[10]

Teachers will find in Ruth Sawyer's *The Way of the Storyteller* inspiration and practical help as they seek to bring joy to children through telling stories to them.[11]

Various techniques for telling stories are also described in *Elementary English,* a publication which includes some tested procedures of skillful teachers.[12]

The prime consideration, then, in storytelling is to expose children to listening to a good storyteller. Interest in literature may be further increased by having children develop the art of storytelling. One technique for involving children in storytelling is described by John DeBoer and Martha Dallmann:

> With primary grade children it is sometimes effective to have a storytelling period with a make-believe microphone. Such simulated "broadcasts" may serve to encourage the shy child who normally would hesitate to speak before a group. Programs may take the form of dramatizations, interviews, or direct storytelling . . . . the

---

[10] Marie L. Shedlock, *Art of the Story-Teller* (New York: Dover Publications, Inc., 1951).

[11] Ruth Sawyer, *The Way of the Storyteller* (New York: The Viking Press, 1942).

[12] Paul Witty (editor), *Creative Writing and Story Telling in Today's Schools.* Reprinted from *Elementary English* (March, 1957) and distributed by the National Council of Teachers of English.

focus will be on the books themselves and on the exciting activity of sharing book experiences.[13]

Oral Reading

Reading stories aloud requires familiarity with the material to be read. The teacher must keep in mind that he himself should provide a model for oral reading; his attitude and enthusiasm, in addition to skill in the use of his voice and in his enunciation and pronunciation, will set the pattern for the class.

The reading aloud of a chapter, or part of a chapter, gives the teacher a good opportunity to acquaint children with a particular book. Discussion of the author, the illustrations, the title, and something about other parts of the book will stimulate pupil interest and a desire to read more. The books selected to be read aloud must, of course, be appropriate to the age group with respect to the characters, setting, plot, elements of humor, description, and so forth. As stories are read aloud, the teacher may observe children's changing attitudes toward books and may note at times the awakening of a genuine interest in reading.

Audience Reading

Closely related to oral reading is audience reading. In audience reading a child reads orally from a book to which no other child has access. Because of the many values derived from this type of oral reading many teachers in their instructional program use a form of audience reading in which they have other children in the reading group close their books while one child reads a certain passage aloud.

According to Russell, audience reading in the literature program "implies an enjoyable situation in which the class listens to new stories which are read with fluency and skill."[14] Thus we see one important value of audience reading—enjoyment. Another value is that audience reading correlates the language-arts skills of listening and reading. Reading skills are improved because a child develops necessary skills by carefully preparing material for oral presentation to the class. Still another value of audience reading is that it may expose the listener to a wide range of literary material.

---

[13] John J. DeBoer and Martha Dallmann, *The Teaching of Reading,* rev. ed. (New York: Holt, Rinehart & Winston, Inc., 1964), p. 278.
[14] David H. Russell, *op. cit.,* p. 125.

Obviously, the teacher must provide time during the school day for this activity. It is also necessary for a teacher to give individual help to children who are preparing material for audience reading. The time is well worth the effort because "oral reading of carefully prepared materials . . . will do more to benefit a child's oral reading than continued practice on poorly prepared materials."[15]

Dramatization

Dramatization provides an effective way to help children experience the color and the charm of certain types of literature. It may consist of a simple dramatic reading of a selection by groups of children, or a performance of a play, or the presentation of puppet shows. The performance may range from a very informal activity in which pupils simply read parts aloud to occasions in which costuming, properties, and memorization are required. Too, the material used may range from prepared dialogues often found in basal and supplementary readers to original scripts written by the pupils. Each type has its advantages and values.

The selection of the story for dramatization is important. It should, of course, have literary quality as well as appeal to both the actors and the audience. It should be worthy of the time spent in preparation and presentation. The central idea should be well developed and not clouded by numerous episodes. In addition, each episode must lead toward a climax and a quick, satisfying ending; the characters should be true to life, and the dialogue should be natural.

Sharing Experiences with Books

Currently there is considerable criticism, and rightly so, of the use of formal written and oral book reports. Though their value is often doubtful, both for the one who prepares the report and also for the reader or listener, the teacher should be familiar with some techniques for ascertaining and recording the effects of experiences in reading upon pupils. The pupil too should learn to record and appraise his reading.

The book report is only one way of judging and recording pupils' reading. When it is employed, it should be short and designed in such a way that the pupil will give his unique response to a book.

[15] *Ibid.*

LaVerne Strong suggests that the effects of reading a book may be judged by the teacher if he observes his pupils in various situations in which they are asked to:

> depict the most exciting scene in the story through a picture and then tell what is happening in it;
>
> design bright-colored book jackets on which will appear in miniature form all the characters and significant objects;
>
> enlist the help of two or three friends to enact exacting or favorite parts through dramatization, through the use of a simple stick or hand puppets, through a shadow play;
>
> construct a three-dimensional shadow box;
>
> model in clay special or favorite characters;
>
> design a book poster centered around a central character;
>
> make a frieze or mural of a story that all have enjoyed together;
>
> produce a class-made anthology of favorite poems complete with their own illustrations.[16]

As pupils share their experiences with books, the teacher may observe and evaluate the effects of books upon them. Readily apparent will be children's response to characters and events as well as their tendency to note details and their ability to communicate their ideas. Through exchanges of ideas in discussion, opinions may be tested and conclusions may be questioned or verified. Thus, discussion of books can become a meaningful and valuable experience. When discussion-type activities are used, the groups should be small so that a free exchange of ideas can take place.

EVALUATING THE LITERATURE PROGRAM

Several factors should be considered when the literature program is evaluated. Of primary importance is the quality and suitability of the

---

[16] LaVerne Strong, "Enjoying Literature Together," Curriculum Letter no. 3, 1953–54. Department of School Services, Wesleyan University, Middletown, Connecticut.

materials read. Of importance too are the results of reading and the extent and nature of the influence of books upon boys and girls.

Evaluation of Books

Teachers who seek to guide pupils to find appropriate books usually consider certain criteria by which such books are selected. Following is a check list which teachers and librarians have found helpful in evaluating children's books.[17]

CHECK LIST FOR EVALUATING CHILDREN'S BOOKS

A. *Difficulty*
1. Can the group (or child) with whom the selection is to be used read it with reasonable ease?
2. Are the concepts within their (or his) comprehension?

B. *Content*
1. Is the content in keeping with the interests or needs of the class?
   a. Will the children really enjoy the book?
   b. Will it contribute understandings which will enable them to make needed personal and social adjustments?
2. Will it extend the range, the depth, and the quality of their understanding and experience?
   a. Will it lead them to broader and deeper appreciation of people, places, times, nature, science?
   b. Will it lead to higher ideals? Are the heroes and heroines seeking worthy ideals?
3. If the book is a storybook, will it give the child a true picture of life? Will it lead him to seek sincerity and truth in the books he reads?
   a. Do the characters talk and behave like real people?
   b. Could the story actually happen? Are the obstacles to be overcome real obstacles? Do the characters and situations interact to produce the events that happen, or does the author force certain outcomes?

C. *Quality of Presentation*
1. Is the book well written?
   a. Is it free from careless, slipshod, crude English?
   b. Does it have simplicity, beauty, or an imaginative quality?
2. Does it have organic and artistic unity?
   a. If factual information is contained in the book is it direct and concrete, or are the facts lost in the conversation and activities of characters?

[17] Paul Witty, *Reading in Modern Education* (Boston: D. C. Heath and Co., 1949), pp. 130–131.

  b. If stories are offered, do they move directly toward a good point or climax?
 D. *Physical Makeup*
  1. Are the type face and the size of type suitable for the age level at which the book is to be used?
  2. Is the binding durable and attractive?
  3. Are illustrations simple, artistic, suited to the content, and meaningful to children?

May Hill Arbuthnot suggests that for different types of literature, varied criteria are appropriate. Thus, "A biography should be true to all the facts known about the subject's life, and it should treat its subject objectively." She adds, "Of course the hero of a biography must be heroic in stature, but he should be a real-life hero, with real-life faults, weaknesses and doubts."[18]

Books which present information require accuracy as a major criterion, while poetry has its own special standards.

> Most important are the melody and movement which, more than any other qualities, distinguish it from prose or from doggerel. Its words, too, are important. They may be exciting new words, or everyday words used in new ways and combinations, but they must not be pedestrian. The rhymes must seem appropriate, not just convenient. The whole poem should give fresh significance to life.[19]

The use of certain criteria for the selection of books is illustrated by the way in which award books are chosen each year. The best known of these awards are the Caldecott and Newbery awards. The Newbery Medal is given each year to the writer of the most distinguished book for children. The purpose of the award is:

> to encourage original and creative work in the field of books for children. To emphasize to the public that contributions to the literature for children deserve recognition as do poetry, plays, or novels. To give to those librarians who make it their life work to serve children's reading interests an opportunity to encourage good writing in this field.[20]

Each year a book is selected by the Children's Services Division of the American Library Association from books published in the United States during the previous year. Frederic G. Melcher, now chairman of the board of the R. R. Bowker Company, who originated the idea of

---

[18] May Hill Arbuthnot, *Children and Books* (Chicago: Scott, Foresman and Co., 1957), p. 26.
[19] *Ibid.*
[20] Irene Smith, *A History of the Newbery and Caldecott Medals* (New York: Viking Press, Inc., 1957), p. 50.

the medal, suggested the use of the Newbery name and became the donor. The medal was suitably named for John Newbery, who was "perhaps the first bookman to appreciate that the reading interests of children were worthy of especial and individual attention."[21]

Interest in giving a medal to honor picture books with outstanding illustrations arose more than two decades after the first Newbery Medal was awarded. There was general agreement "that younger children's books had not fared well in competing for the Newbery Medal."[22] The Newbery Medal awards emphasized distinguished writing, which was more frequently found in books for older rather than younger children. Beautiful and outstanding pictures, on the other hand, were more often found in the books for younger children. Accordingly, it was suggested that another medal be given to the illustrator of the most distinguished picture book, and Mr. Melcher recommended that it be named after the eminent pioneer illustrator of children's books, Randolph Caldecott. In 1937 the children's librarians of the American Library Association passed the following resolution:

> Resolved: That the Picture Book Medal offered by Mr. Frederic G. Melcher be accepted. The name of this medal shall be the Caldecott Medal. This medal shall be awarded to the artist of the most distinguished American Picture Book for Children published in the United States during the preceding year. The award shall go to the artist, who must be a citizen or resident of the United States, whether or not he be the author of the text. Members of the Newbery Medal Committee will serve as judges. If a book of the year is nominated for both the Newbery and Caldecott awards, the Committee shall decide under which heading it shall be voted upon, so that the same title shall not be considered on both ballots.[23]

The Newbery and Caldecott medals have provided a pattern for awards offered by other groups seeking to encourage the writing and illustrating of superior children's books. Many teachers look forward each year to these awards. Some of the award books have not only become very popular, but have also enriched greatly the reading experiences of boys and girls. The Appendix of this book contains titles of books which have been given Newbery and Caldecott medals.

Appraising the Literature Program

In one sense the effects of literature cannot be measured, for they are sometimes too subtle to identify by our conventional approaches; but

---

[21] *Ibid.*
[22] *Ibid.*, p. 63.
[23] *Ibid.*, p. 64.

the teacher can observe some external and often obvious signs of change in pupils. What are some outward indications of pupil growth in and through literature? These outward signs may appear as the teacher tries to appraise the effects of the total reading program and the extent of pupil growth as estimated by observations, conferences, and reports of parents and teachers. The pupil's own evaluation is a valuable indicator, too, of the effectiveness of reading.

1. *Evaluation of the total program.* Jean Betzner has suggested the use of the following and similar questions as a way of appraising the effectiveness of the overall program of literature:

> Is the literature program consistent with the total school program?
> Is literature consistent with other arts? Does it overshadow other art forms or is it used to bring other art forms close to those who do not gain as much from the printed page?
> Is the literature program consistent with itself? (Is its function clearly conceived? Are its methods and procedures for evaluation borrowed from other areas of human experience?)
> Is evaluation applicable at any point? Bringing out values into the light of frequent examination and application is the surest means of improving them.
> Is evaluation determined by all who are engaged in this work? Administrators, teachers, children, parents and community agencies should have a part in determining how literature can best serve the needs of children.[24]

2. *Teacher-pupil evaluation* may take several forms, but from time to time the teacher will find it helpful to discuss a specific story with a pupil. The following questions might be utilized:

> Did the plot of the story hold your interest?
> Did you enjoy reading the story?
> Are you glad you read the story?
> Do you feel as if you really know the characters?
> Did the story make you want to share it with others?
> Did the story make you want to write a story or poem of your own?
> Did the descriptions make you see and feel what was being described?
> Did the story give you some definite feeling?
> What book would you like to read next?

3. *Teacher evaluation* involves day-by-day observations which are recorded. Russell believes the teacher can appraise pupil interest, enjoyment, and overall growth through such items as the following:

> The kind and number of books read
> The use made of magazines, newspapers, and pamphlets
> The desire of pupils to read other selections they have enjoyed

---

[24] Jean Betzner, *Exploring Literature with Children* (New York: Bureau of Publications, Teachers College, Columbia University, 1943), pp. 65–74.

> The desire to tell stories that have appealed to them
> The participation in dramatization of stories read
> The quality of children's expressive activities, such as original stories or paintings developing from stories
> The extent to which children bring available books from home to share with others
> The number of books borrowed for home reading
> The use of books in free periods
> The ease and enjoyment with which children memorize poetry or other selections
> The quality of choices in radio and television programs, recordings, and films
> The form and maturity of pupils' comments about their tastes and preferences[25]

4. *Parent-teacher evaluation* can take place informally before and after PTA meetings, during parent visits to the school or class, or following scheduled conferences. Information which will be helpful to the teacher may be obtained from conferences guided by questions such as these directed to the parent:

> How much time is devoted to reading at home?
> Does he have his own personal library?
> Are books and magazines available at home?
> Does he have a library card?
> Do you encourage him to make frequent trips to the library?
> Are books and magazine articles discussed in the home?
> Does he or do other members of the family practice reading aloud at home?

5. *Self-appraisal conferences.* Teachers may also wish to confer with each child to obtain his own opinion of his reading growth and needs. Questions such as the following may be suggested for the child to use in evaluating his own reading:

> Am I reading more books at home than I read last year?
> Am I going to the library regularly?
> Am I giving too much time to books on one topic?
> Am I reading books in many fields? Or am I reading in too many fields and not concentrating in some areas?
> Am I reading books of various types—stories, biographies, factual materials, and so forth?
> Am I reading poetry?
> Am I finding answers to my school and home problems in books?
> Am I enjoying reading more and more as I read widely?

---

[25] David H. Russell, *op. cit.*, pp. 439–440.

As we have already pointed out some of the values of reading elude evaluation. How do you know that reading a book has changed a pupil's self-concept? Do you have evidence that a book has made a significant change in a child's understanding of reality? We cannot answer these questions with finality, but we can gain insight into pupils by observing their behavior and noting their attitudes. We can also obtain pertinent information in conferences with their parents and teachers. These approaches will enable us to judge the nature and extent of pupils' growth in and through reading, and will provide the basis for further guidance.

CONCLUDING STATEMENT

Books may afford a never-ending source of pleasure for children and youth. The challenge to the teacher is to bring the wonderful world of books and pupils together in the happiest and most productive relationship. To do so, the teacher must know each child's nature and needs, and must be thoroughly acquainted with children's books—old and new. He must be able, also, to interest children in reading and share joyfully their discoveries in books.

Parents play an important role, too, in determining children's attitudes toward literature. They should cooperate with the teacher to encourage extensive reading by children, and should work with the teacher in providing records of the amount and nature of children's reading and of the effects of reading upon them.

The school librarian will also cooperate in a balanced reading program. He will send to each classroom assortments of books, altered and augmented as the interests and needs of the children expand and change. He will also instruct teachers and pupils in the use of library aids, reference books, catalogs, indexes, and bibliographies. He will be informed as to the availability of visual and auditory aids for school use. He may encourage creative writing by the pupils themselves. Reviews of books by the children, informally voiced or written, will do much to advertise books.[26] In addition, a display in the school library of children's art work depicting scenes and characters from their favorite stories will encourage reading.

The school library will make provision for many timid children to prove themselves necessary members of various groups—for the possibilities of helping in the library are numerous. There are book jackets

---

[26] Phyllis R. Fenner, *Our Library* (New York: The John Day Co., Inc., 1942).

to be displayed, magazine racks to be kept in order, volumes to be repaired, and books to be arranged on shelves. Such activities often interest poor readers or indifferent boys and girls. In handling books, apparently only to help the librarian, some children may for the first time in their lives develop an interest in books that will lead to extensive voluntary reading.

Although the task of becoming acquainted with children's literature may seem overwhelming to some teachers who have depended in the past almost entirely upon the use of a single textbook for instruction in reading, most modern teachers recognize the need for a broader approach and for a balanced program in reading. In such a program children's literature has an important place.

In this chapter some practical ways by which the teacher can become acquainted with children's literature have been suggested. Procedures have been described, too, through which the teacher may become skilled in evaluating stories and books and in choosing "the right book for the right child."

Selected References

Arbuthnot, May Hill, *Children and Books* (Chicago: Scott, Foresman and Co., 1957).

Arbuthnot, May Hill, *Time for Poetry* (Chicago: Scott, Foresman and Co., 1952).

Dallmann, Martha, "Year Round with Books," *Grade Teacher,* 34:98–99 (November, 1957).

Fenner, Phyllis R., *The Proof of the Pudding* (New York: The John Day Co., Inc., 1957).

Frank, Josette, *Your Child's Reading Today,* rev. ed., (Garden City, New York: Doubleday and Company, Inc., 1960).

Freeland, Alma, "Growing with the Curriculum" in the 1951 Yearbook of the *National Elementary Principal* (Washington, D. C.: National Education Association, 1951), pp. 248–253.

Garvey, Leone, "What Is Children's Literature? III. Children's Literature—Old," *Elementary English,* 41:475–483 (May, 1964).

Hanna, Geneva R., and Mariana McAllister, *Books, Young People, and Reading Guidance* (New York: Harper & Row, Publishers, 1960).

Hofer, Louis B., "What Do Sixth-Graders Really Like in Poetry?" *Elementary English,* 33:433–438 (November, 1956).

Huck, Charlotte S. and Doris A. Young, *Children's Literature in the Elementary School* (New York: Holt, Rinehart and Winston, 1961).

Huck, Charlotte S., "What Is Children's Literature? I. Children's Literature—Defined," *Elementary English,* 41:467–470 (May, 1964).

Huck, Charlotte S., "What Is Children's Literature? II. Children's Literature—New," *Elementary English,* 41:471–474 (May, 1964).

Huus, Helen, "How a TV Program Can Be Used as a Springboard to Further Reading," *Elementary English,* 34:81–88 (February, 1957).

Jenkins, William A., "What Is Children's Literature? V. Illustrators and Illustrations," *Elementary English,* 41:492–499 (May, 1964).

Larrick, Nancy, *A Parent's Guide to Children's Reading* (Garden City, New York: Doubleday and Co., Inc., 1958).

Larrick, Nancy, *A Teacher's Guide to Children's Books* (Columbus, Ohio: Charles E. Merrill Books, Inc., 1960).

Meigs, Cornelia L. and others, *A Critical History of Children's Literature* (New York: The Macmillan Co., 1953).

Rasmussen, Margaret (editor), *Literature with Children* (Washington, D. C.: Association for Childhood Education International, 1961).

Rollins, Charlamae (compiler), *Christmas Gif'* (Chicago: Follett Publishing Co., 1963).

Roos, Jean Carolyn, *Patterns in Reading* (Chicago: American Library Association, 1954).

Sawyer, Ruth, *The Way of the Story Teller* (New York: The Viking Press, Inc., 1942).

Smith, Dora V., *Fifty Years of Children's Books* (Champaign, Ill.: The National Council of Teachers of English, 1963).

Smith, Lillian H., *The Unreluctant Years* (Chicago: American Library Association, 1953).

Strang, Ruth, "Interest as a Dynamic Force in the Improvement of Reading," *Elementary English,* 34:170–176 (March, 1957).

Strang, Ruth, *Helping Your Child Improve His Reading* (New York: E. P. Dutton & Co., Inc., 1962).

Strang, Ruth and others, *Gateways to Readable Books* (New York: The H. W. Wilson Co., 1952).

Tooze, Ruth, *Storytelling* (Englewood Cliffs, N.J.: Prentice-Hall, Inc., 1959).

Tooze, Ruth, *Your Children Want to Read* (Englewood Cliffs, N. J.: Prentice-Hall, Inc., 1957).

Walker, Elinor, *Book Bait* (Chicago: American Library Association, 1957).

Walter, Nina Willis, *Let Them Write Poetry* (New York: Holt, Rinehart & Winston, Inc., 1962).

Witty, Paul (editor), "Creative Writing and Story Telling in Today's Schools," *Elementary English* (March, 1957).

Witty, Paul, *Helping Children Read Better* (Chicago: Science Research Associates, Inc., 1950).

Witty, Paul (guest editor), "Interests of Children and Youth: Research and Applications," *Education,* 83:450–506 (April, 1963).

Witty, Paul, "Meeting Developmental Needs Through Reading," *Education,* 84:451–458 (April, 1964).

Witty, Paul (guest editor), "Satisfying Needs Through Reading," *Education,* 84:451–492 (April, 1964).

8

THE ROLE OF LANGUAGE DEVELOPMENT

Language is one of the means by which we communicate. Our facial expressions, gestures, and actions also can express our feelings and ideas of things. However, verbal expression remains the essence of full and complete communication.

When referring to language as the essential tool of communication, one must consider the elements of language used to convey a message and the elements used in receiving it. For example, if one uses oral communication—speech—to convey a message, then the audience must use listening to receive the ideas. If a communicator uses the printed symbol—writing—to convey his ideas, then the receiver must use reading as the means of receiving them.

These elements need not be designated as either speech-listening or writing-reading. For example, writing may be used with listening if the reader chooses to read aloud a printed message which may then be recorded by members of an audience. Various other interrelationships of these elements of language expression are, of course, possible.

The Interrelationship of the Language Arts

The language arts have been defined as the communicative elements of writing, reading, speaking, and listening. In reality, however, there is no sharp division of the language arts. The Commission on the English Curriculum emphasizes that although the language arts do include speech, listening, reading, and writing, these parts rarely function independently.[1]

[1] National Council of Teachers of English (Dora V. Smith, Director), *The English Language Arts* (New York: Appleton-Century-Crofts, 1952).

Until somewhat recently it has been customary to give attention to each area in the traditional subject-matter approach to education. Some schools are now following a practice which began about thirty years ago and which has resulted in a combined, or merged, program.

One of the earliest publications to stress the interrelationship among the language arts was that of the National Council of Teachers of English. In 1935 the Council published the monograph *An Experience Curriculum in English*.[2] This was followed by the Twentieth Yearbook (1941) of the Department of Elementary School Principals under the title *Language Arts in the Elementary School,* in which a similar approach was recommended.[3] A few years later the Forty-third Yearbook of the National Society for the Study of Education, Part II, *Teaching Language in the Elementary School,* continued this emphasis.[4] These early reports made a significant impression on the thinking and writing of many educators and teachers and on classroom practice. However, a number of factors contributed to a shift from instruction in a single-subject approach to an integrated approach.

Study of the nature of our language, of course, has always indicated the interrelation of the language arts. A child learns to speak through listening. Reading is dependent upon speech patterns and a listening vocabulary. Finally, writing is influenced by listening, speaking, and reading vocabularies in addition to speech and reading patterns.

It remained for educational organizations, research, and the thinking of certain individuals to make evident these relationships to teachers of the language arts. The relationships were further emphasized by additional research findings from other disciplines.

Factors of Importance in Producing a Change in Classroom Practice

A change in learning theory was one factor which fostered the acceptance of the newer approach to the language arts. Research demonstrated that learning proceeds best when it is organized around meaningful, focused areas of interest. The relevance of these findings

[2] National Council of Teachers of English, W. Wilbur Hatfield (chairman), *An Experience Curriculum in English* (New York: Appleton-Century-Crofts, 1935).

[3] National Education Association, Department of Elementary School Principals, *Language Arts in the Elementary School,* Twentieth Yearbook (Washington, D.C.: National Education Association, 1941).

[4] M. R. Trabue (chairman), *Teaching Language in the Elementary School,* Forty-third Yearbook of the National Society for the Study of Education, Part II (Chicago: University of Chicago Press, 1944).

to the language arts may be illustrated through numerous examples. For example, an ancient practice in the schools was to have children memorize a meaningless passage and then deliver it to an audience. Research has indicated that when speech is developed and used in a meaningful and functional manner learning is more effective. In this case, the ability to listen is enhanced too.

A. Sterl Artley has pointed out that the present approach in the language arts is attributable in part to a deeper insight into the psychology of language as well as to the psychology of child development:

> The transition that took place was an inevitable one, growing as it did out of a greater understanding of the psychology of language, as well as the psychology of child growth and development. This greater understanding resulted first in a change of philosophy of language teaching—away from the mechanics, the niceties and detailed correctness to emphasis on expression, appropriateness, and individuality, growing out of situations in which the pupil uses language. It resulted in the recognition of the fact that the language arts are allied, both in content and purpose; that they are tied together through their common base of meaning and symbolism. Like a closely knit family with similar heritage, commonness of purpose, and an inherent unity, so are the language arts.[5]

As we have stated in many situations one language art may influence another, with each contributing to the development of the other. Thus, Gertrude Hildreth describes the way reading influences and fosters other language acquisitions:

> From reading the pupil gains knowledge of vocabulary, sentence structure, grammatical form used in speaking and writing. Reading enriches vocabulary.
> From reading the pupil derives generalizations about words and word building.
> Reading develops language sense and gives practice in using language correctly.
> Reading furnishes ideas to write about and furnishes a basis for discussion. . . .
> Reading furnishes the stimulus and ideas for creative writing.[6]

To the degree that the development of skills in one of the language arts fosters the development of skills in another, correlated learning takes place. Such learning is advantageously planned in numerous situ-

---

[5] A. Sterl Artley, "Research Concerning Interrelationships among the Language Arts," *Elementary English,* 27:527–537 (December, 1950).

[6] Gertrude H. Hildreth, *Child Growth through Education* (New York: The Ronald Press Co., 1948), pp. 228–229.

ations. In fact, the skills and goals sought in one language art may be almost identical with those sought in another. For example, the relationship between oral and written composition is particularly close because they require similar general abilities and skills. In speaking as well as writing the communicator is concerned with such matters as the topic, the content, the point of view, and the use of appropriate vocabulary. Punctuation marks indicate the pauses in writing, while the emphasis in speaking is shown in various ways such as intonation.[7]

We should not assume that the acquisition of communication skills in a related manner always implies equal development of the separate skills. However, it has been shown that, in general, high achievement in one language ability tends to be associated with higher than average achievement in others.[8] But this relationship is by no means uniform or invariable.[9] Although it is desirable to emphasize language-arts skills independently, it is also important to develop them in related forms.

Robert C. Pooley presents two major premises to support the view that it is the obligation of the teacher to cultivate the development of each language art, but to keep in mind also the related nature of the language arts. He indicates, too, the importance of understanding the relatedness of growth in the language arts to the total growth pattern of each child:

> . . . first, that growth in the language arts is intimately related to physical, mental, emotional, and social growth of the individual student. . . .
> The second major premise is that just as a child varies from other children in his relative advancement in physical, mental, emotional, and social factors, so does he also vary in his advancements of growth in the language arts: listening, reading, speaking, and writing.[10]

Separate skills need to be cultivated in each of the language arts. These skills are best learned when they are expressed in the context of the total development of the person. The interrelatedness of the parts should be recognized.

---

[7] Willard F. Tidyman and Marguerite Butterfield, *Teaching the Language Arts*, 2nd ed. (New York: McGraw-Hill Book Co., Inc., 1959), pp. 5–6.

[8] Vergil H. Hughes, "Study of the Relationships among Selected Language Abilities," *Journal of Educational Research*, 47:97–106 (October, 1953).

[9] Clyde I. Martin, "An Investigation of the Developmental Relationships among Language Variables in Children of the First Grade," Ph.D. dissertation (Austin, Texas: University of Texas, 1952); John J. DeBoer, "Oral and Written Language," *Review of Educational Research*, 25:114–115 (April, 1955).

[10] Robert C. Pooley, "Reading and the Language Arts," in Paul Witty (chairman), *Development In and Through Reading*, Sixtieth Yearbook of the National Society for the Study of Education, Part I (Chicago: University of Chicago Press, 1961), p. 36.

SPEAKING AND READING

Reading and speaking, two areas of the language arts, are highly influenced by experiential background. And both areas are affected by vocabulary development. A brief discussion of these factors and the outcomes of providing experiences for children follows.

Reading, Speaking, and Vocabulary Development

Within the span of a few short pre-school years a child usually develops from a babbling infant into an individual who uses a vocabulary of perhaps two to four thousand words. He acquires his speaking vocabulary by listening, and he uses it to express his needs, thoughts, and feelings.

The cultivation of vocabulary is a responsibility of all persons whose lives touch those of boys and girls. According to authorities the first word is used when a child is about twelve months of age. He acquires a considerable number of words each month thereafter until he is able to employ, when he is about two years of age, approximately 250 different words, each having a definite meaning with a specific relationship to his basic needs and purposes. The importance of these acquisitions is revealed by the fact that after the child has acquired a few words, he is not only able to make his needs known directly, but by the use of questions he is capable of acquiring information.

During the age interval from two to six, the child adds to his vocabulary hundreds of words each year. According to some authorities the number of new words added each year is about 600. Almost incredible is the fact that by the time the typical child is ready to go to school he actually uses or has used about 2500 different words. In addition to these words there are many more whose meanings he knows. When one reflects upon the rapidity of this development, the importance of providing careful guidance and nurture during the pre-school years is obvious.

The development of a reading vocabulary is just as dramatic. The child may enter the first grade knowing possibly one or two words he can read. Within a few months he may have a sight vocabulary of 50 to 100 words and with the teaching of phonic and structural analysis his reading vocabulary may increase to several thousand words. It should be noted that the meaning of the printed symbols a child reads is highly dependent upon his speaking vocabulary and his past experiences.

One important obligation of parents, then, centers in the provision of an atmosphere favorable to wide experience and experimentation with language. To make mistakes comfortably is a privilege which children should enjoy; and parents should display patience, appreciation, and interest as the child attempts to convey his understandings and feelings through words. They should provide good models in their own speech, making sure that their own language is reasonably correct and clear. Even after the child enters school it is necessary for the teacher to continue to provide a good model and experiences for vocabulary development because the child's speech and vocabulary continue to develop throughout his school years.

Moreover, clarity in communication should be the basic test by which parents and teachers evaluate children's language acquisitions. They should inquire: "Is the child finding genuine pleasure in his expanding vocabulary? Are meanings clear and associations accurate?" In other words, is the child communicating successfully and with pleasure?

Promoting Firsthand Experience

Children need wide and varied firsthand experience as a basis for expression and for the development of clear concepts associated with words. During their first year at school they should learn the meanings of words that stand for common objects they have seen and for others they will soon encounter at home or elsewhere. Children are too frequently required to "learn" new words simply by repeating them aloud or by completing exercises in workbooks. For example, one of the writers discussed with a fourth-grade pupil the problems in arithmetic he was attempting to solve in his workbook. One problem required that he find the number of acres in a section of land. After referring to the answer in the back of the book, he tried several approaches until he finally obtained the correct answer. When he was asked, "What is an acre?" he promptly replied, "It's a park." The park nearby was an acre in size. This association was the only one his experience had provided for the word *acre*. Obviously, teachers at every grade level should make a diligent effort to insure that the words which convey the essence of passages are understood.

The role of experience is of special significance when the child is introduced to reading materials. The first words to be read should be related to his own experiences at home and in school. The use of pupil-dictated charts offers an effective way of providing reading materials associated with firsthand observation and experience; from such charts a vocabulary can be developed to constitute each child's basic stock of sight words. In establishing the meanings of these words, the use of a multiple-sensory approach is desirable. Clarity will be given to the meaning of a word such as *chair* by having children observe a real chair, handle it, sit in it, and in other ways sense its essential characteristics. Thus a variety of reactions will insure understanding of the word and its referents. The child should be offered an opportunity for similar experiences with several kinds of chairs in order that he will not associate the word *chair* with a particular type of chair only and experience confusion when he finds that other kinds of chairs are also referred to by this word.

Speaking and English Usage

Emphasis on experience and skill in speaking does more than build a reading vocabulary; it also provides opportunities for the development of correct English usage. Pooley criticizes current classroom practices in the teaching of good usage:

> Teachers tend to use blackboard exercises, workbooks and mimeographed materials, relying upon reading and silent seat work to teach usage, overlooking the fact that faulty usage is learned by ear and can be best corrected by ear. So far as is possible in the classroom from the kindergarten up, the child should hear nothing but acceptable patterns of speech and should hear himself using them.[11]

Acquaintance on the part of the teacher with the customary language expression of various cultural groups is highly desirable. Such a knowledge will not only enable him to understand the unusual and sometimes incorrect usage of certain pupils, but will offer an opportunity for comparing various kinds of expression which are acceptable in different groups. Such comparisons will lead children to discriminate among and accept different ways of communicating ideas.

The basic relationship between speaking and reading is generally recognized, and emphasis on speaking activities has become accepted practice in the beginning stages of teaching children to read. Primary teachers usually plan for preparatory discussion of "what is to be read, to draw inferences from pictures, and to discuss personal experiences which might bear upon the material about to be read."[12]

Gertrude Hildreth suggests some experiences with speech to foster all-around language growth in practical, everyday situations:

[11] Robert C. Pooley, *op. cit.*, p. 44.
[12] Robert C. Pooley, *op. cit.*, p. 46.

Pupils read with greater ease things they have talked about.

Oral statements made in class discussion become reading material when recorded and edited by the teacher.

Oral language reveals the experiences a child has had, which in turn suggest reading interests.

The pupil reports on his reading orally.

The pupil reads aloud.

The class works on word pronunciation—both for speaking and for oral reading.

The same phonetic skills are used in speaking and reading.

The pupil explains the meaning of reading text and pictures.

Pupils dramatize a book they have found in their reading.

Pupils give a book assembly or school program based on reading done in curriculum units.[13]

In addition to the foregoing suggestions many authorities feel that choral reading may foster language facility. Choral reading can be an effective activity for individual children, for small groups, and even for large groups.

LISTENING AND READING

A teacher employing phonics in a reading program is well aware of the interdependence of listening and reading. There are many other relationships between these two phases of the language arts. A brief discussion of the significance of listening, the kinds of listening, and activities for the maintenance and improvement of listening skills follows.

Significance of Listening

No one would seriously question the fact that children and young people spend many hours a day in listening. They listen to their teachers. They listen to their classmates. They listen to radio and television. Studies have been made that show children and young people spend an average of some twenty hours per week viewing and listening to television. In 1950 Miriam Wilt found that children devote 57.5 per cent of classroom time to listening.[14] The large number of hours in a day given to listening makes it essential that efforts be made to teach children to listen effectively.

---

[13] Gertrude H. Hildreth, *op. cit.*, p. 229.

[14] Miriam E. Wilt, "A Study of Teacher Awareness of Listening as a Factor in Elementary Education," *Journal of Educational Research,* 43:626–636 (April, 1950).

Until recently, as has been repeatedly shown, little instruction was offered children in acquiring this significant and essential skill. In fact, little attention has been given to listening by educators generally. For example, although thousands of studies have been reported in the field of reading, fewer have appeared in the area of listening.

In 1958 Witty and Sizemore examined the literature on listening. The first review focused on the relative value of oral and visual presentations of material to be learned; after examining the studies, it was concluded:

- (a) Listening is an effective method of learning certain materials.
- (b) Listening, as compared with reading as a way of learning, seems more effective in early childhood, but its superiority is not consistently demonstrated even at this level.
- (c) Listening seems less effective than reading as an adult way of learning certain materials, as in cases where critical discrimination and analysis are involved. But, here again, a trend only is indicated, and the results of experiments are contradictory.
- (d) Listening as a way of learning is sometimes reinforced by other avenues for learning such as are found in the simultaneous use of visual and kinaesthetic approaches. But, once again, the data are inconclusive or contradictory.
- (e) A high correlation is found between the ability of groups to learn through visual, auditory, and kinaesthetic approaches.
- (f) Individual differences are great in all types of learning, and the person who is successful with one type of presentation tends to be successful with another.
- (g) Success in learning through any avenue depends upon the nature of the task to be learned and the way the materials are to be employed.
- (h) Success in learning through any sensory approach seems to depend to a considerable degree on the individual's experience in that type of learning.
- (i) Little relationship exists between the method of presentation and the retention of materials.[15]

A second report by Witty and Sizemore was a review of studies of the relative value of listening to materials presented in lecture form as compared with reading the same subject matter. It was found that, in general, the studies revealed little difference in the results of the two approaches. When listening *versus* reading as a way of learning was compared, inconsistencies appeared in the reports. When a comparison was made of the effectiveness of seeing pictures *versus* reading a story, again the results of the studies were inconsistent and inconclusive.

---

[15] Paul A. Witty and Robert A. Sizemore, "Studies in Listening: I. Relative Values of Oral and Visual Presentation," *Elementary English,* 35:538–552 (December, 1958).

Studies of the relative value of listening to an examination administered orally and reading the same examination indicated there was little difference in the results obtained by either method.[16]

In these studies learning through listening or reading appeared to be equally efficient. The visual approach and the auditory approach were apparently used with equal success. However, it was clear that learning could be enhanced through the simultaneous use of the auditory and visual approaches.

A third report concerned the effectiveness of visual and auditory presentations with changes in age and grade level. The studies seemed to indicate that with younger pupils auditory presentations are more successfully used than their visual equivalents. The superiority of the auditory approach was less evident at higher age levels; in fact, it appeared that learning through visual presentation became somewhat more effective with advance in age. Many of the investigations, however, failed to consider adequately the influence of factors such as the type and difficulty of the materials employed at various levels.

The writers concluded:

> Any difference in learning efficiency may be traced not to the visual or to the auditory presentation, but, instead, to factors such as the difficulty or nature of the material to be learned, the way in which it is presented, and its suitability in terms of the experience and interests of the groups studied.[17]

Rather than attempting to ascertain the superiority of one avenue of presentation over another, therefore, the researchers advocated that answers to questions such as the following should be sought:

1. What should be the relative emphasis given to silent and to oral presentation in teaching reading throughout the elementary grades?
2. What combinations of the reading-listening skills are most effectively used with different types of subject matter?
3. How can the act of seeing and hearing (through films and filmstrips, for example) be employed most successfully to reinforce learning through reading?
4. How can the interest of children in TV and other media of mass communication be most effectively utilized in promoting learning through listening and through reading?[18]

[16] Paul A. Witty and Robert A. Sizemore, "Studies in Listening: II. Relative Values of Oral and Visual Presentation (Lectures, Movies, Examinations, and Advertising Materials)," *Elementary English*, 36:59–70 (January, 1959).

[17] Paul A. Witty and Robert A. Sizemore, "Studies in Listening: III. The Effectiveness of Visual and Auditory Presentations with Changes in Age and Grade Level," *Elementary English*, 36:130–140 (February, 1959).

[18] *Ibid.*, p. 139.

It is important to note that most of the experiments in listening failed to take into account, or even recognize, the significance of interest. Pupil interest in television, radio, or various subjects has not been utilized to determine the relative or combined value of listening and reading in promoting learning.

The Nature, Levels, and Kinds of Listening

Observation and research make it clear that listening is too important to be left to chance. In the improvement of the instructional program teachers should acquire knowledge about the nature, the levels, and the kinds of listening. There seems to be general agreement that there are at least four kinds of listening:

1. *Passive or marginal listening.* This level of listening is operating when an individual studies with the radio on and tunes in just enough to be conscious of background music.
2. *Appreciative listening* operates when the learner's intent is to enjoy a dramatization, a story, or a poem. The individual may wish to identify with the characters or the experience, and may listen for this purpose.
3. When accuracy of comprehension is essential, the individual uses *attentive listening* for following directions, understanding announcements, and responding to introductions. When conversation and discussion are involved, this is properly labeled *responsive listening.*
4. When pupils reach intermediate and high-school level, they should be given an opportunity to use *analytical listening.* In this type of listening the individual "weighs what is heard against personal experience and is alert to attempts of the speaker to sway his opinion by the devices of propaganda."[19]

It is essential, too, that teachers know the nature of the skills that are involved in listening. L. E. Pratt has suggested a list which may be developed through appropriate and planned instruction at the upper intermediate and high school levels. The similarity to reading skills will be noted in the list which follows:

    I. Word perception
       A. Recall of word meaning
       B. Deduction of meaning of unknown words
   II. Comprehension ideas
       A. Noting details
       B. Following directions

[19] National Council of Teachers of English, *Language Arts for Today's Children* (New York: Appleton-Century-Crofts, 1954), pp. 80–81.

      C. Organizing into main and subordinate ideas
      D. Selecting information pertinent to a specific topic
      E. Detecting clues that show the speaker's trend of thought
  III. Using ideas to build understanding
      A. Evaluating an expressed point of view or fact in relation to previous learning
      B. Making justifiable inference[20]

Some authors have stressed the relatively greater importance of the critical factor in listening as compared with reading. Continuity in the process and the role of sustained attention are also emphasized. In reading, a student may pause or look back. When listening, however, a lengthy pause would cause him to miss the ensuing presentation (or part of the presentation) of the speaker. Such differences should be recognized as a program in listening is planned.

Development of Listening Skills

The development of listening skills and habits involves not only the attitude of each pupil toward listening, but his adjustment of listening skills to different types of presentations. Further, the teacher is an important factor in developing readiness for listening and checking, evaluating, and guiding pupil development in this skill.

The following guides are presented to teachers as aids in developing good listening habits in their pupils:

Readiness. Preparation for listening to different types of presentations is essential, and the most advantageous background or "set" should be provided. An introduction to the topic that is to be considered and interest in the topic, as well as attention to experiential or vicarious background, are essential elements for the cultivation of effective listening.

Purpose. The purpose of a listening activity should be clearly in the mind of the teacher; but more important, the child should be aware of reasons for listening. At times the purpose may be to listen for directions, at other times for certain ideas, and at still other times to compare the ideas of the speaker with some other source. Whatever the purposes for listening, they should not be too numerous or too complex. Edgar Dale believes that listening would be improved on many occasions if one idea or point were stressed at a time.

---

[20] L. E. Pratt, "The Experimental Evaluation of a Program for the Improvement of Listening in the Elementary School," Ph.D. dissertation (Iowa City: State University of Iowa, 1953). Cited by Paul C. Burns, "Teaching Listening in Elementary Schools," *Elementary English,* 38:12 (January, 1961).

We don't listen because we are fed up. Too many people are firing too many different ideas at us. We can't absorb them that fast. A poor speaker covers ten points. A good speaker *uncovers* one.[21]

Duration. The periods that require children to listen should be kept reasonably short. Actually, people usually can read, write, or speak for a longer period than they can listen. Teachers should consider the demands of different listening situations and plan periods for listening of appropriate length. The age of the child, the complexity of the material, and the purposes for listening are considerations in determining the appropriate length of listening activities.

Environment. The setting for listening should be conducive to building good listening habits. Proper temperature of the room, freedom from distractions within and outside the room, and a pleasing quality of a speaker's voice are factors that should be considered when stressing listening activities.

Standards. Utilization of varied self-standards for listening rather than exploring general class standards is usually more effective in developing good listening habits. Some children may need to remove all objects from the top of their desks in order to avoid distractions; others may enhance their listening by having a clear view of the speaker. From a discussion of many standards for good listening a child should be guided in selecting his own standards—those standards that will help *him* to listen better.

Preparation. The speaker has a responsibility to his audience. He should be well prepared and his message should be appropriate to the level of his audience. The ideas should be new, for as Dale suggests:

> Is the . . . speaker presenting new ideas unavailable in textbooks . . . ? Or could the student get this information more effectively by reading it outside of class? Our classrooms must not be places where students practice inattentive listening to repetitious discussion.[22]

The responsibility of the teacher is great in offering guidance to students as they learn to listen with increasing effectiveness. It is obvious, too, that the teacher himself should cultivate appropriate habits of listening and should provide abundant and varied opportunities for pupils to be heard. Ralph Nichols and Leonard Stevens offer valuable counsel for the teacher in the volume entitled *Are You Listening?*[23]

---

[21] Edgar Dale, "Why Don't We Listen?" *The News Letter* of the Bureau of Educational Research, Ohio State University, 22:2 (February, 1957).

[22] *Ibid.,* p. 4.

[23] Ralph G. Nichols and Leonard A. Stevens, *Are You Listening?* (New York: McGraw-Hill Book Company, 1957).

Specific Activities for the Development of Listening

Two activities mentioned by numerous authorities that are of value in the development of good listening habits are the use of films and the use of oral reading. Both are of sufficient importance to warrant discussion here.

The Use of Films. Many writers recommend the discriminating use of films as a basis for the improvement of listening. The authors already have referred briefly to the role of films in teaching listening and have stressed the potentialities of approaches which utilize films and film-readers. The seeing of films may be combined with the use of film-readers and the hearing of scripts projected through the magnetic sound track or on tape. Films such as Arne Sucksdorff's *The Hunter and the Forest, Adventures of the Baby Fox,* and *A Tale of the Fiords* (distributed by Encyclopaedia Britannica Films) offer excellent opportunities for training in listening. Teachers' guides which give detailed suggestions for cultivating skill in listening and writing are provided for these films.

In using films, pupils should be encouraged to listen for various purposes and in different ways. At times it is appropriate for them to listen largely for pleasure, with little attention to organizing facts or ideas. At other times it is desirable to view a film in order to observe certain facts or note certain outcomes. On some occasions pupils should give special attention to the commentaries and examine their validity. Pupils should be encouraged also to attend to details, to note controversial items presented in certain films, and to observe the concepts introduced. When closed-circuit television is employed, it is highly desirable to prepare students for successful viewing by previous training or by guidance in listening to various types of subject matter.

Reading Aloud. Today more than ever before adults appear to be turning to oral reading with great frequency and enthusiasm. One finds examples of the enjoyment of listening to stories and poems read aloud among adults who are attending theaters devoted to the oral presentation of the works of Carl Sandburg, Edna St. Vincent Millay, George Bernard Shaw, and Charles Dickens.

Evidence of interest in reading aloud may be found, too, in accounts of parents reading aloud to children. Thus, in Gilbert Chapman's provocative article entitled *An Experiment in Reading,* we discover how the adults of a Tennessee village, by reading aloud to their children, inspired and fostered a love of good books.[24]

---
[24] Gilbert W. Chapman, "An Experiment in Reading," *Harper's Magazine,* 213:73–75 (December, 1956).

One of the objectives of a national committee on reading, of which Mr. Chapman was president, was to try to establish lifetime reading interests in children and to rekindle a love of reading among adults. The Committee was stimulated to undertake this enterprise by the realization that the United States, despite its high literacy rate, is nevertheless a nation with an extraordinarily low reading record. For example, in one study it was reported that although 55 per cent of the people in England read books regularly, only 17 per cent in the United States do so.

The Committee believed that reading can be both a challenge and a delight—provided appropriate books are available. Through its efforts, shelves of children's books to be read aloud were placed for ready access to the workers in the Yale and Towne plant in Gallatin, Tennessee. Forty-five children's books were included for the workers to take home to read aloud to their children. The idea gained popular acceptance, and the parents were soon enjoying with their children books such as *Katy-No-Pocket, 500 Hats of Bartholomew Cubbins,* and *Grimm's Fairy Tales.* Two months later the number of children's books was increased to seventy-four. Although there were no library cards to sign, not a single book disappeared from the stock of coveted volumes during the six-month period.

The results of this endeavor were widespread and varied. For one thing, the experiment demonstrated the value of oral reading as a way of engendering interest in books. For parents and children alike it was shown that reading need not be drudgery but instead can become an exciting, enjoyable experience, as well as a means of valuable learning.

We are slowly coming to recognize that oral reading is a necessary and indispensable part of a balanced reading program. Among its irreplaceable values are these:

1. The reading aloud of individual and group experience charts constitutes beginning reading. The experience chart is often made after a group has taken part in some activity such as a trip or an excursion, or a tour of the neighborhood. The teacher leads a discussion about the experience and offers guidance to make sure that the expression is simple and accurate. He records the story as it is told, either in manuscript writing or by use of a rubber-type printing press. Then the story is read aloud by the children.

2. Oral reading via the chart enables children to discover and demonstrate their knowledge of words derived from their own experience. The key words used in the stories are placed on cards which are rapidly displayed to encourage correct pronunciation and rapid recognition. The

card is employed too as a check on the accuracy of meanings attached to each word.

3. Oral reading continues to be a way of encouraging good speech habits and correcting defects in pronunciation as children mature. Thus the young pupil who reads aloud and then learns by heart jingles or rhymes may be led to overcome gradually his tendency to slur or mispronounce words. The rhymes of Dr. Seuss are particularly suitable for this purpose, as are other rhymes old and new. Accordingly, seven-year-old Bill, who showed marked irregularity in speech at first, was having a very profitable lesson in pronunciation as he happily read aloud jingles such as the following:

> There once was a cat and three kittens
> And all of the kittens had mittens
> They played with a mouse
> Who hid in the house
> In one of the kitten's red mittens.[25]

4. Checking on varied and incorrect speech habits may be effectively and helpfully done by listening to children read aloud. Although serious errors can be detected also by the use of objective tests, the important day-to-day progress and gradual improvement of each child can be best appraised and guided by the teacher in the classroom. Underlearned and incorrect habits in oral reading can be readily observed and appropriately treated.

5. Success in oral reading is often closely related to efficiency in reading silently, and like silent reading, oral reading should be stressed throughout the elementary school. Although the teacher should stress the significance of silent reading, he must not minimize the importance of oral reading throughout the course of a balanced reading program.

Although the uses of oral reading are many and its value unquestioned, the teacher should be especially careful not to use oral reading to the detriment of good listening. Virgil Herrick and Leland Jacobs emphasize the cautious use of oral reading:

> Listening to others read may be a rich, rewarding experience, or it may be a grave threat to intelligent listening. In many of our classes, we are asking children to listen to others read materials which they have already read silently. Since many of them know the content,

---

[25] Paul Witty, *Reading in Modern Education* (Boston: D. C. Heath and Company, 1949), p. 61.

they are bored when asked to listen; and not only do they not listen, but they often become behavior problems. The most natural thing in the world is for the child to close his ears in this situation . . .[26]

The judicious use of oral reading is vital. Especially in relation to the other language arts, oral reading, used wisely, can enhance a child's speaking, listening, and writing abilities.

WRITING AND READING

The foregoing values of oral reading will be appreciated by most teachers. Many of them will recognize, too, the fact that not merely is oral reading one phase of reading, but it is also one aspect of the language arts. They will grant further that the related and coordinated development of the varied aspects of the language arts is one objective of an effective program. For example, creative writing is intimately associated with reading. As children write and later read their compositions, the teacher may sense their feelings and discern their individual needs. Thus from the long serial story written by a boy and dedicated to "the three dogs I have loved best — one who died, one who was killed and one I wasn't allowed to keep," a teacher was able to learn much about the way one small boy really felt.

Similarly, a child who is unduly embarrassed or worried may reveal his feelings in a composition such as the following:

GIRAFFES
If I were a giraffe, I would not show myself to the people.
I would be ashamed of myself.
When I go to the zoo all the people laugh at the giraffes.
I wouldn't want the people to laugh at me.
I feel sorry for giraffes.

Sometimes a child's feeling about himself is relieved simply by writing and perhaps reading aloud this type of expression:

MONKEYS
A monkey is so black
At night I cannot see him
But I know a monkey can see
Such a white-headed me.

[26] Virgil E. Herrick and Leland B. Jacobs (editors), *Children and the Language Arts* (Englewood Cliffs, N. J.: Prentice-Hall, Inc., 1955), p. 160.

Among the most important functions of creative writing, shared through oral reading, is the pleasure this art affords. Can anyone question the genuine pleasure derived from this product of a fifth-grade child?

        GOING TO SLEEP
Mother says it's easy
Father says so too.
But I think that going to sleep
Is the hardest thing to do.

Sister says that counting sheep
Would be good for me;
But who wants to count old sheep
That you can't even see?

Mother says a glass of milk
Sends you right off to sleep.
But I don't think it's any better
Than counting dull old sheep.

I lie in bed just looking at the sky
And watch the moon go sailing by.
And sometimes when it's very late
The owls start a little chat.

And sometimes there's a lot of yowls
That's Rover chasing our old cat
It's nice but I've tried everything
From milk to counting sheep
It's no use, I'm giving up.
I just can't get to sleep.[27]

A combination of listening skills and creative writing skill is elicited by the use of a film such as Arne Sucksdorff's *The Hunter and the Forest*. On an experimental basis this film was shown in seventy-nine classrooms in forty schools located in thirty-four cities.[28] All grades were represented. The eight-minute motion picture was presented without narration or dialogue but with a musical score and some sound effects to accompany the appearance of birds and animals. At the begin-

---

[27] Several of the foregoing compositions were presented by Ethel E. Smith (Hoeber) in a Ph.D. dissertation on "Creative Writing," submitted at Northwestern University, 1943.

[28] Paul Witty, "The Use of Films in Stimulating Creative Expression and in Identifying Talented Pupils," *Elementary English*, 33:340–344 (October, 1956). See also Paul Witty and William Martin, "An Analysis of Children's Compositions Written in Response to a Film," *Elementary English*, 34:158–163 (March, 1957).

ning of the picture the subtitle, "A Story Without Words," provided an introduction to the pupils who were invited to write their own stories about the film. A film guide, developed for teachers, suggested related language experiences and some steps to be followed in eliciting genuine expression from children.

Over two thousand compositions written by children after viewing the film were evaluated according to the degree to which the writer reflected (a) genuine feeling; (b) sensitivity to the value of particular words, phrases, and larger units in expressing his reactions; (c) recognition of the film-maker's intent and the significance of symbolic presentations; and (d) correct and appropriate use of English. About 10 percent of the total number of compositions were judged to be outstanding and to suggest potential ability on the part of the writers. Not only were all pupils provided with an opportunity to express themselves in creative writing, but talent or giftedness in writing might be identified.

It can be said that all writing, creative or factual, is closely related to reading. Hildreth summarizes the relationship in this way:

> Writing reinforces word recognition and sentence sense. It increases awareness of the characteristic features of words.
> Writing is an aid to the pupil in building a sight vocabulary.
> Writing words from memory aids word recognition.
> The pupil writes reports of his reading.
> Writing is done in reading exercises.
> Vocabulary development, the study of word meanings, word building, and the use of the dictionary in writing are all aids to reading.
> The study of sentence structure and attention to grammar and punctuation in writing aid reading.
> The pupil tends not to use in writing words that are not in his reading vocabulary.
> The pupil writes reports about his reading, [and writes] notices about new books and other reading material.
> The pupil writes material to be read by himself and others in the class. What he writes is easy for him to read because it is in his own language, and consequently the text is meaningful to him.[29]

CONCLUDING STATEMENT

It is generally conceded today that the language arts—including speaking, reading, listening, and writing—have one goal in common: that of fostering clear communication. It has also been found that any one of these arts is usually developed more readily when reinforced by

---
[29] Gertrude H. Hildreth, *Child Growth Through Education* (New York: The Ronald Press Company, 1948), pp. 229–230.

the others. It is true that most children hear or listen to the speech of others before they themselves attempt to speak. Later in their development children are taught to read and write, but instruction in any one of the language arts need not be given in isolation. For example, studies have indicated that reading comprehension is enhanced through discussion of materials read, through dramatization, through sharing favored materials by reading them aloud, and through writing of personal reactions.

The unit of work or centers of interest in social studies and science offers an opportunity for language experiences and is frequently used by teachers at all levels of the school program. After pupils have engaged in activities through which they acquire information conducive to the development of concepts, writing activities provide a most effective method to determine the extent to which the learner has grown in the ability to think critically, to organize ideas, to pass judgment, to follow directions, to classify material, to show awareness of sequence, to draw conclusions, to make inferences, and to see relationships. In other words, writing and speaking activities are integral aspects of reading; it would be impractical, if not impossible, to isolate reading from writing and speaking.

It is evident that effective writing depends upon a number of factors. Two of the mechanical factors are (1) accurate spelling and (2) punctuation. Practice in these areas should be designed to foster growth in both reading and writing. Punctuation is particularly important in the interpretation of reading content, while spelling often becomes a determinant of what words will or will not be used by students in writing. When practice in these two areas is an isolated matter and scant attention is paid to their vital relation to effective writing as well as to comprehension in reading, the results are usually disappointing.

Dora Smith presents her point of view on the interdependence of the language arts as follows:

> Developing a program in the language arts today may be likened less to building a wall by carefully laying brick upon brick than to nurturing growth in a tree by enriching the soil, furnishing the proper environment, and judiciously pruning as certain branches get out of control. The problem is not so much one of looking at English and determining the order of topics to be studied as it is of looking at the learner and the society of which he is a part and aiding his growth both in and through the elements of reading, listening and expression necessary to effective living today.[30]

[30] Dora V. Smith, preface, in National Council of Teachers of English, *The English Language Arts* (New York: Appleton-Century-Crofts, 1952), p. v.

Selected References

Anderson, Paul S., *Language Skills in Elementary Education* (New York: The Macmillan Co., 1964).

Anderson, Verna Dieckman and others (editors), *Readings in the Language Arts* (New York: The Macmillan Co., 1964).

Bensen, Minnie P., *Kindergarten, Your Child's Big Step* (New York: E. P. Dutton & Co., Inc., 1959).

Burrows, Alvina Treut, *Teaching Children in the Middle Grades* (Boston: D. C. Heath and Co., 1952).

Burrows, Alvina Treut, Doris C. Jackson and Dorothy O. Sanders, *They All Want to Write,* 3rd ed. (New York: Holt, Rinehart & Winston, Inc., 1964).

Dawson, Mildred A., and Marion Zollinger, *Guiding Language Learning* (New York: Harcourt, Brace & World, Inc., 1957).

Greene, Harry A., and Walter T. Petty, *Developing Language Skills in the Elementary Schools,* 2nd ed. (Boston: Allyn and Bacon, Inc., 1963).

Hayakawa, Samuel I., *Language in Thought and Action* (New York: Harcourt, Brace & World, Inc., 1949).

Herrick, Virgil E., "Handwriting and Children's Writing," *Elementary English,* 37:248–258 (April, 1960).

Herrick, Virgil E., and Leland B. Jacobs (editors), *Children and the Language Arts* (Englewood Cliffs, N.J.: Prentice-Hall, Inc., 1955).

Keller, Paul W., "Major Findings in Listening in the Past Ten Years," *Journal of Communication,* 10:29–38 (March, 1960).

Lee, J. Murray and Dorris May Lee, *The Child and His Curriculum,* 3rd ed. (New York: Appleton-Century-Crofts, 1960).

MacCampbell, James C. (editor), *Readings in the Language Arts in the Elementary School* (Boston: D. C. Heath and Company, 1964).

Mearns, Hughes, *Creative Youth,* 2nd. ed. (New York: Dover Publications, Inc., 1958).

National Council of Teachers of English, *Language Arts for Today's Children* (New York: Appleton-Century-Crofts, 1954).

National Society for the Study of Education, *Teaching Language in the Elementary School* (M. R. Trabue, chairman), Forty-third Yearbook for the Study of Education, Part II (Chicago: University of Chicago Press, 1944).

Petty, Walter T., *The Language Arts in Elementary Schools* (Washington, D.C.: The Center for Applied Research in Education, 1962).

Rollins, Charlemae, "Story-Telling: Its Value and Importance," *Elementary English,* 34:164–166 (March, 1957).

Sawyer, Ruth, *The Way of the Storyteller* (New York: The Viking Press, Inc., 1942).

Schramm, Wilbur L., Jack Lyle and Edwin B. Parker, *Television in the Lives of Our Children* (Stanford, California: Stanford University Press, 1961).

Shane, Harold G., June Mulry, Mary Reddin, and Margaret Gillespie, *Improving Language Arts Instruction in the Elementary School* (Columbus, Ohio: Charles E. Merrill Books, Inc., 1962).

Smith, Dora V., "Learning to Listen, Listening to Learn in the Elementary School," *NEA Journal,* 47:100–101 (February, 1958).

Strickland, Ruth G., *The Language Arts in the Elementary School,* 2nd ed. (Boston: D. C. Heath and Company, 1957).

Tidyman, Willard F., and Marguerite Butterfield, 2nd ed. *Teaching the Language Arts* (New York: McGraw-Hill Book Company, 1959).

Tooze, Ruth, *Storytelling* (Englewood Cliffs, N. J.: Prentice-Hall, Inc., 1959).

Walter, Nina, *Let Them Write Poetry* (New York: Holt, Rinehart & Winston, Inc., 1962).

Witty, Paul A., *Reading in Modern Education* (Boston: D. C. Heath and Company, 1949).

Witty, Paul A., "Some Results of Twelve Yearly Studies of Televiewing," *Science Education,* 46:222–229 (April, 1962).

Witty, Paul A., "The Use of Films in Stimulating Creative Expression and in Identifying Talented Pupils," *Elementary English,* 33:340–344 (October, 1956).

Witty, Paul A., and William Martin, "An Analysis of Children's Compositions Written in Response to a Film," *Elementary English,* 34:158–163 (March, 1957).

Witty, Paul A., and Robert A. Sizemore, *Studies in Listening,* reprinted from *Elementary English,* vols. 35 and 36 (Champaign, Illinois: National Council of Teachers of English, 1958–1959).

9

READING INSTRUCTION IN THE PRIMARY GRADES

We have seen that, to appraise readiness, the teacher must ascertain each child's physical, mental, social, and educational status. Progress depends on the successful interaction of these factors in the cultivation of habits and skills in reading. In a developmental program, the skills are sequentially introduced, with greater emphasis given to certain ones at different times.

To promote continuous, successful accomplishment among pupils in the primary grades, the teacher must recognize the significance of the following procedures used in an experience chart–basal reader approach, which will be treated in the first part of this chapter: (a) studying children's interests and experiences; (b) using experience charts; (c) introducing pre-primer materials; (d) fostering word study and growth in vocabulary; (e) promoting auditory and visual perception; (f) fostering word analysis; (g) developing word, phrase, and sentence meanings; (h) encouraging reading for varied purposes; (i) using basal reading materials effectively; (j) developing and employing skills in silent and oral reading; (k) helping pupils acquire the ability to select source materials independently.

The student of reading should be aware of several new approaches in the teaching of reading that are variations within the structure of basal reading programs. The New Castle Plan or Film Approach, the Denver Approach, the Initial Teaching Alphabet Plan, and the Linguistic Approach are all regarded as programs in the teaching of reading. The characteristics and values of these approaches will be discussed in the second part of this chapter.

EXPERIENCE CHART—BASAL READING APPROACH

Studying Children's Interests and Experiences

Although there are several possible approaches in learning to read, one of the most practical procedures is the use of experience charts. But what experiences provide the best basis for the development of the experience chart? Experiences are extremely varied and may be direct (firsthand) or indirect, as in situations where films, television, or filmstrips are employed. We should recognize the importance of both types of experience. Although children do not have direct contact with objects in a TV program, their imagination permits an identification which often comes very close to a real experience for them.

The first-grade teacher who wishes to utilize effectively the background that children bring to the initial reading stage does well to discover the extent and nature of children's experiences. To achieve such an understanding, the use of an interest inventory will prove helpful. One inventory, part of which is designed especially for use with primary grade-children, contains questions related to the child's social relationships and experiences.[1] Some of the questions are concerned with matters of personal adjustment:

> If you could have three wishes that might come true, what would be your first wish? second wish? third wish?
> Are you afraid of many things? Name some of the things you fear.
> Would you rather play by yourself or with other children?

Additional questions relate to activities such as collecting, making trips, and visiting nearby places of interest, such as a farm or a zoo. Inquiries pertain also to books and stories:

> Do you have storybooks that you can read yourself? How many books do you have of your own? Name some. What other books would you like to own?

Still other questions deal with the amount and nature of televiewing, favorite radio programs, and movie preferences.

This approach is directed toward ascertaining the nature and extent of children's experience. The use of an interest inventory may prove helpful in making experience charts and in guiding and motivating children's reading. This is, of course, only one approach to the study of interests. Information about interests may be obtained also through

[1] Paul A. Witty, *Reading in Modern Education* (Boston: D. C. Heath and Company, 1949). See also Chapter 3 for a more detailed discussion of interests.

the use of other techniques, such as the anecdotal record and the questionnaire.

The Use of Experience Charts

Use of the inventory will give the teacher the basis for a better understanding of the strong interests of his group. After discussion of certain interests an experience chart may be made, centering around the group or individual experiences entered on the inventory. Records may be made also of a class visit to a farm, a zoo, or an airport. The class discusses the visit and composes a story, which the teacher prints. In such cases the teacher helps the children formulate simple sentences setting forth the essential features of their experience. This account is often recorded by the teacher in manuscript writing, or the story may be transferred to oak-tag (twenty-four by thirty-six inches) and pictures added. The following account illustrates how one teacher developed such a chart:[2]

> Before the teacher called the reading group, the children had been at work on various activities. Some were working in the garden out of doors; others had been painting the playhouse. A group of girls was making new curtains for the house, and still another group was just playing in the house.
> The teacher gathered a small group around her. After all were sitting comfortably, the following conversation developed:
>
> TEACHER: Do you think we could tell a story about the interesting things we have done today?
> CHILDREN: Yes.
> TEACHER: What could our story be about?
> CHILD: The family who lived in our playhouse today.
> CHILD: Our home.
> CHILD: Our garden.
> TEACHER: Yes, all those would be interesting. Did anything happen today that has not happened before? Do you remember our surprise today?
> CHILD: Oh, yes.
> CHILD: The seeds are coming up.
> CHILD: I saw seeds in our garden.
> CHILD: Seeds.
> CHILD: Seeds are growing in our garden.
> TEACHER: Do you think we could tell an interesting story about what has happened in our garden?

[2] Lillian A. Lamoreaux and Dorris M. Lee, *Learning to Read Through Experience* (New York: Appleton-Century-Crofts, 1943), pp. 132–136.

>(*All the children agreed. Then, following a period of free discussion about the garden . . .*)

CHILD: We can call our story "Our Surprise."
CHILD: I know a story. We can say, "Our seeds are up."
TEACHER: Do you all think "Our Surprise" is a good name for our story? (*Teacher wrote on the board:* "OUR SURPRISE")
CHILD: We need to say, "We have a garden."
TEACHER: All right. How many think that is a good way to begin our story?

>(*All agreed. Teacher wrote on the board under the title:* "We have a garden.")

TEACHER: What else should we put in the story?
CHILD: We should tell where the garden is.
CHILD: We should tell how we made our garden.
CHILD: We should tell about watering.
TEACHER: These are good suggestions. How would you like to tell where the garden is, Romero?
ROMERO: (*Shyly pointing*) It is out there.
TEACHER: Yes, it is. You can tell us where our garden is, Ann.
ANN: Our garden is in our school yard.
TEACHER: Do you like Ann's sentence, Romero? Is that the way you meant to say it?
ROMERO: (*Nodded* "yes")
TEACHER: (*Teacher wrote Ann's sentence under the first one.*) Let us read the sentence. You look while I read it to you. (*The teacher ran her hand under Ann's sentence and read*):

We have a garden.
Our garden is
in our school yard.

CHILD: We left out seeds. We must say, "We planted seeds in our garden." (*Some thought they should tell about digging and making rows. After discussion they agreed to say:*)

We made five rows
in our garden.

CHILD: Now we can say, "We planted seeds."
TEACHER: Do you all agree? Do you think we should tell where we planted the seeds?
CHILD: In the garden.
CHILD: We planted seeds in the rows.
TEACHER: How many like John's sentence, "We planted seeds in the rows"?
CHILD: It is all the same. The rows are in the garden.

TEACHER: That is right. Now let us read our story again.
(*Teacher read, running her hand under each line from left to right under the sentence*):

Our Surprise
We have a garden.
Our garden is in
our school yard.
We made five rows
in our garden.
We planted seeds
in the rows.

TEACHER: Now the surprise. Who wants to tell us about it?
CHILD: The seeds are up.
CHILD: Two little seeds are up.
TEACHER: Which sentence shall we use? They are just alike except that Sue told us how many seeds are up.
CHILD: Let's use Sue's sentence.
TEACHER: (*Wrote*): Two little seeds are up. Now who would like to show us where you will begin and how you will read the story? Slide your hand under the sentence as I did.
(*Child followed directions, running hand from left to right under each sentence.*)
CHILD: I can read it.
TEACHER: Let us all read it softly together while I move my hand.

Our Surprise
We have a garden.
Our garden is in
our school yard.
We made five rows
in our garden.
We planted seeds
in the rows.
Two little seeds
are up.

Some teachers use filmstrips to record pleasant and significant experiences of their pupils. For example, one teacher photographed the activities of his first-grade group during the interval in which the pupils participated in caring for an animal that was brought to school. The descriptive phrases and sentences of the children were placed in proper order under each picture and the continuous filmstrip constructed. The showing of this filmstrip, which depicted the children's own activities, made it possible for them to master a stock of familiar words and to find great pleasure and success in reading their own compositions. Similarly, other teachers are assembling pictures or actual photographs to furnish a basis for developing experience charts.

Such informal reading experiences serve to:

1. Motivate interest in reading
2. Provide a thoughtful approach to reading
3. Introduce and develop a new vocabulary with appropriate and clear concepts
4. Stimulate group participation
5. Develop word grouping, accompanied by phrase and sentence recognition

In such endeavor the teacher should encourage children to:

1. Compose short simple sentences
2. Use accepted manuscript form
3. Space the words and phrases uniformly, leaving somewhat larger spaces between phrases
4. Avoid breaking words or phrases at the end of the line
5. Involve all the students—individually and in groups
6. Foster word, phrase, and sentence recognition

Introducing the Pre-primer

Experience charts not only provide interesting reading material but, more than that, they also help greatly in the development of a sight vocabulary. Some authorities believe that, after 50 to 80 words are learned from experience charts, silent reading of pre-primers and short stories may be introduced advantageously. The selection of the first pre-primer is most important. Often an attitude toward reading is formulated at this time which tends to persist throughout the school year or indeed throughout the pupil's school life. The initial experience with pre-primers should be interesting and enjoyable and should provide the child with a feeling of success and achievement. The vocabulary of the pre-primer should be sufficiently large to present a lively story which will challenge the children. The teacher will be helped in making the best selection if he checks his choice against the following criteria:

1. The content must be interesting and close to children's firsthand experience.
2. The concepts should be within the realm of the understanding of children.
3. The stories should encourage sequential thinking.
4. Words and sentence structure should be as closely related to natural conversation as possible.

5. Repetitions of new words should be frequent enough to promote retention.
6. The illustrations should be attractive and should provide cues to the verbal content.

Pre-primers can make a worthwhile contribution to the child's development. In addition to the story they contain vivid illustrations which help the pupil obtain the meaning of the story; they foster interest in books through the presentation of familiar incidents or activities in attractive story form; they extend and enrich experience; and they provide the basis for an orderly introduction of vocabulary. The guides and practice materials accompanying the pre-primers contain suggestions and exercises to develop skills in phonics and word analysis. They should be used judiciously, in accord with individual and group needs.

In addition to the experience provided by appropriate pre-primers, two further types of activity need to be stressed to develop clear concepts and promote rapid growth in reading: (1) continued and varied firsthand experience—e.g., games, trips, caring for animals, etc. and (2) wide use of supplementary readers and picture books. Children's general interest in animal stories, for example, should be satisfied first through direct experience in observing animals. Supplementary pre-primers and some trade books contain animal stories of home and school life—topics of general appeal to primary children. Not only should pre-primers and other books contain stories close to children's own first-hand experience, but the value of imaginative tales should not be overlooked. Through such books children enjoy the world of fantasy.

There should be books of widely varying difficulty in the classroom in order to meet the individual differences of pupils. A general principle that has often been stated is that books for independent reading should be at an easier level than the book from which children are being instructed. However, the vocabulary in some books may be somewhat above children's instructional level because the brighter children can profit from reading these more challenging volumes, in which they learn to derive the meaning from context or from picture clues. If the teacher reads such a story aloud to the class, pupils will often attempt to read the book themselves, applying skills they have already acquired. The significant point of having a variety of books available is that books are needed to reinforce words, develop concepts, and foster interest for children at different levels of development.

Fostering Word Study and Growth in Vocabulary

An immediate reading problem for the first-grade teacher is to assure the retention of the reading vocabulary. Anyone who has attempted to learn a foreign language with its unfamiliar symbols will appreciate the difficulties involved in learning and retaining such associations. The first-grade child usually needs help to assure the retention of his sight vocabulary. The teacher may profitably utilize some of the following approaches to help him:

1. Match words on cards with words on a chart or on the chalkboard
2. Frame phrases or sentences which answer questions
3. Point to the picture which corresponds to a sentence
4. Find a word in the book or on the board called by another student or the teacher
5. Locate repetitions of words, phrases, or sentences
6. Re-create the story from word and phrase cards
7. Use the vocabulary to construct new stories.

After the child has developed word analysis skills, he will be able to attack new words without much help, but he will continue to need to review words in order to insure retention. The development of word-analysis skills involves a number of factors: auditory and visual perception and discrimination, recognition of word parts, and knowledge of principles governing structural and phonetic analysis.

Promoting Auditory Perceptions

Most boys and girls who attended a kindergarten before entering the first grade have played games in which they imitated sounds of animals, machines, the wind, etc. This background is of value for the first-grade teacher, who may build auditory discrimination on such experiences. Soon after children enter the first grade, they may be introduced to games and appropriate exercises to promote skill in auditory perception and discrimination. Games such as the following may be employed:

1. The sounds made by dogs, cats, cows, bees, ducks, and horses may be simulated and repeated by the children to improve the ability to distinguish differences in sounds. If this exercise is introduced as a game, interest may be heightened. Children almost invariably find pleasure in simple games of this type; moreover, such games enable the teacher to identify children whose auditory acuity requires attention.

2. A group of words all but one of which begin with a certain sound may be pronounced by the teacher. The pupils may be asked to clap when the word beginning with a different sound is heard. After skill in recognizing initial sounds has been developed, a similar game may be introduced in which words ending with the same sound are employed.
3. Attention may be directed to the beginning sound of a word such as *cat*. Then the pupils may be asked to name other words that start with the same sound.
4. Exercises similar to those described in 2 and 3 above may be employed to help children recognize common initial speech sounds, such as *wh,* *th,* and *sh.*
5. Practice in hearing and recognizing rhyming words when they are presented orally fosters the ability to recognize likenesses in sound. After the meaning of *rhyme* has been explained, the pupils may be asked to name the words that rhyme in a list of words pronounced by the teacher, or in familiar rhymes and jingles such as those found in *Mother Goose.*

Many authorities have emphasized the importance of auditory ability in learning to read. In beginning reading the importance of knowledge of the various phonemes and ability to discriminate among them appears to be established. Jeanne Chall and others have measured another auditory factor and its relationship to success in reading—auditory blending. Auditory blending develops a child's ability to blend phonemes contained in a word into words. The investigators found that auditory blending ability is "positively correlated with oral and silent reading ability through the fourth grade."[3] One can conclude from the opinion of authorities and results of investigations that the development of auditory abilities of children must include: (1) hearing likenesses and differences of separate sounds, and (2) synthesizing separate sounds heard into words.

Improving Visual Perception

Practice to improve visual perception and discrimination should accompany an ear-training program. Accurate visual recognition is fostered through attention first to the total form of words, and later to details such as capital letters and inflectional endings. The following exercises are helpful in promoting word recognition in the beginning stage of reading:

---

[3] Jeanne Chall, Florence G. Roswell, and Susan Hahn Blumenthal, "Auditory Blending Ability: A Factor in Success in Beginning Reading," *Reading Teacher,* 17:113–118 (November, 1963).

1. The length of words should be noted. For example: *but* is short, *balloon* is long.
2. Differences in the configuration of words of the same length should be stressed. The words *suddenly* and *suitcase* are the same in length and begin with the same letter, but their configurations are significantly different.
3. Words of similar length and form may be compared in order to provide practice in visual discrimination. Lists of words may be selected from the children's textbook, placed on the chalkboard, and compared for appearance and for meaning.
4. Attention may be directed to the difference in the appearance of words beginning with capital and small letters. Two columns of words may be written on the chalkboard with the words capitalized in one column and with the same words, not capitalized and in mixed order, in the other column. The children may then be asked to draw lines between two words that say the same thing.
5. Differences should be observed in the singular and plural forms of words written on the chalkboard, as *balloon, balloons, hat, hats.*
6. Practice may be given in recognizing the root form of words to which *ed* or *ing* has been added. The derived form may be written on the chalkboard, and the children may be asked to make another word by erasing a part of it. Or the basic form may be given and pupils may be asked to build new words by adding suffixes.
7. Exercises to foster the recognition of rhyming words in jingles or in lists of words may be introduced.
8. Attention may be called to the two little words which make up a compound word, as *sunshine, sidewalk.*

Thus we have seen how children are exposed to sight words, auditory perception, and visual perception as the basis for a word-analysis program. When children have developed a considerable degree of auditory and visual perception, they are prepared for exercises in word analysis.

Developing Word-Analysis Skills

Some of the current basal reading programs develop auditory and visual perception in readiness work, begin reading by introducing 50–100 sight words, then begin word-attack skills through the development of auditory-visual perception of initial consonants in the first grade. For many years some authorities believed that instruction in phonics should be delayed until the second grade because a mental age of seven years was thought desirable if pupils were to apply principles of phonics successfully. More recent studies such as the Denver Program and the use of the Initial Teaching Alphabet, which will be discussed later in this chapter, lead one to question these earlier assumptions. Moreover,

Albert Harris feels that many first-graders will succeed in phonics,[4] and Paul McKee suggests that as soon as three or four words containing a common phonic element are learned, the common element may be stressed.[5] Similarly, A. F. Watts states that when the normal six-and-a-half-year-old child has learned from 100 to 200 sight words, he is ready for phonics.[6]

With due regard for individual differences in readiness, practice should be given in both auditory and visual perception in order to increase pupil skill in attacking new words. Once a child can hear likenesses and differences among sounds in words, can see likenesses and differences among words, and has learned a basic stock of sight words, he is ready for the word-analysis program. Major principles in a word-analysis program are:

1. Auditory-visual perception of consonants in initial, medial, and final position of words.
2. Auditory-visual perception of long and short vowel sounds; auditory-visual perception of vowels followed by *r*.
3. Auditory-visual perception of digraphs and diphthongs.
4. Adding endings to words that do not involve changes of the base word.
5. Adding endings to words that involve changes in the base word before adding endings:[7]
    (a) A word ending in *y* after a consonant usually changes the *y* to *i* before adding an ending, except when the ending begins with *i* (*cry, cried, crying*).
    (b) A one-syllable word ending in a single consonant preceded by a short vowel usually doubles the consonant before adding an ending that begins with a vowel (*hot, hotter, hottest*).
    (c) Words of more than one syllable ending in a single consonant usually double the final consonant if the accent is on the last syllable (*begin, beginning, travel, traveled*).
    (d) A word ending in silent *e* usually drops the *e* when adding an ending that begins with a vowel.
6. *Contractions and the apostrophe as an indication of letters left out.* These should be explained when they occur. Children may be asked to name the two words in a contraction, or to make a contraction of two given words.

[4] Albert J. Harris, *How to Increase Reading Ability,* 4th ed. (New York: David McKay Co., Inc., 1961), p. 329.
[5] Paul McKee, *The Teaching of Reading in the Elementary School* (Boston: Houghton Mifflin Co., 1948), p. 200.
[6] A. F. Watts, *The Language and Mental Development of Children* (London: George G. Harrap & Co., Ltd., 1946), p. 96.
[7] Although the generalizations are presented here for the benefit of the teacher, children may develop their own generalizations to insure optimum learning.

7. *Prefixes and suffixes.* To aid recognition, the children may be asked to underline the root form to which a syllable such as *a* or *un* has been prefixed or a suffix such as *y, ly, ful,* or *ness* has been added. Practice in building new words by the addition of prefixes and suffixes should also be provided.
8. *Alphabetizing and syllabication.* The children should prepare for efficient use of dictionaries and other reference materials. Preliminary steps may be taken by providing practice (1) in arranging words in alphabetical order and (2) in recognizing syllables in words both by sound and by sight.

Only the major principles have been outlined above, since most manuals describe the skills, development program in detail. It has been noted by Theodore Clymer, however, that some skills that are developed have little utility. In his study he used four reading series and found that 121 different generalizations were developed. An arbitrary selection of 45 generalizations revealed that only nine generalizations had 100 percent utility:

1. When *c* and *h* are next to each other, they make one sound.
2. When the letter *c* is followed by *o* or *a* the sound of *k* is likely to be heard.
3. When *ght* is seen in a word, *gh* is silent.
4. When a word begins wih *kn,* the *k* is silent.
5. When a word begins with *wr,* the *w* is silent.
6. When a word ends in *ck,* it has the last sound as in *look.*
7. When *ture* is the last syllable in a word, it is unaccented.
8. When *tion* is the last syllable in a word, it is unaccented.
9. When the first vowel element in a word is followed by *th, ch,* or *sh,* these symbols are not broken when the word is divided into syllables and may go with either the first or second syllable.[8]

Similarly, Clymer found that thirteen generalizations had less than 50 percent utility. For example, the generalization that when two vowels occur together the first is long and the second silent was true for only 45 percent of the 2600 words that contained two vowels together from the composite list of words from the four basal series used in the study.[9]

The implication of the study cited above is that we must scrutinize the skills taught in a word-identification program in terms of their usefulness to pupils. Moreover, we must also look closely at the methods used to develop useful skills. It has been recognized that the skills-

[8] Theodore Clymer, "The Utility of Phonic Generalization in the Primary Grades," *Reading Teacher,* 16:252–258 (January, 1963).
[9] *Ibid.*

development program in word identification is a vital part of teaching children to read. We must conclude, however, that further study is needed to determine the most useful skills and the methods in teaching them effectively.

Developing Word, Phrase, and Sentence Meanings

Word meanings.—Skill in analyzing words and skill in getting their meanings are both essential and are related phases of learning to read. If children do not acquire correct meanings for words, analytical skills may be fruitless. Usually the first words learned in the classroom have concrete referents in the forms of objects or pictures. Frequently action words can be demonstrated to clarify meanings. But most words have many meanings, and children need experience in finding these different meanings—beginning with the most common meanings within children's experience and gradually expanding and refining meaning as concept development proceeds.

Many words offer difficulty because there are no objects to which they refer. They should be introduced and taught with extreme care. *Over, under, down, up, here, there* are examples of such words which frequently confuse the beginner. They may be written on the chalkboard and used in as many different ways as the children can suggest. For example:

> The airplane flew *over* the field.
> The rain is *over*.
> The car ran *over* the boy's hat.
> John read the story *over* and *over*.

Pictures provide an excellent means for clarifying and enriching the concepts for some familiar words which have many meanings. Characteristic qualities that contribute to understanding the full meaning of the word may be brought out by a discussion of photographs or pictures of, for example, different kinds of *dogs, houses,* or *chairs.*

Association by classification will also extend meaning. Words may be grouped under such headings as:

THINGS WE DO	THINGS WE WEAR	THINGS WE EAT
play	coat	cake
work	hat	sandwiches
run	socks	peaches
ride	bathing suit	meat

Relationships between words may be clarified by the use of exercises involving the association of one word with another word with which it obviously belongs. Children may be asked to draw a line from a word in one column to a related word in a second column, such as:

        pig   eat
        truck   drink
        food   drive
        water   squeal

The same type of exercise may serve to clarify further relationships between words. Certain words may be written in one column and words that mean the same thing in another, with the instruction to draw a line connecting the two words that mean the same or almost the same. For example:

        little   sea
        boat   car
        ocean   small
        automobile   ship

Similarly, a group of words may be written in one column and their opposites in another, and the children asked to draw lines connecting the words that are opposite in meaning, as:

        big   up
        black   little
        yes   white
        down   no

Phrase recognition.—The recognition of phrases as thought units is another aspect of meaningful reading. Although this skill, sometimes overstressed, should be given only its necessary and appropriate share of attention, phrase recognition may be improved by using exercises such as the following:

1. Titles for stories and pictures may be written on the chalkboard and their suitability discussed; then pupils may be asked to suggest other phrases that would make equally appropriate titles.
2. The class may be directed to locate in their books certain phrases which are written on the chalkboard; and the children may be asked to find other phrases that answer questions.
3. Phrases that have an unusual or, perhaps, colloquial connotation may be written on the chalkboard and their meaning discussed; for example, *keep an eye on*. These phrases may be used in sentences, and substitute expressions found for them.

4. A column of phrases may be written on the chalkboard opposite the sentences in which they appear, and the children may be asked to find the same phrases in the sentences and underline them.
5. Another exercise, similar to 4, may be devised in which the phrases in the column are arranged in mixed order. The children should be asked to draw a line from each sentence to the phrase which it contains.
6. Phrases may be written in one column on the chalkboard and words or other phrases that mean the same in another column. Children may be asked to draw lines connecting two items that have the same meaning.
7. Pupils may be asked to locate in their books sentences that contain given phrases.
8. A series of two phrases which, together, make a sentence may be written on the chalkboard in two columns. Different children may then be asked to draw a line from each phrase at the left to the one at the right with which it belongs in a meaningful sentence. The two phrases that belong together should not be placed directly opposite each other.

Sentence meaning.—In order to improve pupils' ability to obtain accurate meaning from sentences, and to recognize them quickly as units of thought, the following exercises are suggested:

1. Children may be asked to relate in complete sentences some interesting experience they have enjoyed together. One child may be called upon to give a sentence and others may add sentences until the experience has been fully related. The sentences may be written on the chalkboard, arranged in the most appropriate order, and read aloud.
2. Questions may be asked by the teacher which can be answered by a phrase or by a sentence. The answers, consisting of phrases and sentences, may be written on the chalkboard by the teacher. The pupils may then be asked to find the sentences and phrases and read them aloud.
3. Sentences which are found in the textbooks may be written on the chalkboard by the teacher. The pupils may then be asked to locate each sentence in their books.
4. The teacher or a pupil may ask questions that can be answered by sentences to be found in the textbook. Other pupils may then be asked to locate in their books sentences that answer the questions.
5. The children may be asked to find a sentence in their books that would make a good title for a story or a picture.
6. The pupils may be encouraged to make up sentences that describe various pictures in their books.
7. The children may be requested to arrange a group of sentences which are presented out of sequence in the order necessary to por-

tray the way events in an episode took place in the story in their books.
8. The teacher may place on the chalkboard several sentences in which the words are not arranged in their correct order. The pupils should be asked to rearrange the words so as to make meaningful sentences.
9. The children's attention may be directed to certain sentences in their textbooks. A pupil may be asked to read each sentence aloud. Then the other children may be asked to make up different sentences which say the same thing as the sentence in the book. Each new sentence should be placed on the chalkboard to be read aloud by different pupils.

Although the foregoing exercises for studying words, phrases, and sentences are recommended for promoting growth in reading, the skills so developed must be considered secondary to the broader and more significant function of reading, namely, to obtain appropriate meanings from reading materials presented in whole units, episodes, or stories. Properly stressed in this larger setting, these exercises have value and significance.

Reading for Different Purposes

Consistent with the developmental reading philosophy is the idea of making reading an experience which will enable children to obtain various kinds of information needed in diverse situations. As they develop reading skills, they should be using these skills for functional as well as recreational purposes.

Reading in light of a purpose is a much-needed experience. When a child reads for the purpose of acquiring information, answering questions, or following simple directions, he is putting his reading skills to immediate use. Reading becomes a tool by which the specific purpose is realized. A remarkable characteristic of learning is that as children use reading skills to achieve specific purposes, they usually attain not only the purpose but also, in the process, improvement in reading skills. Learning by use or application is basic to reading growth.

Another significant form of reading is primarily to obtain pleasure or recreation through reading. To achieve this purpose it is desirable to provide materials that are somewhat easier to read than those in the text and related materials. It is then possible for the pupil to experience success in reading a story without the frustration of encountering too many unknown words and unfamiliar concepts. His goal is to enjoy the sounds of words, story themes, meaningful pictures. To meet individual differences, the primary-grade teacher will supply books from pre-primer level for the slow pupil, to levels two or three years in advance of the grade for the accelerated child. At times, the teacher will encourage self-selection of materials by the children; at other times he will find it desirable to guide the children in selecting books of appropriate difficulty to satisfy their interests. It is rewarding to stimulate interest by posting attractive book covers, introducing discussion of colorful characters that appear in books, encouraging children to tell stories they have read, and having them read aloud portions of well-liked books. The teacher should be acquainted with children's literature including series and trade books of many kinds. Almost all young children will enjoy the simple *Walt Disney Story Books,* the *True Books, The Little Owl Stories,* and the *I Want to Be* series. For more advanced readers the *First Books* are suitable. Although certain time-honored favorites continue to attract pupils today, children's books appear each year which rightly become popular. Hence, the teacher should examine new books, or reviews of them in periodicals such as *Junior Libraries, Childhood Education, Elementary English,* and the *Horn Book.* The teacher should strive not only to provide books to challenge the superior child but also to meet the needs of the slower pupil. Very simple primer materials, such as *Peanuts the Pony, Frisky the Goat,* and stories such as Hall's *Watch the Puppy Grow,* Dr. Seuss's *The Cat and the Hat,* and McCloskey's *Make Way for Ducklings* are examples of books which contain a low vocabulary load, simple sentences, and stories of high interest. Simply written stories appearing in magazines such as *Highlights for Children, Jack and Jill,* and *Humpty Dumpty* will enrich the program. The use of *My Weekly Reader* will also provide extension and application of reading skills.

Using Basal Materials Effectively

As in the selection of pre-primers, the teacher should seek to obtain primers and first, second, and third readers that contain varied materials including:

1. Stories written in a natural, interesting manner presenting a wide assortment of children's literature of varied difficulty.
2. Stories which challenge the imagination of the children and lead to a deeper appreciation of books as sources of pleasure.
3. Stories which will satisfy the characteristic needs of primary children.
4. Stories related to specific but varied areas of interest of the class.
5. Stories employing suitable and varied vocabularies.

6. Stories having illustrations which heighten interest but do not disclose outcomes.
7. Stories of increasing length so that children may develop attention and interest spans.
8. Stories of increasing difficulty so that children will grow in reading skills.
9. Stories that deal with topics found in the content areas.

When a teacher selects a second or third reader, he will want to choose a book which contains familiar words and concepts. Transition of children from one book to another should be accompanied by encouragement which will make them confident of success in further reading. Emphasis may be placed on the common vocabulary which is often a major factor in the ease with which children adjust to new books.

Teachers must be cognizant of the fact that basal reading materials are the vehicles by which many reading skills are introduced and practiced. The most important aspects of basal reading materials are that they develop skills sequentially, control vocabulary, promote language growth, and offer practical aids and suggestions through the teachers' manuals. The basal reading program, then, by its very nature, is only one aspect of a school's total reading program.

Developing Skills in Silent and Oral Reading

Silent reading.—Children need much practice to develop effective skills in silent reading. An important goal of silent reading is to foster the understanding of thought units. Children should be encouraged to recognize continuity, sequence, cause-and-effect relationships, and internal consistency of story presentation. Thought units should increase in length and complexity with progressively more advanced books.

As children advance in school, they must rely more and more on independent study; and they must learn, beginning in the primary grades, to adjust their rates of reading to different purposes. They must learn to scan pages for quick location of certain facts, to read slowly to recognize and absorb details, and to read quickly to find main ideas, note sequence, or predict outcomes.

Occasionally a child will read silently, using the lip and throat movements common to oral reading. Corrections sometimes need to be made. In such cases children should be provided with a wealth of easy materials and encouraged to read larger and larger units at a glance. Preventing lip movement by placing a finger over the lips may sometimes be helpful.

The main objective of reading instruction in the primary grades is the development of competency in silent reading. It is through efficient silent reading that an individual gains the greatest number of ideas and the most understanding. Only by knowing what he reads can one share his ideas with others through, for example, oral reading.

Oral reading.—First experiences in oral reading may consist merely of reading words or phrases found in an experience chart. The children may have memorized the words after hearing the teacher read them, but they may not have had sufficient experience in associating sounds with words to read them aloud themselves. They must have practice in learning words presented orally in order to be able to differentiate sounds and word parts, but they need also to be able to read the words themselves.

Throughout the developmental reading program children should read orally and be led gradually to improve and apply their skills. They need to read not only fluently but with proper phrasing and inflection. Often the teacher can use actual experiences to demonstrate how we say certain things under specific conditions. Thus, if a child is frightened, the word "Oh!" has quite a different inflection from that when he says "Oh!" in joy over receiving a gift. Children should learn to appreciate the fact that oral reading is often most effective and enjoyable when it approximates real conversation. Further, because English is idiomatic, children should be helped to see that printed words may be expressions similar to or identical with conversational expressions. Emphasis on this relationship may help children appreciate a common purpose of both oral and written expression, namely, to promote clear communication.

Oral reading provides many opportunities for sharing experiences, proving points, supplying information, answering questions, and giving pleasure to the class. The reading of poetry which contains melodious repetitions will be enjoyed and will provide a basis for later interest in poetic presentations of various kinds.

Helping Pupils Select Source Materials Independently

Primary children should learn some basic library skills which will increase their independence in selecting books and heighten their ability to find books according to different purposes and interests. Following are some skills which are desirable for primary children to acquire:

1. Locating books, pamphlets, and magazines in the library
2. Withdrawing and returning books in the room, school, or public library

3. Caring for books
4. Repairing books
5. Using book lists
6. Learning library arrangement
7. Learning how to use a card index
8. Learning desirable library behavior

The school librarian usually encourages primary classes to visit the library so that library facilities and procedures may be presented and discussed. At this time the librarian may help the children develop competency and satisfaction in using the resources of the library.

Grouping Children for Instruction

Today there is considerable controversy concerning the use of group or individual methods in reading instruction. Results from research seem to warrant the use of both group and individual procedures, as well as flexible grouping plans. In some classrooms children are divided into groups and given instruction in skills according to their varied needs. Such a practice necessitates the use of skill-building materials on different levels of difficulty. Pupils are also grouped, from time to time, for reading according to interests or topics, these groups being flexible; their memberships may be readily altered as individual differences transpire. In this type of grouping, an assortment of reading materials of different kinds on varied levels of difficulty is essential.

Margaret McKim, recognizing the difficulty of assessing the relative values of particular classroom organizations or groupings for reading, makes the following points:

> Regardless of the organizational pattern for reading instruction, established practices can be identified in the reports of programs which have produced good results. These, if practiced consistently, seem likely to lead to favorable pupil development *in* reading and *through* the process of learning to read.
> 1. *Instruction must be paced to the developmental pattern of the individual.* Whatever the classroom organization, there must be allowance for the fact that individuals grow at different rates. Every teacher should be prepared to work at several grade levels and be provided with teaching aids selected accordingly.
> 2. *Instruction must focus upon the specific strengths and weaknesses of individuals.* Regarding a series of readers and workbooks as "basic" in the sense that they provide a guarantee that a child who works through them sequentially will automatically learn all the reading skills he needs seems certain to result in ineffective learning. Only intelligent decisions by the teacher regarding needed new experiences will guarantee maximum growth.

3. *Instructional time with the teacher must focus on developing many types of skills.* Any stereotyped round-robin oral reading; detailed discussion of a story, page by page; routine assignment of questions for written answers; routine use of workbooks; an individualized session spent in the same way each time with the teacher—will fail to achieve maximum growth. Teachers must be alert to the special possibilities in each new situation and skilled in providing new and challenging reading problems.
4. *Increased independence in reading must be capitalized upon.* Pupils must be given the feeling of competence that comes with independence. Procedures which give help with problems that pupils are capable of solving for themselves restrict reading growth, threaten feelings of competence, and dampen interest and zeal to learn. Open to question are such practices as telling pupils new words when they are capable of figuring them out, reading a story page by page when pupils are capable of grasping it as a whole, and devoting time to routine work-type activities when pupils are capable of extensive reference and recreational reading.
5. *Teacher leadership should be such that children grow in understanding their own reading skills.* Discussions of errors, assignments of special practice activities and introductions of new ways of working should be planned so that the child understands the nature of the skill he needs and the points at which to focus his attention as he practices.[10]

NEW APPROACHES TO THE TEACHING OF READING

In recent years many approaches to the teaching of reading have been proposed. Four of these approaches will be described briefly: The New Castle Approach, the Denver Plan, the Initial Teaching Alphabet Method, and the Linguistic Approach. It should be recognized that these approaches are sincere attempts to improve reading instruction.

The New Castle Plan

The New Castle Plan teaches reading in the primary grades through the use of filmstrips that accompany reading texts. One frame in the filmstrip accompanies each page of the text. Textfilm manuals are provided for the teacher. An example of the procedures for a typical lesson is as follows:

[10] Margaret G. McKim, "Reading in the Primary Grades," in Paul Witty (chairman), *Development In and Through Reading, Part I,* Sixtieth Yearbook of the National Society for the Study of Education (Chicago: University of Chicago Press, 1961), pp. 281–282.

The teaching procedure varies according to the type of lesson being presented. There are lessons in skills, phonics, vocabulary, paragraph reading, etc. The one described here is the beginning page of a story at the primer level. . . .

The children prepare for the reading class. One adjusts the screen; another turns on the projector; a third turns off the room lights. Now the teacher has the entire lesson before the class in vivid color and adequate size (the image is four feet wide and three feet high). Teacher and pupils (every child in the class) will spend a delightful forty-five minutes with this image, studying and talking about the animals, examining the new words, and reading the story. . . .

The lesson begins as the teacher initiates the carrying out of various suggestions contained in the textfilm manual. She will talk about the picture first. What are the animals the children see? Who can point to each one? These activities promote class interest and opportunities for inviting the less aggressive children to go to the screen where they lead the discussion.

Then attention is given to the story title. What do the three words say? Why are they at the top of the page (or frame)? What does the word *title* mean? Why do we have titles? How many bears are there? In the title who can find and point to a word that tells how many bears there are? At this point the word *three* is also thoroughly examined phonetically.

Then the class will talk about why the first word in the first line is indented. Every pupil will fully understand before the topic is terminated that this is done to indicate paragraphing. Some child will go to the screen, measure the length of indentation, and mark it off for all to see.

At this point in the lesson teacher and pupils will examine the structure of the other new word *once,* after which they will proceed with the reading of the story.

Now, who can read the entire story for the class? After this has been accomplished satisfactorily by several children, the class reviews the structure of various words they have had before.

When this part of the lesson has been completed to the entire satisfaction of the teacher she may say, "Now, boys and girls, find this story in your books. There is more story there than you read at the screen. Let's see what else we can find out about the three bears?". . .[11]

Other lessons that are extensions of the story include work-type materials concerned with vocabulary development, comprehension, and word-study. Many of these lessons are developed on the screen and in workbooks or on ditto sheets.

Certain advantages of this visual method are increased interest, in-

[11] Glenn McCracken, *The Right to Learn* (Chicago: Henry Regnery Company, 1959), pp. 149–150.

creased attention span, greater facility in promoting class discussion, and according to the author, "the significance of the New Castle experiment is that it begins at the beginning."[12] The program introduces phonic instruction in the first grade, and increased emphasis occurs in the second grade.

The Denver Plan

A preliminary study concerning the effectiveness of teaching beginning reading to kindergarten children was undertaken in Denver under the direction of Paul McKee and Lucile Harrison in 1959. The Denver public schools received a grant for a five-year study from the U. S. Office of Education on the basis of the preliminary study.

A unique feature of the plan is that children receive instruction in the pre-school years via educational television. In addition to the educational television programs, parents are provided with a manual suggesting games for developing auditory and visual perception, letter cards for teaching the alphabet, phonic cards, and suggestions for supplying missing words in oral context.

The Houghton-Mifflin Reading Series develops these and other skills during the readiness program in the kindergarten. It is not necessary for a child to have pre-school experiences prior to the readiness program. Major emphasis is placed on the use of oral context and initial consonants. Superior results are reported from the Denver experiment.

The Language-Experience Approach

The advocates of the language-experience approach agree that reading should not be taught independently as a separate assembly of skills; that instead it should be reinforced as a part of the total set of communication skills which also involve speaking, listening, and writing.

An excellent treatise on the language-experience approach is *Learning to Read Through Experience,* by Dorris M. Lee and R. V. Allen. This book expresses the view ". . . that experiences encompassing all the language arts contribute to reading development."[13]

Among the premises inherent in this view are:

> The communication skills of listening, speaking, reading and writing are closely interrelated.

---

[12] *Ibid.,* p. 219.
[13] Dorris M. Lee and R. V. Allen, *Learning to Read Through Experience* (New York: Appleton-Century-Crofts, 1963), p. 1.

> Reading is concerned with words that arouse meaningful responses based on the *individual experiences* of the learner.
> Words have no inherent meaning.
> Written words are visual symbols which, when associated with known sound symbols, arouse meaning in the mind of the reader.
> Reading is developing meaning from patterns of symbols which one recognizes and endows with meaning. *Reading arouses or calls up meanings.*[14] It does not provide them.

With these premises in mind, the authors cite instructional practices for the primary grades.

In the kindergarten, the teacher fosters thinking and creative expression. "Each day she encourages some children to share their thoughts with the class and she records some of this with the individual child observing her or with the whole class watching as she does the writing." A child may tell a long involved story from which she will select only a few important statements to write.

A variety of creative activity is encouraged. The children are proud of the charts and paintings which accompany their stories. The connection between oral language and writing is reinforced in many other ways as children find out that "reading is just talk written down."

At this time, the teacher is, however, "the only person expected to read print." Each day she reads aloud to the children their stories and other stories as well. And she helps the children to enrich their experience through films, trips, group discussion, and other means.

In the first grade, the teacher expects the children, as they dictate stories to her, to discriminate in subject matter, word choice, and structure of sentences.

As the child dictates, the teacher "talks about such things as letter formation and the conventional symbols which represent the oral sounds which the child makes. She helps children discover words which are alike, words that begin alike, and words that end alike." These children are being prepared for independent writing of common words they recognize.

As the teacher works with a small group or with an individual child, the experience of the other children is enriched and extended by activities at the science table or creative work with paint or clay. Others read books brought from home or from the school library.

It is indicated that ". . . a major breakthrough occurs when an individual child wants to write his own story." At this time, children are introduced to varied resources including:

[14] *Ibid.,* pp. 1–2.

"High frequency word lists.
Word lists of common interest.
Word lists on one topic.
Picture dictionaries.
Children's written material.
Labels in the general environment."

Word mastery is fostered by techniques requiring: completing sentences, reading collections of other children's writings made into their own books, and making and examining resource books for social studies. Children who have difficulty are given help from published sources in accord with specific needs.

In the third grade the teacher helps pupils develop their ability to read and tries, through the introduction of a wide variety of books, to cultivate in them a lasting interest in reading as well as improvement in their own writing ability. Children read as a leisure pursuit; they read to find answers to questions, they read to extend their knowledge in interesting areas, and they read to appreciate excellence of style and form in writing. Participation in "seminars" is also designed to heighten their appreciation of good writing and to increase their own writing ability.

Many simple readers, trade books, and volumes on various topics are made available as source materials to help children expand their ability to write and to read their own writing and that of others.[15]

In teaching young children, this approach is logical and may have great value. It is in accord with the conclusions of some semanticists and linguistic scholars who recommend that pupils be encouraged to read from the beginning materials similar to their own language patterns.

An advocate of a procedure closely related to the language-experience approach is Sylvia Ashton-Warner. In this approach, designated "organic reading," the teacher asks each pupil in the "infant group" to name each day the word he wants to learn. It is placed on a large card which the child keeps for the day and reviews the next morning. Then it is placed in a box with other words. Soon there are enough words to write stories. The stories increase in number and eventually become the child's "book."

> "I reach a hand into the mind of the child, bring out a handful of the stuff I find there, and use that as our first working material."[16]

---

[15] Adapted from Dorris M. Lee and R. V. Allen, *Learning to Read Through Experience* (New York: Appleton-Century-Crofts, 1963), *passim,* pp. 100–105.

[16] Sylvia Ashton-Warner, *Teacher* (New York: Simon and Schuster, 1963), p. 34.

Outstanding results have been obtained through the use of this approach by this sympathetic and skilled teacher.

Emphasis on creative writing has been shown to yield products of value as reading materials. Certainly teachers such as those who prepared *They All Want to Write* have succeeded in eliciting results which have enriched children's reading materials.[17] Mauree Applegate also has demonstrated the value of associating reading with other communication skills.[18]

It would seem desirable in grades beyond the primary level to extend instructional materials by use of supplementary readers and other books related closely to children's interests and needs. Such an approach is described by Helen F. Darrow and Virgil M. Howes in *Approaches to Individualized Reading*.[19] The use of "conferences" with children, and other procedures might also be employed in the way described by Walter B. Barbe in *Educator's Guide to Personalized Reading* to assure the development of skills.[20]

The effectiveness of language-experience type of instruction is suggested by the cooperative work of R. Van Allen, Director of Curriculum, and his associates in San Diego County. The approach is described in a series of publications by R. Van Allen. A brief report is found in an article entitled "More Ways Than One." The writer states: "This study probed into methods, materials, and the learning process. Its basic point of view was that no single approach to the teaching of reading can be *the* best or *only* solution."[21] In another article he continues: "During the course of the study, the language-experience teachers ruled out all other approaches for a period of time. Children in their classrooms made as much or more progress in reading skill development (as measured by standardized tests) as did the children who had direct teaching of skills in the classes using the *basic* and *individualized reading* approaches."

Allen then raises a number of provocative questions concerning the use of a predetermined, controlled vocabulary and the unnatural presentations in first-grade materials, and inquires whether we are sacrificing certain values and developing conformity in language and thought.

---

[17] Alvina T. Burrows, Doris C. Jackson, and Dorothy O. Saunders, *They All Want to Write* (New York: Holt, Rinehart, and Winston, 1964).

[18] Mauree Applegate, *Easy in English* (New York: Harper and Row, 1960).

[19] Helen F. Darrow and Virgil M. Howes, *Approaches to Individualized Reading* (New York: Appleton-Century-Crofts, 1960).

[20] Walter B. Barbe, *Educator's Guide to Personalized Reading* (Englewood Cliffs, N.J.: Prentice-Hall, 1961).

[21] R. Van Allen, "More Ways Than One," *Childhood Education*, vol. 38, (November, 1961), pp. 108–111.

George D. Spache indicates some desirable features of language-experience reading and also cites some limitations.

> "If the language-experience approach is continued much beyond early primary levels, there is a possibility that it may retard the full development of reading. If the child's own written expression is the major source of reading materials in grades above the primary level, his reading experiences and development will be extremely limited. Still following this approach in the intermediate grades would limit the child's learning in almost all areas to review of the facts he already knows or has just learned."[22]

One may inquire how far the language-experience approach should extend throughout the elementary grades and how and when the deviations between various kinds of vocabularies should affect the subject matter offered children.

Care should be taken to see that pupils acquire effective skills in the subject fields, yet the language-experience approach has many desirable features which should be considered seriously by all students of Developmental Reading.

The Linguistic Approach

Several texts and articles have appeared recently concerning linguistics and reading. Marked differences are found in these varied procedures. As yet, no fullfledged experiment has been carried on to give statistical evidence concerning this approach.

The relationship between reading and linguistics is explained by Charles Fries:

> Learning to read . . . is *not* a process of learning new or other language signals than those the child has already learned. The language signals are all the same. The difference lies in the medium through which the physical stimuli make contact with his nervous system. In "talk," the physical stimuli of the language signals make their contact by means of sound waves received by the ear. In reading, the physical stimuli of the same language signals consist of graphic shapes that make their contact with his nervous system through light waves received by the eye. The process of learning to read is the process of transfer from the auditory signs for language signals which the child has already learned, to the new visual signs for the same signals.[23]

[22] George D. Spache, *Reading in the Elementary School* (Boston: Allyn and Bacon, Inc., 1964), p. 140.
[23] Charles C. Fries, *Linguistics and Reading* (New York: Holt, Rinehart & Winston, Inc., 1963), p. xv.

In essence, linguistics is concerned with the structure of language. The structure of language consists of phonemes, the smallest speech unit; morphemes, the smallest linguistic units that have meaning—for example prefixes and suffixes; words, the smallest linguistic unit that has meaning and can stand alone; and utterances, a series of words spoken at one time. Studying the structure of words is called morphology, and the study of the structure of utterances is called syntax. Although the terminology is different, the similarity of factors in reading and linguistics is apparent.

A major question still to be answered is: How can the science of language become a functional part of a reading program? Some efforts toward implementation have been made, but at the cost of children's interest. For example, in the Bloomfield-Barnhart approach children would read:

>   Can Pat tag Nan?
>   Pat can tag Nan.
>   Can Nan tag Dad?
>   Nat can tag Dad.[24]

Obviously, there is much more to the varied systems of linguistics than has been presented here. Many questions among linguists are yet unanswered, and the applications to effective reading instruction have yet to be validated. Moreover, the approaches of different linguistic scholars must be reconciled. Many workers in the field of reading believe that these scholars should consider also findings from the science of psychology and child study. Together scholars from various disciplines may be best able to promote more effective instruction in reading.

The Initial Teaching Alphabet Method

The initial teaching alphabet (referred to as i.t.a.) was invented by Sir James Pitman of England, and much of the early experimental work has been performed by John A. Downing.

A major reason for the creation of the i.t.a. was that Pitman felt that many reading problems occur because of the inconsistency of the letter-sound factor in traditional orthography (referred to as t.o.). The i.t.a. has forty-four symbols and each symbol represents one sound. For example, the long *e* sound is represented by the symbol ɛɛ. The word *feet* would be spelled *fɛɛt* and the word *leaf* would be spelled *lɛɛf*.

[24] Leonard Bloomfield and Clarence L. Barnhart, *Let's Read, a Linguistic Approach* (Detroit: Wayne State University Press, 1961), p. 64.

Also, each word in i.t.a. has only one "look-and-say" pattern instead of the two or more in t.o. For example, *AND, And, and, &* would be four patterns to represent a single word; but in i.t.a. the only pattern would be *and*. There are no capital letters in i.t.a. thus, a sentence might read:

        ie sεε fiev fεεt.   (I see five feet.)

The i.t.a. is intended for beginning reading, and the children make the transition to traditional orthography as soon as they have completed i.t.a. materials. Rather widespread investigations indicate that children in an i.t.a. program can read more i.t.a. words than pupils in t.o. programs can read t.o. words. The differences suggest that traditional spelling of English represents an obstacle in learning to read.

A second factor, that of transfer from i.t.a. to t.o., represents a key question in the use of this new approach. Pitman has kept such symbols as *c* and *k* which represent the phoneme at the beginning of *cat* and *key,* in order to make both alphabets as similar as possible. Results of early studies indicate that rather complete transfer occurs within 40 hours of teaching and that children in i.t.a. groups have maintained their superiority over t.o. groups after transfer.

Although the evidence is nowhere near that which is necessary to recommend an immediate change, experimentation continues on a wide scale. In the academic year 1964–65, numerous experiments in i.t.a. are in progress or are being planned throughout the United States and England. Further, it should be noted, those working closely with i.t.a. experimentation request that final judgment be reserved until results of widespread studies have been reported and validated by comprehensive investigations extending over a sufficiently long period of time to warrant recommendations. The reader will find it advisable at this point to consider, in relation to these innovations, the note of caution and wisdom expressed in Chapter 2 of the book by A. I. Gates. (See page 19.)

Teaching the Very Young to Read

Many projects are being reported currently in which young children are being taught to read. Widely publicized efforts have included the provision of opportunities for children to learn to read in the kindergarten—and even earlier. A revealing and provocative study was made by Dolores Durkin, who found that one-third of a group of children who had learned to read before entering first grade had IQ's 110 and below—

these youngsters were not superior or gifted according to intelligence ratings.[25] It is suggested that many other five-year-old boys and girls will acquire reading skills if they are offered appropriate opportunities and stimulation at this time.

Conspicuous also is the success of Montessori materials when employed with "disadvantaged" pupils. C. E. Silberman in the book *Crisis in Black and White* reports that this approach appears to be especially suitable for fostering the development of slum children. Thus, sensory stimulation through experiences with blocks, bells, and sandpaper letters, and opportunities to tie knots, button clothing, and build towers afford the basis for developing perception and understanding that has been typically denied "disadvantaged" children. But such activities appear to be inappropriate and unnecessary for use with most older children.

Parents should guard against assuming that infants should generally be taught to read. The value of these early acquisitions should be seriously weighed against the worth of other seemingly more suitable experiences in promoting the maximum development of children. But many activities essential to later reading, such as wide sensory experience and varied activities, should be encouraged. Particularly suitable as a background for reading are experiences in perceiving and hearing language patterns in varied and natural patterns. Linguistic scholars assert that textbooks which utilize a highly repetitious and limited vocabulary should be avoided. Instead the first reading should be from materials that are written in a manner similar to the vigorous and natural speech patterns of young children. At the present time, we should probably not attempt to teach most very young children to read but should try to prepare them for successful later reading. However, it is becoming clear that many children of kindergarten age can learn to read under favorable conditions.

Our best efforts then will help in providing a wholesome background for children's development. Parents should strive to offer rich language experience for their children and they should read aloud to children, listen to their stories, and help them to cultivate wholesome interests and a love of books. To accomplish these goals, materials and experiences suggested in the Guide for the *First Adventures in Learning Program* of the Golden Book Educational Services appear to

[25] Dolores Durkin, "Reading Instruction and the Five-Year-Old Child" in *Challenge and Experiment in Reading* (G. Allen Figurel, editor), IRA Proceedings, vol. 7, 1962, Scholastic Magazines, Inc.

be more suitable for parents of young children to use than are the more formal programs of instruction in reading.[26]

CONCLUDING STATEMENT

Children come to school with great expectation, most of them highly motivated to learn to read. It becomes the responsibility of the teacher to plan instruction carefully and to attempt to provide the maximum motivation for continuous effective learning. Careful introduction of reading skills, continuous guidance according to varied needs and interests, frequent use of encouragement and praise, and periodic checks on progress will contribute to the maximum growth in reading skills and appreciations for every child. The importance of attitude toward reading at this time cannot be overestimated. Failure during the initial stages in learning to read may influence the child's attitude toward reading for many years, or indeed throughout his entire life; it may be associated also with avoidance of reading or continued failure. Maximum effort should therefore be put forth to help each child acquire effective skills and to find satisfaction in his first experiences in reading.

Traditionally, reading instruction in the primary grades has stressed mainly a mastery of the mechanics of reading. As knowledge of child growth and development has increased and as factors promoting good learning have been identified, shifts in attitude toward the role of reading at the primary level have occurred. The importance of motivating learning through a utilization of children's interests has been increasingly recognized until today teachers are beginning to give greater attention to children's needs and their fulfillment through reading.

In the chapter on developmental needs, we have discussed reading to satisfy needs and have indicated how the reading of certain books has resulted in the attainment on the part of the pupils of greater security and enhanced pleasure in working with others. Better personal and social relationships are thus engendered and fostered through reading.

It is now generally conceded that books may be effectively used to satisfy basic needs not only in the upper grades and high school, but also in the primary grades. Even the picture book can give the young child a source for understanding strange objects or events in a sometimes hostile world. Stories, too, will satisfy, even in these early years, the

[26] The Golden First Adventures in Learning Program, Associated Educational Services Corporation, Golden Books Division, One West Thirty-ninth Street, New York, N.Y. 10018.

child's curiosity about how to meet problems involving other people and their behavior under varied circumstances.

Selected References

Allen, Harold B. (editor), *Readings in Applied English Linguistics* (New York: Appleton-Century-Crofts, 1958).

Barbe, Walter B., "Personalized or Individualized Reading Instruction?" *Education,* 81:537–539 (May, 1961).

Benjamin, Dayton and Alice Burton, "The Experience Approach to Beginning Reading," *Elementary English,* 31:346–349 (October, 1954).

Braddock, Richard, *Introductory Readings on the English Language* (Englewood Cliffs, N.J.: Prentice-Hall, Inc., 1962).

Dawson, Mildred A. and Henry A. Bamman, *Fundamentals of Basic Reading Instruction* (New York: David McKay Co., Inc., 1959).

Dolch, Edward W., "Four 'Methods' of Teaching Reading," *Elementary English,* 31:72–76 (February, 1954).

Downing, John, *Experiments with an Augmented Roman Alphabet for Beginning Readers* (New York: Educational Records Bureau, 1962).

Downing, John, "Teaching Reading with i.t.a. in Britain," *Phi Delta Kappan,* 45:322–329 (April, 1964).

Fries, Charles C., *Linguistics and Reading* (New York: Holt, Rinehart & Winston, Inc., 1963).

Gates, Arthur I., "Vocabulary Control in Basal Reading Material," *Reading Teacher,* 15:81–85 (November, 1961).

Hildreth, Gertrude, "New Methods for Old in Teaching Phonics," *Elementary School Journal,* 57:436–441 (May, 1957).

Leestma, Robert, "The Film-Reader Program," *Elementary English,* 33:97–101 (February, 1956).

Lefevre, Carl A., "Language Patterns and their Graphic Counterparts: a Linguistic View of Reading," in J. Allen Figurel (editor), *Changing Concepts of Reading Instruction* (New York: Scholastic Magazines, Inc., 1961).

Lefevre, Carl A., *Linguistics and the Teaching of Reading* (New York: McGraw-Hill Book Co., 1964).

McCracken, Glenn, "The New Castle Reading Experiment," *Reading Teacher,* 9:241–245 (April, 1956).

McCracken, Glenn, *The Right to Learn* (Chicago: Henry Regnery Co., 1959).

McCullough, Constance M., "Changing Aspects of Reading Instruction," in J. Allen Figurel (editor), *Changing Concepts of Reading Instruction* (New York: Scholastic Magazines, Inc., 1961).

McDavid, Raven I., Jr., "The Role of Linguistics in the Teaching of Reading," in J. Allen Figurel (editor), *Changing Concepts of Reading Instruction* (New York: Scholastic Magazines, Inc., 1961).

Meeker, Alice M., *Teaching Beginners to Read* (New York: Holt, Rinehart & Winston, Inc., 1958).

Owen, George H., "Linguistics—An Overview," *Elementary English,* 39:421–425 (May, 1962).

Petty, Walter T., "Critical Reading in the Primary Grades," *Elementary English,* 33:298–302 (May, 1956).

Russell, David H., "Opinions of Experts about Primary-Grade Basic Reading Programs," *Elementary School Journal,* 44:602–609 (June, 1944).

Smith, Henry L., *Linguistic Science and the Teaching of English* (Cambridge, Mass.: Harvard University Press, 1956).

Witty, Paul A., "Some Issues in the Teaching of Reading," *The Packet. A Heath Service Bulletin for Elementary Teachers,* 18:3–15 (Spring, 1963).

Zirbes, Laura, "The Developmental Approach in Reading," *Reading Teacher,* 16:347–352 (March, 1963).

10

READING INSTRUCTION IN THE INTERMEDIATE GRADES

Since a developmental reading program begins with the kindergarten and extends into the college level, the program for the intermediate grades is but one stage in an unbroken series of purposeful experiences designed to foster individual growth in and through reading. Every stage of development, however, has its own unique characteristics and requirements. David H. Russell suggests that:

> A reading program in the post-primary grades of the elementary school and in junior-high-school classes must be built upon (1) the reading abilities the pupils have acquired in the primary grades, (2) the expanding interests of later childhood and early adolescence, (3) the need for continued development of skillful, fluent, and differentiated reading abilities, and (4) the reading demands of the total curriculum and out-of-school activities.[1]

Thus the continuous nature of reading growth is recognized, and skills appropriate to the needs and abilities of pupils are introduced and developed sequentially.

Continuity Characterizes the Reading Program

No sharp line divides the reading program of the primary and intermediate levels. The acquisition of the skills, attitudes, and appreciations appropriate for the intermediates is gradual and continuous. The "expanded" goals in reading to be achieved by pupils as they progress from the primary grades to the intermediate grades include using reading as a tool to serve many purposes as pupils become increasingly

[1] David H. Russell, *Children Learn to Read,* 2nd ed. (Waltham, Mass.: Blaisdell Publishing Company, 1961), p. 229.

skillful in adjusting reading techniques to their needs and become more adept in locating information, handling complex technical materials with ease.[2]

Although there is continuity in the reading program, certain aspects of learning should be stressed in the intermediate grades. Constance McCullough makes the following suggestions in regard to "developmental aims to be achieved":

> Successful guidance at the intermediate-grade level results in producing a democratic and resourceful person, who not only knows how to help himself in reading and study activities but also how to improve his performance. He reads for different purposes in many kinds of materials, using learning techniques which he has found useful. He follows written and oral directions for specific reading tasks. The level of his reading skills is appropriate for one of his ability, maturity, and opportunity. Through reading and discussion, he has become sensitive to an author's message and has a growing awareness of the writer's techniques, skills, and purposes.
>
> Reading for pleasure and information is an established part of the pupil's school and home life. His reading interests are being broadened and refined as well as extended along one or two lines of current interest. He is adept at finding material in magazines and newspapers. He uses the ideas gained in reading as resources for his many activities, as information and entertainment for his friends, as a basis for comparing or developing his own ideas or for critical appraisal.
>
> Through reading and through listening to the oral reading of well-written material, the intermediate-grade pupil begins to look for more than surface value in a good piece of literature. Developing a personal standard of understanding what he reads and saying what he means, he is becoming impatient with vague or confused expression. He is curious about and interested in the use of words and of different literary forms. Gradually he is learning to note the style of a given author or illustrator and to anticipate the kind of product he will offer.[3]

The intermediate grades may be identified as the period of rapid progress in the acquisition of habits and skills. When a child enters the middle grades, he discovers that special reading skills in subject fields such as science, social studies, and other areas are more frequently required than in the primary grades. Extensive use of reference books and other aids to develop competency in locating information, associating ideas, organizing materials, and adjusting rate are skills needed by

---

[2] Margaret G. McKim and Helen Caskey, *Guiding Growth in Reading,* 2nd ed. (New York: The Macmillan Co., 1963), pp. 263–266.

[3] Constance M. McCullough, "Reading in the Intermediate Grades," in Paul A. Witty (chairman), *Development In and Through Reading,* Sixtieth Yearbook of the National Society for the Study of Education, Part I (Chicago: University of Chicago Press, 1961), pp. 289–290.

the intermediate-grade pupil. The location and use of reading materials in order to obtain a better understanding of himself and his personal problems or to fulfill other needs may become a goal of the middle-grade pupil.

READING HABITS AND SKILLS FOR THE INTERMEDIATE GRADES

Just as the development of reading skills was a vital part of the primary program, so it is in the intermediate-grade program. An outline and a discussion of some specific habits and skills which should be developed in the intermediate grades follow:

I. Developing Comprehension
   A. Following directions and finding information
   B. Finding answers to personal and social problems
   C. Reading a story for various purposes
   D. Understanding words
II. Reading to Remember
   A. Remembering important ideas
   B. Remembering significant details
III. Associating Ideas and Materials
   A. Finding proof
   B. Finding information relevant to particular problems
   C. Examining basic assumptions
   D. Studying the adequacy of presentations
IV. Organizing Ideas and Materials
   A. Arranging events in sequence and making outlines
   B. Summarizing
V. Increasing Speed of Silent Reading
VI. Improving Oral Reading

Developing Comprehension

Comprehension is not a separate and distinct skill to be taught at a given level, for it is an integral part of the total reading program. Yet there are specific ways in which it may be fostered or improved. Comprehension may be increased to some extent by stressing vocabulary growth and concept building. Further, specific exercises in purposeful reading may lead to improvement in this skill at various levels. Smith and Dechant trace the development of comprehension as follows:

1. As the child grows in general experience his ability to take meanings to words will increase and his potential for comprehension will increase.

2. As his proficiency in recognizing words (and their meanings) grows, his ability to comprehend develops.
3. As his comprehension develops, his skill in reading larger and larger thought units develops.
4. As his skill in reading larger thought units develops, his skills of comprehension and his ability to understand more involved (complex) thoughts will increase.
5. And as his ability to read larger and more complex thought units increases, his comprehension and potential for comprehension will develop.[4]

In the intermediate grades, comprehension may be developed by providing experiences which encourage pupils to follow the sequence suggested by Smith and Dechant. Following are some skills—with suggestions for their cultivation—which require greater emphasis in the intermediate grades than in the primary grades:

Following Directions and Finding Information

Intermediate-grade pupils should develop the ability to read more and more complex directions with a high degree of comprehension, and they should also be able to find various kinds of information readily. Guidance and encouragement should be given in order that steady progress in following directions of increasing difficulty may be made by each pupil. It is sometimes advisable for the teacher to make a check list of different types of directions which students must follow in order to be successful in various activities. By ascertaining each pupil's ability to read and carry out directions of different types and degrees of difficulty, the teacher will be able to give individual help as it is needed.

Exercises in practice books may be utilized to foster further improvement in the ability to follow directions and to find information, since the pupil is now expected to work independently. The following are some additional suggestions that may be given to pupils:

1. Make sure that you have the right directions.
2. Before you start following any set of directions, make sure you know what they mean.
3. Read the directions all the way through.
4. Follow the directions in the order they are given.[5]

[4] Henry P. Smith and Emerald V. Dechant, *Psychology in Teaching Reading* (Englewood Cliffs, N.J.: Prentice-Hall, Inc., 1961), pp. 217–218.
[5] Paul Witty, *How to Improve Your Reading* (Chicago: Science Research Associates, Inc., 1956), pp. 70–71.

The foregoing suggestions apply particularly to finding information for various purposes.

Finding Answers to Personal and Social Problems

Growth and development imply the successful resolution of problems. Freeland states:

> The intermediate-grade teacher's responsibilities for helping children to acquire the understandings, the attitudes, and the patterns of behavior essential to their personal welfare and social progress through reading are not unlike those of teachers of other levels. He will endeavor to help pupils to gain the abilities they need to interpret and apply what they read to their own problems; to gain new insights, self-concepts, and social concepts.[6]

Reading for Varied Purposes

There are many purposes for reading. Some of the more general reasons might be to discover the outcome of the story, to enjoy humorous happenings, to compare different plots, and to prepare to tell or dramatize an episode. For the intermediate-grade pupil, the following more specific purposes are also important: (1) reading for principal ideas; (2) reading for details; (3) reading to find the answers to specific questions; (4) reading for implied meanings; and (5) reading critically.

Understanding Words and Increasing One's Vocabulary

The development of vocabulary should receive continuous attention in the intermediate grades. In addition to learning how to use dictionaries and encyclopedias effectively, pupils need to increase word-analysis skills. Although some pupils acquire adequate skills in word analysis in the primary grades, there are many others who require additional help and review. Moreover, it is desirable to assist middle-grade pupils in attaining greater independence in analyzing words in order that they may read rapidly with a high degree of comprehension.

David Russell has listed the skills sequentially for the various grade or reader levels. The middle-grade teacher will find it helpful to examine each pupil's acquisition of these skills. Following is Russell's listing for grade 3 through the higher levels—a listing not intended as a prescription for each level but rather as a general guide.

[6] Alma Freeland, "Intermediate Grade Reading and Needs," *Education* (April, 1964), p. 466.

Third-reader level. Applying word-analysis techniques to words of more than one syllable: further recognition and use of phonograms; study of derivatives formed by adding prefixes and suffixes; further practice in combining phonetic, structural, context, and other clues in word attack; strengthening the generalization that vowels have different sounds—affected by *r*, second one silent in digraphs such as *ai*, etc.; compound and hyphenated words; possessives and contractions that drop more than one letter; readiness for dictionary usage by alphabet study, recognizing variant meanings of words, etc.; readiness for syllabication by mention that syllables contain one vowel sound, by seeing words with first syllable or known words, such as *beside*, by beginning work on accent, etc.

Fourth-reader level. Achieving independence in using a wide variety of word-recognition techniques: further practice in combining visual, auditory, and context clues in recognizing words; reviewing work on consonant and vowel sounds and digraphs which pupils cannot use easily; extension of knowledge and use of commonest phonograms; use of the glossary and dictionary and its various guides in determining pronunciation and meaning; further study of synonyms, antonyms, homonyms, and multiple meanings of words; applying word-analysis techniques in spelling situations.

Higher grades. Continuation of program of earlier grades as needed: review of phonograms; structural analysis of more difficult words; skills and habit of dictionary usage established. Amount and type of instruction determined even more by the child's individual needs.[7]

The implications of such an outline for the intermediate grades are clear. Increasingly complex word-analysis skills should be developed, and skills acquired earlier should be reinforced as they are needed in the middle grades.

Word analysis and word study will help pupils both in pronouncing words and in obtaining the meanings of new words. Analytic word study should start with known words; the total characteristics of words should be noted and then their parts examined. Pupils should be led to analyze new words visually and to develop the habit of noticing similarities and differences in words. Studying the results of adding prefixes and suffixes will also prove helpful; but this endeavor, like all forms of word analysis, should be considered secondary to emphasis on meaning, understanding, and the correct use of whole words.

Vocabulary development and concept building should receive continuous attention throughout the middle grades. Of paramount importance in this respect is the development of clear concepts for words

---

[7] David H. Russell, "Outline of a Developmental Program of Word-Analysis Activities" (developed with the assistance of Verna L. Wadleigh), in *Children Learn to Read, op. cit.,* pp. 315–316.

as general vocabularies grow, along with a knowledge of specialized words and phrases employed in the subject fields.

Reading to Remember

Pupils must remember much of what they read in order to grow as students and to know themselves and their environment. Remembering should be considered far more important than the simple recall of facts and information.

What are some of the best ways to remember what is read? Early research by Gates indicated that recitation may be especially helpful for third- and fourth-graders.[8] He found that material read and discussed was remembered longer than that which was read but not discussed.

It is worthwhile to use materials that are meaningful because of their association with the children's own experience. Pupils tend to remember meaningful material for a longer period of time than nonmeaningful material. There are various ways to promote the remembering of different kinds of materials. For instance, historical passages involving cause and effect are better learned and retained when pupils inquire:

1. What are the causes of the events?
2. In what order did the events occur?
3. Was the development orderly?
4. Can the events be rearranged in a correct order?

Remembering Important Ideas

Pupils frequently have difficulty remembering important ideas because they are not certain which ideas in a paragraph are significant. They need practice in identifying facts which determine the unifying ideas of paragraphs. It may help them identify the most important ideas by observing that the significant fact often, but not always, appears in the first or second sentence of a paragraph. Further, examining the headings and subheadings provided by the author may enable them to locate the main ideas. Or they may be helped by looking for the main ideas as presented in the summary of chapters. Once the important ideas have been identified they may be organized into meaningful relationships to facilitate their retention and their relative significance.

---

[8] Arthur I. Gates, "Recitation as a Factor in Memorizing," *Archives of Psychology*, 6:45 (September, 1917).

Remembering Significant Details

Not all reading necessitates the recall of specific details, but some passages contain essential details which serve to create a clearer image of a person or an event. Moreover, some details are fundamental in disclosing the sequence of events or in revealing the steps in solving a problem. Pupils, especially poor readers, need guidance to determine what constitutes significant details, and practice books containing exercises to improve this ability may be used to advantage at times. The teacher may contribute to the development of this ability by having pupils indicate words or phrases which are significant in descriptions of persons or in explanations of events in the textbook. Simple exercises may also be made by the teacher for such practice.

Stories that are rich in sensory imagery offer an opportunity for pupils to react to details. When such stories are read, pupils may be asked to find items involving sight, hearing, taste, or smell. True-false tests may be devised to estimate the pupils' ability to note significant details in such stories. DeBoer and Dallmann suggest that:

(a) Taking notes on points sometimes helps retention.
(b) Practicing recall aids retention.
(c) Distributed practice is superior to nondistributive practice.
(d) Overlearning is important for recall.
(e) Organizing into a meaningful whole the facts to be recalled aids retention.[9]

Associating Ideas and Materials

The complex array of abilities involved in critical reading includes various kinds of associations between ideas and materials. George Spache refers to the following six skills as essential in critical reading:

(1) Investigating sources
(2) Recognizing author's purposes
(3) Distinguishing opinion and fact
(4) Making inferences
(5) Forming judgments
(6) Detecting propaganda devices[10]

Critical reading, as Spache suggests, involves more than mere comprehension of what is on the printed page; it involves the interpretation

---

[9] John J. DeBoer and Martha Dallmann, *The Teaching of Reading,* rev. ed. (New York: Holt, Rinehart & Winston, Inc., 1964), p. 380.
[10] George D. Spache, *Toward Better Reading* (Champaign, Illinois: Garrard Publishing Co., 1963), Chapter 5.

of ideas and facts in terms of related experiences and knowledge. Various types of exercises may be devised to stimulate pupils (1) to find proof, (2) to locate information relevant to particular problems, (3) to examine basic assumptions, and (4) to study the adequacy of various presentations. Through this approach critical reading may be fostered.

Finding Proof

Verifying statements involves such skills as the ability to select relevant ideas and to reject irrelevant ones. Certain exercises of a type found in widely used practice books in which pupils are asked to select passages that support fact are particularly helpful in furthering these skills.

> Below is a statement of fact, and following it several sentences which prove its truth. Included is one sentence, however, which does not offer proof that the statement is true. Cross out the wrong sentence.
>
> As a boy Columbus had many interests.
>
> 1. The sailors' talk interested Columbus more than the weaving in his father's house, for he was fond of hearing about travel.
> 2. He was fair skinned and bright eyed.
> 3. He liked geography and he liked maps.
> 4. He was interested in geometry and astronomy.
> 5. He enjoyed reading and took an interest in science.

Investigations have shown that some middle-grade pupils may pass standard tests in reading and skills and still be unable to tell whether certain materials are relevant to particular problems presented to them. Other studies stress the fact that many pupils are unlikely to examine the authenticity and accuracy of reports. Hence, attention should be given to various forms of critical reading. These acquisitions comprise a complex array of habits and skills which depend on the type of material read and the child's purpose in reading.

Finding Information Relevant to Particular Problems

Two important types of training must be undertaken to develop the ability to find information relevant to particular problems. One skill concerns the locating of information and the other requires the critical evaluation of the information to determine its relevance to the solution of a problem.

Skills in locating information include the use of:
1. Tables of contents
2. Dictionaries

3. Encyclopedias
4. Indexes
5. Maps, graphs, charts, diagrams, tables
6. Card catalogs

Boys and girls should learn to turn quickly to the appropriate source for answers to different problems. They need also to know how to use to best advantage the library card catalog, the *Readers' Guide to Periodical Literature,* and other indexes. And, after they have found an appropriate book or article, they must know how to read its index and how to use its table of contents to locate relevant facts.

Considerable experience is necessary before pupils can use reference materials effectively, since this ability involves much more than simply the quick location of materials. Children must be able to scan materials and reach a decision as to their relevancy, adequacy, and authenticity. In their quest for authentic materials, they need not only actual experience, but also expert guidance.

Examining Basic Assumptions

Some pupils even in the fifth or sixth grade, as well as many in the seventh or eighth, will be prepared to engage profitably in exercises designed to make them increasingly critical of basic assumptions in printed materials. To foster critical reading, teachers are employing with success a number of interesting approaches. For example, pupils are encouraged as a first step to read simple passages of historical importance and to answer certain cause-and-effect questions. They are then presented with more complex materials from social studies, which they scrutinize to ascertain the author's purposes. Scientific reports may also be examined, and pupils led to inquire: "What are the facts upon which the author bases his case?" "How does he interpret the facts?" If the reading matter is in story form, pupils may be encouraged to examine the plausibility of the story: "Could the events occur?" "Is the author qualified and experienced in the field in which he writes?" "Are the characters and situations distorted and unreal?"

Studying the Adequacy of Presentation

Clearly associated with competency in examining basic assumptions is another skill which should be emphasized in the intermediate grades. The student should examine each of several presentations on a particular topic in order to determine its adequacy. He should inquire:

Is the account reasonably complete?
Is the author's conclusion justified?
Are more data needed?
Are sources for further study and for checking the presentation suggested?
Is the account prepared by a qualified person?

Organizing Ideas and Materials

Certain skills are needed to promote the ability to organize ideas. Pupils in the middle grades should be encouraged to follow more complex instructions, designed to help them organize the materials found in various sources. They should learn to make a sequential arrangement of ideas, to classify and outline, and to summarize. Guidance and training should be provided for individuals or groups in acquiring these skills.

Arranging Events in Sequence and Making Outlines

Exercises for the practice of these skills should be carefully graded as to difficulty. Some early exercises may be devoted to classifying words and phrases as they pertain to or illustrate ideas. Pupils may be encouraged to list details related to specific topics. They may fill in charts designed to guide the organization of ideas. Later, when skills in the making of outlines are being developed, pupils may be provided opportunities for:

1. Finding main ideas and listing supporting ideas
2. Arranging outlines sequentially
3. Making progressively more complex outlines

Pupils should be encouraged to make outlines on various topics in different content areas.

Summarizing

In a similar manner, training in summarizing should progress from simple to more difficult tasks. In the initial stages of learning to summarize, the exercises may consist of a series of statements, presented by the teacher, to be arranged in the right order. The statements, when arranged correctly, should present the main events in a story. Discussing a summary, making cooperative summaries, and writing one-sentence summaries are helpful techniques. In later stages, the pupils may be expected to write, in their own words, the main ideas developed by an author in whole chapters and to arrange the sentences in correct sequence. They should then be encouraged to prepare summaries of different kinds on various topics.

Increasing Speed of Silent Reading

Because the attainment of reading skills is an individual matter, it is difficult to state specifically the speed each individual should attain for reading different kinds of materials silently. By the time pupils have reached the third or fourth grade, they should generally be able to read silently at a much faster rate than they read orally. At this time, moreover, they are ready for experiences designed to enable them to adjust rates for varied purposes. Smith and Dechant caution that rate should not be increased without correlated attempts to improve comprehension:

> These relationships between rate and comprehension are important to the teacher for he must decide when to stress rate improvements and when to emphasize comprehension skills. A reader who is low in both comprehension and rate generally will not benefit from an emphasis on speed. He needs training in basic comprehension skills. One who reads rapidly but with low comprehension likewise needs comprehension training. However, one who reads all materials slowly but with good comprehension may well profit from training in speed.[11]

By the time pupils have reached the sixth grade, some may have achieved a rate of 300–500 words per minute in reading relatively simple materials silently. More important than rapid reading rate is flexibility. As we have pointed out, good students are flexible readers, able to adjust their reading rates to varied materials and purposes. Poor students often tend to read almost everything at the same rate.

Periodic checks on rate are desirable, but they should not be planned for the purpose of achieving a standard performance; instead, they are designed to insure continuous development and to help each child attain acceptable rates in reading different kinds of materials—some that require careful reading for detail, and others that need only to be skimmed for general information.

A simple way to measure the reading rate of a class is to start the reading of a selection at a given time, watch a timepiece, and record on the chalkboard the passing of time in quarters of a minute. When

---

[11] Henry P. Smith and Emerald V. Dechant, *op. cit.*, p. 224.

a child completes the article, he looks up and notes the last number written on the chalkboard. Later he divides the number of words in the article (estimated by counting the words in a line and multiplying by the number of lines) by the number of minutes which have been used in reading the selection. The student or teacher may then compute the number of words read per minute. Monthly comparisons of rates of reading different types of materials are stimulating to many pupils, if too great importance is not attached to them.

Developing Oral Reading

Oral reading is more common in the first three grades of school than in the later grades. Indeed, because of overemphasis, some students must eradicate the tendency to read orally as they learn to read silently. They must cease to form words with their lips and tongue, and must limit throat muscle activity. Simple drills in the silent reading of easy, familiar materials will usually help such pupils. Despite its limitations, oral reading is useful and important at all levels. Students repeatedly have occasion to read aloud a book report, or a newspaper story, or a poem, or some sentences from a textbook. Their purposes in oral reading are usually different from their purposes in silent reading. When they read silently, they may be primarily concerned with acquiring information, but when they read orally they wish to transmit information or give pleasure to others.

Pupils in the middle grades often need encouragement and help in oral reading. Some suggestions for the student follow:

1. Keep in mind *what* you are reading and *why* you are reading it.
2. Watch both your enunciation—the sharpness and clarity with which you say the words—and your pronunciation, the way you say them.
3. Relax and try to be at ease. Remember that you have something interesting to read to your audience.
4. Don't hurry through your reading. Your listeners will learn more if you read slowly.
5. Read word groups rather than word by word.
6. Use pauses to punctuate your reading.
7. While you are reading, speak up so that your whole audience can hear you.
8. Put expression into your reading.
9. Look at your listeners.[12]

[12] Paul Witty, *op. cit.*, pp. 156–159.

READING IN THE CONTENT FIELDS

Skills needed to achieve effective reading in the content fields include the ability to discover the main idea, organize materials and ideas, interpret facts and information, draw conclusions, and critically evaluate the subject matter. Pupils must become flexible in adjusting their rate of reading to the requirements of materials in different content fields.

In the intermediate grades—where pupils have, of course, greater need for skillful reading in the content areas—a number of difficulties arise as they attempt to apply their reading skills widely. As Lillian Gray points out:

> Reading in the basic reader constitutes an easier task for children than reading in the content fields. Various important factors are controlled in the basic readers which cannot be similarly controlled in books dealing with subject-matter content. For example: vocabulary in the content fields is usually more difficult; new terms are introduced faster and with fewer repetitions; more facts are presented to the reader; greater retention is expected; and references to previous facts occur with more frequency in historical, geographical, and other such materials.[13]

Differences in experiential background and in ability are bound to create readiness problems in the various content fields. Hence, the teacher should study each pupil's readiness for reading materials in social studies, mathematics, science, and the language arts. The use of standard tests supported by observations will help in ascertaining such readiness.

Social Studies

Effective reading of materials in the social studies requires the application of certain skills. Smith and Dechant suggest "three principal difficulties that require the development of specialized background and skills" for reading in social studies:

1. The vocabulary may be highly specialized and the reading material is likely to be heavily loaded with complex concepts.
2. The diagrammatic materials require considerable interpretive skill for their effective use.
3. The content frequently is emotionally loaded and controversial. A critical evaluation rather than blind acceptance is required.[14]

---

[13] Lillian Gray, *Teaching Children to Read,* 3rd ed. (New York: The Ronald Press Company, 1963), p. 330.
[14] Henry P. Smith and Emerald V. Dechant, *op. cit.,* p. 356.

Vocabulary in the social studies is often highly abstract and difficult. For example, how do you as a teacher present concepts such as *equality, freedom,* and *pursuit of happiness* so that pupils can grasp clearly what is meant? Obviously, the teacher must spend time in every subject area, building a background for the understanding of such abstract terms. Since the social studies require an understanding of many concepts, special care should be taken to provide it, sometimes even before the pupils read a selection. Some teachers have found it desirable to appoint committees which will use reference books and dictionaries to find meanings for key words from which a class will profit before they read certain social studies material. Students may also keep notebooks in which they list words not clear to them; later they should look up the definitions and enter them too in the notebook. Special and technical vocabularies as well as a general vocabulary may be developed in this way.

The use of *diagrammatic materials* appears to be increasing as one compares modern social studies texts with those of just a few years ago. Successful reading of maps, graphs, charts, tables, and pictures requires a high degree of application and the mastery of certain skills. A pupil who does not, for example, know the meaning of the words *relief, scale,* and *tropic* as they relate to maps, would be greatly handicapped in interpreting a map correctly. Wallace Howell found definite improvement in pupils from the fourth through the eighth grades following training in reading and interpreting diagrammatic materials. Gains were made also in the ability to employ efficiently the dictionary, reference material, and indexes.[15]

Mathematics

Reading in the field of mathematics demands skills not always required in the social studies. The mastery of mathematics necessitates careful, detailed reading with less opportunity to employ context clues for meaning. Almost every word in a mathematics problem may be important. Many concepts in this field are highly specialized and require understanding before new concepts or more advanced concepts can be introduced. "This necessity for building new learnings on old learnings means that in mathematics, possibly more than in any other area, what is worth teaching must be taught well."[16]

[15] Wallace J. Howell, "Work-Study Skills of Children in Grades IV to VIII," *Elementary School Journal,* 50:384–389 (March, 1950).
[16] Henry P. Smith and Emerald V. Dechant, *op. cit.,* p. 367.

It must be recognized, too, that many symbols used in mathematics must be learned. For example, $8 - 6 = x$ is a thought expressed by a series of different symbols—different, that is, from words. In reading such a series of symbols the pupil must not only read them accurately but must also interpret each sign correctly.

Mildred Dawson and Henry Bamman suggest a consideration of the following questions to help the pupil read a problem in mathematics:

>What does the problem tell me?
>What am I asked to find out?
>What process(es) should I use in finding out?
>What would be a reasonable answer?[17]

Thus, it is clear that detailed, accurate reading is more important in the field of arithmetic while critical, evaluative reading is more important in reading the social studies.

Science

Reading in science requires the understanding of highly specialized vocabularies as well as skill in the use of problem-solving techniques. A student may have an excellent vocabulary in general but little ability to comprehend complex scientific terminology. For example, *gravity, vector, electricity,* and *oxygen* are terms for which clear concepts, although difficult to acquire, are necessary for understanding certain passages. The teacher must offer help to pupils in building such concepts in various fields of science. Discussion of terms after seeing films or filmstrips is one effective means of providing the necessary background for understanding such terms.

The development of scientific terms prior to assigning reading in a science text is useful and necessary. From this activity pupils can make their own science vocabulary notebook. Drawings as well as written definitions of words are aids in developing vocabulary. Direct, firsthand experiences (such as experiments) are also helpful in developing vocabulary and concepts in science.

The understanding and solving of problems are important aspects of successful endeavor in science. Dawson and Bamman suggest the following questions to assist in problem-solving:

>What, exactly, is stated?
>What is expected? What is to be found?

[17] Mildred A. Dawson and Henry A. Bamman, *Fundamentals of Basic Reading Instruction,* 2nd ed. (New York: David McKay Company, Inc., 1963), p. 274.

What do we really know about this?

What are the possible steps which we might take to reach a solution or conclusion?

Where can we find additional information which might give further aid toward solving the problem?

Do we see clearly the steps which we must take in attempting to solve the problem?

Is our conclusion or answer reasonable?

Do we now have proof which we can present to others?[18]

Certainly, it is clear that reading in the content fields demands a high level of thinking. Although each field has its unique requirements for successful reading, there are a number of skills and techniques which are common to all areas, summarized by Russell as follows:

1. Establishing the purpose for which the content is to be read.
2. Making a quick preliminary survey of all the material.
3. Checking from the dictionary or other sources the meanings of technical or specialized words occurring in the material.
4. Giving complete attention to the material in the light of the understood purpose.
5. Using related pictures, maps, charts, and tables to verify ideas in the verbal materials, particularly those dealing with locations, quantitative data, and time sequence.
6. Becoming accustomed to verbal clues which give ideas of size, a sense of the passage of time, and sequence of events or topics.
7. Checking the accuracy of the sources of information.
8. Reflecting on the ideas presented in the printed materials in the light of related past experiences.
9. Applying previous knowledge in order to make new generalizations and plans.
10. Where possible, subjecting these conclusions to the test of practical operation.[19]

MATERIALS AND RESOURCES FOR READING

It is apparent that a wide assortment of materials must be made available to middle-grade pupils to satisfy diverse interests and to meet the varied needs of individuals and groups. Materials must be considered in light of the instructional tasks of the middle grades. Two major tasks in the middle grades are development of skills sequentially and the broadening of students' concepts and skills.

[18] *Ibid.,* pp. 277–278.
[19] David H. Russell, *op. cit.,* p. 251.

Materials for Sequential Skills Development

Research has suggested the value of continuous and sequential emphasis on reading skills. Some teachers depend primarily on a basal readers approach to assure their development while others use a combination of readers and workbooks. Some employ supplementary readers and other books in various combinations. In other instances, courses of study provide the guides followed to varying degrees. Still other teachers employ individualized reading with success, utilizing pupil-conferences to assure sequential skill development. Larger and larger numbers of teachers are recognizing that there must be flexibility in the use of all these skill-building approaches because of the wide variation in the attainments and rates of progress of the individual members of each class. But the goal of the teacher is to help every child develop and apply continuously and sequentially the basic reading habits and skills which we have described earlier in this chapter. One method of application will be through the use of skill-building materials in textbooks and related books in the various subject areas.

Materials for Broadening Concepts and Skills

Obviously, the middle-grade reading program as well as any other program at any other grade level is not limited to textbooks. An assortment of materials that supplement a basic program and extend concepts and skills includes:

1. *Workbooks and practice materials.* Workbooks or practice books may prove helpful for some teachers and pupils, although various points of view have been expressed concerning their value. In a provocative article, Robert L. Docter presents a comparison of workbook and nonworkbook approaches to reading instruction.

> Since the development of this tool in the early twenties, questions about the value of such material have been raised by reading experts, parents, teachers and administrators. Just about everyone has had an opinion. Often, particular opinions have correlated highly with particular points of philosophical orientation. Many times, individuals who believed that the reading program should be carefully constructed along individual lines appropriate to the needs of individual students rejected the workbook idea as a form of lock-step busywork.
> On the other hand, individuals who held the idea of simple presentation and acquisition of sequential subject matter believed that the

workbook had great value in assisting the teacher to achieve this objective. There appeared to be very little middle ground.[20]

After pointing to some further advantages and disadvantages of workbooks, Docter showed clearly that the use of workbooks is not an either-or question. It was not surprising that many teachers in his study favored the use of workbooks in appraising the acquisition of skills. There is, of course, always the tendency of some teachers to allow workbook usage to become desultory, monotonous, and repetitious. This unfortunate practice is often not a fault of the workbooks so much as a violation of their intelligent use. Docter concludes:

> It is no surprise that teachers favor workbooks in basal reading programs. When they are not used, a large part of the teacher's preparation time is spent in reproducing follow-up lessons on hectograph machines and charts. Teachers feel that this time might better be spent in preparation of the lesson itself. Indeed, the results of this study clearly indicate the workbooks are a boon, not busywork, to the instructional staff and pupils as well.[21]

There are, of course, numerous examples of situations in which the use of workbooks has become routine, almost futile busywork. However, this need not be the case. We can find other examples in which elementary school classes or individuals have been helped appreciably by careful selection of workbook material according to individual needs. Moreover, systematically developed textbooks consisting primarily of work-type exercises prepared for secondary school pupils who are retarded in reading have been employed with unusual success in many instances.

2. *Materials in the content areas* are parts of a balanced reading program. Stories such as those included in the booklets on social studies published by Harper and Row provide relevant reading experiences in this area. Easy science materials are found in the "All About" Series of Random House, and in the Harper and Row science booklets. The Educational Development Library contains excellent materials for building study skills and for developing the ability to use source materials effectively.

3. *Supplementary reading texts* offer opportunities for further skill development in other than basal readers. The D. C. Heath Reading Caravan Series, for example, presents a concise skill-development pro-

---

[20] Robert L. Docter, "Reading Workbooks: Boon or Busywork?" *Elementary English,* 39:224 (March, 1962).
[21] *Ibid.,* pp. 228, 230.

gram with materials of high interest. Study-skills are developed in an interesting manner in the Harper and Row supplementary reading series. These types of materials are important adjuncts to a balanced reading program.

4. *Experience charts* offering opportunities for recording and sharing firsthand experiences are especially useful in building vocabulary and in aiding the poor reader.

5. *Duplicated materials* prepared by the teacher can prove helpful for sharing experiences and for providing practice materials. A real advantage of teacher-made materials is that they can offer specific practice on particular skills pupils need to develop. Through the use of these materials a teacher can meet individual needs directly.

6. *Reference books, encyclopedias,* the World Almanac, and similar resources are essential in a balanced reading program. Promoting growth in the ability to use these materials independently is one of the major goals of the program in work-study skills.

7. *Dictionaries* are essential in the classroom that promotes steady growth in reading; in fact, each pupil should have his own copy by the time he enters the fourth grade. The development of the dictionary habit at an early age pays large dividends.

8. *Newspapers* designed for children foster application of skills and provide a basis for the acquisition of knowledge about present-day happenings. *Newstime, My Weekly Reader,* and *Current Events* are distinctly useful in the middle grades.

9. *Children's magazines* aid reading growth and foster enjoyment in reading. Effective use of children's magazines requires the application of work-study skills as well as the cultivation of appreciation and taste in reading. In the middle grades *Children's Digest* and *Highlights for Children* are unusually helpful. *Highlights for Children* contains monthly presentations in science of unusual timeliness as well as biographies and stories that extend and enrich interests.

10. *Maps, globes,* and related materials are useful for providing referents and backgrounds essential in helping pupils to read effectively in certain content areas.

11. *Pamphlets, bulletins,* and *files of pictures* contribute to reading by providing supplementary or illustrative materials.

12. *Audio-visual equipment* may be employed to promote growth in reading. The use of tape recorders, the radio, television, recordings of prose and poetry, films, and filmstrips may also contribute greatly to the development of children's background for concepts and understandings necessary in effective reading.

13. *Classroom collections of library books* to meet the immediate needs and interests of pupils offer an opportunity for pupils to apply skills, extend interests, and learn to read independently. In a developmental reading program individual reading plays a significant role.

14. *School and community library facilities* contribute to the attainment of one of the major goals of reading at the intermediate-grade level—the development of interest in and taste for good literature. Wide use of libraries is essential if pupils are to satisfy their interests, meet their needs, and continue to develop through reading.

EVALUATIVE PROCEDURES IN THE MIDDLE GRADES

A comprehensive treatment of evaluation may be found in Chapter 17. Following are suggestions offered by Herbert Klausmeier *et al.* to aid teachers in making an appraisal of children's growth in reading throughout the elementary grades:

1. Observe children's vocabulary, speech, and usage in informal conversation, class discussion, and teacher-pupil conferences.
2. Appraise the children's oral reading of graded textbooks.
3. Discuss with the class the meaning they obtain from silent reading of graded textbooks.
4. Appraise the children's speech in choral reading and verse speaking.
5. By means of discussion, determine how much of the author's intended meaning the children grasp from reading a story silently.
6. Have the children record in a diary the words learned, books read, poems enjoyed, and the like.
7. Have the children make a class dictionary, and appraise their understandings and skills in using it.
8. By means of multiple-choice and other types of test items check the children's comprehension of the content of a story.
9. Administer a standardized reading readiness test late in the kindergarten year or early in the first grade.
10. Administer a standardized reading achievement test in any grade.
11. Appraise mental maturity and identify visual and hearing handicaps by means of other standardized tests.[22]

Self-appraisal by teachers themselves is important, too, in a developmental program. Teachers need to evaluate from time to time their methods of teaching and their attitudes toward the reading process.

---

[22] Herbert J. Klausmeier, Katharine Dresden, Helen C. Davis, Walter Arno Wittich, *Teaching in the Elementary School* (New York: Harper & Row, Publishers, 1956), pp. 235–236.

Bernice E. Leary suggests one type of self-evaluation made possible by answering the following questions:

1. How do I look upon reading?
2. How does my reading program reflect my understanding of children?
3. How does my reading program foster readiness for successive stages in learning?
4. What is included in my reading program?
5. Is my reading program organized for the good of all?
6. In what kind of environment does my reading program operate?
7. Does my reading program help the child to grow *in* reading and *through* reading?[23]

THE IMPORTANCE OF DEVELOPMENTAL NEEDS AND TASKS

The developmental approach to reading recognizes continuity in children's physical, mental, social, and other characteristics; one anticipates that some needs will be similar from year to year or grade to grade. Yet there are other needs, traceable to accumulated experiences or maturation, that require special emphasis at certain levels. Trends in development are noticeable in lists of "developmental tasks" which require fulfillment at various levels in order that the maximum attainment of each child may be realized and his well-being established.

Reading to Meet Developmental Needs

We have already indicated in Chapter 4 some ways by which needs may be met or partially fulfilled through reading, but it is fitting to stress again the importance of satisfying the needs of middle-grade pupils in this way. Thus we have seen that the middle-grade child often faces the task of freeing himself from primary dependence on adults, as well as acquiring an understanding of adults and their values. Some girls find help in meeting this need by reading Marguerite de Angeli's *Thee, Hannah,* a story which makes the meaning of a child's gray, drab bonnet a key to understanding adults and their values. Similarly, boys may enhance their appreciation by reading William Lipkin's *Boys of the Islands.* Both boys and girls often find enjoyment in Kate Seredy's *The Good Master,* and at the same time gain in appreciation of

[23] Bernice E. Leary, "What Am I Doing About Reading?" Unpublished manuscript (Madison, Wisconsin: University of Wisconsin).

family relationships and dependencies. Social values and satisfactions connected with family life may also be fostered by identification with characters in Eleanor Estes' *The Moffats* and the *Middle Moffat,* and in Sidney Taylor's *All-of-a-Kind Family.* Many types of families are presented in Laura Ingalls Wilder's *Little House in the Big Woods* and other books, which offer an excellent opportunity for pupils to identify themselves with different kinds of individuals and gain in this way a greater understanding of people.

Intermediate-grade pupils are extremely curious. They often yearn to find out about the world beyond their own homes and community; they may even want to learn about people in other lands. Factual presentations, biographies, and series books will prove helpful in such a pursuit.

A story such as Robert Lawson's *They Were Strong and Good* may afford an understanding of the strengths of America. Likewise, *America Is Born, America Grows Up,* and *America Moves Forward,* by Gerald W. Johnson, and many of *The Landmark Books* provide boys and girls with valuable information about people and events in our country. *First Under the North Pole,* by Edwin Tunis; *Communication: From Cave Writing to Television,* by Julie F. Batchelor; *The First Book of Space Travel,* by Jeanne Bendick; and *All About Famous Inventors and Their Inventions,* by Fletcher Pratt are examples of books that cover a wide range of topics and offer a challenge to the expanding and broadening horizons of boys and girls in the intermediate grades.

Learning to understand others and their hopes and ambitions may be increased through books which enlarge children's social concepts and deepen their understanding of other people. The following are examples of books to fulfill this need: *Onion John,* by Joseph Krumgold; *The Beatinest Boy,* by Jesse Stuart; and Reba P. Mirsky's *Thirty-one Brothers and Sisters.* Lois Lenski's books, which are authentic descriptions of life on varied socioeconomic levels, are especially suitable for expanding the background of boys and girls regarding the American scene. For example, life in the Florida lake region is described in *Strawberry Girl.*

If the reader will examine Chapter 3 on interests, he will find that the middle-grade child spends a very large amount of time with the mass media. Television is of course the favorite activity, and grade 6 the peak in the amount of viewing time. The time spent on the mass media is three or four times that given to reading. One of our responsibilities, therefore, is to encourage boys and girls to read more widely and to extend their interests, so that a wider assortment of books will be enjoyed.

As we have already indicated, the antidote to TV is helping children enjoy the act of reading and also the results. This they will do when they have acquired sufficient skills and are able to read varied kinds of materials with success and satisfaction. And they will usually enjoy the results of reading when reading experience is associated with their interests.

Recently we have made extensive studies of the reading interests of middle-grade boys and girls.[24] Among the mass media, television undeniably consumes the largest amount of children's time. But there are, of course, other activities to which children turn frequently for recreation. We asked middle-grade pupils to state their preferences for various activities, including TV, radio, the movies, and other leisure pursuits in and out-of-doors. Their answers give us clues in choosing relevant reading.

One question was designed to ascertain the pupils' favorite outdoor activities regardless of season. The number of pupils who stated that they took part in outdoor sports was large. Clearly, baseball and football were hardy perennials in the favorite activities of boys, as shown in Table X.

TABLE X

OUTDOOR ACTIVITIES ENGAGED IN BY PUPILS IN GRADES 3 THROUGH 6
(95 percent return)

BOYS	PERCENT	GIRLS	PERCENT
Playing baseball	59.0	Playing baseball	17.0
Playing football	57.1	Swimming	16.0
Playing basketball	16.8	Ice skating	11.1
Swimming	7.5	Riding a bicycle	8.6
Playing soccer	6.0	Playing hide-and-seek	7.2

The pupils were requested also to name their favorite indoor games and activities. Quieter games were more popular with the girls, while the more active nature of the boys was reflected in the high frequency of organized games, as indicated in Table XI.

One question related to building or construction, in answer to which a larger number of boys (65.6%) than girls (58.7%) reported actually making things. The objects most frequently constructed by boys were boats and airplanes, whereas the girls most frequently made doll clothes and doll houses.

[24] Paul Witty, "Studies of Interests of Children," *The Packet*, vol. 16, no. 2, D. C. Heath and Company (Winter 1961–62), pp. 15–21, 24–33.

TABLE XI
INDOOR ACTIVITIES ENGAGED IN BY PUPILS IN GRADES 3 THROUGH 6
(88 percent return)

BOYS	PERCENT	GIRLS	PERCENT
Playing basketball	12.2	Playing checkers	12.4
Playing ping-pong	11.8	Playing ping-pong	9.4
Playing checkers	8.7	Bowling	7.0
Bowling	7.5	Playing with dolls	6.3
Playing monopoly	6.0	Playing bingo	6.1

A question on pets showed that over sixty percent of the boys and girls owned pets, as shown in Table XII. Both boys and girls favored dogs, but girls cited birds a little more often than did the boys. The responses of the boys and girls were strikingly similar.

TABLE XII
PETS OWNED BY PUPILS IN GRADES 3 THROUGH 6
(97 percent return)

BOYS	PERCENT	GIRLS	PERCENT
Dog	56.6	Dog	53.4
Bird	25.7	Bird	32.9
Fish	21.4	Fish	21.2
Cat	17.2	Cat	19.4
Turtle	6.7	Turtle	6.2

Varied responses were obtained to the question concerning the three wishes of the pupils. The first wish of both boys and girls in grades three through six was for wealth. The second wish expressed by the boys was for a bicycle, while that of the girls was for a horse. The third wish of the boys was for a horse; of the girls it was for a dog.

In answer to one question which pertained to preferred types of reading, the pupils chose fiction as the kind of reading they liked best. Boys selected fiction, articles in newspapers and magazines, and biography as their first three choices. The girls, on the other hand, expressed a greater liking for poetry and plays than did the boys. While no one kind of story was an outstanding favorite, the boys did rate adventure first and the girls showed a slight preference for mystery stories. The book titles listed by boys in order of preference were *Black Beauty, Davy Crockett, Daniel Boone, Robin Hood, Thirty Seconds over Tokyo* and *Custer's Last Stand;* the girls listed *Little Women, Cinderella, Snow White, Heidi,* and *Black Beauty.*

Table XIII reports the favored nonfiction reading of boys and girls.

TABLE XIII
NONFICTION READING OF PUPILS IN GRADES 3 THROUGH 6
(84 percent return)

BOYS	PERCENT	GIRLS	PERCENT
Space travel	28.7	Famous people	25.0
Famous people	18.5	People from other lands	17.7
Handicrafts	12.8	Handicrafts	16.1
Travel	12.7	Travel	12.7
Careers	10.3	Space travel	11.5

The pupils indicated that their reading was not confined to books but also included frequent reading of magazines. Table XIV gives lists of magazines read frequently by boys and girls in grades three through six.

TABLE XIV
MAGAZINES READ BY PUPILS IN GRADES 3 THROUGH 6
(86 percent return)

BOYS	PERCENT	GIRLS	PERCENT
Life	28.8	*Life*	26.3
Boys' Life	22.5	*Look*	14.1
Look	12.0	*Saturday Evening Post*	6.9
Saturday Evening Post	6.5	*Jack and Jill*	6.7
Sports Illustrated	3.0	*American Girl*	4.6
Ebony	3.0	*Better Homes and Gardens*	4.6

Finally, an inquiry was made concerning vocational preferences of the pupils in grades three through six. Doctor and scientist were first and second choices of the boys, while teacher, nurse, and secretary were the majority choices of the girls.

These, then, are some of the interests characteristic of middle-grade boys and girls which can be counted on generally as dependable motivators of reading. Baseball and football, for example, will attract readers among the boys. Many middle-grade boys can be expected also to turn avidly to books concerning such vocations as airplane and space pilot, doctor, or scientist. Accordingly, books such as the Tunis stories of baseball heroes and the *First Books* on topics connected with space and airplane travel, medicine, and science usually will have strong appeal.

Similarly, middle-grade girls are generally attracted to such topics as nursing, teaching, and swimming. Hence biographical accounts and factual information about some of the women included as heroines in biographies found in the Landmark series or in a story such as that of the courageous teacher in Lenski's *Prairie School* will undoubtedly have strong appeal for many girls. Freeland concludes:

> The teacher who knows children and books will have little trouble in bringing them together if she is also blessed with enthusiasm and a genuine desire to share her interest in books with the children. The teacher who recognizes the potential value of books for promoting children's personal and social growth will take advantage of every opportunity to stimulate personal reading.[25]

CONCLUDING STATEMENT

In the intermediate grades there is need for extending and enriching reading through increased attention to the interests and developmental "tasks" of boys and girls. There is need, too, for the cultivation or further development of the habits and skills which enable pupils to become independent and resourceful in selecting and employing reading materials. In addition, there is need for emphasis on reading in the content fields with appropriate experience designed to extend and enrich the pupils' backgrounds in various fields. Pupils should also at this time become increasingly proficient in adjusting their rates of reading to their increasingly varied purposes.

In this chapter we have indicated habits and skills essential in the developmental program for the middle grades, and have set forth the conditions for assuring their sequential development. We have suggested sources of reading materials required for a developmental program, and have indicated some ways to evaluate growth in and through reading.

Finally, we have presented some recent studies of the interests of middle-grade pupils and have suggested ways by which these interests may be used to motivate reading.

Selected References

Betts, Emmett A., *Foundations of Reading Instruction*, rev. ed. (New York: American Book Company, 1957), Chapters 6 and 7.

Betts, Emmett A., "Reading Problems at the Intermediate-Grade Level," *Elementary School Journal*, 40:737–746 (June, 1940).

Burrows, Alvina T., *Teaching Children in the Middle Grades* (Boston: D. C. Heath and Co., 1952).

Carlson, Thorsten, "Evaluating Materials for Reading Instruction—Inter-

[25] Alma Freeland, *op. cit.*, p. 471.

mediate Grades," in J. Allen Figurel (editor), *Challenge and Experiment in Reading* (New York: Scholastic Magazines, Inc., 1962), pp. 190–193.

Daw, Seward E., "The Persistence of Errors in Oral Reading in Grades Four and Five," *Journal of Educational Research*, 32:81–90 (October, 1938).

Dolch, Edward W., "Goals in Intermediate Reading," *Elementary School Journal*, 35:682–690 (May, 1935).

Fay, Leo C., "Promoting Growth in Ability to Interpret When Reading Critically: In Grades Four to Six," in *Promoting Growth Toward Maturity in Interpreting What Is Read*, Supplementary Education Monographs, No. 74 (Chicago: University of Chicago Press, 1951), pp. 144–148.

Gainsberg, Joseph C., "Critical Reading Is Creative Reading and Needs Creative Teaching," *The Reading Teacher*, 6:19–26 (March, 1953).

Glock, Marvin D., "Developing Clear Recognition of Pupil Purposes for Reading," *The Reading Teacher*, 11:165–170 (February, 1958).

Gray, Lillian, *Teaching Children to Read*, 3rd ed. (New York: The Ronald Press Company, 1963).

Gray, William S., "Growth in Understanding of Reading and Its Development Among Youth," in *Keeping Reading Programs Abreast of the Times*, Supplementary Education Monographs, No. 72 (Chicago: University of Chicago Press, 1950), pp. 8–13.

Hansen, Carl W., "Factors Associated with Successful Achievement in Problem Solving in Sixth Grade Arithmetic," *Journal of Educational Research*, 38:111–118 (October, 1944).

Hudson, J. S., "Reading Readiness in the Intermediate Grades," *Elementary English*, 19:134–137 (April, 1942).

Jelinek, James J., "Literature and the Development of Critical Thinking," *The Clearing House*, 30:462–463 (April, 1956).

Johnson, Marjorie Seddon, "Readiness for Critical Reading," *Education*, 73:391–396 (February, 1953).

Knapp, Jessie V., "Improving Reading Skills in Content Areas," *Elementary English*, 24:542–550 (December, 1947).

Lorge, Irving, "Reading, Thinking, and Learning," in Nancy Larrick (editor), *Reading in Action*, International Reading Association, Conference Proceedings (New York: Scholastic Magazines, Inc.), 2:15–18 (1957).

McIntire, Alta, "Reading Social Studies Materials in the Middle Grades," *Elementary English Review*, 21:262–266 (November, 1944).

McLendon, Jonathon C., *Teaching the Social Studies: What Research Says to the Teacher*, American Educational Research Association and the Department of Classroom Teachers, vol. 20 (Washington, D. C.: National Education Association, 1960).

Malter, Morton S., "Children's Ability to Read Diagrammatic Materials," *Elementary School Journal*, 49:98–102 (October, 1948).

Morton, R. L., "Language and Meaning in Arithmetic," *Educational Research Bulletin*, 34:197–204 (November, 1955).

Parker, Bertha M., "Reading in an Intermediate-Grade Science Program," *Elementary School Journal*, 38:38–43 (September, 1937).

Russell, David H., *Children Learn to Read*, 2nd ed. (Waltham, Mass.: Blaisdell Publishing Company, 1961).

Russell, David H. and Marion A. Anderson, "Professional Opinions About Basic Reading Programs in the Middle and Upper Grades of the Elementary School," *Elementary School Journal,* 46:81–88 (October, 1945).

Schubert, Delwyn G., "Science Teachers: What You Can Do to Help Your Students to Read More Efficiently," *The Clearing House,* 30:83–84 (October, 1955).

Smith, Dora V., "The Goals of the Literature Period and the Grade Sequence of Desirable Experiences," in *Improving Reading in All Curriculum Areas,* Supplementary Educational Monographs, No. 76 (Chicago: University of Chicago Press, 1952), pp. 188–194.

Smith, Henry P. and Emerald V. Dechant, *Psychology in Teaching Reading* (Englewood Cliffs, N. J.: Prentice-Hall, Inc., 1961).

Spache, George D., "Types and Purposes of Reading in Various Curriculum Fields," *The Reading Teacher,* 11:158–164 (February, 1958).

Spache, George D., and Paul C. Berg, *The Art of Efficient Reading* (New York: The Macmillan Co., 1955).

Strang, Ruth and Dorothy Kendall Bracken, *Making Better Readers* (Boston: D. C. Heath and Company, 1957).

Strang, Ruth, Constance M. McCullough, and Arthur E. Traxler, *The Improvement of Reading,* 3rd ed. (New York: McGraw-Hill Book Co., 1961).

Taba, Hilda, "The Problems in Developing Critical Thinking," *Progressive Education,* 28:45–48, 61 (November, 1950).

Witty, Paul A. (chairman), *Development In and Through Reading,* Sixtieth Yearbook of the National Society for the Study of Education, Part II (Chicago: University of Chicago Press, 1961), Chapters 13, 16, and 17.

Witty, Paul, "Meeting Developmental Needs Through Reading," *Education,* 84:451–458 (April, 1964).

Witty, Paul, "Reading of Social Studies Materials," *Elementary English,* 27:1–8 (January, 1950).

Witty, Paul, "Studies of Children's Interests—A Brief Summary," *Elementary English,* 37:469–475 (November, 1960), 38:540–545 (December, 1960), 38:33–36 (January, 1961).

Witty, Paul and associates, *A Study of the Interests of Children and Youth.* Northwestern University in Cooperation with the Office of Education, U. S. Department of Health, Education and Welfare, 1960.

Wren, F. Lynwood, "What Are the Goals of Instruction in Arithmetic and Mathematics and the Grade Sequence of Understandings and Skills?" *Improving Reading in All Curriculum Areas,* Supplementary Educational Monographs, no. 76 (Chicago: University of Chicago Press, 1952), pp. 144–149.

II

READING INSTRUCTION IN JUNIOR AND SENIOR HIGH SCHOOL

The development and improvement of basic reading skills was once regarded as the unique function of the elementary school. In the early school years the pupil learned to read and later, in the more advanced grades, he learned through reading. During the last three decades, however, "Concern for the improvement of reading has extended beyond the primary grades into college and adult years."[1] It is recognized today that "reading can no longer be regarded as a number of simple skills which can be taught once and for all purposes in a few formal reading lessons" and that "even the superior learners profit by continued guidance in reading throughout the elementary school and into higher levels."[2]

Evidence of interest in the improvement of reading skills of older pupils was found when the editor of *The Nation's Schools* sent letters to school superintendents asking them to submit questions concerning their major problems and needs in the field of reading instruction. The superintendents repeatedly requested information about the characteristics of, and ways to establish, an effective reading program for pupils in the junior and senior high schools. This information was provided by Paul Witty in four articles which appeared in this journal in January through April, 1958.

---

[1] Ruth Strang, Constance M. McCullough, and Arthur E. Traxler, *The Improvement of Reading*, 3rd ed. (New York: McGraw-Hill Book Company, 1961), p. 440.

[2] Arthur I. Gates, "What Research Says about Teaching Reading," *National Education Association Journal*, 42:402 (October, 1953).

NEED FOR DEVELOPMENTAL READING PROGRAMS

Why is there such a keen awareness of the need for developmental reading programs at the junior and senior high school levels? The following facts will suggest some of the reasons.

Need to Provide Appropriate Educational Opportunities

From statistics compiled by the United States Office of Education one writer notes that "Only four percent of the youth of our country were graduated from high school in 1870, in contrast to 59 percent in 1950, not quite one hundred years later."[3] Thus, increased enrollments throughout the secondary school have added to the problems of administrators, and one of the main problems today is to provide appropriate educational experiences for many pupils who formerly would have dropped out of school. Large numbers of these pupils are poor readers who, with suitable opportunities, could greatly improve their reading abilities. M. Agnella Gunn notes that:

> The general population of the United States tripled from 1870 to 1940; during that same interval the secondary school population became ninety times as large. After World War II there was a tremendous increase in the number of children in the population. At the same time there was an increase in the number of pupils being retained in school who formerly would have been dropped. . . .
> Even more important than the change in the size of the school population is the change in its nature or character. This stems in part from a modification of our philosophy of education. Our attitude toward the purpose of the secondary schools has altered basically. No longer is their main function conceived to be, in effect, the providing of a proving ground for the academic pupil who is headed for college. Today their function is also considered to be the providing of a training ground for the pupil whose abilities are more limited or more "practical."[4]

Need to Meet Varying Abilities

In addition to the continuing increase in school enrollments, the widely varying reading abilities and attainments of large numbers of

[3] Ruth C. Penty, *Reading Ability and High School Drop-Outs* (New York: Bureau of Publications, Teachers College, Columbia University, 1956), p. 1.
[4] M. Agnella Gunn, "What Does Research in Reading Tell the Teacher of English in the Secondary School?" in *What We Know About High School Reading,* prepared by the National Conference on Research in English and reprinted from the *English Journal,* 1957–58 (Champaign, Ill.: National Council of Teachers of English), pp. 4–5.

pupils have created additional problems. A wide range in ability and a marked amount of poor reading will be found in almost every class throughout both the junior and the senior high school. Reading retardation, as indicated by high frequencies of reading scores decidedly below norms, will vary, of course, from community to community and from school to school. For example, it was found that, in one school located in a section of relatively low socioeconomic status in an industrial city, about half of the eighth-grade pupils made scores one year or more below the norms for their grades. And there were relatively few high scores earned by the pupils in this school. In a more prosperous Illinois community, on the other hand, it was found that among 518 eighth-grade pupils only 89 fell at or below the seventh-grade norms, while 154 attained ninth-grade standards and 171 reached or exceeded tenth-grade attainment according to the California Test norms.[5]

Although variation in school achievement within classes has long been recognized, today it appears that there are more very low scores made by junior and senior high school pupils than formerly. Wide variation in school achievement, as W. S. Gray points out,

> has always existed and results largely from the fact that pupils vary widely in background, motives, and capacity to learn. The teachers of former decades were conscious of differences in rates of learning, just as teachers are today, and were just as deeply concerned about them. Few techniques of adjustment had developed, however, and pupils who were unable to profit from the uniform instruction which was customary often repeated given grades several times and finally dropped out of school.[6]

The results of a provocative study by Ruth Penty also indicate that poor reading ability may be an important factor in the failure of many students to finish high school today.[7] Two groups of tenth-grade students attending a large Midwest high school were the subjects of the study.

(1) 593 tenth-grade students who were in the lowest quarter of their class at the time of their last reading test (of these, there were 296 who dropped out of school, 270 who remained to graduate, 27 who transferred);
(2) 593 tenth-grade students whose scores were in the highest quarter of their class at the time of their last reading test (of

---

[5] Glenn Myers Blair, *Diagnostic and Remedial Teaching* (New York: The Macmillan Company, 1956), p. 5.

[6] William S. Gray, "Educational News and Editorial Comment," *The Elementary School Journal,* 46:482 (May, 1946).

[7] Ruth C. Penty, *op. cit.,* p. 12.

these, there were 86 who dropped out of school, 481 who remained to graduate, 26 who transferred).

It was found that:

> More than three times as many poor readers as good readers dropped out of school before graduation; the peak of the school leaving among the dropouts was during the tenth grade. There was no significant difference between the reading scores at the tenth grade level of the poor readers who dropped out of school before graduation and of the poor readers who remained in school until graduation.
> The interview data emphasized that difficulty in reading played a very important role in the school leaving of boys and girls, especially when certain other problems and pressures were also present.[8]

It is evident that many pupils need remedial instruction. Certainly the presence of considerable numbers of junior high school pupils who read at the fourth-, fifth-, or sixth-grade level discloses sharply the need for additional instruction in reading. Even the more competent readers require guidance in reading as well as emphasis on the reading skills used repeatedly in the various subject areas.

Need to Develop Reading Interests

Additional evidence of the need for developmental programs throughout the junior and senior high schools is found in the lack of interest in reading exhibited by many young people and adults today.[9] Yet it is generally recognized that to cope successfully with occupational and civic demands of modern life, skill in reading, as well as a tendency to read widely, is a desirable and often a necessary acquisition. Regrettably, however, many studies over the past twenty years have revealed a relatively small amount of reading (apart from textbook assignments) among junior and senior high school students. It is not surprising, then, that adults generally read little—although there are, fortunately, many exceptions.

Many schools are attempting to create a more general and lasting interest in reading by establishing elementary school libraries and by extending greatly secondary school library facilities and opportunities. Moreover, there is a growing tendency to establish reading programs designed to help students satisfy their interests and meet their needs.

[8] *Ibid.*, pp. 73–74.
[9] An excellent series of books designed for pupils who "need to begin reading in low gear" and with the purpose of changing these pupils' negative attitudes toward reading are the *Teen-Age Tales,* Books 1, 2, 3, 4, 5, 6, A, B, and C, published by D. C. Heath and Company, Boston, Mass.

THE DEVELOPMENTAL PROGRAM

Characteristics of an Efficient Developmental Program

After reviewing the literature on reading programs and after observing some of the programs in action, most authorities will agree that developmental reading programs having the following characteristics should be provided in our schools.

First, a developmental program aims to cultivate mastery of the skills needed for effective reading. It has already been pointed out that the core of a reading program is the teaching of skills. In this light, it must be recognized that the reading program on the junior and senior high school level must teach those skills not learned by pupils and must cultivate mastery of those skills inadequately learned previously by students. Only when skills are mastered can the reading process prove most enjoyable and beneficial.

Second, the developmental approach recognizes various purposes and needs for reading. Some needs relate to common attainments, at times referred to as "developmental tasks." Other needs are highly personal, but nonetheless significant for individual welfare. Obviously some needs are temporary; others may constitute a basis for long-range planning to be fulfilled at various times. A worthy developmental program seeks to evaluate needs and plans for their fulfillment at the most appropriate time.

Third, a developmental program depends on other experiences and activities operating in association with reading. In meeting the needs of youth, reading must be construed as only one factor—and not relied on solely to meet needs. Adequate satisfaction implies an effective relationship of reading to other experiences in the individual's total activity pattern. Three elements are involved with this characteristic: one item involves the teacher's efforts to gain an understanding of each pupil, his background of experience, and his needs; another relates to the provision of varied reading materials and experiences to satisfy interests and needs; and a third concerns the teacher's efforts to evaluate each pupil's growth in and through reading.

Fourth, a developmental program encompasses the entire faculty. The mistaken notion that reading is the sole task of the English teacher has been prevalent for many years. Actually, every teacher should be a teacher of reading because the subject-matter areas represent the actual use of the total spectrum of reading skills. Robert Karlin extends this idea:

One thing at least is certain: it is unrealistic to expect the English teacher or the reading expert to teach all the needed reading skills. A total reading program demands the cooperation and work of everyone—classroom teacher, librarian, guidance counselor, supervisor, and administrator. It is probably the most difficult school program to initiate and to implement, and also the most worth while.[10]

Some Present Practices in Administering Reading Programs

There is heartening evidence that efforts to improve the reading of junior and senior high school students are often most successful and that many pupils are now reading more effectively. In Elizabeth Simpson's book a number of such high school programs have been described and evidence of their success has been offered.[11] Margaret Early, who has also given examples of reading programs in grades nine to twelve, makes the following comments in regard to them:

> Reading programs vary according to the size of the school, the type of community, the abilities of the pupils and their needs now and in the future, the curriculum offered, the attitudes and skill of the teachers, the size of the staff, and the consultant help available. No one pattern can be described as "most likely to succeed." Furthermore, experience with reading programs in the high school is still extremely limited. Most of those reported in the literature are fairly recent developments, and few practices have been evaluated in objective experiments. Promising practices and trends on trial are the most that can be reported at this early stage.[12]

She goes on to point out:

> if the various types of reading programs that have been suggested by competent authorities or tried out in actual practice were arranged according to comprehensiveness of approach, at the top of the ladder would stand the all-school developmental program.[13]

Thus the teaching of reading, like education itself, is regarded by many educators as a developmental process in which the maximum development of every boy and girl should be sought according to his or her unique nature and needs. Most educators now insist that reading experiences should be meaningful from the beginning, and that reading

---

[10] Robert Karlin, *Teaching Reading in the High School* (Indianapolis, Indiana: The Bobbs-Merrill Company, Inc., 1964), pp. 260–261.

[11] Elizabeth Simpson, "Examples of High School Reading Programs in Action," in *Helping High School Students Read Better* (Chicago: Science Research Associates, Inc., 1954), Part II, pp. 93–142.

[12] Margaret J. Early, "What Does Research Reveal about Successful Reading Programs?" in *What We Know about High School Reading, op. cit.*, p. 7.

[13] *Ibid.*

instruction should continue as long as the student has need for guidance or for the refinement of his skills in reading.

Many problems have to be solved, however, in extending effective reading programs into the junior and senior high schools. William Sheldon indicates that the role of the junior high school has not been fully identified, that some secondary school teachers have little training or experience in coping with the reading problems of their pupils, and that the administration and faculty in junior and senior high schools are just beginning to realize the need for continuing instruction in reading.[14]

Likewise, Margaret Early points out that there are many problems to be solved by individual school systems in their efforts to provide an all-school reading program extending into the senior high school. She maintains that many reading programs are "compromise programs" because of teacher attitudes, teaching methods, and decisions of teacher-committees.[15] She goes on to describe the characteristics of some of these "compromise programs" as practiced in school today.

> In an attempt to provide systematic instruction in reading before a total program has been fully developed, many secondary schools offer special classes in reading. In some cases these classes are additions to the regular curriculum. Frequently they are labeled "developmental" to show that they provide for all pupils—slow, average, and superior—at a given grade level. Sometimes they are called "corrective" when they are designed for students with specific reading disabilities. When individual or very small group instruction is provided for retarded readers, the program is sometimes designated as "remedial," although this term has fallen into disrepute because it carries unattractive connotations.
>
> In place of the regular English course, corrective classes sometimes are offered for a semester or two. This type of program is different in objectives and organization from the type described next.
>
> Another common approach, especially in smaller schools, is to charge English teachers with the responsibility of developing the reading skills of all students as part of the regular English courses. Occasionally, especially in the junior high school, the teaching of reading is a specific area of instruction within the core course or, as in one laboratory school, an integral part of a problem-centered core.
>
> Emphases differ and variations occur within these patterns, but essentially these four types—the special reading class, the substitute Eng-

---

[14] William D. Sheldon, "Reading Instruction in the Junior High School," in Paul Witty (chairman), *Development In and Through Reading,* Sixtieth Yearbook of the National Society for the Study of Education, Part I (Chicago: University of Chicago Press, 1961), pp. 305–306.

[15] Margaret J. Early, *op. cit.,* p. 9.

lish class, instruction within the regular English class, and developmental reading as part of the core course—are the practices commonly recommended and followed.[16]

The preceding four patterns are finding expression in our schools. The special reading class is being organized in some schools, while in others the substitute English class is providing much-needed help in reading. The third practice, too, is being initiated by high school teachers of English who are trying to offer help in reading to all students within the regular class. This practice may be incorporated as a part of the developmental approach which elicits the services of all teachers —perhaps the most desirable and promising of the four practices. Though difficult to inaugurate and maintain, it is undoubtedly the most effective and rewarding procedure.

It is gratifying to discover that, despite its complexities, the developmental approach is being undertaken in some high schools. For example, the reading program in the Evanston (Illinois) Township High School is introduced through the film *Better Reading*. The Reading Accelerator and the Flashmeter are employed only as motivating devices. Filmstrips and the tape recorder are used in building vocabularies. The textbook *How to Become a Better Reader* is followed in the reading-improvement program. Some features of this work are described below:

> A full-time reading consultant has been appointed and has been given ample time and diversified materials for use with individuals. One of the major purposes of the program is to encourage the improvement of reading within every classroom rather than merely to offer remedial services. This developmental program has emphasized four types of instruction to improve reading: (1) remedial classes are substitutes for freshman English, (2) skill classes for upperclassmen, (3) individual diagnostic work for students having special problems, and (4) emphasis upon growth in reading in all classrooms. . . .
> To coordinate the reading program with the regular English course (for example), units on grammar and special topics were included. Shakespeare recordings were employed to familiarize the group with plays such as *The Merchant of Venice*. Enthusiastic discussions, dramatizations, and question-and-answer panels made these plays interesting to students who otherwise might not have enjoyed them. . . .
> More important, perhaps, than the reading gains made by these groups was the students' change in attitude toward reading. Practice and knowledge of efficient reading skills stimulated interest and prepared students to attack assignments in other classes. This led to a

[16] *Ibid.*, pp. 9–10.

change in attitude toward reading in the different subject areas, as well as to improvement in the mental health of the students. It is the purpose of the school's reading committee to promote a school-wide acceptance of this type of reading instruction and to establish developmental conditions for reading and learning activities within the classrooms of all the content fields.[17]

A developmental reading program designed to increase speed and comprehension was established in the high schools in Des Plaines–Park Ridge, Illinois. Committees planning the reading improvement programs in both schools consisted of the principal, assistant principal, director of student personnel, reading specialist, head librarian, and department chairmen. A unique feature of this program was that every teacher was considered a teacher of reading. All teachers stressed the need for developing better reading abilities, which was accomplished, for example, through homeroom activities, class discussions, and bulletin board displays. Moreover, the reading clinics at the high schools continued to give specialized instruction to all freshmen and juniors, and plans were made for expansion of the clinics so that they could aid the entire school program.[18]

It may be seen that some schools are courageously attacking the reading problem. Various plans are being followed with success, but regardless of the plan followed, certain responsibilities must be assumed by the teachers. In fact to engage successfully in *any* of these approaches the teacher must be prepared to ascertain each pupil's ability and potentiality and to study his interests and his needs; he must also be qualified to obtain and use efficiently the varied but necessary materials of instruction; and he must be equipped to appraise and evaluate the results of instruction in terms of the objectives of the program.

It will be found that in some successful programs on the junior and senior high school level administrators have assumed certain responsibilities. Probably their most important task has been to provide educational leadership. Frequently, this leadership involved, first, motivation and second, guidance of the staffs. Once the program began to function, the principal then coordinated the efforts of guidance counselors, department chairmen, and reading specialists, who in turn guided the efforts of the teachers. As was pointed out in the Des Plaines-Park

---

[17] Phyllis Bland, "Adjusting Instruction to Individual Differences in Grades Ten to Fourteen," in William S. Gray (editor), *Improving Reading in All Curriculum Areas,* Supplementary Educational Monograph No. 76 (Chicago: University of Chicago Press, 1952), pp. 44–45.

[18] "Planning a Developmental Reading Program for Maine East and Maine West," *Parents' Bulletin,* October, 1960, pp. 1–2. A publication of Township High School District No. 207, Des Plaines–Park Ridge, Illinois.

Ridge Plan, the remedial program continued to function within the framework of the total developmental program. Attempts are made in a developmental program for help to be given to individuals—even to seriously retarded readers. This is sometimes accomplished through the services of a reading consultant, a clinician, or an especially skilled teacher.

It is now generally conceded that the modern high school should not only continue to offer guidance in reading, but should also encourage the students in assuming the responsibility for their own growth and improvement in reading skills and appreciation. Thus Bond and Kegler say:

> The primary goal of reading instruction at the senior high school level is independence in reading. Within the broad framework of this fundamental goal, the methods of instruction, for most students, will revolve around systematic extensions of previously learned abilities, further refinements of basic skills, and in many cases, the acquisition of new techniques required for dealing with the variety of reading materials available to young adults. These methods of instruction must be direct rather than incidental; in any reading activity there must always be the dual purpose of increasing independence in reading and mastering the content of the subjects.[19]

DETERMINING PUPIL NEEDS

Studying the Reading Status of Pupils

It is obvious that before initiating instruction in reading at any level, the teacher should have data regarding the mental maturity as well as the reading attainment of every pupil in the class. This information can be obtained in part from the results of standardized tests—which, however, should be interpreted judiciously with an awareness of their limitations as well as their values.

Widely used mental tests designed for group testing which have forms suitable for junior and senior high school pupils are:

> *California Test of Mental Maturity*, s-form, 1963. Level 3 for Grades 7, 8, 9; level 4 for Grades 9–12. (California Test Bureau, Del Monte Research Park, Monterey, California.) Working Time: Approx. 40 minutes.

---

[19] Guy L. Bond and Stanley B. Kegler, "Reading Instruction in the Senior High School," in Paul Witty (chairman), *Development In and Through Reading*, Sixtieth Yearbook of the National Society for the Study of Education, Part I, (Chicago: University of Chicago Press, 1961), pp. 330–331.

Henman-Nelson Tests of Mental Ability, High School Form for grades 7–12. (Houghton Mifflin Company, 2 Park Street, Boston, Massachusetts.) Working time: 30 minutes.

Otis Quick-Scoring Mental Ability Tests, Beta form for grades 4–9, Gamma form for grades 9–12. (Harcourt, Brace and World, Inc., 757 Third Avenue, New York, New York.) Working time: 30 minutes.

SRA Primary Mental Abilities Test, grades 6–9 and grades 9–12. (Science Research Associates, Inc., 259 East Erie Street, Chicago, Illinois.) Working time: 55 minutes.

In addition to ascertaining pupils' mental ability it is also necessary to determine their achievement level in reading. Reading tests such as the following may be administered to groups of junior and senior high school students:

California Reading Test, 1963 edition, junior high school form for grades 7–9, advanced form for grades 9–14. (California Test Bureau, Del Monte Research Park, Monterey, California.) Test measures vocabulary and reading comprehension.

Cooperative English Test: Reading Comprehension, 1960 rev., Level 1 for grades 9–12, and Level 2 for grades 7–12. (Educational Testing Service, 2 Chambers Street, Princeton, New Jersey.) Test measures recognition vocabulary, speed of comprehension, and level of comprehension.

Iowa Silent Reading Tests, new edition, Elementary form for grades 4–8, Advanced form for grades 9–12. (Harcourt, Brace and World, Inc., 757 Third Avenue, New York, New York.) Test measures rate of reading, comprehension, and ability to use skills in locating information.

Kelley-Greene Reading Comprehension Test, Grades 9–13 (Harcourt, Brace and World, Inc., 757 Third Ave., New York, New York.) Test measures ability to comprehend paragraphs, ability to find answers to questions, ability to retain what is read.

Metropolitan Reading Tests, Advanced form for grades 7–9 (Harcourt, Brace and World, Inc., 757 Third Ave., New York, New York.) Test measures word knowledge, word discrimination, and comprehension.

Nelson-Denny Reading Test, Grades 9–12 (Houghton Mifflin Company, 2 Park Street, Boston, Massachusetts.) Test measures vocabulary, comprehension, and reading rate.

Traxler High School Reading Test, Grades 10–12 (The Bobbs-Merrill Company, Inc., 4300 West 62nd Street, Indianapolis, Indiana.) Test measures rate of continuous reading of material in the field of social science and also measures ability to locate main ideas.

In addition to ascertaining the pupils' general reading proficiency, the teacher should evaluate each pupil's ability to read from varied sources, such as materials in the social sciences and natural sciences. A test designed for this purpose is the *Iowa Test of Educational Development*.[20]

Although standardized tests provide important information concerning both mental maturity and reading achievement, further information about each pupil is needed before reading instruction can proceed most effectively. Study of the interests and needs of each pupil contributes important additional information.

Studying Pupils' Interests

Throughout this book we have stressed the importance of studying the interests and needs of pupils. To engage successfully in the guidance of reading, the teacher requires, as we have already pointed out, more than reliable information concerning the reading ability of each pupil. To offer effective guidance, the teacher must also take account of information pertaining to each pupil's personal and social adjustment. Some helpful procedures are now being used to obtain such data. Interest inventories often yield clues of value,[21] as do anecdotal records and similar approaches. Examination of pupils' personal writing may also help; through

> ... personal writing, the teacher's and pupil's insight into a problem may be increased. The teacher may become less concerned with split infinitives and more concerned with split personality; unity and coherence in the paragraph may become subordinated to unity and coherence of the self.[22]

Through approaches of these kinds, the teacher may acquire a somewhat valid basis for suggesting reading especially valuable for promoting the personal and social adjustment of the reader. Books, of course, will not be "prescribed," nor reading considered the sole method through which improved adjustment could be sought. Varied experience, discussion, and investigation are also significant aspects of the process.

Research on the interests of high school boys and girls has been meager in recent years. One extensive newer study investigated pupils'

---

[20] *The Iowa Tests of Educational Development* contain nine subtests that provide a practical appraisal of educational development in English, mathematics, natural sciences, and social sciences. Alternate forms X and Y are available for students on the high school level. Published by Science Research Associates, Inc., 259 East Erie Street, Chicago, Illinois.

[21] See Appendix for inventories.

[22] David H. Russell and Caroline Shrodes, "Contributions of Research in Bibliotherapy to the Language-Arts Program, II," *The School Review*, 58:418 (October, 1950).

interests in grades 9 through 12.[23] The interest areas included: (1) television, radio, and movies, (2) recreation and hobbies, (3) vocational ambitions and educational choices, and (4) the amount and nature of reading. A number of important facts concerning interests of high school youth came to light.

The results of this study are similar to others in demonstrating the popularity of television as compared with other media of mass communication. Indeed, television appears as the favorite leisure activity of youth, with radio a close second.

The students in this investigation appear to be somewhat more realistic in their occupational preferences than pupils in studies made a decade or more ago. Witness their selection of a relatively small number of occupations—occupations which hold possibilities of absorbing many people today. Girls mentioned more frequently than in earlier studies such occupations as teacher, nurse, and secretary. The boys today frequently choose engineer and scientist.

One of the most interesting and significant facts revealed by this study is the very high percentage of both boys and girls who planned to go to college. Seventy-eight percent of the boys said that they were planning to attend college; and higher percentages of the parents, too, wanted their children to go to college. A college education for his children is clearly the dream of the typical American parent today.

Another noteworthy finding is the close relationship between the subjects liked best by the pupils and those in which they received their highest marks. Such a relationship suggests the importance of attitude in determining a child's successful school endeavor.

The results of this investigation in the field of reading are provocative. Thus we find that while the mass media consume three or more hours daily, reading is accorded only about an hour each day by these pupils. Most of the books reported fell in the category of fiction; poetry, essays, and drama were less often read. In the nonfiction group, stories of famous people were best liked. The most popular books of the boys fell under the headings of adventure and mystery, though boys were attracted to science fiction too. Girls turned more frequently to stories involving romance. There was frequent mention of superior series books, such as the Landmark Series and Teen-age Tales, with occasional mention of paperback books. Magazine reading for the older

---

[23] Paul Witty, "A Study of Pupils' Interests, Grades 9, 10, 11, 12." *Education*, 82:39–47 (September, 1961); 82:100–110 (October, 1961); 82:169–174 (November, 1961).

pupils was limited largely to *Life, Look, The Saturday Evening Post,* and news periodicals.

Collectively, these data present a picture of youth today surrounded by intriguing mechanical devices and opportunities for "purchased" vicarious recreation. Throughout the entire investigation of interests the influence of standardizing forces and the power of the ubiquitous mass media were reflected. The teacher may question whether the present pattern of interests of these pupils is not too heavily weighted with activities associated with the mass media—particularly television. The antidote to the undesirable aspects of TV and other mass media, as well as to other standardizing influences, lies in the provision of a constructive program of guidance. Below are a few suggestions which parents and teachers might follow to advantage in working to improve not only television but the pupil's total pattern of interests and activities.

1. Extend the recreational opportunities of your school and of your community. Try to offer boys and girls abundant opportunities for varied play activities and for creative pursuits of many kinds that will balance their craze for sedentary activities.

2. Use child study to understand pupils and their needs. Find out the programs they are seeing on television and the amount of time they are giving to TV, the radio, and the movies. Discuss the merits and limitations of favorite programs. Investigate the extent to which they take part in other leisure activities. Study the amounts and nature of their participation in outdoor activities and offer constructive suggestions so as to bring about balanced programs of recreation. Discuss strong interests, and whenever possible relate them to hobbies or creative pursuits. Offer individual guidance in recognition of the uniqueness and varied needs of each pupil.

3. Keep in mind the fact that some of the satisfactions obtained from television are similar to those derived from the movies, the radio, and comic books. Find out the amount of time pupils devote to each activity and try to offer constructive individual and group guidance.

4. Strive to improve the offerings on television and the radio. There is a unique opportunity for teachers to participate in a widespread movement aimed at the presentation of better TV programs. Talk over with pupils the ratings given to TV presentations by various magazines.

5. Help students to develop more efficient reading habits and skills so that they will enjoy the act of reading as well as the results. Become well acquainted with literature for youth. Try to provide an assortment of reading materials to satisfy and extend wholesome interests.

MATERIALS OF INSTRUCTION

Analysis of tests will reveal large variability in reading ability within any typical high school class. Some pupils, although superior in total scores on standard tests, will show certain weaknesses. Guidance in reading will be needed by most high school pupils, including the generally good readers. Some superior students are inclined to read all materials in about the same way; others are restricted in their development of special vocabularies. Some need to become more proficient in critical reading, and still others who read little and lack the ability to use source materials effectively need direction and encouragement.

Studies show that large numbers of junior and senior high school pupils need to develop more fully some of the subtle reading skills such as determining the nature of proof, examining the validity of basic assumptions, and distinguishing fact from fiction. In the two books *How to Improve Your Reading,* designed for the junior high school pupil, and *How to Become a Better Reader,* prepared for the senior high school and college students, suggestions are offered for the development of such skills.[24] These books pay considerable attention to word analysis and vocabulary building and also stress the skills essential to the reading of different types of subject matter on advanced levels.

Another aid for the student in improving his reading independently is the SRA Reading Laboratory.[25] Laboratory III is designed for the use of grades 7–9 and Laboratory IV for grades 9–12.

A helpful book for vocabulary development of junior and senior high school students is *Developing Your Vocabulary,*[26] a book which may be used by students independently or under the supervision of the teacher.

The Textbook

A textbook in reading for high school pupils provides for the systematic development and use of reading skills. Almost all students in the junior and senior high schools, we have said, need practice in applying skills such as the ability to note significant details, follow clues,

---

[24] Paul Witty, *How to Improve Your Reading* (Chicago: Science Research Associates, Inc., 1963); and *How to Become a Better Reader* (Chicago: Science Research Associates, Inc., 1962).

[25] Science Research Associates Reading Laboratory: III for Junior High School or Early High School, grades 7–9; IV for High School and College, grades 9–13 (Chicago: Science Research Associates, Inc., 1957).

[26] Paul Witty and Edith Grotberg, *Developing Your Vocabulary,* (Chicago: Science Research Associates, Inc., 1960).

determine the authenticity of different presentations, recognize and appreciate different types of literature, and find and use reference materials. These and many other basic skills should be developed systematically. In addition, good texts contain suggestions for helping students expand their vocabularies.

A good textbook also contains suggestions for helping pupils discover, record, and improve their rates of reading in various kinds of subject matter. Wide reading practice tends to foster improvement in rate of reading. Pupils should be led to check systematically their rates of reading different kinds of material. Selections which are easily read for pleasure, and primarily for the story value, should be read at a faster rate than those used to obtain detailed factual information. A good textbook provides a variety of subject matter to help students adjust their rates of reading to purpose or need. Because the range of reading abilities within a high school class is often large, there must be stories on many levels of difficulty.

Textbooks in reading, as we pointed out in Chapter 10 of this book, have been prepared recently for junior and senior high school pupils. For some series teachers' guides have been designed to help the teacher in studying the needs of pupils and in finding appropriate reading materials for each pupil. The materials in these texts cover topics of strong appeal to young people today, such as sports, radio, space travel, television, and other expressions of twentieth-century life. Such textbooks, through the inclusion of stories of high interest which are presented in readable style, invite the student to read. The Reading Roundup Series is an example of textbooks designed for the purposes noted above.[27]

Many adolescents at one time or another are concerned with such matters as: conflicts arising from family and school relationships, decisions about matters of etiquette and acceptable behavior, a desire to "belong" to the group and to follow the group pattern, the longing for personal success in sports and other activities, the choice of an occupation, devotion to an ideal or purpose, enjoyment of the natural world, enjoyment of humor, and many others. The reading of appropriate stories, plays, poems, biographies, and autobiographies may help young people meet many of their own problems successfully. Biographies as well as narrative materials afford analysis of the lives of people in a thought-provoking manner; and students in the course of discussion often come to recognize the importance of character traits in determining achievement as well as the significance of interest, effort, and opportunity.

[27] Reading Roundup Series, for Grades 7, 8, and 9 (Boston: D. C. Heath and Company).

Literature both of the past and of the present may help students expand their understanding of the world and the people about them. The point is not, however, whether literature is of the past or contemporary, but whether it is within the emotional and intellectual grasp of the reader. It is true that a considerable amount of literature of the past, in spite of universal themes, contains elements of language and manners and customs often baffling to pupils today. These works should usually be introduced after students have been prepared for them by acquiring the necessary experience, historical background, and understanding. Certain American classics, however, such as Mark Twain's *Tom Sawyer* and *Huckleberry Finn,* are often quite as comprehensible to modern youth as to pupils in earlier times.

There are many selections from contemporary authors as well as from the classics that can be readily enjoyed by young readers today and will touch their lives vitally. Young people should have the opportunity to read about man's hopes, fears, and struggles, his failures and successes in overcoming physical difficulties, and his ceaseless attempt to build a kind of world in which he can live harmoniously and happily with others.

Varied Types of Reading Matter

In order to engage successfully in a developmental reading program, the teacher should become acquainted with a large number of books published for young people, as well as with reliable sources for obtaining additional materials. Indeed, the success of the reading program is in part dependent upon the teacher's own interest in the world of books—an interest reflected in his teaching, since enthusiasm is contagious. Such an interest is heightened and intensified through increasing familiarity with books as well as through sharing reading experiences with others. Each year thousands of books roll from the presses. To become acquainted with all of them is impossible, but a systematic program of reading or even of examining a certain number of books each month, will, over a period of time, build valuable literary background for the teacher, will lend insight and understanding concerning the range of materials available, and will help him greatly in relating books to the needs of students. In such efforts the teacher will of course cooperate closely with librarians.

Manifestly, a broad reading program geared to individual needs will take into account a wide variety of purposes and utilize many types of reading matter: fiction, biography, drama, essays, poetry, informative prose, and so forth. Such an approach, moreover, necessitates the use of various kinds of printed matter—books, magazines, and newspapers. Some books will already be known to teachers of junior high school pupils; others may be chosen from selected lists and book sources such as *A Basic Book Collection for Junior High Schools*[28] and *Your Reading, a Book List for Junior High School*.[29] Special book lists in the areas of human relations, developmental values, and character development are: *Reading Ladders for Human Relations*[30] and *Character Formation Through Books*.[31]

The Basic Book Collection for High Schools[32] is one type of book list compiled primarily for use with senior high school students. *Book Bait*[33] is a special type of book source containing a list of adult books which are popular with young people. The long annotations, including a summary of the story, should be of assistance to teachers who may have missed reading the books. Excellent suggestions for guiding the reading of young people are found in *Books, Young People, and Reading Guidance*.[34]

In directing young people to suitable reading materials, collections of poetry should be included. Poetry is a very personal matter. It may evoke an intense personal response when it re-creates an individual's experience or when it deeply stirs the reader's or listener's sympathy. Poetry should be chosen which will afford enjoyment either through its appeal to the ear or through the associations it awakens; some young people will enjoy the music and the rhythm without much concern about the meaning or the verse pattern. Through poetry, many students may be led to a deeper appreciation of words and meanings. Sensitivity to the use of the word that is most appropriate or most exact in describing an experience often comes with the reading of poetry, for true poetry fulfills the definition of Coleridge: "The best words in the best order."

---

[28] American Library Association, *A Basic Book Collection for Junior High School*, 3rd ed. (Chicago: American Library Association, 1960).

[29] National Council of Teachers of English, *Your Reading, a Book List for Junior High School* (Champaign, Illinois: National Council of Teachers of English, 1954).

[30] Margaret M. Heaton and Helen B. Lewis, *Reading Ladders for Human Relations*, rev. ed. (Washington, D. C.: American Council on Education, 1955).

[30] Muriel Crosby, *Reading Ladders for Human Relations*, 4th ed. (Washington, D. C.: American Council on Education, 1963).

[31] Clara J. Kircher, *Character Formation Through Books*, 3rd ed. (Washington, D.C.: Catholic University of America Press, 1952).

[32] American Library Association, *The Basic Book Collection for High Schools*, 6th ed. (Chicago: American Library Association, 1957).

[33] Elinor Walker, *Book Bait*, compiled for the Association of Young People's Librarians (Chicago: American Library Association, 1957).

[34] Geneva R. Hanna and Mariana K. McAllister, *Books, Young People, and Reading Guidance* (New York: Harper & Row, Publishers, 1960).

Poetry, both of the past and of the present, of a type which has wide appeal and unique suitability for adolescents, should be known to the teacher.[35] Several publishers have made available suitable poems for young people chosen from the writing of such contemporary poets as Edna St. Vincent Millay, Robert Frost, and Carl Sandburg.

Audio-Visual Materials

In addition to the using of recordings, many schools employ visual aids with success. It must be noted, however, that although these visual and auditory materials enhance teaching and reinforce it, they are not designed as a total instruction method nor the sole purveyors of content. Films, for example, may assist in the development of many reading skills. Although they are invaluable aids, they should not dictate the curriculum or course content. Films and filmstrips may be used to improve speed in reading; and when their use is coupled with other procedures, rapid progress often results.

Other materials and their use have been recognized by Bond and Kegler:

> Other types of visual aids which are sometimes used in reading classes are the mechanical aids frequently used at the senior high school level. These run the gamut from machines which offer training in hand-eye co-ordination to machines designed to improve speed. Within certain limits, these machines may be used in the general program of instruction in high schools and colleges. They may be aids to, but they are not substitutes for, instruction in reading. They do not take the place of a variety of instructional materials suitable for reading courses in general.[36]

An important use of films, filmstrips, and recordings is that they offer an excellent source for the development of background prior to or in conjunction with the study of literature. Again and again it has been shown that comprehension is increased through the use of audio-visual aids.

EVALUATING GROWTH IN AND THROUGH READING

In recent years attention has been called to the need for considering evaluation as a significant phase of a developmental reading program.

---

[35] Helen J. Ferris, *Favorite Poems, Old and New, Selected for Boys and Girls* (Garden City, N. Y.: Doubleday & Company, Inc., 1957)).
[36] Guy L. Bond and Stanley B. Kegler, *op. cit.,* p. 332.

In order to estimate the amount and character of growth the teacher in charge of the program must at the beginning have obtained a fairly comprehensive understanding of each pupil's status. There was a time when many educators accepted with little question the results of standardized tests as valid indicators of reading status; initial and final test scores were compared, and gains in reading estimated. As the concept of the reading process was broadened, however, this simple practice fell into disfavor. Today standard test scores are generally viewed as only partial, though valuable, indicators of reading status and attainment. Significance is also attached to factors usually not measured by tests: for example, the pupil's success in reading different kinds of materials, his attitude toward reading, his reading pattern, the influence of reading on his behavior, and his own evaluation of his status and needs.

Systematic records should be kept of each pupil's progress in acquiring effective habits and skills, judged by periodic testing and observation. The extent of his reading experience and the development of appreciation may be estimated by reference to notations concerning his reading in and out of school, and his growth in personality traits may be appraised roughly by the use of additional ratings and judgments resulting from interviews.

Toward the end of a term and again toward the end of the year the teacher may profitably inquire: To what extent have goals been attained, and to what extent has the pupil improved? The following questions may serve to show where both the teacher and the pupil have succeeded or failed:

1. Have you noticed improvement in the pupil's reading:
    (a) in the amount, the breadth, and the quality of his reading?
    (b) in the speed and accuracy with which he reads silently? orally?
    (c) in his vocabulary?
2. Have you noticed improvement in his attitudes toward his reading, especially in his gains as an independent reader? Is he using the school and public library effectively?
3. Have you observed improvement in his personal and social adjustments which may be an outgrowth of his reading:
    (a) in his recreational activities?
    (b) in character traits such as self-confidence, tolerance, and so forth?
4. Does he show greater interest in reading and owning books?
5. Is he enjoying reading?

To this estimate of progress made by the teacher, the pupil's own evaluation of his gains may add appreciably.

CONCLUDING STATEMENT

The need for a developmental reading program in the junior and senior high school is great, as is suggested by surveys which disclose a wide range of ability among junior and senior high school pupils. Many students are clearly in need of assistance in building their skills, while others require guidance to make full use of their ability. Developmental needs of boys and girls must also be met at these levels, as well as help in meeting the reading demands of various subject areas. Moreover, most pupils require stimulation or assistance in acquiring an interest in reading and in developing individually appropriate patterns of reading. They can also use help in improving their rates and in learning to adjust their rates readily to varied types of materials.

Clearly, a developmental reading program is essential to satisfy these needs in a modern junior or senior high school. In such a program systematic instruction in the acquisition of basic reading skills should be given both in the junior high school and in the high school, whenever the need is apparent. At both levels every teacher should be encouraged to contribute to the developmental program. In this chapter we have set forth some essentials of such approaches, together with examples of schools in which programs have been established.

Selected References

Bland, Phyllis, "Adjusting Instruction to Individual Differences in Grades Ten to Fourteen," in *Improving Reading in All Curriculum Areas,* Supplementary Educational Monograph no. 76 (Chicago: University of Chicago Press, 1952), pp. 44–45.

Boeck, Clarence H., "The Inductive-Deductive Compared to the Deductive-Descriptive Approach to Laboratory Instruction in High School Chemistry," *Journal of Experimental Education,* 19:247–253 (March, 1951).

Bond, Guy L. and Stanley B. Kegler, "Reading Instruction in the Senior High School," in Paul A. Witty (chairman), *Development In and Through Reading,* Sixtieth Yearbook of the National Society for the Study of Education, Part I (Chicago: University of Chicago Press, 1961), pp. 320–335.

Conant, James, *The American High School Today* (New York: McGraw-Hill Book Company, 1959).

Fay, Leo C., "Adjusting Learning Activities and Reading Materials to Individual Differences: In Grades Seven to Nine," in *Improving Reading in All Curriculum Areas,* Supplementary Educational Monographs no. 76 (Chicago: University of Chicago Press, 1952), pp. 36–40.

Ferrell, Frances Hunter, "Methods of Increasing Competence in Interpreting Social-Studies Materials: In Grades Ten to Fourteen," in *Improv-*

ing Reading in All Curriculum Areas, Supplementary Educational Monographs no. 76 (Chicago: University of Chicago Press, 1952), pp. 183–187.

Gray, William S., "Growth in Understanding of Reading and Its Development among Youth," in *Keeping Reading Programs Abreast of the Times,* Supplementary Educational Monographs no. 72 (Chicago: University of Chicago Press, 1950), pp. 8–13.

Gunn, M. Agnella, "What Does Research in Reading Tell the Teacher of English in the Secondary School?" in *What We Know about High School Reading,* prepared by the National Conference on Research in English and reprinted from *The English Journal,* 46:391–394 (October, 1957).

Hanna, Geneva R. and Mariana K. McAllister, *Books, Young People, and Reading Guidance* (New York: Harper and Row, 1960).

Huelsman, Charles B., Jr., "Promoting Growth in Ability to Interpret When Reading Critically: In Grades Seven to Ten," in W. S. Gray (editor), *Promoting Growth Toward Maturity in Interpreting What Is Read,* Supplementary Educational Monographs no. 74 (Chicago: University of Chicago Press, 1951), pp. 149–153.

National Association of Secondary School Principals, Committee on Curriculum Planning and Development, "English Language Arts in the Comprehensive Secondary School," *The Bulletin,* 44:46–58 (October, 1960).

North, Marie, "Reading at North Central High School," *Journal of Developmental Reading,* 11:62–64 (Winter, 1959).

Penty, Ruth C., *Reading Ability and High School Drop-Outs* (New York: Bureau of Publications, Teachers College, Columbia University, 1956).

Pressey, L. C. and W. S. Moore, "The Growth of Mathematical Vocabulary from the Third Grade Through High School," *School Review,* 40:449–454 (June, 1932).

Russell, David H., "A Reading Program for the Seventh and Eighth Grades," *Contributions in Reading* no. 13 (Boston: Ginn and Company, 1958).

Schubert, Delwyn G., "Science Teachers: What You Can Do to Help Your Students to Read More Efficiently," *The Clearing House,* 30:83–84 (October, 1955).

Sheldon, William D., "Reading Instruction in Junior High School," in Paul A. Witty (chairman), *Development In and Through Reading,* Sixtieth Yearbook of the National Society for the Study of Education, Part I (Chicago: University of Chicago Press, 1961), Chap. 17.

Smith, Nila Banton, "Implementing Change Through Productive, Free-flowing Interrelationships," in J. Allen Figurel (ed.), *Changing Concepts of Reading Instruction,* Proceedings of the International Reading Association Conference (New York: Scholastic Magazines, 1961), pp. 61–64.

Stewart, L. Jane, Frieda M. Heller, and Elsie J. Alberty, *Improving Reading in the Junior High School* (New York: Appleton-Century-Crofts, 1957).

Witty, Paul, "The Improvement of Reading Abilities," in David A. Clift (chairman), *Adult Reading,* 55th Yearbook of the National Society for the Study of Education, Part II (Chicago: University of Chicago Press, 1956), pp. 251–274.

Witty, Paul, Miriam E. Peterson, and Kathryn P. Welsh, "The Need for Developmental Reading in Grades Seven, Eight and Nine." *The Packet,* a Heath Service Bulletin for Elementary Teachers, 13:3–18 (Spring, 1958).

Witty, Paul and Margaret Ratz, *A Developmental Reading Program for Grades 6 Through 9.* A Handbook for Teachers, Counselors, and Administrators in Elementary, Junior High, and High Schools (Chicago: Science Research Associates, Inc., 1956).

Wren, F. Lynwood, "What Are the Goals of Instruction in Arithmetic and Mathematics and the Grade Sequence of Understandings and Skills?" in *Improving Reading in All Curriculum Areas,* Supplementary Education Monographs no. 76 (Chicago: University of Chicago Press, 1952), pp. 144–149.

12

READING INSTRUCTION FOR COLLEGE STUDENTS AND ADULTS

Reading instruction for college students and adults receives more attention at the present than in the past because of a number of conditions. First, the increasing number of high school graduates going to college has produced a more general need for reading proficiency; and second, the increasing demands on adults to read effectively in order to adjust well and happily in contemporary life have been recognized and have led to a widespread interest in the improvement of reading ability.

Today a very large number of high-school graduates go on to college, a condition which presents a striking contrast with that existing thirty or forty years ago. Students now find a greater need for effective rapid reading in larger college classes with little individual attention.

Moreover, the demands on reading ability made by college textbooks are greater than those of textbooks used in high school. Phillip Shaw and Agatha Townsend point to the relatively greater difficulty of college textbooks and emphasize the difference between high school and college teaching methods as factors contributing to reading problems experienced by many college students:

> At the outset, the student reacts quite logically and correctly to the rise in reading difficulty of the college text as contrasted with the high school text. In the second place, he reacts to a real difference between high school and college teaching. Not only is he faced with a more difficult reading task, but he is expected to deal with it more independently.[1]

[1] Phillip B. Shaw and Agatha Townsend, "Diagnosis of College Reading Problems by Use of Textbooks," *The Reading Teacher*, 14:30 (September, 1960).

Although the problems associated with difficult textbooks and the need for greater independence in studying on the part of the college student, as compared with the pupil in high school, have long been recognized, the presence of reading problems has become more and more conspicuous as enrollments in college have increased. Today the need for reading instruction by many college students is generally acknowledged. As a result, large numbers of colleges have initiated remedial programs.

Few colleges have assumed responsibility for reading instruction as a developmental process; yet this need, too, is increasingly recognized. Shaw and Townsend point to the tenuous position of developmental reading at the college level:

> As a new field, developmental reading on the higher level is on the defensive. Efforts to indoctrinate educators to believe that every college freshman can improve his reading proficiency have been frustrated by the misunderstanding that this developmental educating is the same as "remedial" help. Programs of both types are vital.[2]

The larger numbers of students and the gradual penetration of the developmental reading philosophy at the college level have both contributed to an increased interest in the extension of reading instruction. In addition, recognition of the greater need for efficient reading on the part of adults today has brought an increased tendency to offer young people generally an opportunity to improve their reading. The demands for efficient reading are numerous and varied in present-day life. In our highly technological age it is necessary to read rapidly. Many adults, especially business executives, recognizing this fact, have sought to improve their own reading rate and comprehension in order to function more adequately in their work. But rapid reading is not sufficient. The adult, like the younger person, needs to adjust his rate to different kinds of materials and to different objectives. Newspapers require one kind of reading; scientific articles another; and novels still another. Professional journals, common in industry and the professions, require special reading skills in addition to the general reading abilities which many adults have not acquired.[3]

Those concerned about reading for the college student and the adult

---

[2] *Ibid.*, p. 30.
[3] William S. Gray, "How Well Do Adults Read?" in David H. Clift (chairman), *Adult Reading,* Fifty-fifth Yearbook of the National Society for the Study of Education, Part II (Chicago: University of Chicago Press, 1956), pp. 29–56. (See also Paul Witty, "The Improvement of Reading Abilities," in above Yearbook.)

need, however, to look beyond the factors of increased college enrollment and greater reading demands on adults today. Although these two factors are important, they are related to changes in our society, in our education, and in our concepts of the nature and function of reading.

THE CHANGING ROLE OF COLLEGE AND ADULT READING

When our culture was primarily agrarian, reading played a minor role in living. It was valued mainly for the opportunity it provided to know the Bible and religious materials of various kinds. As our nation grew, reading came to be a significant way of disseminating political information. Later, it was prized highly in an expanding economy which offered varied services in addition to production. Reading to meet job specifications and economic and social problems, and reading to gain information concerning the many complexities of life, are some of the demands being made on readers in recent times.

Obviously, if the culture demands decisions based on a critical evaluation of ideas, those members of the culture who wish to participate in making such decisions should be able to read not only well but critically. College students, therefore, should be offered training in reading that will enable them to read not merely with increased understanding but also with critical acumen and discrimination. Critical reading is, of course, an acquisition which we have stressed throughout the developmental reading sequence.

In addition to long-range needs, the college student has the immediate task of mastering materials in many fields. Moreover, the amount of knowledge and information available in various fields literally increases daily. The scope of any given field requires constant efforts to grasp, organize, understand, and evaluate materials. The slow reader is greatly handicapped and can never really achieve a high degree of academic success with such a limitation. Because he is required to deal with increasing amounts of information, he needs extended reading skills to meet his requirements.

How Much Do College Students and Adults Read?

It has been pointed out that college students and adults generally do not read widely. Many college students confine their reading largely to textbooks, and do little reading beyond class assignments.

Accordingly, it is not surprising to find that other adult groups similarly read little, although there are, of course, many exceptions.

The small amount of reading done by the typical adult has been commented on frequently, and attention has often centered on the fact that not more than ten percent of our adults can be considered "readers" of library books. More specifically, according to Lester Asheim, "We know that almost everyone does some newspaper reading; about two-thirds of the adult population read one or more magazines with some regularity; and that books—reaching about a quarter of the adult population—are read less than any other medium of print."[5]

Why Don't College Students and Adults Read Widely?

Certainly there are many factors which contribute to the relatively small amount of reading by college students and other adults. It is obvious, of course, that poor reading habits alone do not account entirely or even largely for the condition. Among other causes, for instance, is the lack of ready access to public libraries.

Closely associated with the problem of the availability of books is interest in reading. Many schools are attempting to develop a more general and lasting interest in reading by establishing elementary school libraries and by extending secondary school library facilities. Moreover, there is a growing tendency to initiate developmental reading programs designed to satisfy students' interests and meet their needs and hence to lead them to enjoy reading and to read widely. Some people generally recognize the validity of emphasis on the importance of the interest factor.[6]

Despite the small amount of reading, there is evidence that a rather large number of adults are reading more today than ever before. One factor leading to more extensive reading is the publication of inexpensive, paper-bound books, thus making reading material more accessible. Additional evidence of growing interest in reading is found in the increased participation by adults in book clubs, discussions about "Great Books," and courses designed to improve reading ability.

---

[5] Lester Asheim, "What Do Adults Read?" in David H. Clift (chairman), *Adult Reading,* Fifty-fifth Yearbook of the National Society of the Study of Education, Part II (Chicago: University of Chicago Press, 1956), pp. 9–10.

[6] George W. Norvell, "Some Results of a Twelve-Year Study of Children's Reading Interests," *English Journal,* 35:536 (December, 1946).

DEVELOPMENTAL READING FOR THE COLLEGE STUDENT AND ADULT

The fourfold approach of the developmental reading philosophy applies to college students and adults as well as to younger people. Continuous, systematic instruction, utilization of interests, fulfillment of developmental needs, and the relationship of experience in reading to other types of worthwhile activity are as important to them as to any younger person. Yet most colleges do not provide systematic, continuous instruction in reading, and not often do adults outside college receive such instruction.

At Northwestern University one group of undergraduates who were having reading difficulties displayed the following characteristics:

1. They adopted a very slow, uneven rate of reading for most materials.
2. They lacked the ability to adjust their rate of reading to different types of material or to their immediate purpose for reading.
3. They were more successful in reading very short passages than in getting the meaning from longer presentations.
4. They lacked accuracy in reading. They comprehended little of the materials read and, in many cases, gained a false impression.
5. They lacked the ability to concentrate upon difficult materials and frequently were unable to complete their assignments in a reasonable amount of time.
6. They had poorer-than-average vocabulary scores. They lacked an understanding of the precise meaning of many words. They were weak in "specialized vocabularies."
7. They did very little leisure reading.
8. They lacked the ability to comprehend important details in many types of presentations.
9. They were unable to organize materials read and to present the facts in concise outline form.
10. They read uncritically and were unable to discern contradictions or inconsistencies in many presentations.[7]

These college students, because they had not developed in reading as they should have in order to function effectively in college, were handicapped in their reading development as are many high school students. Being no longer in high school, yet with reading problems comparable to those of high school students, they were given reading

[7] Paul Witty, Theodore Stolarz, and William Cooper, "Some Results of a Remedial Reading Program for College Students," *School and Society,* 76:378 (December 13, 1952).

instruction in many ways similar to what should have been included in the high school program. In short, these experiences were designed to meet the students' developmental needs and to offer systematic instruction as required. The activities included:

1. *Rapid reading of fairly easy, interesting materials.* The selections which the students read at first were short stories or magazine articles of eighth- or ninth-grade difficulty. The Reading Accelerator was used in practice periods.

2. *Leisure reading.* An inventory was used to ascertain the areas of greatest interest to each student. Appropriate reading materials of suitable difficulty were read in accord with any particular interest. In addition, some students chose to read novels they had planned to read "some day," and others read nonfiction ranging in type from legal cases and mechanical manuals to popular biographies.

3. *Speed-reading practice.* Periods for practice in rapid reading each day in addition to the time for the reading program were arranged for each student. Records of rate and comprehension were kept by the student in his daily effort to improve speed and comprehension.

4. *Training in recognizing short phrases on the tachistoscope.* This practice was designed to encourage rapid recognition of groups of words. Two or three students worked with the tachistoscope while the rest of the group was occupied with other activities. This training was limited to about ten minutes per day. Most of the students became very proficient in this skill and discontinued practice after a few weeks.

5. *Vocabulary building.* Exercises were planned to enable students to obtain the meanings of unfamiliar words from their context. Students also kept records of new words encountered in various types of reading. The importance of vocabulary in each subject area was stressed throughout the program, and students kept lists of key words and their meanings. These lists were frequently reviewed and related to assignments and to textbook reading.

6. *Attack on specific reading skills.* In reading assignments as well as in the use of manuals, emphasis was placed upon exercises to facilitate the mastery of important reading skills such as skimming, reading for details, getting the general thought of paragraphs, and critical reading. Competent advisers aided students in the exercise of discrimination in selection of materials and in the choice of the method to be used in reading. They learned to select materials for skimming, for precise reading, for leisure reading, and for other purposes.

7. *Frequent individual conferences.* Particular problems and needs of the students were studied, and materials and methods to overcome difficulties were discussed in individual conferences.

8. *Help in reading textbooks.* Students were taught to interpret

graphs, illustrations, and charts, and the special vocabulary of each subject was studied.[8]

Gains made from this program were significant and led to a better adjustment of the students generally. Similar results have been reported by other investigators. For example, Donald Smith and Roger Wood conducted an experiment with seventy-four University of Michigan freshmen over a 60-week period in an improvement of reading course and compared their results with a control group not taking the course. They concluded: "Significant superiority in academic status (increasing with time) is demonstrated by experimental subjects over both control and representative freshman subjects when study and examination skills are emphasized during the training period."[9]

It is recognized that college students benefit from reading programs geared to their developmental needs. Yet some colleges today are curtailing such opportunities for reading improvement. University authorities occasionally take the position that high schools should provide training in reading and that the universities should not be obliged to meet this need. The argument sounds not unlike the one heard a few years ago to the effect that reading skills should be mastered before sixth grade and no junior or senior high school teacher should be expected to teach reading. The fact that many colleges and universities do not require a course in reading or a course in the teaching of reading for prospective junior and senior high school teachers—including prospective English teachers—is also regrettable.

At the adult level considerable evidence is available to show that reading may be improved as the result of a planned reading program. Max Siegel, for example, reports a "five-year experimental program of reading improvement for adults conducted jointly by the Brooklyn Public Library and Brooklyn College, during the period September, 1955, through June, 1960. He found that the "principal motivations for entering the program appeared to be a general desire for better understanding of books and for an increased rate of reading." Moreover, "significant gains in reading comprehension (high and low level) and/or reading speed were found for most groups of students participating in the program."[10]

---

[8] *Ibid.*, pp. 378–379.

[9] Donald E. P. Smith and Roger L. Wood, "Reading Improvement and College Grades: A Follow-up," *Journal of Educational Psychology,* 46:158 (March, 1955).

[10] Max Siegel, "Adult Reading Improvement: A Five-year Report," *The Reading Teacher,* 15:246 (January, 1962).

Methods and Devices to Improve Reading Rate

Speed of reading has been a topic of interest to reading specialists for many years. Knowledge concerning the possibility of increasing the speed of reading has been widely disseminated in recent years, as business concerns have produced various devices for studying and controlling eye movement.

Interest in the conditioning of eye movements has resulted in the making of tachistoscopic devices such as the *Reading Accelerator,* the *Flashmeter,* the *Controlled Reader,* and the *Harvard Reading Films,* the use of which has become a feature of "accelerated reading programs." George S. Speer emphasizes the current demand for such programs and points out that although schools have for many years been concerned about remedial and developmental reading, "accelerated reading has been largely neglected."[11] Pointing to the gradual development of reading instruments, he concludes:

> All of the instrumental technics have demonstrated their value at all grade and age levels above the seventh grade. . . . The successes, however, have encouraged many teachers to extend the work to lower grade levels.[12]

Accelerated programs have proved unusually successful with adult groups, as have other efforts to improve the efficiency of adults' reading. Numerous studies report significant gains in reading speed under various types of programs. Undoubtedly, accelerated reading programs have brought gains in speed of reading as measured by the tests employed. But it is well to inquire whether such gains are really worthwhile and whether one is justified in concluding that phenomenal gains in rate of reading carry with them a correlated improvement in comprehension.

For example, David Gliessman and Robert Hodell report that in a study with 139 adult students a significant gain in reading speed was made, but there was a slight drop in comprehension.[13] A study by Frederick Westover and William Anderson reported a forty-eight per cent increase in speed but none in comprehension.[14] From these and

---

[11] George S. Speer, "Using Mechanical Devices Can Increase Speed of Reading," *The Nation's Schools,* 48:45 (October, 1951).

[12] *Ibid.,* p. 48.

[13] David Gliessman and Robert D. Hodell, "The Value of Improved Reading Skills to Businessmen," *Journal of Developmental Reading,* 1:30–40 (Autumn, 1957).

[14] Frederick L. Westover and William F. Anderson, Jr., "A Reading Improvement Course at the University of Alabama, *School and Society,* 83:152–153 (April 28, 1956).

other studies it becomes apparent that gains in rate of reading do not necessarily carry a commensurate growth in comprehension. A recent study by William Liddle indicated that an experimental group read fictional and nonfictional materials at a higher rate of speed than a control group. No significant difference was found between the two groups in comprehension of nonfictional material, but the control group scored significantly higher in reading fiction.[15]

We believe that a good perspective concerning speed reading can be gained from Paul McKee's comments:

> Speed in itself has no value. . . . Every pupil should learn to adjust his speed of reading in a given situation to the purpose for which he is reading and to the difficulty of the reading material which he has at hand. . . . He should have several speeds, each to be used as needed, within the limits of adequate understanding.[16]

It is clear, then, that reading rate will vary with the type of reading one does, and that one should not expect that a *general* rate of reading can be established which will apply to all situations. Rate of reading, moreover, may not be found to be so closely associated with comprehension as we have been led to believe from reports in which high coefficients of correlation have been cited.

Limitations of Tests of Reading Speed and Comprehension

Coefficients of correlation between speed and comprehension are affected by the types of materials read and the procedures used to measure reading speed and comprehension. Standard tests of reading speed are obviously limited to particular kinds of materials covered. The materials included in such tests are frequently inadequate samples of the different kinds of materials people read or need to read. In addition, the tests are sometimes too short to afford reliable measures of speed or of comprehension. A much larger amount of reading material is needed than that found in many standard tests if one is to measure rate of reading reliably. Even more important is the type of material used in tests of reading comprehension.

One of the most obvious limitations of tests of reading comprehension is the fact that they are "timed," thus introducing the element of

---

[15] William Liddle, "Results of Experimentation on the Wood Reading Technique," in Clay A. Ketcham (editor), *Proceedings of the College Reading Association* (Easton, Penn.: College Reading Association, 1962), pp. 13–15.

[16] Paul McKee, *The Teaching of Reading in the Elementary School* (Boston: Houghton Mifflin Company, 1948), pp. 109–110.

speed in the measurement of comprehension.[17] Another limitation, as found by Ralph Preston and Morton Botel, is that test designations of "comprehension" are in reality partly tests of speed.[18] Other studies have found that comprehension depends less upon speed than upon intelligence, purposes of the reading, difficulty of the material read, opportunities for verifying questions of comprehension, and the continuity of the text.[19]

Yet despite the relatively low correlations between speed and comprehension and the limitations of testing, it is clear that most people can improve greatly in their rate of reading as well as in their understanding of various kinds of materials.

The Role of Mechanical Devices in Developing Speed

A controversial issue in the field of reading, especially when considering the development of speed, is the role of mechanical devices. Research has compared groups that used tachistoscopes with those that did not employ mechanical devices.

One study was made by presenting relatively simple reading material to students and merely emphasizing the aspect of speed. Fifty times during the year students were given one-minute drills in reading the material and reporting their results. During the drills the researcher insisted that all students read at least 350 words a minute without regard to comprehension. After two months of such practice the class members were reading at speeds varying from 250 to 1,000 words per minute.[20]

A somewhat different procedure, which is recommended by another teacher, Alan Snyder, involves the use of the "flashreader"—a device covering, then exposing several lines of print. The researcher concluded: "In conjunction with other aspects of the reading program it seems to justify the 200-minute role it plays in the production of rapid readers."[21] Perhaps the most important aspect of this approach is its value in stimulating and maintaining interest.

[17] Frederick B. Davis, "Comprehension in Reading," *Baltimore Bulletin of Education,* 28:16–24 (January–February, 1951).

[18] Ralph C. Preston and Morton Botel, "Reading Comprehension Tested Under Timed and Untimed Conditions," *School and Society,* 74:71 (August 4, 1951).

[19] J. Harlan Shores and Kenneth L. Husbands, "Are Fast Readers the Best Readers?" *Elementary English,* 27:52–57 (January, 1950).

[20] Joe W. Andrews, "An Approach to Speed Reading," *The English Journal,* 41:352–356 (September, 1952).

[21] Alan Snyder, "The Flashreader in the Reading Laboratory," *The English Journal,* 41:269 (May, 1952).

While many enthusiastic claims are made by those conducting research using machines and devices, some cautions need to be injected. Arthur Gates warns, for example, that "in general, the elaborate mechanical devices should be regarded as last resorts to be used when other methods have failed or when there are some tangible reasons for selecting them at the earlier stage."[22]

College students and adults may become more interested in reading and the improvement of rate when they use mechanical devices such as the Reading Accelerator or the Reading Rate Controller. That such devices are necessary for conducting a successful program has yet to be demonstrated; but they may become a factor, if judiciously used, in fostering interest in and zeal for learning.[23] It is clear, however, that at every level of instruction the chief requirements for effective reading are: careful diagnosis of each student, a variety of books and reading experiences, high motivation, and sufficient time to enable the student to develop skills in reading to meet his most pressing needs. Many students and adults will of course require exercises to increase speed of reading different kinds of materials. The aim of this endeavor should not be to develop a rapid *general* rate of reading but rather a capacity to adjust the method of reading to meet different demands. The objectives will vary with the types of materials to be read as well as with differences in student needs.

READING INSTRUCTION FOR THE EDUCATIONALLY RETARDED AND THE DISADVANTAGED

A new problem has arisen in many of America's large cities. It is not confined to metropolitan centers only. However, its magnitude in large centers of population is so great that it may become a threat to the welfare of many communities unless it is recognized and dealt with realistically.

We refer to the increasing incidence of children who are described as "disadvantaged" or "culturally deprived." Frank Riessman has estimated that in 1950 approximately one child out of every ten in the fourteen largest cities of the United States was culturally deprived. By 1960 *this figure has risen to one in three.* If rapid migration to certain

---

[22] Arthur I. Gates, *The Improvement of Reading*, 3rd ed. (New York: The Macmillan Company, 1947), p. 67.
[23] Paul Witty, Theodore Stolarz, and William Cooper, "Some Results of a Remedial Reading Program for College Students," *op. cit.*

large cities continues, this proportion may increase by 1970 "to one deprived child for every two enrolled in the schools in these cities."[24]

Robert Havighurst has described this group as "socially disadvantaged." The socially disadvantaged have personal, family, and social characteristics that impair their chances for successful participation in urban life. Their frequency in general is perhaps 15 percent.

> Since these children and their families tend to concentrate in the large cities, while upper-income people tend to move out from the cities to the suburbs, the socially disadvantaged children are in big cities in larger proportions than 15 percent. Probably *30 percent of the children* in such cities as New York, Chicago, Philadelphia, Washington, Detroit, Cleveland, and Baltimore fall into the socially disadvantaged category.[25]

During the past year, the needs of disadvantaged pupils have been repeatedly emphasized and a number of programs have been developed for pre-school children. The new head-start programs have also been initiated. Perhaps the most notable of these efforts are the nursery school centers in ten New York public schools and five day-care centers developed under the direction of Martin Deutsch.

The results of these projects have already dramatically shown the need for extending education down to the nursery level. It is reported that:

> The youngsters in Deutsch's experimental classes show significant improvement in IQ test scores. The more profound effects may be less measurable, but they are striking to anyone who spends even a few weeks in one of the classrooms observing children; they change under the observer's eye. Kindergarten teachers who receive youngsters exposed to even as little as six months of Deutsch's experimental program are almost speechless with enthusiasm; in all their years of teaching, they say, they have never had slum youngsters enter as intellectually equipped, as alert, as interested, or as well-behaved.[26]

Another noteworthy program was started in the schools in the Banneker area of St. Louis in 1958 in which the population is largely Negro. Pre-school experiences were provided which extended and enriched the backgrounds of young children through field trips, visits to

---

[24] Frank Riessman, *The Culturally Deprived Child* (New York: Harper and Row, Publishers, 1962), p. 1.

[25] Robert Havighurst, "Who Are the Socially Disadvantaged?" Chapter 1 in "Educational Planning for Socially Disadvantaged Children and Youth." *The Journal of Negro Education*, vol. 33 (Summer, 1964), pp. 210–217.

[26] C. E. Silberman, *Crisis in Black and White* (New York: Random House, London: Jonathan Cape Limited, 1964), p. 289.

the zoo, opportunities to use colorful toys, varied language and listening activities. These children achieved scores on tests equal to city averages upon entrance to school and excelled the ratings of children from other slum areas.

Despite the recognition of the limitations of certain approaches by many scholars, authorities are generally agreed that efforts to improve the reading ability of the disadvantaged pupil should recognize:

(a) The need for establishing pre-school or nursery centers to provide the background in language and related experience essential to successful reading.
(b) The importance of enriching the experience of pupils in school so as to equip the pupil with the necessary background which has been denied or precluded.
(c) The significance of the use of materials of instruction which are closely associated with the needs, interests, and experiences of these groups.
(d) The importance of providing help for the education of the disadvantaged throughout the full range, including adult education.

Many college students who are inadequately prepared in reading skills to meet the demands of college curricula are identifiable by socioeconomic status, race, or residence. Thus, Froe[27] found that Negro college-entering freshmen tested below white college-entering freshmen in all aptitude and achievement tests. Newton[28] described the language deficiencies of Negro college-entering freshmen as including limited vocabularies, impoverished use of descriptive or qualifying words, and inability to comprehend figurative language. Folkman,[29] examining the progress of 2200 rural and urban students entering a midwestern university in 1955, found that rural students fell considerably below the urban students in the college entrance examinations.

These groups reflect some patterns of experience and learning which are either different from or less adequate than the experience and learning patterns of other groups.

At present, these students are included in the broader group of socially or culturally disadvantaged children and youth who consistently demonstrate reading and educational retardation.

[27] Otis D. Froe, "Educational Planning for Disadvantaged College Youth," *Journal of Negro Education,* vol. 33 (Summer, 1964), pp. 290–303.
[28] Eunice Shaed Newton, "Verbal Destitution: The Pivotal Barrier to Learning," *Journal of Negro Education,* vol. 29 (Fall, 1960), pp. 497–499.
[29] William S. Folkman, *Progress of Rural and Urban Students Entering Iowa State University, Fall, 1955,* U.S. Department of Agriculture, Economic Research Service, Agricultural Economic Report no. 12 (Washington, D.C.: U.S. Department of Agriculture, 1962).

The evidence has shown clearly that there is a cumulative effect of social and educational deficiencies or disabilities and that the students from these disadvantaged groups who enter college are seriously handicapped.[30]

An examination of the literature has revealed a direct path from the inadequate preparation of disadvantaged youth who enter college back to early language experiences. Deficiencies occur all along the path. Thus the linguistics and language patterns are restricted and underdeveloped.[31] Further, perception, conception, cognition, and vocabulary are all limited in development among disadvantaged youth.[32]

Reading programs for disadvantaged children and youth have used developmental and remedial techniques with considerable success.[33] Grotberg,[34] for example, conducted a study with 35 disadvantaged ninth grade boys and found an average gain of 1.5 years in reading after 30 hours of intensive remedial and developmental work using available commercial materials. The development of perceptual, conceptual, cognitive and vocabulary skills were an integral part of the program.

Another area of concern has been the large number of adult illiter-

---

[30] Froe, *op. cit.*, Newton, *op. cit.*, Martin Deutsch and Bert Brown, "Social Influences in Negro-White Intelligence Differences," *Journal of Social Issues*, vol. 20 (April, 1964), pp. 24–35.

[31] Alexander Frazier, "A Research Proposal to Develop the Language Skills of Children with Poor Backgrounds," *Improving English Skills of Culturally Different Youth*, U.S. Department of Health, Education, and Welfare, Office of Education, Bulletin 1964, no. 5 (Washington, D.C.: Superintendent of Documents, Government Printing Office, 1964), pp. 62–68.

Walter Loban, "Language Ability in the Elementary School: Implications of Findings Pertaining to the Culturally Disadvantaged," *Improving English Skills of Culturally Different Youth, op. cit.*, pp. 62–68.

Eunice Shaed Newton, "Planning for the Language Development of Disadvantaged Children and Youth," *Journal of Negro Education*, vol. 33 (Summer, 1964), pp. 264–274.

[32] Jerome Seymour Bruner, "The Cognitive Consequences of Early Sensory Deprivation," *Sensory Deprivation*, Edited by Philip Solomon (Cambridge: Harvard University Press, 1961).

Martin Deutsch, "The Disadvantaged Child and the Learning Process," *Education in Depressed Areas*, Edited by A. Harry Passow (New York: Bureau of Publications, Columbia University, 1963).

J. Allen Figurel, editor, "Teaching Reading to the Disadvantaged," *Improvement of Reading Through Classroom Practice* (Newark, Delaware: International Reading Association, vol. 9, 1964), pp. 160–175.

[33] *Improving English Skills of Culturally Different Youth*, Edited by Arno Jewett, Joseph Mersand, and Doris V. Gunderson, U.S. Department of Health, Education, and Welfare, Office of Education, Bulletin 1964, no. 5 (Washington, D.C.: Superintendent of Documents, Government Printing Office, 1964).

Programs for the Educationally Disadvantaged, U.S. Department of Health, Education, and Welfare, Office of Education, Bulletin 1963, no. 17 (Washington, D.C.: Superintendent of Documents, Government Printing Office, 1963).

[34] Edith H. Grotberg, "The Washington Program in Action," *Education*, vol. 85 (April, 1965), pp. 490–494.

ates, many of them army rejects or school dropouts. While programs sponsored by the federal government and private groups have been developed to reduce illiteracy among the adult population, one of the largest reading programs for deprived persons was developed during World War II for "functionally illiterate" men in the army. Let us examine that program to determine implications for current endeavor.

Instruction of Illiterate and Non-English-Speaking Men

In order to satisfy the need for manpower in the armed forces, it became necessary to induct large numbers of illiterate and non-English-speaking men. Special Training Units were organized to give these men the academic training they needed to become useful soldiers. The fourth-grade level in reading and related subjects was the standard believed to be essential. Because of the existence of very large numbers of adults in America who had completed less than four years of elementary education, the army found it necessary to accept such men and teach the three R's.[35] By applying established principles of education, the army succeeded in offering a remarkably efficient program which enabled the typical illiterate or non-English-speaking man to acquire the basic academic skills in eight weeks' time. Some men finished the program in less time, while a few non-English-speaking men were allotted thirteen weeks.

Origin of Special Training Unit Men

Some of the men had lived in mountainous or rural districts where schools were inaccessible during several months of the year and poor at all times. Others came from the border and coast states, where immigrants sometimes formed independent groups that managed to get along with very limited proficiency in English. And some came from the foreign communities of our great cities. In one Special Training Unit in Texas 95 percent of the trainees were non-English-speaking men of Spanish or Mexican background. But in other units there were trainees from parts of the country in which educational opportunities were good or superior. In some cases, such men had been faced with family needs which had led them to leave school at early ages. Still others had learned little during their years in school.

---

[35] At that time, it was found that about one-seventh, or 13.5 percent of the recruits might be considered functionally illiterate. In states such as Louisiana, South Carolina, Georgia, and Mississippi, the percentages were much higher.

Tests were employed to classify the men in one of four groups at the beginning of the training cycle. Critical scores showed whether the trainee could be expected to succeed at the most elementary level or whether he would be able to follow the work prescribed at more advanced levels. If a trainee started at the first level, he ordinarily finished the program in eight weeks. If he entered the third section, only four weeks were required to complete the course. Every student had to reach critical scores on tests of reading, arithmetic, and language ability before leaving a unit. Men who failed to make acceptable scores were separated honorably from service and returned to civilian life.

Typically the men were eager to learn. Experience had shown the disadvantage of being unable to read. The men wanted to overcome their handicaps and welcomed their new opportunities. "More than anything else, I want to learn to read," said one man. When asked why, he summarized rather fully the reasons of many of his comrades: "I want to be able to read letters from home. And I want to know what's going on in other places." Finally, he added, "I want to be able to read the things the other fellows do."

The Use of Functional Methods and Materials

The success of the literacy program may be attributed in part to the teaching methods and materials employed. Of significance is the fact that both materials and methods were functional. Accordingly, all subject matter was presented in the form in which it was most readily and most frequently used. The *Army Reader* and the *Army Arithmetic,* textbooks for developing basic skills, dealt with familiar problems such as taking care of the barracks, making purchases at the PX, and keeping a budget. Filmstrips and other visual aids provided additional functionally useful information about how to wear a uniform; when, whom, and how to salute; what to do in the case of an air raid; and how to fire a rifle. Filmstrips were used also to help the men acquire a reading vocabulary.

Before devising instructional materials, a list of the words most frequently used by the soldier in his daily life was prepared from counts of words appearing in the *Soldier's Handbook* and other manuals, as well as from study of word usage in various routine army situations. Consideration was given to the frequency ratings of these words in the preparation of teaching materials. Several specialized lists were also developed for devising instructional materials in military subjects such as *Defense Against Chemical Attack* and *Military Discipline and Courtesy*.[36]

Various ways of introducing the basic words were considered. It was decided to experiment with the filmstrip approach in the presentation of the initial vocabulary. Forty-six nouns of high frequency in the general vocabulary list were employed in the filmstrip *The Story of Private Pete,* which was made up of four series of frames (pictures) dealing with Private Pete's experience in the army. Each series consisted of eight to ten pictures presented as a continuous story of life in the camp. In several breakdowns of each scene, attention was centered on certain objects through the use of word labels. The largest number of labels on any frame was three.

After each series was presented a single frame was used to present all the objects in a new relationship. There were no labels on this frame. The inclusion of all objects previously identified made it possible to check readily the student's recognition of the words. Two summary scenes followed. Under these pictures, a printed story presented all the words. These frames provided additional opportunities for the reading in natural context of words, phrases, and sentences repeatedly used by the men in camp. Two other filmstrips, *Introduction to Language* (Parts 1 and 2), were designed to extend vocabulary and to introduce thirty-one verbs and twelve prepositions. Guides were made to provide the teachers with suggestions for using all materials.

Attention was given in the guides to simple considerations governing effective language instruction based in part upon principles of semantics and linguistics. For example, it was indicated that many important army words were symbols for easily identifiable things or activities. Words such as "gun," "drill," "flag," and "march" could be associated easily with familiar things or routine activity. And other words such as "flags," "airplanes," and "soldiers" could be shown to stand for classes or groups of objects or persons.

The teaching of abstract words such as "brave" and "freedom" received special consideration too. Since the general background of the

---

[36] Paul Witty, "The Conquest of Illiteracy," *School and Society,* vol. 62, (1945), pp. 1–3. Paul Witty, "Some Suggestions for Vocabulary Development in Public Schools, *Educational Administration and Supervision,* vol. 31, (1945), pp. 271–282. Paul Witty and Samuel Goldberg, "The Use of Visual Aids in Special Training Units in the Army," *The Journal of Educational Psychology,* vol. 34, (February, 1944), pp. 82–90. Paul Witty and Golda Van Buskirk, "Beam in the Eye," *Childhood Education,* vol. 21 (October, 1944), pp. 80–85, and Paul Witty, "The Soldier Learns to Read," *National Parent-Teacher Magazine,* vol. 38 (February, 1944), pp. 8–10.

students was wide and varied, they were encouraged to define this type of word in terms of their own experience. Group discussion and exchange of ideas might then be employed to classify further the meanings of such terms.

When the soldiers were able to recognize quickly the words presented in the first language filmstrip (*The Story of Private Pete*), the textbook (*The Army Reader*) was introduced and instruction in silent and oral reading advanced rapidly. Instruction centered on basic skills such as getting the central idea of a paragraph, noting details, organizing information, and following directions. Skill in oral reading was emphasized, with attention given to presentation of thoughts and ideas. Informal discussions and impromptu dramatization of personal experience were also employed as clarity in communication was further encouraged.

The *Army Reader* was developed in four parts, representing roughly the first through fourth grade levels of difficulty. The materials were so arranged as to enable the instructors to emphasize progressively the varied reading skills at each level. All reading materials were closely associated with familiar experiences in army life. Thus, the four parts of the reader were entitled: (1) Private Pete in Camp, (2) Private Pete Writes a Letter, (3) Private Pete Gets Paid, and (4) Private Pete Smith of the Army of the United States.

Supplementary materials offered the men additional reading experiences of direct usefulness. For example, one bulletin—*Your Job in the Army*—provided facts about the various kinds of jobs the men might enter when they completed basic training. A monthly magazine, *Our War,* and a weekly *Newsmap* (special edition) presented additional directly useful information. These periodicals kept the men up to date on the progress of the war and also gave them some understanding of its background. In addition, these periodicals contained descriptions of some outstanding leaders on the fighting front and at home, as well as simple presentations of events of interest to the soldier. Both periodicals were profusely illustrated with pictures, charts, maps, and diagrams to assure understanding and stimulate interest. Not the least important of these items was an informative comic strip which appeared in every issue of *Our War*. Other supplementary reading materials were issued monthly.

In Special Training Units the academic work in reading, writing, arithmetic, spelling, and oral expression was integrated. For example, a reading lesson on army insurance and the purchase of bonds necessitated oral discussion and also required the use of arithmetic in order that each man might know exactly how much money would be taken from his pay. Such activity was often followed by a writing lesson in which letters explained the practices of the army to the families or friends of the soldiers. These letters brought replies which the men read and answered. Thus, many activities in the soldier's life contributed to his education in the three R's. Moreover, further integration occurred, since the teacher of the academic work was also the teacher of military subjects. Three or four hours per day were given over to reading, writing, and arithmetic. And four or five additional hours were devoted daily to military training. The military subjects were presented with the same regard for clear communication and understanding that characterized the presentation of the academic work. Specialized vocabularies were studied in subjects such as sanitation and hygiene, military discipline and courtesy, and rifle marksmanship. Clarity was enhanced through the use of visual aids such as filmstrips, films, and graphic portfolios. Even on the drill field, careful attention was directed to the giving and timing of commands. The entire program was one in which the acquisition of language skills was at all times a vital concern.

The maximum effectiveness of the instructional materials was assured by using them in classes which seldom exceeded twelve members. In classes of this size it was possible to encourage every man to take part in varied individual activities involving oral and written expression, and to overcome initial learning difficulties at their onset. It was possible too to offer individual guidance and encouragement as needed.

The Role of the Teacher

The teachers in the Special Training Units were enlisted men. Most of them had considerable professional and academic training, and many had experience in teaching. Few, however, had specific training or experience in teaching adult illiterates. The materials already mentioned, as well as teachers' manuals and suggestions for the presentation of subjects, were specified. However, the teachers adapted and extended the instructional materials. They made some of their own visual aids, developed reading charts, and prepared supplementary materials.

Perhaps the most important contribution of these teachers was found in the attitude they brought to their work. They emphasized success and steady progress, and made it clear that they expected every man to learn effectively and rapidly. This attitude spread to the students who came to recognize and appreciate their ability to learn. Thus, the cycle began and continued; success brought confidence, and confidence brought further success.

Other factors also contributed to the program's efficiency, as well as to the general well-being of the men. The Special Training Units offered many of these men a better environment from the standpoint of health and hygiene than most of them had ever known. Moreover, they experienced a more secure, well-ordered kind of life. These factors contributed to their adjustment and to their ability to make rapid progress in learning.

The program proved to be extremely successful. With the increased use of these functional materials and methods, the salvage rates rose to above 90 percent in the average instructional period of eight weeks. The materials and methods employed were undoubtedly important factors affecting the program's success.

Some Implications for Education

The program of special training has certainly shown that the mass of American youth are educable. Moreover, it has shown that widespread illiteracy need not continue as a great social problem among adults in America. In addition, it has demonstrated the significance of certain basic principles of learning which are of utmost importance in teaching the educationally retarded and the disadvantaged pupil.

First, the army program for illiterates demonstrated the validity of employing functional methods and materials of instruction. Illiterate and non-English-speaking men were able to acquire the literacy skills needed by the soldier in an astonishingly short period of time. Moreover, the salvage rate in these units advanced progressively with the development and use of functional materials. Reading habits were established and reinforced in situations having maximum meaning because of the close relationship of the goals to the men's firsthand experience.

Second, this program revealed the values of visual aids in accelerating the learning process. The Special Training Units made extensive use of film, filmstrips, graphic portfolios, and other aids. Thus, clear referents were provided for the words and other language symbols employed in reading instruction.

Third, the work of Special Training Units showed the importance of strong interest and motivation in fostering learning. These functionally illiterate men welcomed an opportunity to learn the three R's in order that they might read and write letters, keep informed about what was taking place on the fighting fronts, and enjoy reading the materials available to their comrades.

Fourth, the army program demonstrated the value of clear objectives and specific goals. In Special Training Units, the objectives in every subject were clearly defined. Steps in their attainment were outlined, and tests were used to check progress at regular intervals. In this sense, instruction was "programmed," but it was not limited to pencil and paper goals.

Fifth, the work in the Special Training Units has shown the advantage of correlating activities. Instructors taught both military and academic subjects and attempted to present all training materials in such a way that understanding was unimpaired. The use of special vocabularies, presented through appropriate visual aids, proved an effective means of relating military and academic subjects.

Sixth, the work demonstrated the value of keeping enrollment in classes small. The average class contained only twelve men. Classrooms were equipped for the use of appropriate instructional aids, and every man was issued the necessary books and materials.

Seventh, the use of supplementary materials proved an important means of applying and reinforcing academic skills. Every man received a weekly newspaper and a monthly magazine. The difficulty of these publications did not exceed the fourth-grade level.

Eighth, two methods of instruction, regarded as appropriate for all training activities, were widely followed in the Special Training Units. Demonstrations were frequently given by instructors, and trainees engaged in applicatory exercises to show that they could perform every step in an essential operation.

The foregoing procedures might be employed in the development and use of instructional materials for teaching educationally retarded and disadvantaged pupils. Although principles underlying this program seem to be applicable at almost all levels of reading instruction, they are especially pertinent in the effective education of pupils whose opportunities and attainments have been meager.

CONCLUDING STATEMENT

Reading for college students and adults is one phase of a developmental reading program, emphasizing the continuity in the development and application of reading skills. Fostering reading growth is a responsibility at all educational levels. Although many colleges have not accepted the responsibility for developing reading programs, those which have done so have reason to be pleased with the results of their instruction and guidance. Adult programs outside the schools have also proved successful. Because of increased demands on adults today, both as workers and as citizens, to make intelligent decisions based on critical reading, broad programs of reading instruction are needed. These programs should be continuous with similarly comprehensive programs for skill building in younger persons and for disadvantaged pupils. Moreover, the programs at every level should be similar in emphasizing the satisfaction of interests and the fulfillment of needs through reading.

Selected References

Barbe, Walter B. "Slow Learner: A Plea for Understanding," *Education,* vol. 81 (February, 1961), pp. 323–325.

Bracken, Dorothy Kendall, "Why Teach Reading in College?" in J. Allen Figurel (editor), *Challenge and Experiment in Reading,* International Reading Association Conference Proceedings (New York: Scholastic Magazines, 1962), pp. 52–55.

Carter, Homer L. J. and Dorothy J. McGinnis, *Effective Reading* for College Students (New York: Holt, Rinehart & Winston, Inc., 1957).

Chicago Public Schools. "Services Rendered by the Teacher-Librarian," *Compensatory Education,* Study Report, no. 4, 1964 Series (August, 1964), p. 75.

Clift, David H. (chairman), *Adult Reading,* Fifty-fifth Yearbook of the National Society for the Study of Education, Part II (Chicago: University of Chicago Press, 1956).

Deutsch, Martin. "Social and Psychological Perspectives on the Development of the Disadvantaged Learner," *The Journal of Negro Education,* vol. 33 (Summer, 1964), pp. 232–244.

Educational Policies Commission. *Education and the Disadvantaged American* (Washington, D.C.: National Education Association, 1962).

Featherstone, W. B., *Teaching the Slow Learner.* (New York: Bureau of Publications: Teachers College, Columbia University, 1951).

Figurel, J. Allen (editor), "Teaching Reading to the Disadvantaged," in Part III, Sequence VIII in Improvement of Reading Through Classroom Practice, International Reading Association, 1964), pp. 160–175.

Gray, William S., and Bernice Rogers, *Maturity in Reading: Its Nature and Appraisal* (Chicago: University of Chicago Press, 1956).

Improving English Skills of Culturally Different Youth (Edited by Arno Jewett, Joseph Mersand, and Doris V. Gunderson), U.S. Department of Health, Education, and Welfare, Office of Education, Bulletin 1964, no. 5

(Washington, D.C.: Superintendent of Documents, Government Printing Office, 1964).

Ingram, C. P. *Education of the Slow Learning Child*, 3rd ed. (New York: The Ronald Press Company, 1960).

Johnson, G. O., *Education for the Slow Learners*. (Englewood Cliffs, N.J.: Prentice-Hall, Inc., 1963).

Lowrie, Jean (special editor), "Providing School Library Service to the Culturally Disadvantaged," *ALA Bulletin*, vol. 58 (June, July, August, September, October, December, 1964, January, 1965).

Mazurkiewicz, Albert J., "Means and Ends in College-Adult Reading," in J. Allen Figurel (editor), *Reading as an Intellectual Activity*, International Reading Association Conference Proceedings (New York: Scholastic Magazines, 1963), pp. 69–70.

Newton, Eunice Shaed, "Planning for the Language Development of Disadvantaged Children and Youth," *The Journal of Negro Education*, vol. 33 (Summer, 1964), pp. 264–274.

Norton-Taylor, Duncan, "Why Don't Businessmen Read Books?" *Fortune*, 49:115–117 (May, 1954).

Passow, A. Harry (editor), *Education in Depressed Areas* (New York: Teachers College, Columbia University, 1963).

Programs for the Educationally Disadvantaged, U.S. Department of Health, Education, and Welfare, Office of Education, Bulletin 1963, no. 17 (Washington, D.C.: Superintendent of Documents, Government Printing Office, 1963).

Rankin, Earl F., Jr., "The College-Adult Reading Program as a Research Laboratory," in J. Allen Figurel (editor), *Reading as an Intellectual Activity*, International Reading Association Conference Proceedings (New York: Scholastic Magazines, 1963), pp. 74–77.

Riessman, Frank, *The Culturally Deprived Child* (New York: Harper & Row, Publishers, 1962).

Shaw, Phillip, "Reading in College" in Paul A. Witty (chairman), *Development In and Through Reading*, Sixtieth Yearbook of the National Society for the Study of Education, Part I (Chicago: University of Chicago Press, 1961), pp. 336–354.

Shores, J. Harlan, and Kenneth L. Husbands, "Are Fast Readers the Best Readers?" *Elementary English*, 27:52–57 (January, 1950).

Simpson, Ray H., and Kenneth L. Camp, "Diagnosing Community Reading," *School Review*, 61:98–100 (February, 1953).

Smiley, Marjorie, "Research and Its Implications," in *Improving English Skills of Culturally Different Youth in Large Cities*, U.S. Department of Health, Education, and Welfare, Office of Education, Bulletin 1964, no. 5. (Washington, D.C.: U.S. Government Printing Office, 1964), pp. 35–61.

Smith, Donald E. P., and Roger L. Wood, "Reading Improvement and College Grades: A Follow-up," *Journal of Educational Psychology*, 46:151–159 (March, 1955).

Smith, Henry P., and Emerald V. Dechant, *Psychology in Teaching Reading* (Englewood Cliffs, N.J.: Prentice-Hall, Inc., 1961).

Strang, R., *Diagnostic Teaching of Reading* (New York: McGraw-Hill Book Company, 1964).

Witty, Paul, "The Improvement of Reading Abilities," in David H. Clift (chairman), *Adult Reading,* Fifty-fifth Yearbook of the National Society for the Study of Education, Part II (Chicago: University of Chicago Press, 1956), pp. 251–274.

Witty, Paul, "Needs of Slow-Learning Pupils," *Education,* vol. 81 (February, 1961), pp. 331–335.

Witty, Paul, ed. "Reading Instruction for the Educationally Retarded and the Disadvantaged," (Entire issue) *Education,* vol. 85 (April, 1965).

Witty, Paul, "Guiding Principles in Reading Instruction," *Education,* vol. 85 (April, 1965), pp. 474–481.

Witty, Paul, "Reading Instruction for the Educationally Retarded and the Disadvantaged," in *Invitational Addresses 1965* (Newark, Delaware: International Reading Association, 1965).

13

REMEDIAL READING

Theoretically, the term *remedial reading* has little or no place in a developmental reading program, which provides continuous instruction, guidance, and evaluation for each student as he progresses in reading. Accordingly, the need for remedial reading as traditionally understood is eliminated. Thus the developmental approach makes provision for differences in rate of learning and attempts to lead each pupil to develop a pattern of reading that is individually appropriate and beneficial. By the use of abundant and varied materials of instruction it offers reading experience to satisfy interests and fulfill needs. Under such a program, the need for remedial reading should not exist. Developmental programs, however, are found in few schools and seldom operate with maximum efficiency. As a result, remedial reading is still greatly needed in many schools. Large classes, inexperienced teachers, and meager instructional materials account in large measure for the need.

Studies show a wide range of ability to read and a large amount of reading retardation in the modern school. In 1944 a study of 7,380 graduates from the eighth grade in one large city revealed that 2,169 were reading at or below the sixth-grade level.[1] In 1949, Arthur Traxler reported that "from 10 to 25 percent of the children are two or more grades retarded in reading achievement, as measured by standard tests, by the end of the elementary school."[2] In 1953, one study reported that 50 percent of the 247 entering freshmen for high school fell at or below the sixth-grade level.[3]

[1] William Kottmeyer, "Improving Reading Instruction in the St. Louis Schools," *Elementary School Journal,* 45:33–34 (September, 1944).
[2] Arthur E. Traxler, "Research in Reading in the United States," *Journal of Educational Research,* 42:496 (March, 1949).
[3] Vivian Zinkin, "A Staggering Reading Problem," *The Clearing House,* 28:133–137 (November, 1953).

The amount of retardation varies, of course, from school to school; and reading difficulties appear as early as the first grade and are found in varying degrees throughout the elementary and the secondary school. In Chapter 12, we indicated the need for some corrective work at the college and adult level. The need, then, for remedial work is apparent, and a recent study indicates that many remedial programs are becoming a reality. For example, 54 percent of seventy junior high schools responding to a survey reported having remedial reading courses.[4]

THE RETARDED READER

Identifying Retarded Readers

Children who are not reading up to their capacity have been identified in various ways. One classification includes the pupil with a remedial problem and another, the child with a corrective problem. Roy Kress designates a child with a corrective reading problem as one who

> may be retarded in reading anywhere from a few months to several years below his expected grade level of achievement. . . . His classroom teacher is unable to place instruction on a level which is within the child's present range of word-recognition and comprehension skills . . . there is no basic neurological or psychological learning difficulty present.[5]

A child who has a remedial problem "in addition to being faced with the same inhibiting factors as found in the corrective category . . . is handicapped by a basic neurological or psychological difficulty."[6]

Numerous formulae have been constructed for the purpose of identifying retarded readers. Of the many ways to determine the expectancy level of children, two are worthy of mention here: the Bond-Clymer Formula and the Listening Capacity Test.

[4] M. D. Baughmann, "Special Reading Instruction in Illinois Junior High Schools," *National Association of Secondary School Principals Bulletin*, 44:90–95 (November, 1960).

[5] Roy A. Kress, "When Is Remedial Reading Remedial?" *Education*, 80:540–541 (May, 1960).

[6] *Ibid.*, p. 542.

Bond-Clymer Formula

Reading expectancy is determined by this formula: Estimated Reading Level = Number of Years in School $\times \frac{I.Q.}{100} + 1$.[7] For example, the estimated reading level of a child in the third month of the sixth grade with an I.Q. of 108 would be: $5.3 \times 1.08 + 1 = 6.7$. In view of the child's I.Q. and the years in school we could estimate his reading expectancy level as 6.7. If the child scores a year or more below that level he would be classified as a retarded reader. Whether he is a "corrective" or "remedial" reader depends upon the factors causing the disability.

Listening Capacity Test

A listening capacity test is a teacher-made instrument administered individually. From a graded series of passages a teacher reads to the pupil and checks comprehension of each passage immediately after it is read. The rationale of this type of test is to determine the level at which a child can understand printed matter without having to read it. The difference between the level attained on a listening test and the child's actual reading level would be the amount of retardation. Donald Cleland says of this test: "It is the considered opinion of the writer that a valid and reliable listening test is as good an instrument as can be found."[8]

In retrospect, then, a *retarded reader* is one who is reading one or more years below his expectancy level. The classification of "corrective" or "remedial" then depends on the factors causing the reading retardation. Reading retardation may be estimated through the use of an expectancy formula or a listening capacity test.

Factors Causing Retardation in Reading

Almost all retarded readers are characterized by several factors which contribute to their difficulty. In 1957 Margaret J. Early, reporting a summary of research on the causation of reading difficulty, concluded

---

[7] Guy L. Bond and Miles A. Tinker, *Reading Difficulties: Their Diagnosis and Correction* (New York: Appleton-Century-Crofts, 1957), pp. 76–81.

[8] Donald L. Cleland, "Clinical Materials for Appraising Disabilities in Reading," *The Reading Teacher,* 17:429 (March, 1964).

that "Since causation is multiple, remediation must also use many approaches," and that "diagnosis of the complex process of reading is continuous."[9] Likewise, John DeBoer and Martha Dallmann point out that "the causes of reading difficulty are usually numerous, complex, and interrelated."[10]

Some factors involved in reading retardation follow. These factors may be the effects of reading retardation in some cases and the causes of reading retardation in other cases. Often it is extremely difficult to determine which factor is a cause and which an effect.

Lack of Interest Factor

A study conducted by Witty with a hundred boys and girls identified as poor readers who attended the clinic at Northwestern University indicated the following items associated with reading retardation:[11]

CAUSES	PERCENT OF CASES
Lack of interest in reading	82
Indifference to reading	44
Dislike for reading	43
Emotional maladjustment	42
Problems and conflict in home	40
Defective vision	14
Generally poor physical condition	12
Left-handedness	4
Defective hearing	3

The study indicated that lack of interest in reading occurred in 82 percent of reading disability cases. Interest was determined by the pupils' responses to an inventory; indifference to reading was reported by teachers and examiners. Undoubtedly these items overlap greatly. Whether these factors were causes or effects it seems obvious that they are significant enough to bring about serious problems in learning to read.

[9] Margaret J. Early, "What Does Research Tell the Classroom Teacher About Basic Causes of Reading Disability and Retardation?" *Improving Reading in the Junior High School,* U. S. Department of Health, Education and Welfare, Office of Education, Bulletin 1957, no. 10 (Washington, D.C.: U.S. Government Printing Office, 1957), p. 22.

[10] John J. DeBoer and Martha Dallmann, *The Teaching of Reading,* rev. ed. (New York: Holt, Rinehart and Winston, Inc., 1964), p. 308.

[11] Paul Witty, "Interest and Success—The Antidote to Stress," *Elementary English,* 32:507–513 (December, 1955).

Emotional Factors

It may be concluded from research that most pupils who are retarded or disabled readers display minor or serious personality or adjustment problems. There is, of course, no certainty whether the emotional maladjustment is a cause or an effect of reading disability. Helen Robinson advises caution in relying on the very tentative conclusions drawn from recent research.[12] Albert Harris also states that the "present status of research on the relationship of personality and emotional factors to reading disability is one which is confused and contradictory."[13] To emphasize the complexity of the problem, he cites possible reasons for children's emotional resistance to reading.

> For example, one child may have been negatively conditioned by painful emotional events during early efforts to read; a second may have displaced resistance from mother to teacher or from eating to reading; a third may be emulating the approved behavior pattern of his gang; a fourth may be repressing hostile impulses so hard that little energy is available for intellectual effort . . .[14]

Many studies, however, do show a high frequency of emotional problems and personality limitations in poor readers. Other studies may fail to reveal such a relationship although it may be strongly suspected. George Spache's conclusion in 1954, after analyzing the test results of 50 retarded readers on the Rosenzweig Picture-Frustration Study (ages of subjects were from 6 to 14 with a mean I.Q. of 93 obtained from the Wechsler Verbal Scale), was that the average retarded reader is a "candidate for play-therapy or some other psychotherapeutic approach because of the common social maladjustment present."[15] The findings of a second study reported by Spache in 1957 were consistent with those of the 1954 study.[16]

It is generally conceded that reading disability or failure may in some cases be caused by emotional problems. Witty found, for example, in the investigation referred to earlier in this chapter, that one-third of the

---

[12] Helen M. Robinson, "Personality and Reading," in A. E. Traxler (editor), *Modern Educational Problems,* Report of the 17th Educational Conference, New York City, 1952 (Washington, D. C.: The American Council on Education, 1953).

[13] Albert J. Harris, "Unsolved Problems in Reading: A Symposium II," *Elementary English,* 31:416 (November, 1954).

[14] *Ibid.,* p. 417.

[15] George Spache, "Personality Characteristics of Retarded Readers as Measured by the Picture Frustration Study," *Educational and Psychological Measurement,* 14:191 (Spring, 1954).

[16] George Spache, "Personality Patterns of Retarded Readers," *Journal of Educational Research,* 50:461–469 (February, 1957).

students reported their introduction to reading as unsuccessful, and the experience embarrassing and frustrating.[17] Moreover, it has been found that pupils improve both in reading and in adjustment when given remedial work under desirable conditions. Play therapy has also proved helpful.[18]

Visual Factors

Although other factors contributing to reading disability are less frequently found than is emotional disturbance, one which has been extensively studied is poor vision. A review of the research reveals conflicting points of view.

Certain recent studies are similar to earlier ones in revealing little relationship between visual irregularities and poor reading. Thus Arthur Traxler and Ann Jungeblut conclude that when the usual school population is considered "there is little, if any, relationship between visual anomalies and measured reading achievement. However, refractive error may contribute to the reading failure of some pupils in the elementary school."[19]

As an example bearing on this conclusion, the study of William Edson, Guy Bond, and Walter Cook is relevant. These workers studied 188 fourth-grade pupils and analyzed the data from the Gates Basic Reading Tests, the Bond Silent Reading Diagnostic Tests, and tests of thirteen visual characteristics. The authors found no statistically significant differences between the normal and the defective groups of pupils. They concluded that "within these groups and for the tests employed no evidence was found to lend support to the opinion that achievement in reading is limited by vision."[20]

On the other hand, Albert Harris is of the opinion "that positive findings outweigh negative findings."[21] Harris and other investigators feel that a number of highly controlled studies do indicate a relationship between poor vision and reading disability.

A plausible solution to the problem is to check carefully both near-

---

[17] Paul Witty, *op. cit.*, p. 510.

[18] Robert E. Bills, "Nondirective Play Therapy with Retarded Readers," *Journal of Consulting Psychology,* 14:140–149 (May, 1950).

[19] Arthur E. Traxler and Ann Jungeblut, *Research in Reading During Another Four Years: Summary and Bibliography,* Educational Records Bulletin no. 75 (New York: Educational Records Bureau, 1960), p. 9.

[20] William H. Edson, Guy L. Bond, and Walter W. Cook, "Relationships Between Visual Characteristics and Specific Silent Reading Abilities," *Journal of Educational Research,* 46:451–457 (February, 1953).

[21] Albert J. Harris, *How to Increase Reading Ability,* 4th ed. (New York: David McKay Co., Inc., 1961), p. 235.

point acuity and disabilities in fusion in the diagnosis of any remedial reading case. Further, more adequate tests for measuring visual abilities and detecting visual disabilities appear necessary.

Auditory Factors

Similar to the visual problems, there is also little agreement about the incidence of hearing deficiencies among school children, estimates ranging from 1.5 percent of children to about 40 percent. The variability of incidence is very likely due to the different criteria for defining deafness and the different methods of measuring it. Louis Di Carlo and Eric Gardner came to the conclusion that no single measurement of deafness is adequate and that a need exists for standardization of audiometric procedures.[22] L. A. Dahl's survey of the literature on the relationship of hearing deficiencies to reading led him to conclude that there is general agreement among the experts that language development is somewhat retarded among children with hearing deficiencies.[23] Witty and Kopel added the factor of method of teaching as important in affecting the relationship between hearing loss and reading disability.[24] When the teaching method used is largely oral-phonetic, the child with gross hearing loss is handicapped.

On the other hand, certain recent studies indicate there is little relationship between hearing and reading difficulty. For example, Dorothy Poling studied 58 boys and 20 girls, of ages ranging from 8 to 13 years with I.Q.'s of 100–120. A statistical analysis of test data from the Stanford-Binet Intelligence Scale, the Wechsler-Bellevue Intelligence Scales, the Aurex Audio-Meter, and the Auditory Discrimination and Letter-Memory sections of the Monroe-Sherman Group Diagnostic Reading Aptitude and Achievement Tests led the author to the conclusion that "auditory acuity and auditory discrimination are not widespread causes of inefficient word recognition, but it is possible that auditory memory span is a significant factor in development of adequate word recognition."[25]

Lester Wheeler and Viola Wheeler analyzed data from tests adminis-

---

[22] Louis Di Carlo and Eric F. Gardner, "Comparative Study of the Efficiency of Three Group Pure Tone Screening Tests for Public School Children," *Exceptional Children,* 24:351–359 (April, 1958).

[23] L. A. Dahl, *Public School Audiometry: Principles and Methods* (Danville, Ill.: Interstate Printers and Publishers, 1949).

[24] Paul Witty and David Kopel, *Reading and the Educative Process* (Boston: Ginn and Company, 1939), p. 213.

[25] Dorothy L. Poling, "Auditory Deficiencies of Poor Readers," in Helen M. Robinson (editor), *Clinical Studies in Reading II,* Supplementary Educational Monograph no. 77 (Chicago: University of Chicago Press, 1953), pp. 107–111.

tered to 629 pupils in grades 4, 5, and 6. Tests included an auditory discrimination test, the pitch test from Seashore's Measures of Musical Talent, the Metropolitan Achievement Tests of vocabulary and reading comprehension, and tests of mental ability. The authors decided that "it cannot be assumed that pupils with poor pitch discrimination will tend to be poor readers or that good readers tend to have good pitch discrimination"; and that "difficulties in discriminating phonic elements in words do not appear as serious handicaps in developing reading skills at intermediate grade levels." No apparent basis was found for "relying exclusively on, or over-emphasizing the phonetic or 'sounding' method in teaching reading."[26]

Paul Berg studied data in research studies and conluded that although a relatively high correlation exists between reading and listening, there is a need for further research in this field and also for better instruments to measure listening comprehension.[27]

Lateral Dominance Factor

Paul Witty, working with David Kopel, selected the one hundred poorest readers in grades 3 to 6 and compared them with a group of good readers.[28] A systematic appraisal of the psychological functions underlying vision was made for both groups. Various phases of laterality were measured. Children showing mixed dominance were selected in both the good and the poor reading groups, and their tendency to make reversals was investigated. Although the poor readers made more reversals than the good readers, the children of mixed dominance within the group of poor readers made no more reversals than did the others. Among the good readers, reversals were few. It is noteworthy also that children mixed in dominance made the same average number of reversals as did the other pupils. Reversals, therefore, appeared to be merely symptoms of poor reading. Furthermore, lefthandedness, lefteyedness, and various other conditions of hand and eye dominance were found to be unrelated to reversal tendency.

---

[26] Lester R. Wheeler and Viola D. Wheeler, "A Study of the Relationship of Auditory Discrimination to Silent Reading Abilities," *Journal of Educational Research*, 48:103–113 (October, 1954). Cited by A. E. Traxler and A. Jungeblut, p. 146.

[27] Paul Berg, "Reading in Relation to Listening," in Oscar S. Causey and Albert J. Kingston (editors), *Evaluating College Reading Programs,* Fourth Yearbook of the Southwest Reading Conference for Colleges and Universities (Fort Worth, Texas: Texas Christian University Press, 1955), pp. 52–60. Cited by A. E. Traxler and A. Jungeblut, p. 141.

[28] Paul Witty and David Kopel, *op. cit.,* p. 52.

Traxler and Jungeblut, after reviewing research, concluded that "reversal tendencies are usual and normal among little children," but added that if "reversal tendencies persist beyond the age of nine, they may be a source of difficulty."[29]

Brain Damage Factor

Neurological factors have been studied in relation to reading retardation, and the role of brain damage as a possible causal factor has repeatedly been mentioned. The feeling among some authorities is that there is a much larger proportion of reading disability cases with brain injury than previously suspected.[30] At the present time tests are not available for teachers or reading consultants to identify children with brain damage; hence it is possible for children with minimal brain injury to go undetected.

This factor, however, is one that should not go unnoticed, and certainly there is common agreement that more research is necessary.

Intelligence Factor

Since most intelligence tests tend to be highly verbal in nature, children who earn high I.Q. scores are usually good readers. Ruth Strang found correlations from +.80 to +.84 between the language factor in the *California Tests of Mental Maturity* and scores on the *Gates Basic Reading Tests* among elementary children.[31] It has been suggested that children handicapped in reading should not be expected to score as high on I.Q. tests as children not so handicapped. When Joseph Justman and Miriam Aronow, however, compared I.Q. scores from the *Pintner Intelligence Test,* regarded as highly verbal in nature, and the other from the *Davis Eells Games,* designed to eliminate a heavy verbal weighting, the resulting scores were similar.[32] In some studies the nonlanguage portions of certain tests have been found to yield a low correlation with reading test scores. Thus Traxler obtained a correlation

---

[29] A. E. Traxler and A. Jungeblut, *op. cit.,* p. 9.

[30] Ralph C. Preston and J. Wesley Schneyer, "The Neurological Background of Nine Severely Retarded Readers," *Journal of Educational Research,* 49:455–459 (February, 1956).

[31] Ruth Strang, "Relationships Between Certain Aspects of Intelligence and Certain Aspects of Reading," *Educational and Psychological Measurement,* 3:355–359 (1943).

[32] Joseph Justman and Miriam Aronow, "The Davis-Eells Games as a Measure of the Intelligence of Poor Readers," *Journal of Educational Psychology,* 46:418–422 (1955).

of only +.36 between the scores on the nonlanguage parts of an intelligence test and reading scores, and a correlation of +.69 between the results on the language portions of the test and the *Iowa Silent Reading Test* scores.[33]

Many pupils of low I.Q. make poor scores on reading tests; indeed, the majority of pupils of I.Q.'s 70–90 are retarded readers if reading below grade placement is the criterion used for designating retardation. Yet many of these pupils may be reading in a satisfactory way if reading attainment is considered in terms of their ability. Hence, in designating pupils as retarded readers, we must compare reading attainment with the most reliable measures of ability we can obtain. In terms of reliable measures, the *Stanford-Binet Scale* and the *Wechsler Intelligence Scales,* both individually administered, appear to be valid instruments for determining the mental ability of children and young people. One could conclude that an individually administered intelligence test is necessary when dealing with retarded readers. Thus Harris states: "Verbal group tests above the primary grades do not distinguish between mentally slow children and those with reading disabilities; often the latter are mistakenly categorized as intellectually retarded."[34]

The teacher will want to examine the results of achievement tests too, which may help in arriving at an estimate of ability. The pupil who is a poor reader but who performs well on tests in areas such as arithmetic may be considered to have greater promise for learning than his intelligence test score indicates. Judgment of ability then will be based, in the case of the poor reader, on careful study and observation of each child.

Home and Environment Factors

The socioeconomic level of the home and community contributes to variations in the language experiences of boys and girls, although such variations seem to have a greater influence on readiness than on achievement. Mahmand Khater has reported that patterns of language used by upper-class kindergarten children are, in general, more mature than those of lower-class children. He also found that pronunciation and sentence

---

[33] Arthur E. Traxler, "A Study of the California Test of Mental Maturity: Advanced Battery," *Journal of Educational Research,* 32:329–335 (1939).

[34] Albert J. Harris, "Reading and Human Development," in Paul A. Witty (chairman), *Development In and Through Reading,* Sixtieth Yearbook of the National Society for the Study of Education, Part I (Chicago: University of Chicago Press, 1961), p. 23.

structure among upper-class children are closer to standard English.[35] Nila Banton Smith, in a review of studies designed to determine the influence of socioeconomic status on reading achievement, concluded:

> From these studies and other similar ones it seems that while there is a close relationship between the socioeconomic level of the home and readiness for beginning reading, this relationship usually does not hold to any significant extent in regard to reading achievement in later grades.[36]

Teachers need to become acquainted with the home background of each child in order to estimate the possible effects of impoverished conditions upon his reading status. In some cases the teacher's responsibility is clearly to enrich the pupil's experience and thus to provide the basis for success in reading.

Poor Teaching Factor

The opinion is generally held among reading authorities that poor teaching is a cause of some children's failure in reading. The extent to which poor teaching affects the reading ability of children is unknown.

Two reasons have been given for poor teaching: (1) lack of adequate teacher preparation, and (2) teaching the "text" rather than the "child." Mary Austin and Coleman Morrison, in discussing the first reason, state:

> Teachers and administrative officers agree almost to a person that the preservice preparation of teachers of reading is inadequate. . . . In-service programs, which might well be thought the *sine qua non* for the improvement of existing and future reading programs, commonly evidence weaknesses. Approximately one-third of all the school systems sampled offered no such services, and those that did provided programs so sporadic as to cast doubt on their overall effectiveness.[37]

Coupled with poor preparation is the fact that some teachers lose sight of the individual and their only goal is to "get through" the texts. Covering material has never proved successful in terms of learning. Somehow, however, the mistaken notion that reading a text insures

---

[35] Mahmand R. Khater, *The Influence of Social Class on the Language Patterns of Kindergarten Children*, Unpublished Doctoral Dissertation (Chicago: University of Chicago Press, 1951).

[36] Nila Banton Smith, "Readiness for Reading, II," *Elementary English*, 27:96 (February, 1950).

[37] Mary C. Austin and Coleman Morrison, *The First R* (New York: Macmillan Company, 1963), p. 180.

learning seems to pervade certain classrooms and sometimes entire schools. The importance of meeting children's needs has been pointed out in Chapter 4 in this text. It is desirable then, in many instances, to implement this idea in the classroom. The sound preparation of teachers and strong leadership on the part of principals and reading consultants appears necessary if the teaching of reading in the classroom is to become effective.

DIAGNOSIS OF READING DISABILITY

In order to understand the nature and scope of reading disability, teachers may profit from a consideration of some general principles related to diagnosis in reading. William Sheldon lists six principles:

1. Diagnosis is an essential aspect of teaching and is a preliminary step to sound instruction.
2. Diagnosis should be continuous because child growth in reading depends upon the sequential development of skills, which is promoted through the teacher's knowledge of each child's progress.
3. Diagnosis is an individual task and reflects the fact that each child is different.
4. Diagnosis of reading status demands far more than an assessment of reading because reading difficulties are symptomatic of many causative factors.
5. Because reading is but one aspect of language, teachers must understand the listening, speaking, and writing status of children to fully understand their reading abilities.
6. Because the instruments of diagnosis have not been perfected, the limitation of each instrument must be thoroughly understood.[38]

Bond and Tinker suggest three levels of diagnosis depending upon the extent and nature of each child's deviation:[39] (1) *A general diagnosis* which utilizes group intelligence- and achievement-test results, as well as data from cumulative records. Many students who are not seriously retarded need little more than an evaluation by group tests to determine their status and needs. (2) *An analytical diagnosis* which employs tests to ascertain specific strengths and weaknesses in reading. Children who are markedly retarded in reading but who do not display serious personality problems or irregularities may be profitably studied in this way. (3) *A case-study diagnosis* which includes comprehensive

---

[38] William D. Sheldon, "Specific Principles Essential to Classroom Diagnosis," *The Reading Teacher,* 14:2–8 (September, 1960).
[39] Guy L. Bond and Miles A. Tinker, *op. cit.,* pp. 128–132.

examinations and inquiries concerning the child's total personality pattern is appropriately employed with pupils who exhibit serious retardation accompanied by behavior problems or irregularities.

In general, the extent and seriousness of the reading problem will determine the type of diagnosis employed. When the problem is so severe as to require a case study, many possible contributing factors are investigated, including the pupil's physical condition, his mental ability, his educational status, his interests, his emotional and social problems, and his home background. Detailed study is especially made of his acquisition of reading skills.

It is important to remember that diagnosis and remedial work are not limited to slow learners, but are applicable to all pupils. According to Smith and Dechant:

> Diagnosis and remediation are no longer to be considered the special privileges of the slow learner; they are extended to the gifted and to the average learners as well. Each child deserves diagnosis in order that his abilities, inadequacies, disabilities, and progress can be determined. Then remediation may overcome his disabilities so that he can progress to the extent of his abilities.[40]

Standardized Tests for Diagnosis of Reading Ability

Standardized tests are commonly used as a measure for determining reading performance. They are classified as *survey* tests and *diagnostic* tests. Survey tests measure the level at which a child can read and usually provide an average score which compares the individual tested with other pupils of the same grade. Diagnostic tests indicate strengths and weaknesses of pupils in various reading sub-skills.

Standardized tests should be used judiciously because of their limitations. It should be noted that these tests are only a sampling of selected skills, and therefore a five- or seven-minute test would be less likely to be as reliable as a twenty-minute test. Also, it is difficult to measure certain skills without considering others. For example, a measure of vocabulary on a silent reading test entails identification of words. A child who has a weakness in word-identification skills may score low on vocabulary tests, not because of poor vocabulary but because he couldn't identify the words. Other limitations of standardized tests are given by Donald Cleland:

[40] Henry P. Smith and Emerald V. Dechant, *Psychology in Teaching Reading* (Englewood Cliffs, N.J.: Prentice-Hall, Inc., 1961), p. 407.

> *A score on any test (informal or standardized) is simply a measure of performance on a particular day, at a particular time of the day, and under a particular testing situation. . . .*
> *Tests sample proficiency in selected language skills. . . .*
> *Many tests do not measure the ability to disentangle concepts from complex masses of data. . . .*
> *Some tests do not provide a measure of the ability to evaluate, in depth, an article on a controversial issue. . . .*
> *Not all tests provide an opportunity to substantiate a considered choice between seemingly plausible choices. . . .*
> *Tests cannot directly reveal the depth or subtlety of an appreciation of the finest literature. . . .*
> *Tests cannot measure the capacity or ability to interpret to others one's understanding of an abstract concept or idea. . . .*
> *The pattern of response is usually set by the format of the test, i.e., the subject merely recognizes the most plausible response. . . .*
> *Some tests do not measure the ability to read creatively.*[41]

In spite of their limitations, standardized tests, if used carefully, can yield important information concerning the reading ability—or disability—of an individual or group of pupils. The tests listed in Table XV may be helpful in diagnosing pupils' strengths and weaknesses in reading.

Use of Informal Methods in Diagnosing Reading Disability

Standardized tests are valuable for diagnosis of reading disabilities, but they are limited to certain skills. The teacher may wish to employ more informal methods of diagnosis (1) for following up reading problems and (2) for determining additional needs of seriously retarded pupils. Informal procedures are frequently valuable in such cases. The teacher may decide, after studying the results of a standardized test, that a pupil needs help in word recognition; but he wants to know more about the child's reading in order to offer the maximum help. He may then select paragraphs from a book at the child's reading level and listen to him as he reads aloud. Or the teacher may wish additional information about another child who is easily distracted and inattentive, who looks out of the window, yawns, or annoys his neighbors, scores low on the standardized tests, and appears to lack an interest in and a liking for reading. To such a pupil, an interest inventory may be profitably administered as an aid in finding specific interests which can be fruitfully associated with reading.

---

[41] Donald L. Cleland, *op. cit.*, pp. 429–430.

TABLE XV

SELECTED READING TESTS FOR DIAGNOSIS OF DIFFICULTIES

TEST	PUBLISHER	DATE	HOW ADMINISTERED	FORMS	LEVEL	SKILLS TESTED
American School Achievement Tests	Bobbs-Merrill Company, Inc.	1960	Group	D, E	Primary I (Grade 1)	Word recognition Word meaning
				D, E, F, G	Primary II (Grades 2–3)	Sentence meaning Word meaning Paragraph meaning
					Intermediate (Grades 4–5–6)	
					Advanced (Grades 7–8–9)	
Basic Sight Word Test	Garrard Press	1942	Individual		(Grades 1–2)	Word recognition
California Phonics Survey	California Test Bureau	1963	Group	1	(Grades 7–college)	Diagnosis reversals, confusion of blends, confusion of vowels, letter combinations to spoken sounds.

303

TABLE XV (*Continued*)

TEST	PUBLISHER	DATE	HOW ADMINISTERED	FORMS	LEVEL	SKILLS TESTED
California Reading Test	California Test Bureau	1957 Edition with 1963 norms	Group	W, X	Lower Primary (Grades 1–2)	Vocabulary Comprehension
					Upper Primary (Grades 3 and L4)	
				W, X, Y, Z	Elementary (Grades 4–5–6)	
				W, Y, Z	Junior High (Grades 7–8–9)	
				W, X, Y	Advanced (Grades 9–14)	
Developmental Reading Tests	Lyons and Carnahan	1955	Group		Primer (Grade 1.5)	PV-A Basic vocabulary PG-A General comprehension PS-A Specific comprehension
					Lower Primary	LV-A Basic vocabulary

			(Grades 1.5–2.5)	LG-A General comprehension LS-A Specific comprehension
			Upper Primary (Grades 2.5–3.0)	UV-A Basic vocabulary UG-A General comprehension US-A Specific comprehension
		1959	Intermediate (Grades 4–6)	Basic vocabulary, reading to retain information, evaluate-interpret, appreciate
Diagnostic Reading Scales	California Test Bureau	1963	Individual (Grades 1–8)	Measures oral reading ability. Yields instructional level, independent level, potential level. Also tests basic phonic skills.
Diagnostic Reading Tests (Survey Section)	Science Research Associates, Inc.	1960	Group A, B (Grades 4–8)	Word recognition, rate, study selection, story comprehension, vocabulary
			(Grades 7–13)	Rate, study selection, story comprehension, vocabulary

305

TABLE XV (*Continued*)

TEST	PUBLISHER	DATE	HOW ADMINISTERED	FORMS	LEVEL	SKILLS TESTED
Durrell Analysis of Reading Difficulty: New Edition	Harcourt, Brace and World, Inc.	1955	Individual		(Grades 1–6)	Analysis of silent and oral reading, listening comprehension, word analysis, phonics, writing, and spelling.
Gates Primary Reading Tests	Bureau of Publications, Teachers College, Columbia University	1958	Group		Primary (Grades 1–2.5) Advanced (Grades 2.5–3)	PWR Word recognition PSR Sentence reading PPR Paragraph reading AWR Word recognition APR Paragraph reading
Gates Basic Reading Tests	Bureau of Publications, Teachers College, Columbia University	1958	Group		(Grades 3.5–8)	GS Appreciate general significance UD Understand precise directions ND Note details RV Reading vocabulary LC Level of comprehension
Gilmore Oral Reading Test	Harcourt, Brace and World, Inc.	1951	Individual	A, B	(Grades 1–8)	Analysis of accuracy, comprehension, and rate.

Gray Standardized Oral Reading Paragraphs Test	The Bobbs-Merrill Co., Inc.	1963	Individual	(Grades 1–8)	Analysis of word-recognition ability and comprehension,
High School Reading Test: National Achievement Tests	Acorn Publishing Co.	1952	Group A, B	(Grades 7–12)	Vocabulary, word discrimination, sentence meaning, noting details, interpreting paragraphs
Iowa Every-Pupil Test of Basic Skills	Houghton Mifflin Co.	1945	Group L, M, N, O	Elementary (Grades 3–5) Advanced (Grades 5–9)	Silent reading comprehension Word-study skills Basic language
Iowa Silent Reading Tests: New Edition	Harcourt, Brace and World, Inc.	1942	Group Am, Bm, Cm, Dm	Elementary (Grades 4–8) Advanced (Grades 9–12)	Rate, comprehension, locating information
Iowa Tests of Educational Development	Science Research Associates, Inc.	1962	Group X, Y	(Grades 9–13)	Understanding of basic social concepts, general background in the natural sciences, correctness and appropriateness of expression, ability to do quantitative thinking,

TABLE XV (*Continued*)

TEST	PUBLISHER	DATE	HOW ADMINISTERED	FORMS	LEVEL	SKILLS TESTED
						ability to interpret reading materials in social studies, ability to interpret literature, general vocabulary, use of source materials
Lee-Clark Reading Test	California Test Bureau	1958	Group	A, B	Primer (Grade 1)	Vocabulary and following directions
					First Reader (Grades 1–2)	Vocabulary, following directions, sentence completion, inference
Metropolitan Achievement Tests (Reading Battery)	Harcourt, Brace and World, Inc.	1960	Group	A, B, C	Primary I (Second half of Grade 1)	Word knowledge Word discrimination Comprehension
					Primary II (Grade 2)	
				A, B, C, D	Elementary (Grades 3–4)	Word knowledge Word discrimination

					Intermediate (Grades 5–6)	Paragraph comprehension
					Advanced (Grades 7–9)	
				A, B	High School (Grades 9–12)	
Monroe Revised Silent Reading Tests	The Bobbs-Merrill Co., Inc.	1959	Group	4, 5, 6	Test I (Grades 3–4–5)	Rate and comprehension
					Test II (Grades 6–7–8)	
				1, 2	Test III (Grades 9–12)	
Reading Comprehension Test: National Achievement Tests	Acorn Publishing Co.	1957	Group	A, B	Grades 4–6	Following directions, sentence meaning, paragraph meaning, rate
					Grades 4–9	
Silent Reading Diagnostic Tests	Lyons and Carnahan	1955	Group		Grades 3–8	Word recognition patterns, recognition techniques, and word synthesis

Some teachers wish to determine informally at what reading level a pupil will benefit most from remedial endeavor. An informal method of studying such a pupil consists in having him read paragraphs aloud from books selected on graduated levels of difficulty. The teacher may select for oral reading a number of books from a basal series with which the child is not familiar. As the pupil reads aloud and the teacher records errors on dittoed copies of the materials, the nature and extent of the pupil's difficulties are clearly shown. If he makes a very large number of errors in reading a selection, he should be given an easier one. Most difficult material may be gradually introduced from the level at which he can read easily and fluently. His comprehension may also be studied informally, and appropriate exercises may be devised to help him overcome his varied difficulties. Bond and Tinker describe various reading levels that may be obtained by listening to children read in the manner just discussed:

> 1. The child's *independent reading level* is ascertained from the book in which he can read with no more than one error in word recognition (pronunciation) in each 100 words and has a comprehension score of at least 90 per cent. At this level the child must read orally in a natural conversational tone. The reading should be rhythmical and well phrased. . . .
> 2. The *instructional reading level* is determined from the level of the book in which the child can read with no more than one word-recognition error in each 20 words and has a comprehension score of at least 75 per cent. At this level the child reads orally, *after silent study,* without tension, in a conversational tone, and with rhythm and proper phrasing. . . .
> 3. The *frustration reading level* is marked by the book in which the child "bogs down" when he tries to read. He reads orally without rhythm and in an unnatural voice. Errors and reversals are numerous. Tensions are manifest. The child comprehends less than half of what he is trying to read. The test should be stopped as soon as it is clear that the child is at his frustration level.
> No child should be asked to go on reading at the frustration level when he is being taught or in any other situation. . . .
> 4. The *probable capacity reading level* is shown by the highest book in the series in which the child can comprehen 75 percent of the material when it is read aloud by the examiner. . . .[42]

Instead of the foregoing informal type of analysis, the teacher may wish to use some of the published checklists to record specific errors made by a pupil as he reads silently or orally. The checklist presented here may prove helpful in offering individual guidance and instruction to very poor readers.

[42] Guy L. Bond and Miles A. Tinker, *op. cit.,* p. 170 (from E. A. Betts).

INFORMAL DIAGNOSIS BLANK[43]

Basic Data

Name _____ School attending _____
Chronological age _____ Grade in school _____
Mental test given _____
I.Q. _____ M.A. _____ Mental grade _____

Standardized reading tests given:
 1. _____ Score _____ Reading grade _____
 2. _____ Score _____ Reading grade _____
 3. _____ Score _____ Reading grade _____
 4. _____ Score _____ Reading grade _____
    Average reading grade _____

Reading Levels
 1. Independent reading level, grade _____
 2. Instructional reading level, grade _____
 3. Frustration reading level, grade _____
 4. Probable capacity reading level, grade _____

Oral Reading from Book
 1. Name and grade level of book _____
 2. Rate: words per minute _____
 3. Degree of comprehension _____
 4. Expression _____
 5. Nature of enunciation _____
 6. Skill in phrasing _____
 7. Word-by-word reading _____
 8. Habits during reading: head movements, following with finger, posture, distractibility, tenseness
 9. Attitude toward reading _____
 10. Word-recognition difficulties:
     a. Reversals _____
     b. Wrong beginning _____
     c. Wrong middle _____
     d. Wrong ending _____
     e. Wrong several parts _____
 11. Word-recognition skills:
     a. Use of context _____
     b. Adequacy of sight words _____
     c. Adequacy of procedure in word analysis _____
 12. Other difficulties:
     a. Repetitions _____
     b. Omissions _____
     c. Refusals _____
     d. Other _____

Silent Reading from Book
 1. Name and grade level of book _____
 2. Rate: words per minute _____
 3. Degree of comprehension _____

[43] Adapted from Guy L. Bond and Miles A. Tinker, *op. cit.*, pp. 172–174.

    4. Vocalization (degree of lip movement, whispering, audible speech) _____
    5. Finger pointing _____
    6. Head movements _____
    7. Signs of tenseness _____
    8. Posture _____
    9. Distractibility _____
   10. Other habits _____

Word Pronunciation from Word Lists in Basic Book
    1. Name and grade level of book _____
    2. Nature and phonetic attack _____
    3. Blending skill _____
    4. Resorts to spelling attack _____
    5. No method of word analysis _____
    6. Skill in syllabication _____
    7. Recognition of familiar parts _____
    8. Recognition of parts of compound words _____
    9. Recognition of word roots _____
   10. Handling of suffixes _____
   11. Handling of prefixes _____
   12. Trouble with consonants _____
   13. Trouble with vowels _____
   14. Sounds omitted _____
   15. Sounds added _____

Other Relevant Data
    1. Hearing status _____
    2. Visual status _____
    3. Speech difficulties _____
    4. Other physical difficulties _____
    5. Fluency in language usage _____
    6. Chief interests _____
    7. Ability to concentrate _____
    8. Persistence in tasks _____
    9. Emotional reactions (confident, shy, overaggressive, negativistic, cheerful) _____
   10. Attitudes (toward school, teacher, reading) _____
   11. Handedness _____
   12. Eyedness _____
   13. Home environment _____
   14. Other observations _____

Tentative Diagnosis of Case
    1. Degree of reading retardation _____
    2. Important physical handicaps _____
    3. Adjustment difficulties _____
    4. Lack of voice control and rhythm in oral reading _____
    5. Main word-recognition difficulties _____
    6. Comprehension difficulties _____

REMEDIAL READING PRACTICES AND PROGRAMS

Specialized Procedures

Procedures characterized by varying degrees of specialization have been devised for retarded readers. These approaches are sometimes recommended for use with remedial cases in the classroom; they are employed, too, in special classes.

All of these procedures have been used successfully. Arthur Gates has pioneered in offering poor readers varied experience with appropriately graded materials, directing special attention to the desirability of repeating words in varied contexts.[44] Samuel Kirk, on the other hand, has recommended a reading program for slow-learning children which stresses to a greater extent phonic training.[45] Much drill is provided and is accompanied by repeated associations of objects with sounds. The child says a new sound, writes it, and uses it in words with other sounds he has learned. The Kirk approach is exemplified in the drill exercises devised by Hegge, Kirk, and Kirk,[46] from the use of which outstanding results have been reported.

Highly specialized approaches have been recommended not only for remedial teaching but also for helping the slow-learner. For example, Marion Monroe devised a special phonic approach which she has employed with success with extremely retarded readers.[47]

The *Grace Fernald Method* has also been used effectively with very poor readers. The pupil is taught to write the words and read the printed copy, then to proceed slowly to materials of varied kinds with emphasis on concept expansion and comprehension.[48] The more specialized approaches are perhaps most appropriate to use with cases that do not respond to more eclectic and more directly applicable methods, such as those recommended by Gates. But it is well to bear in mind that one should not rely on a single approach because one method may succeed with certain pupils where another fails.

Any teacher who is carrying on remedial work should note that

---

[44] Arthur I. Gates, *The Improvement of Reading,* 3rd ed. (New York: The Macmillan Co., 1947), p. 310.
[45] Samuel A. Kirk, *Teaching Reading to Slow-Learning Children* (Boston: Houghton Mifflin Co., 1940).
[46] T. G. Hegge, S. A. Kirk, and W. D. Kirk, *Remedial Reading Drills* (Ann Arbor, Michigan: George Wahr Publishing Company, 1945).
[47] Marion Monroe, *Children Who Cannot Read* (Chicago: University of Chicago Press, 1932).
[48] Grace M. Fernald, *Remedial Techniques in Basic School Subjects* (New York: McGraw-Hill Book Company, 1943).

remedial methods and developmental reading methods are similar. Remedial work usually is more time-consuming and necessitates greater repetition, for it is a slow process to break old habits and establish new ones; and time-consuming repetition is often required to strengthen underlearned habits. Indeed, these activities not only require time, but also patience and understanding, on the part of the teacher.

Remedial Reading Programs

A number of comprehensive remedial reading programs have been reported which include thorough diagnosis, systematic guidance, provision of diversified reading materials, and careful evaluation of growth as improvement occurs. Almost without exception, these efforts have been successful.

For example, one such program carried on for three semesters in a Chicago high school demonstrated the educability of the poorest readers in the entering class.[49] Four classes, each enrolling thirty-one pupils, were formed to offer remedial work for the poorest readers entering the ninth grade. All pupils had I.Q.'s above 80; the median I.Q. was 88. On standardized reading tests all pupils made scores below the norms for grade 7; the median attainment fell at 5.2 grade level.

At the first class meeting the reading problem was discussed with the pupils, and it was frankly admitted that the class as a whole was retarded in reading attainment. But it was also pointed out that great improvement was possible. Attractive reading materials were presented; and their contents were discussed and related to individual interests.

During the first week the pupils in each group were encouraged to examine and read books and other materials displayed on tables and racks in the classroom. Meanwhile, the teacher interviewed every pupil. Since each class contained thirty-one pupils, it was necessary to employ study periods and other free time for these informal discussions of each pupil's hobbies, preferences, and favorite leisure pursuits. The conferences were guided by the use of the Witty-Kopel Interest Inventory. (See Appendix C for a similar Inventory.)

Dominant group and individual interests were ascertained, as well as reading experiences and preferences. The responses to a graded book list showed that these pupils had read few books; moreover, most of the books begun had not been completed. Reading was usually associated with disappointment and frustration.

---

[49] Paul A. Witty and David Kopel, *op. cit.*, p. 145.

In the remedial program, structurally simple materials related to the interests of the group were employed. A classroom library was assembled; it included a nucleus of books which had been utilized successfully with ninth-grade classes of very low reading ability. Additions were made from time to time of books suggested by the pupils, the librarian, and the teachers. Periodicals such as *Young America, My Weekly Reader, Boys' Life, Newsweek,* and the *Reader's Digest* were made available for reading in the classroom. The *Unit Study Books* (now known as *Little Wonder Books*) provided materials related to topics in the fields of science and social studies. Many other books and pamphlets of approximately sixth-grade reading difficulty offered the pupils further opportunity to develop or extend worthy interests. The classroom was equipped with open bookshelves, racks for booklets, magazine tables, and attractive pictures.

The program was characterized by an orderly and systematic introduction of materials. First, the students expressed their interests, talked about the books they had enjoyed, and indicated the types of stories they would like to read. They also examined books and periodicals. On the following days assignments from different volumes in a new textbook series were distributed. Each assignment was made in accordance with the pupils' expressed interests and their reading ability. For several weeks specific assignments continued to be made daily, but additional activities were also introduced. On some days periodicals were read, or voluntary reading took place from the books in the room. On other days the class was taken to the school library and helped in locating source materials and in finding information related to group or individual interests. A weekly period was devoted to planning, during which the senior author met with the teachers and librarians and discussed the work of the preceding week, and tentative day-by-day outlines were made for the coming week. Thus, the efforts of the different teachers were concentrated on providing reading experiences in an orderly sequence according to changing interests, needs, and abilities.

To evaluate the students' progress, tests were repeated at the end of the first semester and the interest inventory was again administered. Large gains were displayed on standard tests of silent and oral reading. In addition, pupils reported that they enjoyed reading at school and that they were now finding pleasure in reading at home; their indifference or antagonism had been replaced by interest in reading and, in many cases, by real enthusiasm for the satisfactions and values which can be obtained through it. Improvement was shown, too, in the ability to organize reading content in comprehensive thought patterns, in the capacity to grasp the relationship of new reading to past experience, and in ability to assimilate rather long episodes which called for sustained attention and discrimination. Speed in reading showed a gain from a group median of 160 to 270 words a minute. The number of subject failures in other areas was reduced greatly.

Other approaches in similar programs have also been very successful. Some of these programs employ limited materials for short periods of time and are conducted by the regular classroom teacher. In two such programs, for junior and for first-year high school pupils, careful screening of poor readers preceded the introduction of the Science Research Associates' *Developmental Reading Kit, Secondary Edition.* The ninth-grade pupils met with the teacher during two periods each week for sixteen meetings. Each student took the *Starter Test* to determine his reading level.[50] Then, for two periods a week, he used the reading materials and recorded his growth in the Student Record Booklet. Another form of the SRA Reading Test was administered at the end of the eight-week period, and the results indicated large gains.

Another study, more comprehensive in nature, is reported by Phyllis Bland, who tells how the Evanston Township High School established a twofold reading improvement program—a reading clinic and a developmental reading program.

> The purpose of the former was to assist students who could profit most from remedial or individual work. The purpose of the latter was to aid groups of good or above-average readers who wished to make further improvement.[51]

The principal features of a developmental reading program guided the work in clinical and developmental instruction. A reading consultant worked closely with the teachers to help them guide students in the improvement of reading skills.

> This recognizes that the clinical and developmental instruction conducted by the reading consultant can accomplish only part of the total reading program.
> To understand and to satisfy the needs of students with special reading problems, the school's reading consultant works closely with the teachers who are homeroom directors, and with the staffs of the

---

[50] For a full report of these efforts, see John French, Melvin Donaho, and Edith Grotberg, "A Small School in Beecher, Illinois, Makes Big Strides," *The Bulletin of the National Association of Secondary School Principals,* 43:85–99 (January, 1959).

[51] Phyllis Bland, "The Development of a Reading Program in the Evanston Township High School, Evanston, Illinois," in Elizabeth A. Simpson, *Helping High-School Students Read Better* (Chicago: Science Research Associates, Inc., 1954), pp. 107–115.

library, health center, and guidance department. Also, she often confers with the school psychologist and social-psychiatric workers about students who have mental or emotional blocks to reading improvement.[52]

The remedial program included students whose reading abilities were substantially below their scholastic aptitudes as indicated by entrance tests. These English Reading Classes, which met five times a week throughout the academic year, were substituted for the regular freshman English course. The students learned about successful reading through use of films such as the Encyclopaedia Britannica film *Better Reading* and through reading and discussing two booklets by SRA, *You Can Read Better* and *Streamline Your Reading*. Reading needs and goals were set up in conference with the teacher. Book games, the writing of TV scripts, class-written and class-edited magazines, and special group or individual projects contributed to the appeal of the program. Many books and other reading materials related to interests and needs of the students were made available on varied reading levels. Wide use was made of the tape recorder.

After nine months of instruction the mean score of the freshman group increased from 7.6 to 9.2, as measured by the *California Reading Test*. More important, however, "than the reading gains made by these groups was the students' change in attitude toward reading."[53]

Thus we see that remedial programs may involve a short period of time and may be concerned with improvement of a limited number of skills, or they may be more comprehensive and be concerned with improvement in all subject areas. Remedial work may be carried on by the regular classroom teacher or by teachers or consultants in special classes.

CONCLUDING STATEMENT

Remedial reading might not be required if developmental reading methods were generally found in schools today. Continuous evaluation of student growth would then lead to the prevention of reading disabilities, for special help would be given to students whenever difficulties arose. However, lack of adequately prepared teachers, large classes, and a wide range of ability within classes make remedial instruction necessary in many schools. Complicated psychological or neurological ir-

[52] *Ibid.*
[53] *Ibid.*

regularities also necessitate additional detailed diagnosis and attention.

Diagnosis of reading disability, using both formal and informal techniques, is vital. Standardized tests may aid the teacher in ascertaining difficulties, and informal methods may supplement those findings. Materials for remedial reading may consist of books from basal series, volumes written at a high interest but low reading level, and special materials designed for remedial purposes.

Although a special teacher for remedial work is often to be desired, relatively few school systems employ such a person. Much can be done, however, by the classroom teacher, who is often able to offer effective help by the use of simple procedures. In some schools more comprehensive programs have been undertaken. They have included not only remedial work for the seriously retarded reader, but also extensive opportunities for all students to develop and extend their reading skills and to satisfy their varied interests and needs through reading. These programs have included guidance in the various subject fields and have elicited the cooperation of all teachers in an effort to improve reading throughout the school.

Selected References

Austin, Mary C., "Identifying Readers Who Need Corrective Instruction," in *Corrective Reading in Classroom and Clinic,* Supplementary Educational Monograph no. 79 (Chicago: University of Chicago Press, 1953), pp. 19–25.

Austin, Mary C. and Coleman Morrison, *The First R* (New York: The Macmillan Co., 1963).

Bond, Guy L. and Miles A. Tinker, *Reading Difficulties: Their Diagnosis and Correction* (New York: Appleton-Century-Crofts, 1957).

Dolch, E. W., "Success in Remedial Reading," *Elementary English,* 30:133–137 (March, 1953).

Fernald, Grace M., *Remedial Techniques in Basic School Subjects* (New York: McGraw-Hill Book Company, 1943).

Freeland, Alma, "Helping Parents Understand" in the 1955 Yearbook of the *National Elementary Principal* (Washington, D.C.: National Education Association, 1955), pp. 236–244.

Harris, Albert J., *How to Increase Reading Ability,* 4th ed. (New York: David McKay Company, Inc., 1961).

Johnson, Marjorie Seddon, "A Study of Diagnostic and Remedial Procedures in a Reading Clinic Laboratory School," *Journal of Educational Research,* 48:565–578 (April, 1955).

Kirk, Samuel A. and Orville G. Johnson, *Educating the Retarded Child* (Boston: Houghton Mifflin Company, 1951).

Rasmussen, Glen R. and Hope W. Dunne, "A Longitudinal Evaluation of a Junior High School Corrective Reading Program," *The Reading Teacher,* 16:95–101 (November, 1962).

Robinson, Helen M., "Clinical Procedures in Diagnosing Seriously Retarded Readers," in William S. Gray and Nancy Larrick (editors), *Better Readers for Our Times,* International Reading Association Conference Proceedings, vol. 1 (New York: Scholastic Magazines, 1956), pp. 152–156.

Robinson, Helen M., "Corrective and Remedial Instruction," in Paul A. Witty (chairman), *Development In and Through Reading,* Sixtieth Yearbook of the National Society for the Study of Education, Part I (Chicago: University of Chicago Press, 1961), pp. 357–375.

Roswell, Florence G., "Are Emotional Problems a Block to Reading Achievement?" in J. Allen Figurel (editor), *Reading as an Intellectual Activity,* International Reading Association Conference Proceedings (New York: Scholastic Magazines, 1963), pp. 139–142.

Spache, George, "Integrating Diagnosis with Remediation in Reading," *The Elementary School Journal,* 56:18–26 (September, 1955).

Strang, Ruth, *Diagnostic Teaching of Reading* (New York: McGraw-Hill Book Company, 1941).

Strang, Ruth, Constance M. McCullough, and Arthur E. Traxler, *Problems in the Improvement of Reading* (New York: McGraw-Hill Book Company, 1955).

Traxler, Arthur E., "Critical Survey of Tests for Identifying Difficulties in Interpreting What Is Read," in William S. Gray (editor), *Promoting Growth Toward Maturity in Interpreting What Is Read,* Supplementary Educational Monographs no. 74 (Chicago: University of Chicago Press, 1951), pp. 195–200.

Wheeler, Lester R., "Distinctive Problems Presented by Poor Readers: The Retarded Reader," in *Improving Reading in All Curriculum Areas,* Supplementary Educational Monographs no. 76 (Chicago: University of Chicago Press, 1952), pp. 109–114.

Witty, Paul A., "Problems in the Improvement and Measurement of Growth in Reading," *School and Society,* 78:69–73 (September, 1953).

Witty, Paul A., *Reading in Modern Education* (Boston: D. C. Heath and Company, 1949).

Witty, Paul A. and David Kopel, *Reading and the Educative Process* (Boston: Ginn and Company, 1939).

14

READING INSTRUCTION FOR THE SLOW-LEARNING PUPIL

The term *slow-learner* is neither precise nor always appropriate, but it is often employed today to designate pupils whose I.Q.'s range from approximately 70 or 75 to 90. Such pupils are not retarded enough to be considered mentally handicapped or candidates for special classes. Some of them, particularly among high school students, are treated as if their abilities were greater than they are and expectations set for them exceed their capabilities. On the other hand, slow-learning students are occasionally regarded as if their abilities were lower than they actually are; then they are looked upon as being almost incapable of learning. It is apparent that a thorough diagnosis of ability is necessary to enable teachers to estimate students' abilities more accurately and to make more appropriate prognoses.[1]

Importance of Identifying the Slow-learner

Although slow-learners do have a potential for learning, they also have distinct limitations which should be recognized. According to Ernest Newland:

> They are not mentally retarded or mentally defective. On the other hand, they aren't likely to succeed in, or even want to go to, college. These people should not be criticized. They are more likely to be followers than leaders, but they play an important part in doing the work of the world.[2]

---

[1] Ishmel Utley, "The Slow-learner in the Secondary School," *Education*, 81:341–344 (February, 1961).

[2] Ernest T. Newland, *Help for the Slow-learner,* Booklet no. 11 (Chicago: F. E. Compton & Co., 1957), pp. 5–6.

In many elementary schools slow-learning pupils, according to some estimates, constitute approximately eighteen to twenty per cent of the school enrollment. They frequently repeat grades and often become discouraged by academic assignments that are too difficult for them. In the secondary school slow-learners "make up the majority of school drop-outs."[3]

In both the elementary and the secondary school the needs of the slow-learner are often neglected. In an attempt to provide appropriate and challenging curricula for average and superior students there is an ever-present danger of overlooking the slow-learning pupil. We should avoid this threat by recognizing the importance of the pupil as a potential citizen. Unless his needs are met and he receives adequate preparation for life, the slow-learner may not become a self-sustaining individual. If his needs are met, he will be able to work successfully, carry his share of responsibilities in the community, and provide an adequate home for himself and his children.

The capacity of the slow-learner to acquire the basic reading and language skills on a level commensurate with his ability has been repeatedly demonstrated. One outstanding example was the training of the slow-learning men among the functionally illiterate drafted during World War II. Many such soldiers were transformed from liabilities into assets in the army. The slow-learning pupil is similarly a liability when his potentialities are neglected to such a degree that he understands little of what he reads or studies. It is imperative that we educate these pupils according to their abilities in order that they may derive the greatest benefits from education and be prepared for effective citizenship.

It is essential that curricula be planned so that the slow-learner may experience success. Too frequently he meets failure; and repeated failure has far-reaching effects upon personality and adjustment. On experiencing frequent failure in school, the slow-learner may resort to compensatory reactions—withdrawal, aggression, indifference, lack of interest, or marked anxiety. At home he may reveal his lack of self-confidence by resorting to minor illnesses in order to receive attention or to avoid school attendance. One must take care to appraise reliably the ability of this type of pupil, since average and superior students who fail in school sometimes exhibit similar behavior. Moreover, it is well to bear in mind that some pupils of average and even superior ability may appear to be slow-learners because of language handicaps

---

[3] Ishmel Utley, *op. cit.*, p. 341.

or impoverished home conditions. Accordingly, great care must be taken in diagnosing the slow pupil's learning capacity. This point deserves special emphasis in our large cities today because of the high incidence of disadvantaged pupils. The teacher must become more and more adept in detecting the student of good ability who is performing on the level of a slow-learning pupil because of impoverished background and related factors. Although such a pupil may at present be educationally retarded, he is capable of performing much better and of making progress at a more rapid rate. He needs, however, like the slow-learner, to begin successful endeavor at a level in harmony with his attainment. Under appropriate stimulation and with sympathetic guidance and encouragement, he will often make rapid gains and soon find himself able to function successfully in meeting the requirements of his grade. For many such disadvantaged pupils special educational efforts are often most rewarding.[4] These efforts in behalf of the disadvantaged appear most successful when early childhood and parent education are effectively combined.[5]

Characteristics of the Slow-learner

When the slow-learner has been reliably identified, it will be found that he generally has certain characteristics listed by Robert DeHaan and Jack Kough as follows. The slow-learner

1. Is unable to think abstractly or to handle symbolic material.
2. Is unable to understand and carry through your directions for assignments.
3. Lacks the so-called "common sense" and reasoning level of the class.
4. Is unable to understand complex assignments or game rules.
5. Is slow in all areas: academic, social, emotional, and physical.
6. Breaks rules of conduct or of games and is often unaware of doing so.
7. Is unable to work independently.
8. Is easily confused.
9. Has a short interest and attention span.
10. Is unable to concentrate voluntarily.

[4] Charles G. Speigler, "Give Him a Book That Hits Him Where He Lives," *Improving English Skills of Culturally Different Youth in Large Cities*, U. S. Department of Health, Education and Welfare, Office of Education Bulletin 1964, No. 5 (Washington, D.C.: U.S. Government Printing Office, 1964), pp. 91–92.
[5] Martin Deutsch, "Social and Psychological Perspectives on the Development of the Disadvantaged Learner," *The Journal of Negro Education*, 33:232–244 (Summer, 1964).

11. Finds it is extremely difficult, if not impossible, to keep up with the class in academic work.
12. Is behind normal grade achievement in school.[6]

Slow-learners may tend to be idle during certain school activities and lack the initiative to seek help when needed—particularly when the activities or their significance are poorly comprehended. School tasks and home duties may be left undone by these pupils. The slow-learner will complete assignments or tasks most acceptably when the goals set for him are attainable and their importance is appreciated.

DIAGNOSIS OF EACH CHILD'S NEEDS

It is clear that the teacher should have a considerable amount of information about each slow-learning pupil in order to guide his learning effectively. Such information, which pertains to his total development, covers the following areas: home background, physical condition, mental ability, school history and educational status, interests and attitudes, and personality.

By studying each pupil's status in these areas, the teacher will discern individual strengths and weaknesses and will be able to provide successful and generally beneficial experiences in school. Such information is desirable to have for every pupil; but it is essential for the slow-learner's welfare.

Home Background

Studies show that the home background of slow-learning children usually is culturally somewhat less desirable than that of average and superior pupils. Moreover, there are some children among the slow-learners whose home backgrounds are so deprived of normal experiences that their opportunities to acquire information and knowledge are limited.[7] It is generally found, too, that such handicaps become progressively more limiting with the years. Hence, the teacher needs to evaluate the environmental background of each slow-learning child. This may be accomplished through home visits, through obtaining in-

---

[6] Robert F. DeHaan and Jack Kough, *Identifying Students with Special Needs,* Teacher's Guidance Handbook Vol. II (Chicago: Science Research Associates, Inc., 1956), p. 70.

[7] J. Allen Figurel (editor), "Teaching Reading to the Disadvantaged" in Part II, Sequence VIII in *Improvement of Reading Through Classroom Practice,* International Reading Association, 1964, pp. 160–172.

formation about the community, and through parent interviews. With such information at hand, the teacher can endeavor to counteract environmental handicaps and provide individually suitable experiences. Moreover, to improve conditions generally, the widespread initiation of preschool education coupled with parent education appears to be desirable.

Physical Development

Although the physical development of slow-learners as a group appears to be somewhat below that of average children of similar ages, there is great variability among them. It has been found, too, that slow-learners have slightly more defects in hearing and vision than average pupils. William Featherstone advises that we be especially alert in detecting these defects and that we endeavor to have them corrected because "every physical handicap that can be overcome increases a child's opportunity to make the most of such intellectual capacity as he has, to say nothing of contributing to his comfort and happiness."[8]

His relatively meager environmental background may account for the fact that the typical slow-learner is slightly below average in his physical development. However, the teacher should not overlook the fact that the range in the physical development of slow-learning pupils is similar to that of the remainder of the class. Of course, the teacher should be especially zealous to identify the slow-learning child who has a visual or auditory defect or limitation and should provide corrective or adjustment measures, since such a condition may add to the pupil's difficulty in learning. Similarly, other physical and health conditions may block his progress. Optimum physical development and health should be a goal set for these pupils (and all others). It is highly desirable for the school to provide a record which will accompany the child through school and will cumulatively reveal his development and status. Periodic examination of this record will aid the teacher in understanding the slow-learning child's needs and in planning the most suitable experiences for him.

Mental Ability

Slow-learning pupils, as we have seen, have a mental ability and rate of learning somewhat lower than those of the average pupil and markedly lower than those of the superior student. For most of these

---

[8] William B. Featherstone, *Teaching the Slow Learner* (New York: Bureau of Publications, Teachers College, Columbia University, 1941), p. 5.

children a relatively slow rate of learning will continue to characterize their attainment in school. It is essential, therefore, for the teacher to have access to a reliable rating of mental ability for each pupil in order to formulate reasonable expectations for him. A rating on an individual test such as the *Wechsler Intelligence Scale for Children* or the *Stanford-Binet Intelligence Scale* is desirable. If scores from these tests are not available the teacher should make a request that one of them be administered by a qualified examiner.

The use of group tests tends to be inappropriate with many slow-learners because of their meager experiences and the limited opportunities offered them in underprivileged areas. Others may perform poorly on group tests because of factors such as absence from school for prolonged periods. Non-English-speaking pupils also may experience difficulty, especially on group tests, which rely on the reading ability they have not had an opportunity to acquire. The teacher, therefore, should seek to determine the ability of each pupil by supplementing the results of tests by observations made under various conditions. By observing how each pupil actually learns in highly motivated situations the teacher may better understand and appreciate his needs.

Educational Status

The educational attainment of the slow-learning pupil should be thoroughly appraised. Although he may need help in acquiring the basic habits and skills in all subject areas, his need for assistance in reading is usually both great and persistent. Accordingly, his reading ability should be evaluated with utmost care.

It is most desirable that the slow-learning pupil's status be ascertained when he enters school in order that plans may be made to engender readiness for reading. This program should provide rich and varied activities, including most of the items discussed in detail in Chapter 5. But it is well to bear in mind that the slow-learner usually requires a greater variety of such activities over a longer period of time than is customary for average pupils.

The results of standardized oral and silent reading tests may be used to ascertain the child's attainment as he progresses in school; later on, they may be employed again in estimating his gains. Information should be obtained from such individual oral tests as the *Gray Oral Reading Paragraphs,* the *Durrell Diagnosis of Reading Difficulties,* or *the Gilmore Oral Reading Test.* Silent reading tests such as the *Iowa Reading Tests,* the *Developmental Reading Test,* the *Diagnostic Reading Tests,* and the *S.R.A. Reading Record,* may be used to diagnose silent reading abilities. In addition, the nature and amount of each child's reading in books and other sources should be ascertained. A study of his rate of reading different types of material will yield pertinent and useful data. With such information at hand, it will be possible for the teacher to offer this type of pupil an opportunity to read materials of appropriate difficulty and suitability, and the importance of readiness will thus be recognized at every level.

Determining Interests

The role of interest and how to determine the pupils' interests have been thoroughly discussed in Chapter 3. It may be well to emphasize two points here: (1) if growth is to take place to the optimum extent the pupils' interests must be determined, and (2) the activities in which these pupils engage must be interesting.

Perhaps the most useful technique in determining interests is the use of the interest inventory (see Appendix C).

FACTORS IN TEACHING THE SLOW-LEARNER

The slow-learner has been defined in this chapter as the pupil whose I.Q. may fall between 70–75 and 90; that is, he is not retarded to the degree that education in a special class is necessary or desirable. He should become a happy, contributing member of the regular class, but he will require special attention, since his rate of learning will be slow and typically he will fall below average in his attainment.

The Factor of Readiness

One of the characteristics of the slow-learning child is his inability to learn to read on entering school at a chronological age of approximately six years. But there are varied activities in which he can take part profitably which will prepare him for reading. Extensive provisions should be made for a readiness program that should continue until the slow-learner shows sufficient mental development to learn to read successfully. The readiness program should be broader and richer than the regular one and should be planned for a longer period. Authorities agree that added repetition is essential for slow-learning pupils and that such repetition should be meaningful.

The Factor of Experience

One way to make reading materials meaningful is to associate them with firsthand experiences which may be recorded on experience charts. The experiences are discussed, of course, and the teacher may follow the steps given in Chapter 9 in the construction of such charts. The vocabulary used in the stories on the charts is placed on cards and repeated in various ways until the words are thoroughly familiar and their meanings mastered. Attention is given to the correct pronunciation of each word, which should be used in various sentences composed by the pupils. Slowly the pupils will acquire a basic stock of sight words, which are then studied with attention given to the sounds of the letters and letter combinations in each word. Further familiarity with the letters is given through the varied use of a picture dictionary. Along with considerable individual guidance as the child progresses, there should be group instruction, since these children will enjoy and profit from the sharing of their experiences through discussion. Work in small groups also permits the pupils to tell stories and engage in other activities of mutual interest. Accordingly, it is desirable to introduce first-grade materials of the type devised by Dolch to insure the knowledge of letters, phrases, and sentences.

In the early work with slow-learners there should be wide use of picture books, and the teacher should read aloud frequently to the pupils, who will be encouraged to listen carefully and to discuss and reproduce the materials they hear. Simple exercises in listening may also be devised for additional individual and group practice. The materials published monthly in *Highlights for Children* are especially suitable.

The Factor of Pupil Needs

The recognition of pupil needs is particularly appropriate in the case of the slow-learning pupil, since his needs are so frequently blocked or denied. His progress often appears to depend upon the extent to which his fundamental need for self-respect and self-esteem can be satisfied or restored. It is important too that we seek to help the slow-learning child develop a satisfying and appropriate ideal of self. There are, to be sure, some interests that are general and can be relied on, such as the ubiquitous attraction to television. But most interests are usually less generally found and are often highly personal. Diversity of interest will characterize any group of slow-learners. The teacher may find that the reading of books about individuals whose ideals of self are commendable will help such pupils to modify inappropriate ideals of self and to build more suitable ones. Thus, a slow-learning pupil in an eighth-grade class may find association with the courageous hero in Armstrong Sperry's *Call It Courage* a wholesome antidote to his fears and insecurities.[9]

Experience in reading in itself, of course, will not lead invariably to the fulfillment of needs. We should recognize the fact that many factors determine the impact of reading upon boys and girls. Thus David Russell comments:

> We must hypothesize that impact of reading is determined by the reader's expectations or set, by his overt purpose for reading, by his conscious or unconscious needs, by the personality traits or patterns which affect much of his conduct, and by combinations of these factors.[10]

Aiding a pupil to satisfy his interests and helping him fulfill his needs through reading are two excellent ways to foster the development of self-confidence and feelings of security. Through reading associated with other desirable classroom activities a teacher can help slow-learners develop at a steady rate.

Materials for the Slow-learner

If learning goals are adjusted to the slow-learners' educational status and are geared to their rate of learning, progress will usually be steady. Recognition on the part of the learner of his continuing progress and success may also contribute to his security and affect his general mental health favorably.

Within the regular classroom, provision may be made for the slow-learning pupils' acquisition of reading skills on the appropriate level by the use of multi-level materials such as the SRA Reading Laboratories or the Skilltexts. These materials and others are listed in Appendix B. There are other books, too, which will promote greatly the development of skills. In building the vocabulary of the slow-learner in the secondary school the teacher may wish to refer the pupil to *Developing Your Vocabulary*.[11]

---

[9] Paul Witty, "Meeting Developmental Needs Through Reading," *Elementary English*, 84:451–458 (April, 1964).
[10] David Russell, "Some Research on the Impact of Reading," *The English Journal*, 47:398–413 (October, 1958).
[11] Paul A. Witty and Edith Grotberg, *Developing Your Vocabulary* (Chicago: Science Research Associates, 1960).

The field of biography affords a great opportunity for advancing the level of the pupil's reading gradually through the use of appropriately graded materials. For junior and senior high school pupils of limited ability, *The American Adventure Series* of the Wheeler Publishing Company offers the possibility of coupling the exploits of adventurous heroes such as Buffalo Bill and Wild Bill Hickok with simply written, exciting stories which have been arranged and graded as to difficulty. The Bobbs-Merrill Company also publishes a similar series of books; and the *Landmark* and *World Landmark Series* of Random House provide excellent opportunities for the reading of exciting biographies whose leading characters may be readily associated with heroes and heroines of TV fame.

Very appropriate for the slow-learning pupils in the junior and senior high school are the Teen-Age Tales published by D. C. Heath, simply written and highly exciting stories. The *Reader's Digest* publications for poor readers are appropriate, too. Similarly easy but informative accounts of scientific discovery are provided by Random House in the All-About Books, which present simply written accounts of scientific accomplishment. Lists of series books are to be found in Appendix A.

Various trade books may also be used advantageously with slow-learners. An excellent list of these books may be found in George Spache's *Good Reading for Poor Readers,* revised edition, published by the Garrard Publishing Company in 1962.

The Importance of the Teacher

Perhaps the most significant single factor in determining the success of efforts with the slow-learning child is the teacher. The following letter from an eleven-year-old boy suggests the role of the teacher in affecting a pupil's attitude and behavior:

> I am getting along fine with my work and enjoy going to school very much. I am giving most of the credit to Miss X who taught me during my third year in school. She really dug down deep and started me on the road to learning. Before this I hated school and everything about it. My parents had to drive me off every morning and every time I got a chance I skipped school.
> I had often heard what a wonderful teacher Miss X was but I just couldn't make up my mind about her until I tried her. The very first week she made me understand that school was not a jail house or a cage in which children were kept all day without any privileges or good times, but a place where everyone could work together, play together, share together, and live together. . . . When we worked,

she worked, and when we played, she played. She was right with us in everything we did. . . . She was so patient and kind you could not help but try to learn. She was never too tired or busy when anybody in the class needed help.

A major responsibility of the teacher of the slow-learning pupil is to provide a classroom atmosphere in which success, security, understanding, mutual respect, and opportunity to attain worthy educational goals is all-pervading. In this type of classroom the teacher is prepared to direct children's development in such a way that their emotional life will yield the maximum of human satisfactions and values.

CURRICULUM PRINCIPLES

We have indicated that the slow-learner can make satisfactory progress in a regular classroom setting in which a differentiated curriculum is provided. In such a classroom there will be found emphasis in the curriculum based on the following principles:

1. *Emphasis upon concrete experiences.* Since the slow-learner is limited in his ability to think abstractly or to employ symbolic material he cannot deal successfully with most involved concepts and abstract ideas. His education should be planned so as to rely primarily upon concrete experiences rather than upon abstract, symbolic materials.

2. *Emphasis upon the development of the ability to follow simple directions.* Verbal direction should be carefully worded and made unmistakably clear to insure understanding. Since success in school work depends to a large extent upon comprehending and following directions, it is essential that the teacher formulate all directions carefully. In this connection the teacher may find helpful the use of games and other informal activities as well as more formal exercises. When written directions are used there should be a simple, clear message given and care should be taken to be sure the child understands all words.

3. *Emphasis upon the development of logical thinking.* Following the logical sequence in a discussion or a learning experience will often prove difficult for the slow-learner, who may appear bewildered when logic or "common sense" is demanded. One must have patience to see that the slow-learner progresses methodically from one step to the next one with full understanding of each step. Discussion of plans for, and purposes of, various projects accompanied by the making of sequential outlines, will aid in the development of logical thinking.

4. *Emphasis upon a basic vocabulary.* A basic vocabulary is es-

sential in following directions and rules as well as in other forms of communication. The expansion of vocabulary should be planned with utmost care. The slow-learner frequently lacks a basic vocabulary and will profit from help in acquiring a clear understanding of the words in such lists as the Dolch Basic Vocabulary (220 words). Mastery of these words may be motivated through games, as well as by reading the Dolch collection of simply written books (animal stories, fairy tales, etc.). Similarly the Gates list of 1800 words may be used in building vocabulary; practice material and related stories based on this list may be introduced profitably. For older pupils, the use of books such as *Developing Your Vocabulary* (see page 437) will prove effective.

5. *Emphasis upon specialized vocabulary for study in content areas.* Because the slow-learner tends to be slow in all academic areas, it is especially important that he be enabled to find success in reading the content of the various subject fields. To do so successfully, he must be helped in a number of ways, one of which is in the acquisition of the specialized vocabularies of each field. Direct, firsthand experience is considered to be a most significant factor in the development of such a vocabulary. For example, in the social studies the primary-grade pupil may encounter a number of words related to a topic such as farming. A visit to a farm may provide him with the experience to appreciate the fact that a word such as *tree* may refer to many kinds of trees. Similarly, on visiting an airport, the pupil will find that *airplane* covers many types of planes. Accordingly, the pupil will realize that words have different meanings. Gradually he will come to understand the fact, too, that the meanings of words are influenced by their context and that the meaning of an unknown word often may be derived by a study of its relationship to other known words around it. The study of context should be carefully planned and introduced slowly. The use of films, filmstrips, and various visual aids will help to enrich the pupil's background and enable him to gain an understanding of the meaning of new terms. Discussion of terms often leads to greater understanding. A simplified dictionary may also be used profitably in the quest for the meaning of words in various situations. The use of films is especially appropriate in providing a background for concepts. Films such as *The Mailman* and *The Fireman* present essential information and background to primary-grade pupils. These films have been used effectively preceding the reading of books designed to accompany them. Not only has the practice been associated with the enlargement of vocabulary and the clarification of concepts, but it has also been accompanied by improvement in general reading ability.

Since the slow-learning child is typically retarded in several or many areas of learning, his status should be recognized by every teacher, and efforts should be made to enable him to make suitable progress in all subjects. This will sometimes require the introduction of easier materials than those found in the usual textbook. In addition, the use of the library and other resources should be geared to his ability.

6. *Emphasis upon the varied aspects of the language arts.* Particularly vital to the welfare of the slow-learning child is success in the various areas of the language arts; he should be helped not only to read proficiently, but also to speak with clarity and to write effectively. Moreover, he must improve in comprehension as he listens to various presentations. These acquisitions are of special importance, since they are necessary for success in school as well as in citizenship. Featherstone makes the following comments:

> Every child and youth, slow learner or rapid learner must learn to read, write, spell, compute and solve problems, and speak the mother tongue with reasonable grace and fluency. Without these there is little communication, there is little learning.[12]

Group discussions are beneficial in developing oral facility in the slow-learner. Oral reading also provides an excellent opportunity for these children to learn to speak clearly and convincingly.

The writing of reports and compositions of various kinds is often difficult for these pupils because of the many factors involved—organization, spelling, motor skills. Brief reports that tell one thing with some details offer an effective beginning technique. As the pupil progresses, reports containing two or three ideas, in sequence and with greater detail, provide an extension in learning for the pupil.

7. *Recognition of short attention span.* The teacher must recognize the relatively short attention span of the slow-learner and plan activities of suitable lengths. It is desirable, of course, to try at all times to insure success in learning situations, a consideration which is essential to establish and maintain interest. But motivation depends not only on proper gradation of assignments and materials, but also upon the relationship of the materials to the interests of the pupils. Hence the teacher must be zealous to study interests and, when interests are few, to plan activities and introduce experiences which will engender new ones.

The slow-learning pupil should not be expected to maintain attention and concentration for long periods of time without supervision. Under supervision and guidance he can increase his attention span

---

[12] William B. Featherstone, *op. cit.,* p. 70.

gradually and read successfully longer and more difficult passages. In learning to concentrate for longer periods of time, the pupil must have access to materials not only of appropriate difficulty but also of vital concern to him. It is desirable, too, that short episodes, which can be readily understood, be frequently employed.

8. *Emphasis upon reinforcement of learning.* The slow-learner requires special help and repetition in learning: often the rereading of materials and accompanying discussion are necessary in order to grasp ideas presented. A story having many parts or one containing detailed descriptive passages may prove too difficult for him to grasp at first. He must reread such selections several times, each time noting additional details. Materials that are rich in sensory imagery are especially appropriate. Although he may be encouraged at times to read through a story or a whole chapter at first, he should be expected to note only the most obvious facts; rereading may then enable him to note other details. Oral reading, too, will prove helpful in directing his attention to details, and will enable the teacher to check his comprehension as he responds to questions by reading aloud correct answers.

Although the foregoing suggestions will foster effective learning, the teacher must not assume that these steps will eliminate all the problems. The slow-learner will need much help in overcoming insecurities and in building an appropriate concept of himself and his abilities. Insecurities and anxieties often accompany the slow-learning pupil's awareness of his relative inferiority as he advances from grade to grade. With proper use of recognition and praise by the teacher, however, these feelings may be lessened. The need for safeguarding the slow-learner from needless anxiety exists from the time he enters school. The attitudes of many such pupils are influenced deeply by their experiences in the first grade, where their conspicuous failures may lead them to develop grave doubts concerning their competence, acceptability, and worth. The problem of satisfactory personal adjustment continues to be important at every stage of their development. Frequent frustrations and failure may not only color the child's evaluation of himself, but may also destroy his self-confidence and self-respect.

It is imperative, therefore, that the classroom atmosphere be conducive to the development of self-confidence and self-reliance in the slow-learner. Christine Ingram puts it this way:

> Satisfactory adjustment in life calls for self-confidence, self-reliance, and independence on the part of the individual. The mentally retarded, because of their inability to compete successfully with other children, tend to lack these essential qualities. It becomes, therefore,

the responsibility of the school to provide experiences that will aid this group to become self-confident, self-reliant, independent workers at tasks commensurate with their learning abilities.[13]

CONCLUDING STATEMENT

To offer effective instruction, the teacher should have available not only facts about each slow-learning pupil's reading, but also information pertaining to his interests. To help guide the pupil in attaining the most rewarding outcomes from reading, findings regarding each pupil's needs are also essential. The study of developmental needs differs somewhat from the study of interests, although similar techniques may be used in both cases.

The value of an approach to reading through a concern for interest and need is gradually being acknowledged. Such an approach is particularly appropriate in the case of the slow-learning pupil, because his needs are so frequently blocked or denied. Indeed, his rehabilitation often appears to depend upon the extent to which his fundamental need for self-respect and self-esteem can be satisfied.

It is recognized that experience in reading in itself will not lead invariably to the fulfillment of needs. Nevertheless if reading is used in association with other activities in efforts to fulfill needs it may assist greatly. We must, of course, recognize that many factors determine the impact of reading upon boys and girls.

One aim of a developmental program is to lead the slow-learner to become relatively independent in using the library and other resources for satisfying his interests and fulfilling his varied and changing needs— an objective which will be achieved if the student acquires a reasonable command of silent and oral reading skills and is able to adapt his skills readily to the demands of varied kinds of reading. To achieve such an aim, an efficient, systematic program of reading instruction and guidance is needed throughout the course of his education. The slow-learner must also be enabled to enjoy the results of wide reading, as he will do if reading experience is associated with his interests and needs. In this way slow-learning pupils may become independent readers, successful and competent on their own levels, extending their understandings and satisfactions to the maximum through reading.

[13] Christine P. Ingram, *Education of the Slow-learning Child*, 3rd ed. (New York: The Ronald Press Company, 1960), p. 42.

Selected References

Barbe, Walter B., "Slow Learner: A Plea for Understanding," *Education,* 81:323–325 (February, 1961).

Birch, Jack W. and G. D. Stevens, *Reaching the Mentally Retarded* (Bloomington, Ind.: Public Schools Publishing Company, 1955).

Bond, Guy L. and Miles A. Tinker, *Reading Difficulties: Their Diagnosis and Correction* (New York: Appleton-Century-Crofts, 1957).

Bond, Guy L. and Eva B. Wagner, *Teaching the Child to Read,* rev. ed. (New York: The Macmillan Company, 1960).

Brueckner, Leo J. and Guy L. Bond, *The Diagnosis and Treatment of Learning Difficulties* (New York: Appleton-Century-Crofts, 1955).

Gates, Arthur I., *The Improvement of Reading,* 3rd ed. (New York: The Macmillan Company, 1947).

Harris, Albert J., *How to Increase Reading Ability,* 4th ed. (New York: David McKay Co., Inc., 1961).

Harris, Albert J. (editor), "New Ways of Helping Poor Readers," *The Reading Teacher,* 10:195–224 (April, 1957).

Harris, Albert J. (editor), *Readings on Reading Instruction* (New York: David McKay Co., Inc., 1963), Chapter 18.

Hegge, T. G., S. A. Kirk, and W. D. Kirk, *Remedial Reading Drills* (Ann Arbor, Michigan: George Wahr Publishing Company, 1945).

Hunnicutt, Clarence W. and William J. Iverson, *Research in the Three R's* (New York: Harper & Row, Publishers, 1958).

Ingram, Christine P., *Education of the Slow-learning Child,* 3rd ed. (New York: The Ronald Press Company, 1960).

Johnson, G. O., *Education for the Slow Learners* (Englewood Cliffs, New Jersey: Prentice-Hall, Inc., 1963).

Kirk, Samuel A. (chairman), *The Education of Exceptional Children,* Forty-ninth Yearbook of the National Society for the Study of Education, Part II (Chicago: University of Chicago Press, 1950).

Kirk, Samuel A., *Teaching Reading to Slow-learning Children* (Boston: Houghton Mifflin Company, 1940).

Kirk, Samuel A. and G. Orville Johnson, *Educating the Retarded Child* (Boston: Houghton Mifflin Company, 1951).

Monroe, Marion, *Growing into Reading* (Chicago: Scott, Foresman and Co., 1951).

Robinson, H. Alan (editor), *The Under-achiever in Reading,* Supplementary Educational Monographs no. 92 (Chicago: University of Chicago Press, 1962).

Robinson, Helen M., "Corrective and Remedial Instruction" in Paul A. Witty (chairman), *Development In and Through Reading,* Sixtieth Yearbook of the National Society for the Study of Education, Part I (Chicago: University of Chicago Press, 1961), pp. 357–375.

Smith, Marion F. and A. J. Burks, *Teaching the Slow Learning Child* (New York: Harper & Row, Publishers, 1954).

Strang, Ruth, Constance M. McCullough, and Arthur E. Traxler, *Problems in the Improvement of Reading* (New York: McGraw-Hill Book Company, 1955).

Tinker, Miles A. and Constance M. McCullough, *Teaching Elementary Reading,* 2nd ed. (New York: Appleton-Century-Crofts, 1962).

Vernon, Magdalen D., *Backwardness in Reading: A Study of Its Nature and Origin* (Cambridge, England: The Cambridge University Press, 1958).

Wallin, John E., *Education of Mentally Handicapped Children* (New York: Harper & Row, Publishers, 1955).

Witty, Paul A., "Needs of Slow Learning Pupils," *Education,* 81:331–335 (February, 1961).

Witty, Paul A., *Reading in Modern Education* (Boston: D. C. Heath and Company, 1949).

Woolf, Maurice D. and Jeanne A. Woolf, *Remedial Reading: Teaching and Treatment* (New York: McGraw-Hill Book Company, 1957).

15

READING PROGRAMS FOR THE GIFTED

The recent revival of interest in superior and gifted students is in part a result of the spectacular launching of *Sputnik I*. Actually, however, the interest is much earlier in origin and is consistent with the developmental reading philosophy. When developmental reading concepts are applied to reading instruction the goal is to help every child develop his reading ability to the maximum according to his unique nature and needs. Gifted and superior pupils, of course, are included in this concern. Some writers believe that this group has too often been neglected in our schools and that reading curricula are seldom sufficiently varied and challenging to meet their needs.

Today's interest in the superior student is traceable also to the recent spread of knowledge concerning gifted children and youth. The American Association for Gifted Children, recognizing the need for the dissemination of facts relating to the nature and needs of the gifted, prepared a book entitled *The Gifted Child*.[1] It was widely read and helped to rekindle interest in the education of the gifted. Various chapters presented data from genetic studies, and the work as a whole gave an overview of the nature and extent of educational offerings available to the superior student. Again and again it was shown that gifted children were neglected or inadequately provided for in elementary and secondary schools. A few years later, in what is probably his last written comment on this problem, Lewis Terman stated:

> Failure to make the most of our intellectual resources has been thoroughly documented by several recent researchers, especially by those of Wolfle and the National Manpower Council. Wolfle estimates that 41 per cent of our youths who rate in the top 1 per cent

[1] Paul Witty (editor), *The Gifted Child* (Boston: D. C. Heath and Company, 1951).

337

for tested ability either do not enter college or, if they enter, do not remain to graduate. He further estimates that of those who have the intelligence to earn a Ph.D., less than 2 per cent do so. Of my large group of gifted children with I.Q.'s of 140 or higher who were located in California thirty-five years ago, 15 per cent did not enter college and 30 per cent did not graduate. Though all of these presumably had the ability to earn a Ph.D., M.D., or their equivalent, only 15 per cent of the men and 5 per cent of the women did so.[2]

It is noteworthy, too, that a few writers have stressed for several decades the significance of a broad perspective in dealing with various types of gifted students. Even before the appearance of *Sputnik I,* Paul Witty cited the danger of paying too much attention to the development of scientists with a consequent neglect of the training of necessary leaders of other types. Again and again he proposed that the gifted child be considered as any child whose performance in a worthwhile type of human endeavor is consistently or repeatedly remarkable.[3]

THE IDENTIFICATION OF THE GIFTED

Traditional Concepts

With the introduction of the *Stanford-Binet Intelligence Test* in 1916 and its widespread use, gifted children were defined and selected according to I.Q. Terman designated the gifted as those children who attained an I.Q. of 130 or higher. He was a pioneer in studying a large group of gifted pupils for the purpose of gaining an understanding of their nature and needs. He and his associates assembled facts about their physical development, their family history, their social status, their emotional health, and their educational attainment. Several volumes have been devoted to a genetic study of these subjects in childhood, youth, and adulthood.[4]

Hollingworth[5] and Witty[6] conducted similar studies and added cor-

---

[2] Lewis M. Terman, "What Education for the Gifted Should Accomplish," in Robert J. Havighurst (chairman), *Education for the Gifted,* Fifty-seventh Yearbook of the National Society for the Study of Education, Part II (Chicago: University of Chicago Press, 1958), pp. 15–16.

[3] Paul Witty, "Some Considerations in the Education of Gifted Children," *Educational Administration and Supervision,* 26:512–521 (October, 1940).

[4] Lewis M. Terman, et. al., *Genetic Studies of Genius: Mental and Physical Traits of a Thousand Gifted Children* (Stanford, California: Stanford University Press, 1925), vol. 1.

[5] Leta S. Hollingworth, *Gifted Children: Their Nature and Nurture* (New York: The Macmillan Co., 1926).

roborative data to the findings of Terman. These studies revealed that the typical gifted child was physically superior, attractive, and well adjusted, neither a physical weakling nor a social misfit. He usually excelled in his school work. By the time he had reached the upper elementary grades, he had generally acquired knowledge and skills which surpassed those of children classified two or three grades above him. His superiority persisted, and typically he continued to display outstanding academic ability throughout his high school and college career. The newer image of the gifted, based on research, was in sharp contrast to the previously held view "that intellectual precocity is pathological," and that the gifted are "the product of supernatural causes and moved by forces which are not to be explained by the natural laws of human behavior."[7]

Acceptance of a high I.Q. as the crucial factor in identifying the gifted continued generally for several decades. Moreover, research conducted between 1920 and 1940 involved chiefly descriptive or genetic studies of children of high I.Q. These children were occasionally referred to as the verbally gifted, since the *Stanford-Binet Scale,* the one mainly used for their identification, relied primarily on verbal tests. Similarly, school administrators, concerned with providing better opportunities for such pupils, relied on the intelligence test for identifyng them. Selection of pupils for special groups such as the Major Work Classes in Cleveland,[8] or for schools such as the Hunter College Elementary School,[9] was based in large measure upon the results of intelligence tests.

At present many writers continue to think of the gifted in terms of high I.Q., and provision in schools is often made for children designated according to this criterion. It should be noted, however, that there are expansions of the concept of the gifted which are deeply affecting this practice. The first is the tendency to enlarge opportunities for superior pupils and to include candidates whose abilities, though marked, are not high enough to warrant inclusion in the gifted group if it is delimited by an I.Q. of 130 or higher. The second is the tendency to

---

[6] Paul Witty, "A Genetic Study of Fifty Gifted Children," in George D. Stoddard (chairman), *Intelligence: Its Nature and Nurture,* Thirty-ninth Yearbook of the National Society for the Study of Education, Part II (Chicago: University of Chicago Press, 1940), pp. 401–409.

[7] Lewis M. Terman, *op. cit.,* vol. 1, p. vii.

[8] Theodore Hall, *Gifted Children: The Cleveland Story* (Cleveland: World Publishing Co., 1956).

[9] Gertrude H. Hildreth in collaboration with Florence N. Brumbaugh and Frank T. Wilson, *Educating Gifted Children* (New York: Harper & Row, Publishers, 1952).

expand and alter greatly the concept of the gifted to include a larger number displaying varied types of gifts.[10]

Modern Concepts

While interest in verbally superior and gifted students has been developing, there has emerged another interest, which grew out of the recognition of the limitations of the I.Q. as a means of selecting potentially gifted pupils in art, music, social leadership, and other areas. These limitations, stressed many years ago by Paul Witty, became increasingly evident during the period from 1940 to the present time, when it was repeatedly noted that pupils of rare ability in art, music, or writing were not always found in the very high I.Q. groups. It appeared that different approaches were needed to detect giftedness of these kinds. As a result, it became increasingly recognized that any child whose performance is consistently or repeatedly remarkable in a worthwhile line of human endeavor might be considered gifted.[11] The authors of *A Survey of the Education of Gifted Children* justify the broader concept of giftedness in this way:

> There is a threefold importance in looking for a variety of talent in children. First, such discovery points out to teachers that there are other bases besides intelligence for talent in children. Second, it calls attention to more children than a single-talent criterion does. Third, it encourages the teacher to use a variety of avenues of approach to children, whereas a single measure of giftedness narrows her approach.[12]

This broader concern is also expressed in the Fifty-seventh Yearbook of the National Society for the Study of Education. In that text the gifted person was described as "one who shows consistently remarkable performance in any worthwhile line of endeavor."[13] Thus, this new concept not only included the intellectually gifted but also those who performed outstandingly in the graphic arts, creative writing, dramatics, mechanical skills, and social leadership.

Since there are few reliable measures for gauging creative ability of

---

[10] Robert Iglehart, "Identifying Art Talent," in Bruce Shertzer (editor), *Working with Superior Students: Theories and Practices* (Chicago: Science Research Associates, 1960), Chapter 10.

[11] Paul Witty (editor), *The Gifted Child, op. cit.*

[12] Robert J. Havighurst, Eugene Stivers, and Robert F. DeHaan, *A Survey of the Education of Gifted Children,* Supplementary Educational Monograph no. 83 (Chicago: University of Chicago Press, 1955), p. 6.

[13] Robert J. Havighurst, "The Meaning of Giftedness," in Robert J. Havighurst (chairman), *Education for the Gifted, op. cit.,* p. 19.

various kinds, it would seem that a considerable degree of subjective judgment must be relied on at present in identifying talented youth. Further, studies have suggested that high I.Q. and creativity are not closely related, requiring investigators to seek a new approach for estimating creativity.[14]

The Study of Creativity

Several workers have sought to determine the components in creative behavior. Thus Viktor Lowenfeld, after a comprehensive study which aimed to differentiate creative from less- or non-creative persons in the arts, stressed the following criteria: (1) sensitivity to problems; (2) fluency of ideas; (3) flexibility; (4) originality; (5) redefinition and the ability to rearrange; (6) analysis or the ability to abstract; (7) synthesis and closure; (8) coherence of organization.[15]

Other researchers found that creative pupils have different goals in life and different attitudes towards teachers than those of students with high I.Q.'s; moreover, teachers preferred students of high I.Q. and more frequently recognized their abilities. They pointed out, too, that new concepts of the nature of giftedness, although much needed, are not always readily accepted.[16] Even so, there is a growing tendency to accept a broader criterion and to think of gifted children as those pupils having (a) high verbal ability, (b) unusual potentiality for science and mathematics, (c) promise in arts such as music, creative writing, and dramatics, (d) proficiency in social leadership, and (e) mechanical comprehension and ability.

GUIDING THE READING OF THE VERBALLY GIFTED

In our schools, as we have said, primary attention has been given to verbally gifted pupils. This movement is salutary and significant, although admittedly incomplete in caring for *all* types of gifted pupils.

---

[14] Donald R. Ferris, "Creative Behavior in Fifth and Sixth Grade Elementary School Pupils," Ph.D. dissertation (Urbana: University of Illinois, 1957). Cited by Louis A. Fliegler and Charles E. Bish, "The Gifted and Talented," *Review of Educational Research,* 29:408–450 (December, 1959).
[15] Viktor Lowenfeld, "Current Research on Creativity," *National Education Association Journal,* 47:538–540 (November, 1958).
[16] Jacob W. Getzels and Philip W. Jackson, "The Highly Creative and the Highly Intelligent Adolescent: An Attempt at Differentiation," a paper presented at the American Psychological Association Convention (Washington, D.C., August 28, 1958).

In the verbally gifted, it has been found that one of the most important problems relates to motivation. It is generally agreed that early identification is necessary if the gifted are later to be most successful. An important consideration in fostering motivation is associated with the child's first experiences in school. Many gifted children are able to read on entering school; others are prepared to acquire skills with such rapidity that the typical first-grade program is obviously inadequate. Earl McWilliams points out that "one of the prime reasons for the low level of achievement of many older gifted and superior children is that they were not stimulated to work up to their capacities in early school years."[17]

The problem of stimulating and motivating the superior student deserves penetrating research. At present there are few investigations in this area. A study by Charles Cole has yielded, however, some provocative findings. Cole reports questionnaire responses from 32,750 seniors, considered a random sample of students in public high schools, who also took a brief academic aptitude test. The pupils who were in the upper 30 per cent on the aptitude test (9,689 seniors) replied to questions about their intent to go on to college or their reasons for not planning to attend college.

For twelve per cent of the high-scoring group the most important reason for not planning to go to college was financial need. Although others mentioned financial need as an important consideration, the importance of "lack of college goal" was indicated many times.[18]

Certainly it appears that the ideal of self and the goal a pupil sets for himself are important factors in his realization of adult attainment commensurate with his youthful promise. How and when such goals arise are challenging, little-studied problems; there are, however, some studies which have yielded clues on this perplexing topic. We have already indicated the significance of challenging school programs. In addition, comparative studies of young adults who were identified as gifted children have produced important data. For example, Terman divided his group of gifted young men into groups—the most successful and the least successful. The parents of the most successful group were superior in education, vocational status, and cultural background. Case studies have also revealed the importance of early home and school guidance

---

[17] Earl M. McWilliams, "Reading Programs for the Mentally Advanced Child," in Donald L. Cleland and Josephine Tronsburg (editors), *Controversial Issues in Reading,* A Report on the Twelfth Annual Conference and Course in Reading (University of Pittsburgh, June 18–29, 1956), vol. 12, pp. 135–151.

[18] Charles C. Cole, Jr., "Current Loss of Talent from High School to College: Summary of a Report," *Higher Education,* 12:35–38 (November, 1955).

in determining the goals which gifted students seek. No less important is the acquisition of early attitudes.[19]

Studies suggest, too, that the precocious child who has learned to read at home may have an advantage when he enters school.[20] Such a child may be not only a better reader but his attitude toward reading may be more favorable.

In the quest for an ideal of self, which gifted students may set as a goal, perhaps no other factor is so important as reading. Studies show that despite the fact that gifted pupils typically read more than average pupils, they often neglect biographies, books on vocations, psychology, and other types of subject matter that might help them acquire an understanding of themselves, their capabilities, and the kinds of life patterns they might most appropriately follow. The teacher and the parent have a mutual responsibility to offer more effective counsel and guidance, an effort which should begin early and involve the continued use of reading materials. Teachers and parents can assist greatly both by encouraging reading and by making books readily available.

The Role of the Home

The guidance of the reading of the gifted learner should begin at home. Parents should read aloud to their children. These children frequently request that certain books be read to them again and again, and they will ask the names of words and letters seen in books, on signs, or in pictures. The gifted child's parents can help by supplying accurate answers to such questions and by making books, especially picture books, readily available. The parents may help greatly by encouraging the gifted child to develop interest in reading. Under these circumstances, suddenly and without instruction, the gifted learner will often begin to read before he is five or six years old.

The Role of the School

At school the reading ability of the gifted child should be recognized, developed, and directed. He should have access to a variety of reading materials. In the first grade the gifted child may read rapidly a number of primers, and he will also enjoy simply written stories about

---

[19] Paul Witty and Anne Coomer, "A Case Study of Gifted Twin Boys," *Exceptional Children,* 22:104–108 (December, 1955).
[20] Dolores Durkin, "Children Who Learned to Read at Home," *Elementary School Journal,* 62:15–18 (October, 1961).

animals, home and school life, and everyday happenings. Soon, he will probably like the books by Inez Hogan, Dr. Seuss, Marjorie Flack, Marguerite Henry, Ludwig Bemelmans, Robert McCloskey, Lynd Ward, and others. He may turn with great pleasure to books illustrated by Walt Disney, reading an entire series of these books. He may read many books on a favorite subject and extend his information by using magazines and other sources. He should be encouraged to make contributions to class projects from his reading and should be offered an opportunity to share his discoveries with other pupils.

A major responsibility of the school is to provide for the gifted learner wide and suitable reading experience in the primary grades. Under stimulating conditions, his ability and his interest in reading will develop rapidly, and by the time he reaches the fourth grade he will usually have become an avid and discriminating reader. Despite this promising picture, however, there are many exceptions and many gifted pupils who need special help. In fact, as Terman and Oden have said, each gifted child requires careful study to determine his particular nature and his needs:

> Gifted children do not fall into a single pattern but into an infinite variety of patterns. One can find within the group individual examples of almost every type of personality defect, social maladjustment, behavior problem, and physical handicap; the only difference is that among gifted children the incidence of these deviations is, in varying degrees, lower than in the general population.[21]

One problem teachers sometimes encounter in dealing with gifted children is the tendency of some to concentrate their reading in a single area, to become too specialized in their reading interests. Teachers should help each child establish a balanced program in reading different types of materials in diverse fields. This is especially true of the gifted child who becomes interested in an area such as science, in which he may want to read to such an extent that his total pattern of reading lacks balance. In this instance encouragement of wide reading is especially desirable. In many cases, balance in reading is achieved when the teacher and the librarian work together in behalf of gifted pupils; for example, Lois Fannin reports a program in which she and the librarian cooperated in developing a challenging reading program for superior pupils in the fifth and sixth grades.[22] The pupils met with the librarian once each week for a forty-minute period. Attractive displays of books

---

[21] Lewis M. Terman and Melita H. Oden, "The Stanford Studies of the Gifted," in Paul Witty (editor), *The Gifted Child, op. cit.,* p. 25.

[22] Lois Fannin, "Reading for the Bright Child," *Bulletin of the School Library Association of California,* 20:27–29 (March, 1949).

in particular fields suggested by the teacher were arranged, and under the guidance of the librarian were examined and selections made to be read at home. During the remainder of each week the pupils read books of their own choice, and at the end of each week they met for an informal discussion of their reading. Related experiences were introduced through the use of films, maps, and charts; art and music were correlated with the reading. After eight months the attainment of the experimental group was compared with that of the control group made up of superior pupils who received only regular classroom instruction in reading. The experimental group made greater gains on tests of reading and developed, it appeared, a greater degree of literary appreciation and taste.

Another interesting attempt to encourage "advanced reading" by gifted pupils was reported by Margaret Gregory and William McLaughlin. Twenty superior junior high school students were "invited to volunteer for a reading project in which mostly non-fiction books intended for adults of some maturity were used." They discovered that bright children will respond to an invitation to read stimulating books far beyond what we often assume their reading level to be.[23]

At the high-school level many teachers of English are attempting, in various ways similar to those described by Marion Sheridan, to enrich the curriculum for the gifted. The activities suggested by this writer include independent reading, creative pursuits, and projects related to the mass media of communication.[24]

In a comprehensive article presenting activities for the gifted pupil throughout the elementary and secondary school, Buck Rex describes procedures suitable for use in guiding the work of the gifted in regular classes. His presentation stresses the work of consultants, committees, creative pursuits, and ways of planning and evaluating the endeavor at various levels.[25]

Several writers have emphasized the gifted child's need for training in critical reading throughout the intermediate grades and the junior high school. It has been frequently pointed out, too, that the reading of the gifted pupil should help him to solve personal and social problems, to satisfy his needs, and to extend his interests.[26]

---

[23] Margaret Gregory and William J. McLaughlin, "Advanced Reading for the Bright Child," *The Clearing House,* 26:203–205 (December, 1951).

[24] Marion C. Sheridan, "Teaching English to Superior Students," *National Education Association Journal,* 41:566–567 (December, 1952).

[25] Buck R. Rex, Jr., "The Gifted Child in the Heterogeneous Class," *Exceptional Children,* 19:117–119 (December, 1952).

[26] Frances Hunter Ferrell, "Techniques in Stimulating and Guiding the Reading Activities of Superior Learners in Junior and Senior High Schools," in William S. Gray (editor), *Classroom Techniques in Improving Reading,* Supplementary Educational Monograph no. 69 (Chicago: University of Chicago Press, 1949), p. 171.

The reading of narratives and biographies may help the gifted to meet personal and social problems successfully. Although, of course, children may not always be changed greatly through reading experience alone, nevertheless reading accompanied by discussion and related experience may prove beneficial. In many cases, particular books have been used with remarkable success in helping a bright child meet obstacles to personal or social adjustment. For example, a pupil's indecision about following a career in science may be lessened as he reads books on vocations as well as narratives and biographies about scientists; or a high school senior who has expressed an interest in teaching may be guided to read with profit a number of books about careers in teaching.

Insight concerning personal problems as well as help in the development of an ideal of self may be obtained from books. A story like Elizabeth Yates' *Amos Fortune: Free Man* may provide the basis for wholesome identification of a gifted child with a character who has experienced and met successfully problems somewhat similar to his own. Gifted pupils in the intermediate grades and in the junior high school often find excellent examples of successful accomplishment in the champions of the sports world—Babe Ruth, Knute Rockne, and others whose lives have been described in books. Occasionally, an effective identification is established through the reading of such books. Similarly profitable identification may result in the case of a talented pupil from his reading about courageous inventors—for example, Alexander Graham Bell, whose career is dramatically set forth in Katherine B. Shippen's *Mr. Bell Invents the Telephone*. Or the gifted girl who wants to be a dancer may find inspiration in Gertrude Lawrence's *A Star Danced*.

Gifted children should also be encouraged to turn to poetry, an area of reading sometimes neglected. They should be given opportunities to write poetry, too. Their products are often superior; and in addition, their writing sometimes reveals individual problems or pressing needs. From the first, children should have access to collections of poetry. When they are very young, they will enjoy the writing of Dr. Seuss and A. A. Milne. In the junior and senior high schools they will find the verse of Ogden Nash and Arthur Guiterman amusing. Their acquaintance with other modern poets, such as Millay, Frost, Dickinson, and Sandburg, should be extended greatly as they grow older.

Children should be led to enjoy reading. Some books provide hilarious situations which gifted pupils find most engaging. The humor of Robert McCloskey's *Homer Price* is almost universally appealing to gifted pupils in the elementary school; and junior high school girls often find their taste for humor fulfilled by reading Sally Benson's *Junior Miss*.

Margaret Scoggin's short stories, *Chucklebait* and *More Chucklebait,* appeal strongly to the older boys and girls. Geneva Hanna and Mariana McAllister put it this way:

> The important thing is that if young people are to get pleasure from reading they must have an opportunity to choose from a wide variety of books and acquire the understanding that to read just for amusement and entertainment is a desirable thing to do. We can never expect them to think of books as a source of fun if they never encounter a book that is fun to read.[27]

Information Essential in Directing Pupils to Appropriate Books

To engage successfully in the guidance of a gifted pupil's reading the teacher, too, should have acquired certain knowledges and skills. For one thing, the teacher should be able to employ techniques of child study in order to secure the necessary understanding of each pupil and his needs; this includes facts concerning reading ability.

To offer effective guidance, the teacher requires not only these data, however, but also information pertaining to the pupil's personal life and adjustment. Some helpful procedures have already been suggested in this book for obtaining such information. It has been pointed out that from interest inventories clues may be obtained which will help the teacher understand pupils' attitudes, problems, and adjustment. Occasionally, such a study makes it clear that the teacher's major problem is to develop more varied or worthwhile patterns of interest. Activities and experiences properly chosen are needed by the gifted for enrichment and as a basis for the development of effective and meaningful reading. Despite the fact that the background of the typical gifted child is usually rich and varied, there are some who live in limited or impoverished environments and whose chief need is the extension of experience. Indeed, one of the major problems commonly encountered by the regular classroom teacher who has one or more gifted children in his group is the provision of such enrichment. Earl McWilliams suggests the following enrichment activities for the mentally advanced pupils:[28]

IN THE PRIMARY GRADES:
  Reading fairs for the community.
  Reporting to class on more difficult reading material.

---

[27] Geneva R. Hanna and Mariana K. McAllister, *Books, Young People and Reading Guidance* (New York: Harper & Row, Publishers, 1960), p. 101.

[28] Earl M. McWilliams, "Reading Programs for the Mentally Advanced Child" in Donald L. Cleland and Josephine Tronsburg (editors), *Controversial Issues in Reading, op. cit.,* pp. 140, 142–143, 148–149.

Extra time for free reading.
Writing stories, poems, and plays.
Preparation of bibliographies on items of interest.
Pupils serving as librarians for the class.
Pupils serving as class historians or secretaries.
Visual aids or trips which stimulate curiosity and lead to reading.

IN THE INTERMEDIATE GRADES:
Trips to community library.
Adapting stories for dramatic presentation.
Organizing quiz programs.
Compiling bibliographies.
Reading demonstrations for patrons and parents.
Hobby reading lists.
Poetry of local authors.
Biographies of local men and women of past and present.
Collecting poetry or short stories.
Reading difficult material to summarize for the class.
Group projects requiring library research.
Preparing test questions on reading material.

IN HIGH SCHOOL:
Radio and TV scripts based on outstanding books or plays.
Reports on essays in current magazines such as *Atlantic Monthly* or *Saturday Review*.
Planning and arranging displays for Book Week.
Scrapbook of materials on favorite author.
Interviewing famous writers.
Study of writing of contemporary writers.
American dialects.
Literature with local settings or references.
Collecting and filing critical reviews of books.
Files of biographical and anecdotal material on authors.
"Term papers" requiring literary research.
Debating and other speech activities based on factual information and ideas found in books, magazines, and newspapers.

Many of the foregoing suggestions apply not only to the verbally gifted, but also to pupils of outstanding promise in art, music, creative writing, and other fields. Although such pupils may also be superior verbally, the correlation between proficiencies in the creative fields and verbal ability is low and we cannot take it for granted that a high reading status will always or even generally be found among the talented. Accordingly, we should expect among such students a wide range of scores on reading tests. Many pupils who are gifted in areas other than verbal ability, then, will require special help in the development of basic reading skills. It is important, therefore, that a careful appraisal of their reading ability be made and appropriate instruction be given.

Interest in reading also varies widely among talented children. In some, we may find reading limited to a narrow specialization, while in others there may be only a meager desire for reading as a leisure pursuit. In still others, reading may be seldom engaged in because of unfortunate attitudes concerning its value. Attention to interest and to motivation is essential if unfortunate habits and attitudes are to be altered. In this effort the use of inventories will disclose interests that may often be profitably associated with reading experiences of various kinds. There is, of course, the possibility of helping the creative child discover suitable reading in the area of his talent. Thus, the child who has ability in music will usually find the books by Opal Wheeler on Mozart, Chopin, and other composers a help and an inspiration.

It is the responsibility of the parent, the teacher, and the librarian to locate appropriate books and make them available to such children. Like the verbally gifted, the creative child often has a need for experiences in reading that will enable him to meet personal and social problems and to build an ideal of self consonant with his ability and promise.

A CASE STUDY OF A VERBALLY GIFTED CHILD

A better understanding of gifted pupils as well as the basis for providing an adequate instructional program for them may be derived from detailed case studies. We have chosen an extremely gifted child as an illustration—a child whose reading and language proficiencies are really remarkable:

John was referred to the Psycho-Educational Clinic of Northwestern University by his father, who wished to obtain suggestions for guiding his remarkable son. Accordingly, diagnostic testing was arranged to determine the extent of John's intellectual superiority and to explore the resources that might be drawn upon to enable him to develop his abilities to the maximum. At the time John came to the Clinic, he was 4 years, 10 months of age. The following report was prepared one month later, after four visits had been made to the Clinic.

Family Background

John is the son of a rabbi; he has a two-year-old sister. The family background, although superior, contains few persons whose attainment would suggest childhood superiority approaching this child's status. However, John's parents are well-educated and intelligent people. They both received college degrees. The mother taught deaf children in a university school for four years after she had completed her college work. The father is a graduate of a theological college. John's two-year-old sister, although considered very bright by her parents, does not demonstrate the unusual abilities that John did at her age. John appears to be an anomaly or variant such as is found sometimes in superior families.

Physical Status

John is a well-built, healthy-appearing four-year-old boy. His parents report that his general health is good. He has had only minor physical diseases, from which he has recovered fully. His sleep habits are described as satisfactory. A report by a physician shows John to be in good health.

Intelligence Test Results

The Terman-Merrill Revision of the Stanford-Binet Scale, Form L, was administered. John earned a mental age of eight years and ten months, thus receiving an intelligence quotient of 183. His basal year was VI, and he gave correct responses to items on tests at the XIV year level.

John was extremely active throughout the testing. He questioned the items which the examiner recorded, and displayed more than an average amount of restlessness. But he entered willingly into each task and displayed strong interest when it was challenging. Although he appeared self-confident, he was eager to avoid failure of any kind.

John's highest attainment was on verbal subtests of the Scale, such as Vocabulary, Memory for Sentences, and Reading and Report. His poorest attainment was in those subtests requiring the explanation of pictures and dealing with Verbal Absurdities. John's performance was consistently excellent throughout the test. He displayed originality in many of his responses, speed in reaction, and accuracy in recall.

Educational Test Results

On the California Achievement Tests—Primary Form AA, John received a total grade equivalent of 4.8. While this score is remarkable, it might have been even higher if his interest had been sustained throughout all tests. For example, in the test of multiplication, John solved the first eleven problems, but would not continue to try to solve the remaining items. It appears that John's educational attainment is commensurate with the high level of his capacity as suggested by the intelligence tests.

Noteworthy is the fact that John's educational superiority is general. Although his attainment was highest in reading, he was also proficient in arithmetic and in spelling. John's poorest performance (Mechanics of English) was above third-grade norm. On tests of oral reading, his responses were even more outstanding than on the other educational tests. On the Gray Oral Reading Paragraphs, he received a grade equivalent of 6.1. On the Gilmore Oral Reading Test, his grade equivalent was 8.3 (superior rating) in Accuracy, and 4.1 (superior rating) in Comprehension. His rate score was 84 words per minute (fast). His main errors were mispronunciations made when he was reading far beyond his comprehension level.

This was partly traceable to the fact that he attempted, usually with success, to pronounce all new words. John has mastered an unusual number of sight words and has attained skill in unlocking new words through phonetic analysis. His performance on these tests is really remarkable.

Personality Aspects

John is an interesting, likable four-year-old boy. At first, he was somewhat inattentive. He often wanted to digress from the tests. He preferred not to attempt anything he thought to be "too hard," yet when encouraged he was often quite capable of performing difficult tasks successfully. During the last interview, however, John was more poised and compliant. He appeared eager to continue the testing and was pleased when opportunities to excel were offered. In an effort to obtain recognition and praise, John explained to the examiner how he performed feats of multiplication or how he was able to add four columns of figures.

John's mother reported that he presents no unusual problem at home. He thoroughly enjoys reading and particularly likes to play games. He is cooperative at home, and does chores such as hanging up his clothes, putting away his toys, and setting the dinner table.

He has a strong attachment for his father, and attempts to please him. John's father spends much time and effort in stimulating and guiding

John's development. This boy has few friends outside the family but appears to get along well with other children when he is with them. He is a fairly happy child who seems especially well pleased with himself when others are pleased with him. There are many occasions for this type of satisfaction, since his outstanding mental ability is reflected in almost everything he does.

John attends the kindergarten of a public school in a suburb of Chicago. During the first half of the school year he had few friends within the group. He was chiefly dependent upon a teacher-child relationship at that time. However, it was felt by the school that John has made great gains in his social and emotional adjustment during the school year. He has become friendly with other children and has invited them to his home. His teacher believes that he has benefited greatly from the school experience. He has grown less excitable and restless. Part of this improvement is attributed, both by the parents and by the teacher, to his success in group activities; for example, he was selected to represent the kindergarten at the School Council Meeting. He reported the experience to the members of his class, who expressed their admiration of his ability to tell the story of the meeting. Although the other children know that John can read and write, they do not seem to recognize the extent of his superiority. Therefore, they accept him as one of the group.[29]

There can be no question of John's superior gifts in abstract intelligence. He is not only mentally bright, but he seems to have the drive and motivation that enable him profitably to use his ability. His achievement in reading is extraordinary; he reads test material with success, and also reads books and magazines effectively.

The language development of this boy is so anomalous that one is at a loss to explain its origin. Undoubtedly the encouragement of his parents and his unusual opportunities at home are important factors in his accelerated development. But his ability to apply phonetic principles, to spell unusual words, to solve arithmetic problems, and to engage successfully in many complex learning activities can hardly be accounted for solely in terms of unusual environmental opportunities. John is a boy whose mental ability seems so unusual that one must account for much of his performance in terms of a very fortunate endowment.

What will the future hold for this precocious boy? One can only speculate concerning his development. It is to be hoped that means will

[29] Paul Witty and Rochelle Blumenthal, "The Language Development of an Exceptionally Gifted Pupil," *Elementary English,* 34:214–217 (April, 1957).

be found to direct and foster his future growth in effective ways and to channel his remarkable ability into individually profitable and socially desirable pursuits. Recognition of his outstanding ability is a first step. With the help of intelligent parents and with the opportunities which good schools and understanding counselors may offer, the youthful promise of this boy may be realized in constructive endeavor and in the type of contribution to society which only the most gifted can make.

CONCLUDING STATEMENT

We have in this chapter noted a change in the concept of giftedness held by educators. For many years the gifted pupil was regarded as a child whose I.Q. was 130 or higher. Children of high I.Q. are at present still considered gifted, but as only *one* type of such pupils. A concern is now shown for other pupils whose performance in various worthwhile types of endeavor, such as art, music, or writing, is repeatedly remarkable. Today, this broader criterion of giftedness is widely accepted; it includes pupils whose I.Q.'s may or may not be outstandingly high but whose ability and promise in certain areas are unmistakably demonstrated.

We have also pointed out that all these types of gifted pupils may need guidance in reading. We believe that for them a developmental reading program is most desirable; such a program may enrich and extend their interests and, in association with the other language arts, may lead to personally desirable fulfillment of their needs. Another aim of this program is to help students become successful and independent in using the library and other resources for finding the right book at the right time. This objective is of unusual significance, since the gifted pupil, if he is to develop his full potential, must become skilled in directing and expanding his own education.

Selected References

Barbe, Walter B., "Differentiated Guidance for the Gifted," *Education*, 74:306–311 (January, 1954).

Barbe, Walter B., *Psychology and Education of the Gifted: Selected Readings* (New York: Appleton-Century-Crofts, 1965).

Barbe, Walter B., "A Study of the Reading of Gifted High-School Students," *Educational Administration and Supervision*, 38:148–154 (March, 1952).

Barbe, Walter B. and Dorothy E. Norris, "Reading Instruction in Special

Classes for Gifted Elementary Children," *The Reading Teacher,* 16:425–428 (May, 1963).

Barbe, Walter B. and Thelma E. Williams, "Developing Creative Thinking in Gifted Children Through the Reading Program," *The Reading Teacher,* 9:200–203 (April, 1956).

Bland, Phyllis, "Helping Bright Students Who Read Poorly," *The Reading Teacher,* 9:209–214 (April, 1956).

DeBoer, John J., "Creative Reading and the Gifted Student," *The Reading Teacher,* 16:435–441 (May, 1963).

Educational Policies Commission, *Education of the Gifted* (Washington, D. C.: National Education Association, 1950).

Edwards, Newton, "Education of the Able Student: Social Significance and Goals," in Helen M. Robinson (editor), *Promoting Maximal Reading Growth Among Able Learners,* Supplementary Educational Monographs no. 81 (Chicago: University of Chicago Press, 1954), pp. 1–5.

Flory, Vera, "Special Classes for the Gifted?" *The Clearing House,* 32:22–24 (September, 1957).

Frampton, Merle E. and E. D. Gall (editors), *Special Education for the Exceptional,* 3 vols. (Boston: Porter Sargent, Publisher, 1955–56).

Gray, William S. (editor), *Classroom Techniques in Improving Reading,* Supplementary Educational Monographs no. 69 (Chicago: University of Chicago Press, 1952), pp. 153–171.

Heck, Arch O., *The Education of Exceptional Children,* 2nd ed. (New York: McGraw-Hill Book Co., 1953).

Hildreth, Gertrude H., in collaboration with Florence N. Brumbaugh and Frank T. Wilson, *Educating Gifted Children at Hunter College Elementary School* (New York: Harper & Row, Publisher, 1952).

Justman, Joseph, "Academic Achievement of Intellectually Gifted Accelerants and Non-accelerants in Junior High School," *School Review,* 62:142–150 (March, 1954).

Justman, Joseph, "Academic Achievement of Intellectually Gifted Accelerants and Non-accelerants in Senior High School," *School Review,* 62:469–473 (November, 1954).

Mersand, Joseph, "Reading for Superior Students in a Comprehensive High School," *The Reading Teacher,* 16:442–447 (May, 1963).

Mosso, Asenath M., "A Seminar for Superior High-School Seniors," *School Review,* 53:464–470 (October, 1945).

Murphy, Geraldine J., "The Education of Gifted Children: Suggestions for a Philosophy and a Curriculum," *School Review,* 62:414–419 (October, 1954).

Strang, Ruth, "Basic Issues and Problems in Reading Instruction for Capable Students," in Helen M. Robinson (editor), *Promoting Maximal Reading Growth Among Able Learners,* Supplementary Educational Monographs No. 81 (Chicago: University of Chicago Press, 1954), pp. 6–10.

Witty, Paul A., "A Balanced Reading Program for the Gifted," *The Reading Teacher,* 16:418–424 (May, 1963).

Witty, Paul A. (editor), *The Gifted Child* (Boston: D. C. Heath and Company, 1951).

Witty, Paul A., "The Gifted and the Creative Pupil," *Education,* 82:451–459 (April, 1962).

Witty, Paul A., "The Gifted and the Creative Student," *School and Society,* 92:183–185 (April 18, 1964).

Witty, Paul A., "Reading and the Gifted Child," *The Reading Teacher,* 9:195–196 (April, 1956).

16

THE ROLE OF THE TEACHER

Efficient reading is an individual acquisition. Similarly, learning to read is basically an individual matter. Some writers emphasize the place of self-instruction in the classroom and minimize the role of group work and group guidance by the teacher. Increasingly, materials are being produced for independent use by the pupil and "programmed" for self-instruction.

At various stages pupils may need only a minimum of guidance from the teacher; indeed, one of the goals of reading is to promote independence in reading. Few children, however, learn to read without help from teachers. Moreover, children appear to learn to read most effectively when their needs, interests, and goals are recognized and utilized in a developmental reading program in which both individual and group instruction are provided. In fact, the teacher is considered perhaps the most important single factor in motivating learning and in producing good readers.

Who Is the Reading Teacher?

Before discussing the personal and professional assets of the teacher, it is desirable to answer the question "Who is the reading teacher?" Since reading permeates the entire school curriculum, it is not surprising to find a number of different people involved directly or indirectly in reading instruction. The roles of these people vary considerably, but there is one overall purpose they share—to help every child reach his optimum development in and through reading. In a broad sense, then, we may define the reading teacher as any person who guides children and young people in their efforts to attain maximum efficiency in reading. In this definition, parents, classroom teachers, librarians, and special teachers are included. We shall limit our discussion of the teacher in this chapter, however, to the person who carries the major responsibility for the instructional program in reading. This obligation usually rests upon the teacher in the self-contained classroom. At the junior and senior high school levels it is often assumed by the English teacher.

Teachers of reading vary widely in their competency and training. It is generally recognized that facilities for their improvement should be greatly expanded and enhanced. That much is needed to improve their opportunities for adequate preparation in college, may be readily observed by examining *The Torch Lighters*.[1] Following a résumé of college practices in preparing teachers of reading, twenty-one far-reaching recommendations are made. To "revitalize instruction in the teaching of reading," many departures from current practices are advocated, including: the introduction of the case-study or problem-centered approach; the increased use of tape recordings and films portraying classroom activities; direct observation *via* closed circuit T.V., and the coordination of reading instruction with the practice teaching program.

Not only are improved teacher-training programs needed, but the establishment of helpful in-service programs is essential. To meet the challenge of reading instruction today, it is also imperative that increased attention be given to the mental health and the personality of the teacher himself.

DESIRABLE PERSONAL ASSETS FOR TEACHING READING

The teacher's personality is a powerful factor in determining both the classroom atmosphere for learning and the relationship between teacher and pupil which affects the learning process. Unless there is mutual understanding and a sympathetic relationship between the pupils and the teacher, there is a likelihood that reading instruction will become a process of narrowly conceived mechanical responses.[2] Burton points out that "two teachers of equal intelligence, training, and grasp of subject matter may differ considerably in influence and in the results they achieve." He believes that

> part of the difference is clearly accounted for by the effect of personality on the learners. . . . Everyone can testify to the evil effect,

[1] Mary C. Austin, Coleman Morrison, and others, *The Torch Lighters* (Cambridge, Mass.: Harvard University Press, 1961).
[2] Lyman C. Hunt, Jr., "Let's Not By-pass the Reading Teacher," *The Reading Teacher*, 11:37 (Otcober, 1957).

within a group, of one or two inadequate or warped personalities and to the almost miraculous effect of a few serene, poised personalities.[3]

Each teacher has his own unique characteristics in terms of success in human relationships. Although the particular combination of traits in teachers that promotes the best learning in children is unknown, there are a number of factors which are deemed essential in an effective teacher-pupil relationship.

Personal Reading Is Important to the Teacher

There are few if any personal assets that have a greater influence upon the nature and quality of instruction than the teacher's own tendency to enjoy reading and to read widely. The teacher who reads little is a poor model and an uninspiring example. Moreover, such a person usually lacks the background necessary to stimulate children to understand people and the world around them. He is uninteresting and usually ineffective in directing his students' reading if he does not "know books of all kinds, their content, the way they can meet both curricular interests and specific needs of the individual children."[4]

Teachers should be not only thoroughly acquainted with contemporary children's literature, but they should also be well informed about literature of the past. It is, as Alvina Burrows points out,

> the old question of learning by precept or percept . . . Can we build in children attitudes favoring wide, discriminating, reflective reading, or even of affection for reading, if we do not liberally demonstrate our own satisfaction in it?

Unfortunately, Burrows' recent investigation of teachers' reading values shows

> that teachers as a group are not outstandingly active in the wider reaches of literate pursuits.[5]

There are, of course, exceptions who constitute the inspiring, effective teachers of our day.

Children are imitators; a teacher's enthusiasm for reading usually is reflected in the children's delight in reading. The young reader is often influenced deeply as he notes the teacher's habit of enlarging his personal library, of getting books regularly from the library, of sharing books with

---

[3] William H. Burton, *The Guidance of Learning Activities,* 3rd ed. (New York: Appleton-Century-Crofts, 1962), p. 253.
[4] Ruth Tooze, *Your Children Want to Read* (Englewood Cliffs, N. J.: Prentice-Hall, Inc., 1957), p. 19.
[5] Alvina Treut Burrows, "Do Teachers Read?" *The Reading Teacher,* 11:254 (April, 1958).

friends, and of rereading favorite stories and poems. Children's joy in reading is enhanced by the teacher who brings poetry into class discussions frequently; who speaks of storybook characters as if they were real and cherished friends; and who can as if by magic transport his listeners from the prosaic classroom environment to a setting of high drama in which suspense, excitement, courage, and determination are vividly shown.

Of course, the teacher who has grown up with books around him and has developed an early interest in reading has a decided advantage over the person with a more limited background. It is not an easy matter for a busy teacher to find time to read widely; yet wide reading is a responsibility of the teacher. Many avid readers say that they make a habit of keeping reading material with them and take advantge of the time they must spend in routine activities such as traveling or waiting in the dentist's office. Paperbacks are excellent companions, many teachers find. It is surprising how much reading one can do over a relatively short period of time if books are kept on the bedside table and read regularly. The teacher who recognizes his needs for books will find a way to engage in the kind of reading that broadens and deepens his insight into human behavior, fosters his spiritual and aesthetic appreciation of life, and enlarges his knowledge of the physical, political, and social world of which he is a member.

Closely associated with wide reading is the development of adequate skills on the part of the teacher to enable him to read effectively and adjust his rate of reading to the varied demands of different kinds of materials and situations. It is, therefore, desirable for teachers to examine their own proficiencies. If they find themselves lacking in certain skills, they will usually find that they can improve their own reading by the use of a book such as *How to Become a Better Reader*. With improvement of their own skills, they will usually gain an enhanced understanding of the reading process, and will be better prepared to help children overcome difficulties as well as to read more widely and effectively themselves.

The Teacher Leads a Full, Purposeful Life

Important as it is, however, the vicarious experience derived from reading alone will not suffice to fulfill the teacher's need for a deep understanding and appreciation of people and the world about him. The teacher should try to live a full and purposeful life, made so through a variety of firsthand experiences and interesting pursuits of many kinds.

The good teacher soon realizes that the modern schoolroom is no place for a person who holds tenaciously to outmoded concepts, methods, and materials for teaching reading.[6]

There are unlimited opportunities for the teacher to have rich and rewarding personal experiences. Participation in civic, church, and educational affairs will enable him to develop a broader understanding of the political, social, economic, educational, and spiritual conditions of his community. As a member of a family group he has the opportunity to maintain his identity as an individual and at the same time to enjoy the fulfillment of his basic needs for security, love, and companionship. Such a person usually develops a friendly, sympathetic, understanding atmosphere in the classroom. There are, of course, many other avenues for rewarding experiences—attending concerts, visiting museums and art galleries, traveling, and following hobbies. These experiences give direction and purpose to life, and enrich immeasurably the teacher's background for effective work.

The Teacher Is a Well-Adjusted Person

The mental health of the teacher may have a marked influence upon the effectiveness of his instruction. Investigations suggest that poor results are obtained more often in the classrooms of maladjusted teachers.[7] The well-adjusted teacher has many desirable traits that help to qualify him for the responsibilities involved in the teaching profession, one of the most important probably being his ability to make a fairly objective appraisal of himself both as a person and as a teacher. He is able also to accept readily differences among people in intellectual ability, physical stamina, talents, personal appearance, and other characteristics. Such a teacher recognizes his weaknesses, but he is determined to make maximum use of his own "unique personal equipment as effectively as possible in the interests of the maximum growth of the boys and girls under his care."[8] The teacher who has learned to meet his personal problems with equanimity has a sound basis for guiding children's development in reading.

The significance of the mental health of teachers in relation to chil-

---

[6] Margaret G. McKim and others, *Learning to Teach in the Elementary School* (New York: The Macmillan Company, 1959), p. 14.

[7] Paul Witty, *Reading in Modern Education* (Boston: D. C. Heath and Company, 1949), p. 262. See also Paul Witty, "The Teacher Who Helped Me Most," *Elementary English*, 24:345–354 (October, 1947).

[8] Margaret G. McKim and others, *op. cit.,* p. 4.

dren's learning has been revealed in a number of studies. In one study by Paul Witty the children were asked to write on the topic *The Teacher Who Has Helped Me Most,* and these letters from 14,000 children were analyzed to reveal the character traits of the effective teacher. The most desirable traits according to this study are listed, in order of frequency, in Table XVI.

TABLE XVI

DESIRABLE TRAITS OF TEACHERS AS CITED BY
LETTERS OF 14,000 PUPILS[9]

1. Cooperation, democratic attitude
2. Kindliness and consideration for the individual
3. Patience
4. Wide interests
5. Attractive personal appearance and pleasing manner
6. Fairness and impartiality
7. Sense of humor
8. Good disposition
9. Interest in pupils' problem
10. Flexibility
11. Use of recognition and praise

In a later investigation the author studied the negative or undesirable traits which children attributed to some teachers. These characteristics are presented in order of frequency in Table XVII.

TABLE XVII

NEGATIVE TRAITS OF TEACHERS AS CITED BY PUPILS[10]

1. Bad-tempered and intolerant
2. Unfair and inclined to have favorites
3. Disinclined to show interest in the pupil and to take time to help him
4. Unreasonable in demands
5. Tendency to be gloomy and unfriendly
6. Sarcastic and inclined to use ridicule
7. Unattractive in appearance
8. Impatient and inflexible
9. Tendency to talk excessively
10. Inclined to talk down to pupils
11. Overbearing and conceited
12. Lacking in sense of humor

[9] Paul Witty, *Reading in Modern Education, op. cit.,* p. 263.
[10] *Ibid.,* p. 264.

Since the process of learning is definitely influenced by the relationship between the teacher and the learner, it is important that the teacher provide a good emotional tone in the classroom. He can create a pleasant, friendly, and confident feeling among his pupils if he is a friendly, patient, understanding person himself who likes children and finds satisfaction in teaching.[11]

The Teacher Possesses Good Physical Health

The personality of the teacher is also influenced by his physical health. It is a point of wisdom for the teacher to learn early in his career to conserve his physical strength. Leading a full and purposeful life requires strong physical stamina; teaching children is a demanding task. Proper food, adequate rest and sleep, and interesting recreational activities are conducive to health, but the teacher will also have to arrange and schedule his habits of living so that he does not have to face more responsibilities than he can handle.[12]

PROFESSIONAL QUALIFICATIONS FOR TEACHING

The Teacher Has a Positive Attitude Toward His Profession

The attitude of the teacher toward his profession has a direct bearing upon the way he teaches, the responsibility he feels for personal growth, and his relationship with children and adults. He should feel that he is a member of a group of people who are making not only a significant contribution toward the development of our children and young people, but also one of the most important contributions to our way of life. Pride in his profession should be matched by an equally high degree of that personal satisfaction which is the reward of those who enjoy working with children.

The professional-minded teacher is a growing person; he is constantly on the alert to find ways for improving the procedures he uses in teaching reading. Three factors may be thought of as determiners of the teacher's increase in stature: (1) he must want to continue to grow professionally, (2) he must demonstrate the sincerity of his in-

---

[11] Ruth Strang and Dorothy Bracken, *Making Better Readers* (Boston: D. C. Heath and Co., 1957), p. 159.
[12] Margaret G. McKim and others, *op. cit.*, p. 6.

tention by taking steps toward self-improvement, and (3) he must strive continuously to improve his teaching.

Although the "teacher-on-the-job" must demonstrate an interest in professional improvement and take the initiative in doing something about it, he will find many individuals, groups, and organizations ready to assist him. It is the rule rather than the exception for school systems to encourage teacher growth through participation in in-service study groups; action research projects; observation of master teachers; reading of professional books and periodicals; and local, college, or university workshops featuring specialists in the field of reading. Membership in professional organizations such as the Association for Childhood Education, the National Council of Teachers of English, and the International Reading Association offers avenues of growth through participation in local group meetings and a variety of stimulating activities of other kinds. The publications of these organizations are also helpful to the reading teacher.

Fortunately, teachers, school administrators, persons actively engaged in the education of prospective teachers, as well as teachers in service, are seeking to reach agreement regarding the kind and quality of professional competencies teachers must acquire if they are to give effective guidance in reading and literature. They concur in stressing the fact that the effective teacher is one who knows children's needs and interests, who knows the broad field of reading, and who knows how to bring children and reading together joyfully.

The Teacher Uses Human Resources to Strengthen the Reading Program

Although the reading teacher has the major responsibility for the children in his group, it is not to be expected that he will carry the load alone. Some beginning teachers are reluctant to ask for help in the mistaken notion that such a gesture will be construed as an admission of incompetence. They forget that they live in an age of specialization and that there are persons who by virtue of their training and experience are better qualified than they to handle certain types of situations. It is important that the reading teacher follow three steps when confronted with lack of progress in reading: (1) he should as far as possible identify the needs of children having special reading problems and determine the kind of help each requires, (2) he should make an effort to locate all available resources, and (3) he should take positive action to use these resources constructively. The timely and intelligent use of resources will make it possible for him to solve problems which otherwise would stand in the way of certain children's progress.

In seeking to understand some children's special needs, help may sometimes be obtained from a child's former teachers. They can supplement the data recorded in permanent files and often give a more meaningful interpretation of the child's present behavior. They can also make substantial contributions to new teachers by helping them understand and meet problems of various kinds as they arise.

The school nurse and doctor may be consulted to help in matters pertaining to children's health, and thus enable the teacher to better understand children's present needs. The result of vision, hearing, and speech tests may be consulted to obtain pertinent data related to success in learning to read.

The procedure for the administration and interpretation of standardized tests varies from school to school, but the use of this type of service should not be neglected. Psychologists often make it possible for the teacher to obtain objective data useful in locating current individual weaknesses and strengths in reading skills, interests, and personality traits. Such concrete information can be used in improving instructional procedures and content for special cases as well as for groups of unsuccessful learners.

The increasing demand of classroom teachers for assistance in meeting special reading problems has prompted some school systems to employ specialists trained to help teachers with their more urgent reading problems. These specialists concern themselves with the problems of pupils who for various reasons are unable to succeed under prevailing classroom conditions. These special supervisory staff members are in a position to help the teacher locate and coordinate resources, and can also give concrete suggestions that will enable the teacher to improve his reading program. It is a good idea for beginning teachers and those new to a system to seek suggestions from specialists and to try to set up effective working relationships with them.

On the whole, parents too are eager to serve as resource persons and to assist in the arrangement of excursions and field trips, getting books, and sponsoring projects related to the extension of room and school libraries. Through parent-teacher conferences and in other ways communication can be improved between teacher and parent. Parents are often poorly informed about school practices with the result that they fail to cooperate with the teacher. It is the teacher's responsibility to try to bring about a relationship that is informative, pleasant, and profitable.

From school and community librarians the classroom teacher may obtain much help, for these resource persons have the opportunity to observe children pursuing their interests in an informal setting. The librarian whose knowledge of children's books is extensive may offer the teacher valuable hints in selecting new books for the classroom library, in compiling bibliographies for special projects, in telling and reading stories to pupils, and in sponsoring a variety of activities designed to stimulate an interest in and a taste for good literature.

There are a number of other persons and groups who may contribute to the reading program, but who do so in an indirect way. For example, the school custodian who understands why the reading teacher requests a special arrangement of furniture in the room and who assists in making the adjustments is performing a service. We are reminded of a custodian who smiled in appreciation when he read the "thank-you" notes from the second-grade children after he had helped them construct and paint an "apple-box" library corner in their room.

Similarly, we might single out other groups whose roles in improving the instructional program in reading, though significant, are carried out in an indirect way. There are the principal and other administrative personnel, whose responsibilities include the selection of appropriate equipment and materials and adequate guidance and supervision of teachers. There are persons in the community who also help in various ways. Included in a list of local resources people who had made a definite contribution one year to the reading program in one fourth grade were: an artist who had illustrated a favorite book, an author of a supplementary reader used by the group; a parent who presented a puppet show, a retired college teacher who had taught courses in children's literature for many years and who was an accomplished reader of poetry, an artist who helped the children paint scenery for a play they had written, and two student teachers from a university who helped to plan a trip to the local television station where the children presented book reviews for the Book Week program.

The Teacher Provides a Challenging and Stimulating Learning Environment

In planning the reading program, the teacher must give attention to the physical, emotional, and intellectual environment of the classroom. All three factors are vital when effective results from the reading curriculum are to be achieved.

The Physical Environment

The physical environment should make the children feel comfortable and relaxed. Attention to lighting, ventilation, and arrangement of furniture is the responsibility of the teacher, although he does not always have a part in the choice of such items.

Room dividers make it possible to set off areas for group reading, independent reading, art, dramatic presentations, and other activities. Such dividers also make it possible for pupils to be "by themselves in a quiet place apart from the group."[13] Pupils should have a voice in planning and working to develop an attractive room. As they move through the grades, they can assume greater and greater responsibility in such efforts. Reading experiences become more meaningful to children who have had a part in developing an exciting, interesting, and attractive environment. As Annette Frank points out, a reading center

> will have more meaning for the children if they have helped to choose the available books according to class interest and have helped to organize a place where they can go to read for pleasure, find information, engage in independent reading activities, record evaluations and progress.[14]

Pupil participation, according to this author, should also include taking part in arranging bulletin boards; making posters, displays, exhibits; housekeeping chores, and similar activities that will help them to develop a sense of responsibility for an "interesting, vital, and aesthetically satisfying environment."[15]

Accessibility of reading material is a factor of primary importance in the reading program, for it is a well-known fact that children will read what is at hand and readily available; hence, the teacher must feel responsible for the quality as well as the quantity of reading materials.

The Social and Emotional Environment

The atmosphere of the classroom should promote social and emotional well-being. As we have pointed out earlier in this chapter, there seems to be general agreement that the "personality of the teacher sets the emotional tone in the classroom." Children need happy, well-adjusted teachers; teachers who are sensitive to beauty and order;

---

[13] Annette Frank, "Organization and Arrangement for Middle Grades," in *Space, Arrangement, Beauty and Schools* (Washington, D.C.: Association for Childhood Education International, 1958), p. 10.
[14] *Ibid.*
[15] *Ibid.*

creative persons who can guide pupils in making proper adjustments and achieving happy relationships with their peers. "As the teacher is," says Ruth Tooze, "so are her students."[16] A warm, friendly atmosphere helps pupils feel secure in the love, esteem, and friendliness of others, adequate to the task expected of them, and important to the work of the group. Children learn best in an atmosphere where they are free from fear, and free, too, from unnatural physical restraints.

The daily schedule of living has a marked effect upon the emotional tone of the classroom. It should be flexible to the extent that the teacher is not compulsively driven to try to "cover" a specified amount of work each day or to follow a rigid time schedule. The activities of each day should be planned to avoid haste, nervous tension, and discouragement on the part of either children or teacher. Pressures from administrative sources and unrealistic expectations of parents should be kept at a minimum. Careful planning helps the teacher to eliminate the unnecessary and irrelevant and to emphasize the important.

The Intellectual Environment

The teacher is charged with the responsibility of making the classroom "a laboratory of learning"—a place where questions are raised, a desire to find out is exhibited, and problems are solved by the process of discovery. In order to provide this favorable climate for learning, the teacher should arrange opportunities for pupils to help plan and participate in purposeful reading experiences. This means that the pupils must attain an understanding of the variety of purposes for reading and the importance of reading in the light of purposes. They must have a chance to learn the essential skills in everyday, functional situations. For example, emphasis upon the development of work-study skills as they are needed in problem-solving situations in social studies, science, and other content areas will give meaning to reading and encourage pupils to use reading skills in solving their own problems.

The Teacher Makes Provision for Broad, Well-Balanced Reading Experiences

Teachers should plan a balanced reading program which will insure for each individual experiences and repeated practice in the many aspects of reading. In a comprehensive review of research and opinions

---

[16] Ruth Tooze, *op. cit.*, p. 54.

of authorities, John Pescosolido identified ten goals that should be sought in a well-balanced reading program:

1) To maintain a continuous, systematic reading program
2) To recognize individual differences among children
3) To provide and use a variety of instructional materials
4) To develop purpose for reading
5) To develop word-study techniques
6) To develop comprehension skills in reading
7) To develop study-skills in reading
8) To provide opportunities for wide and varied reading
9) To develop oral and silent reading skills
10) To appraise children's progress in reading[17]

Two things may be deduced from such a list: *first,* a balanced reading program includes a number of goals, and *second,* since all are components of a balanced reading program, one goal cannot be taught to the exclusion of others.

In a developmental program children are given systematic training in the development of skills, habits, and attitudes essential to proficiency in reading, although the approach used to insure such development varies.[18] Some teachers attempt to offer a balanced reading program through a completely individualized reading approach; others find greater security in following a combination of individual and group approaches.

The content subject areas offer excellent opportunities for the application of reading skills and the development of power in reading. These opportunities include study-type exercises and experiences in reading subject matter of various kinds in arithmetic, health, safety, science, and social studies materials.

In making his long-term as well as weekly plans, the teacher should bear in mind that not all pupils need the same type or amount of guidance in each of these areas of reading, but he must not lose sight of the fact that all pupils need an opportunity to grow increasingly more proficient in each area. The most effective reading programs are those based upon the point of view that "children differ—so should programs."[19]

In earlier chapters we have pointed to the fact that the teacher of reading must have a thorough understanding of the principles of child

---

[17] John Pescosolido, *The Identification and Appraisal of Certain Major Factors in the Teaching of Reading,* unpublished Ph.D. dissertation (Storrs, Conn.: University of Connecticut, 1962), p. 17.

[18] Newark, New Jersey, Board of Education, *Language Arts in Our Schools: A Guide to Improvement of Instruction,* September, 1950, p. 9.

[19] F. Pauline Hilliard, "Children Differ—So Should Programs," *Childhood Education,* 29:155 (December, 1952).

growth and development and of the role of interest in the motivation of children's reading.

The Teacher Provides for Individual Differences in Reading

A sound background in child development will help the teacher understand his own pupils and enable him to make an effective appraisal of their varied needs as a basis for instruction in reading. It is not an easy task, but the teacher must know the individual's strengths and weaknesses and interests before he can give the kind of guidance that will assure each child's optimum growth through reading. For example, the teacher must challenge the

> child with superior abilities to realize his potentialities; the child who progresses at normal rate should be stimulated to maintain maximum growth; while the slow-learning child must be encouraged and carefully guided in order that his growth in reading, although gradual, shall be continuous and the best of which he is capable.[20]

Current practice suggests that there are several factors to be taken into consideration in planning for individual differences. First, the teacher must accept the point of view that each child needs a custom-made program that takes into consideration his unique nature and needs.[21]

Second, the teacher, to identify the strengths and weaknesses of the individual members of the group, must use all available resources. Previous reference has been made in this book to a number of possibilities for obtaining data that give reliable clues to the needs of each pupil. For example, *classroom observations* of children often reveal symptoms which are related to reading difficulties. The results of *standardized tests* of silent and oral reading yield information that may lead to a better understanding of abilities with respect to speed, accuracy, comprehension, vocabulary, and other aspects of reading skill. *Informal tests* and other *teacher-made materials* can be used to assess important phases in the development of skills. Examination of *cumulative records* may make it possible for the teacher to study the patterns of growth of children over a period of time.

Third, children with meager backgrounds require enrichment of their experiences. Teachers often find it worthwhile to provide activities such as listening to stories, songs, and records; viewing films; taking trips;

---

[20] Newark, New Jersey, Board of Education, *op. cit.,* p. 10.
[21] Edith Thomas, "Grouping in the Classroom," *Childhood Education,* 30:69 (October, 1953).

dramatizing stories; singing; drawing; and reading widely from varied sources.

Grouping for instructional purposes provides another means of meeting individual differences. When children are placed in small groups according to interests, they can make contributions to discussions after they have read materials on different levels of difficulty, thus enabling every child to have a part and to recognize the value of reading.

Experimentation is now in progress to determine the practicality of still another plan for meeting individual differences, namely, individualized reading. Proponents of this approach claim that it meets individual differences more effectively than do the conventional grouping practices. They believe that children have a better chance to pursue their individual interests and enrich their experiences when they are permitted to exercise self-selection and pace their own reading. Studies are being made to ascertain also the comparative efficiency of plans that combine individualized and group procedures in varying ways.

Regardless of the procedure used to guide children's growth in reading, there is a need for much and varied reading material. Basal and supplementary readers, children's magazines and newspapers, and books of many kinds are necessary to satisfy the individual reading abilities and interests of pupils within each class.

The teacher of reading should attempt continuously to appraise each child's progress and note his evolving needs. Flexibility of organization is essential as the reading program is adapted to individual requirements. If grouping is looked upon only as a tentative arrangement, pupils can be readily shifted from one group to another as they grow in certain abilities or change in needs—but not unless there is constant appraisal of progress. Suggestions for appraising children's growth in reading are given in the following chapter.

CONCLUDING STATEMENT

It has been observed that the hygienic classroom is one permeated by a spirit of friendliness, sympathetic concern, and genuine affection. In such a setting, happiness and success in individually suitable and challenging tasks are powerful contributors to wholesome personality development. A sense of "belonging" to a group is another psychological imperative in the creation of an atmosphere for effective learning. Similarly essential in promoting growth is the changing, evolving curriculum through which children may express, enrich, and develop their varied interests in terms of their unique needs. Throughout this book, reading has been presented as one phase only of such a curriculum. The essential principles stressed have been shown to apply to every subject and to every area of instruction. They are grounded in a respect for children and youth and in a sincere recognition of the needs and rights of every individual—the teacher as well as the student. Widely followed, such an approach will be a guarantee of great and far-reaching gains in human welfare and human happiness. The reading process will then assume its role as a powerful factor in improving the welfare and in fostering the happiness of all our people.

Selected References

Burrows, Alvina Treut, "Do Teachers Read?" *The Reading Teacher,* 11:254–255 (April, 1958).

Burton, William H., *The Guidance of Learning Activities,* 3rd ed. (New York: Appleton-Century-Crofts, Inc., 1962).

Corson, Hazel, "Who Will Help Me?" *Childhood Education,* 29:252–285 (February, 1953).

Crosby, Muriel, "The Totality of the Reading Program," *Elementary English,* 36:374–379 (October, 1959).

Freeland, Alma, "Planning with the Staff for Guidance" in the 1954 Yearbook of the *National Elementary Principal* (Washington D.C.: National Education Association, 1954), pp. 36–41.

Gray, Lillian, *Teaching Children to Read,* 3rd ed. (New York: The Ronald Press Company, 1963).

Gray, William S. (editor), *Basic Instruction in Reading in Elementary and High Schools,* Supplementary Educational Monograph no. 65 (Chicago: University of Chicago Press, 1948).

Gray, William S. (editor), *Keeping Reading Programs Abreast of the Times,* Supplementary Educational Monograph no. 72 (Chicago: University of Chicago Press, 1950).

Hilliard, F. Pauline, "Children Differ—So Should Programs," *Childhood Education,* 29:155 (December, 1952).

Hunt, Lyman C., Jr., "Let's Not By-pass the Reading Teacher," The Reading Teacher, 11:37–41 (October, 1957).

Kyte, George C., *The Elementary-School Teacher at Work* (New York: Holt, Rinehart & Winston, Inc., 1957).

Lazar, May, "Individualized Reading: A Dynamic Approach," *The Reading Teacher,* 11:75–83 (December, 1957).

McCall, Lucie Ann, "Beauty Around Us," *Space, Arrangement, Beauty in Schools* (Washington: Association for Childhood Education International, 1958).

McKim, Margaret G., Carl Hansen, and William L. Carter, *Learning to Teach in the Elementary School* (New York: The Macmillan Company, 1959).

Mehl, Marie A., Hubert Mills, and Harl R. Douglass, *Teaching in Elementary School,* 2nd ed. (New York: The Ronald Press Company, 1958).

Russell, David H., *Children Learn to Read,* 2nd ed. (Waltham, Mass.: Blaisdell Publishing Company, 1961).

Stendler, Celia B., *Teaching in the Elementary School* (New York: Harcourt, Brace & World, Inc., 1958).

Strang, Ruth M. and Dorothy K. Bracken, *Making Better Readers* (Boston: D. C. Heath and Company, 1957).

Thomas, Edith M., "Grouping in the Classroom," *Childhood Education,* 30:69–71 (October, 1953).

Thomas, Lawrence G., Lucien B. Kinney, Arthur P. Coladarci, Helen A. Fielstra, *Perspective on Teaching* (Englewood Cliffs, N.J.: Prentice-Hall, Inc., 1961).

Tooze, Ruth, *Your Children Want to Read* (Englewood Cliffs, N.J.: Prentice-Hall, Inc., 1957).

Witty, Paul A., "The Mental Health of the Teacher," Chapter 13 in Witty, Paul A. (chairman), *Mental Health in Modern Education,* The Fifty-fourth Yearbook of the National Society for the Study of Education, Part II (Chicago: University of Chicago Press, 1955).

Witty, Paul A., *Reading in Modern Education* (Boston: D. C. Heath and Company, 1949).

17

EVALUATION OF DEVELOPMENT IN READING

Hundreds of standard reading tests have appeared in the past fifty years. Many of these are periodically revised and widely used, while many others have become obscure or have vanished. Research literature abounds with reports on the nature and development of reading abilities, analysis and diagnosis of reading skills, and tests which aid in the evaluation of reading growth. A major problem in evaluation, however, involves determining what can or should be measured.

ESSENTIAL FACTORS IN EVALUATION

What Measurements Are Possible?

A perusal of reading-test manuals discloses a vast array of reading skills considered measurable. These may include such general skills as paragraph comprehension and rate of reading or the more definite skills of visual perception and word analysis.

Research workers have attempted to identify the basic skills in the reading process. Frederick Davis, for example, concluded from his study that word knowledge and reasoning were definitely independent factors which could be measured.[1] He felt too that finding inferences, determining literal meanings, and following the organization of a reading selection were perhaps measurable as independent factors. Margaret Conant concluded, however, that there were no measurable independent abilities in study-type reading.[2] Chester Harris came to a similar conclusion after

---

[1] Frederick B. Davis, "Fundamental Factors of Comprehension in Reading," *Psychometrika,* 11.249–255 (December, 1946).

[2] Margaret M. Conant, *The Construction of a Diagnostic Reading Test for Senior High School Students and College Freshmen* (New York: Teachers College, Columbia University, Contributions to Education No. 861, 1942).

examining seven supposedly separate reading skills; he considered that only one general reading ability was to be found which related to success on these tests.[3]

Roger Lennon, in a review of research on reading factors, pointed out that most of the research had been confined to high school and college levels:

> It is certainly conceivable that at lower grade levels reading ability is much less highly organized than it is at the high school, college, and adult levels. We may readily suppose that in the beginning stages of reading, emphasis is on the perceptual and mechanical aspects of the task to a greater extent than on central thought processes; and that, since the requisite perceptual skills are being acquired at varying rates by children, there may exist among pupils more readily differentiable degrees of proficiency in various components of reading ability.

He also sets forth this caution:

> We still have little experimental evidence about the reality of the distinctions that are made among the various reading abilities and about the validity of supposed diagnostic profiles of reading skills.[4]

Lennon, nevertheless, identified four components of reading ability that might be measured reliably:

> (1) a general verbal factor, (2) comprehension of explicitly stated material, (3) comprehension of implicit or latent meaning, and (4) an element that might be termed "appreciation."[5]

Scope of Evaluation

The problem, then, of evaluating growth in reading is complicated by the limitations of standard tests. Does this mean that evaluation of reading growth is not possible? Not necessarily. It does mean, however, that in our efforts we must include informal methods of evaluation as well as standardized approaches. Moreover, since reading growth should be considered in terms of the goals of the developmental reading program, the teacher should be interested not only in gains made on standard tests, but also in estimating changes or gains in children's attitudes toward reading, reading habits, taste in literature, and certain other aspects of behavior.

---

[3] Chester W. Harris, "Measurement of Comprehension of Literature: II, Studies of Measures of Comprehension," *School Review*, 56:332–342 (June, 1948).
[4] Roger T. Lennon, "What Can Be Measured?" *The Reading Teacher*, 15:332 (March, 1962).
[5] *Ibid*, p. 333.

The tests and procedures used for evaluation vary with grade levels and with the changing goals throughout the school years. Evaluation must always be considered in association with the goals sought. Thus the goals for beginning reading would include the following acquisitions:

1. Ability to identify a basic stock of words at sight
2. Recognition of words, phrases, and sentences
3. Proficiency in using context clues and picture clues
4. Skill in auditory and visual discrimination among letters and words
5. Capacity to apply knowledge in new reading situations
6. Tendency to find pleasure in reading
7. Use of a thoughtful approach to reading
8. Ability to adjust to different reading situations
9. Skill in reading simple passages silently and orally

The goals for the eighth grade would be quite different from those of beginning reading. By the time a pupil has reached the eighth grade, he should have acquired many skills involved in efficient silent and oral reading. Thus eighth-grade goals might include the acquisition of:

1. Extensive general and specific vocabularies
2. Accurate concepts for words in the content areas
3. Ability to employ study-skills effectively
4. Facility in applying phonetic and other word-analysis skills
5. Tendency to apply complex reading skills independently
6. Inclination to read extensively and intensively in accord with varied interests and developmental needs
7. Ability to read and interpret different kinds of materials
8. Improvement of behavior through reading
9. Rapid reading rate and high comprehension of materials in the content areas
10. Heightened interest, taste, and appreciation in reading

Because of difference in goals, evaluation of a reading program will differ markedly from level to level, as new skills are introduced, new purposes established, and new abilities developed. But there are some constants in evaluation which, broadly interpreted, pertain to all grades. The process of evaluation should enable the teacher of any grade (1) to ascertain the child's present level of ability and attainment, (2) to estimate the amount, rate, and quality of his learning, and (3) to offer effective guidance and direction for future growth. Teachers at various grade levels must relate these overall evaluative principles to the goals of their particular grade.

Complexity of Evaluation

The goals adopted by a teacher at any given level will be derived from a number of sources. Teachers' manuals which accompany basal series may provide objectives for particular grades as well as statements of desired outcomes. Courses of study may also serve as sources. Some pupils are not able to attain the reading goals of their grades, while others surpass these goals by wide margins.

In evaluating reading progress it has often been the custom to measure improvement solely by gains shown on standardized tests—sometimes compared with expectancies based on mental test ratings. It is the responsibility of the teacher to attempt to appraise each child individually in consideration of his ability, his interests, his attitudes, the amount and nature of his reading, and his success in applying reading skills in many fields.

It is highly desirable for an entire school to plan a continuous development program in which goals are sequentially set forth. In such a school all teachers work together in setting up the goals and estimating the progress of groups and individuals. Anyone who has been fortunate enough to have a part in designing such a developmental reading program will appreciate the advantages of the school-wide approach. Teachers help each other learn what is expected of pupils in different grades. Thus, the senior high school teacher may realize perhaps for the first time that one of the slow readers in his room needs some basic skill instruction; this teacher may obtain helpful suggestions from teachers in the lower grades. Thus teachers of one grade level become resource persons for teachers of other grades.

EVALUATION PROCEDURES

It is obvious that diagnosis, guidance, and appraisal should be considered closely related phases of reading instruction. Only when the teacher knows thoroughly each child's beginning status can progress be estimated accurately. Successful teachers of reading are therefore devoting the first few weeks of the school year to a study of each child, using techniques similar to those repeated at a later time to judge the amount of growth. It is desirable to record findings systematically so that they can be used in formulating objectives, in planning guidance, and in estimating progress.

Many teachers have employed simple record forms on which to enter the results of their initial study of the child. The information thus recorded may be supplemented from time to time by observations made in the classroom, on the playground, and elsewhere. Periodically, perhaps once a month or bimonthly, these teachers may examine and compare test results and other entries. In this way evaluation contributes important insights concerning children's changing needs. Thus the process continues: diagnosis, guidance, appraisal—and further diagnosis, further guidance, further appraisal—an unending cycle.

Evaluative procedures that a teacher may use will be both formal and informal.

Informal Evaluation

Informal evaluation includes the use of observation by teachers, anecdotal records, cumulative records, checklists, informal tests, inventories, interviews, and self-appraisal conferences.

Teacher Observations

In various reading situations, the teacher observes each child as he works with the teacher, with small groups, with the total class, or independently. Items observed and considered important in the various situations should be recorded. The teacher may note, for example, that the child works and reads well alone or with the teacher, fairly well in a small group, but seems to lose interest in reading in larger groups. The teacher will recognize that the child is not experiencing a reading difficulty so much as a problem of social adjustment. Such a child needs support and sympathetic guidance, for he is lost in a crowd. His reading may be exactly what is to be expected for his age, grade, and abilities, but adjustments must be made to promote his social development.

Continuous daily observation is important, since it is only by a recognition of the sequence and direction of development that a relatively accurate picture of growth is attained. Noting only the errors a child makes may prove misleading. His strengths are as important as his weaknesses and should be noted. Moreover diagnosis of needs should be made from several or repeated observations. Thus a teacher might observe that on a particular day Bill is not reading as well as usual. Rather than decide, on the basis of one day's observation, that Bill needs some special help, it is better to study him for several days to determine if the initial observation is justifiable. *Needs should be estimated from adequate samples of a child's behavior.*

Anecdotal Records

Keeping records of children's behavior should not consume too much of the teacher's time, for he cannot be expected to take copious notes of every child's behavior and spend long hours writing up the results. There are events, however, which illustrate clearly something significant about a child's reading attitudes and skills. There are occasions when a marked change in attitudes or abilities may take place. Such times and events are worthy of record, since they highlight the child's direction of growth. When the teacher evaluates the child's growth over a semester or a school year, the anecdotal record may serve to provide landmarks of growth. These records are usually extremely helpful to the "next teacher," too. Some teachers discuss in their conferences with pupils the anecdotal records and attempt to guide the pupils into an appreciation of their own behavior and its significance.

Anecdotal records can be an important part of reading evaluation, but such records need not be too lengthy or too frequently made. Records that describe succinctly a child's stage of growth are desirable. A few such entries in the record throughout a semester may be sufficient.

Cumulative Records

Schools increasingly are using cumulative records which accompany pupils as they progress from grade to grade. The most desirable place to keep these records is in the classroom, where the teacher has ready access to them. Since cumulative records at their best include an overall view of the child's total development, they are especially helpful to the teacher of developmental reading; such items as health, achievement test results, and evaluations of behavior often afford essential help in offering guidance. It is in the cumulative records that anecdotal reports belong, since they often afford insight concerning a child's previous development that helps to explain his present status.

At the beginning of each school year the teacher needs to become acquainted with the pupils as individuals. If he has access to cumulative records and has had an opportunity to examine them well before the first day of school, he will be able to treat his new pupils with greater understanding and appreciation.

An example of a useful record form is reproduced here.

[6] Cumulative Student Records. Courtesy of the New Britain Public Schools, New Britain, Connecticut.

PUBLIC SCHOOLS — OBJECTIVE TEST RECORD — GRADES KGN VIII — NEW BRITAIN, CONNECTICUT

NAME _____ (Last) _____ (First) _____ (Middle)

BIRTHDATE _____ (Month) _____ (Day) _____ (Year)

INTELLIGENCE TESTS (Including Readiness Tests)

Grade	Date	TITLE OF TEST	Form	C.A.	M.A.	I.Q.	Standard Score	Local %ile

ACHIEVEMENT TESTS

Grade	Date	TITLE OF TEST	Form	C.A.	Grade Place.	Standard Score	Local %ile

SPECIAL TESTS

INTEREST TESTS %ILE

0	1	2	3	4	5	6	7	8	9

EDUCATIONAL RECORD - GRADES IX-XII

PUBLIC SCHOOLS   **NEW BRITAIN, CONNECTICUT**

NAME _____ (Last) _____ (First) _____ (Middle)

BIRTHDATE _____ (Month) (Day) (Year)   ADDRESS _____ (At time of graduation)

IX
Date Entered _____   Name of School _____

COURSES	1st Qtr.	2nd Qtr.	3rd Qtr.	4th Qtr.	Av.	Per.	Attendance and Credit	Teacher
English							Days Absent / Days Tardy / Dismissed / Promoted / Dbl. Promoted / Not Promoted / Average Year / Credit Forward / Credit Year	
Phys. Ed.							Total Credit	

Date Withdrawn (Grade IX) _____   Reason _____

X
Date Entered _____   Name of School _____

COURSES	1st Qtr.	2nd Qtr.	3rd Qtr.	4th Qtr.	Av. Cr.	Attendance and Credit	Teacher
English						Days Absent / Days Tardy / Dismissed / Promoted / Dbl. Promoted / Not Promoted / Average Year / Credit Forward / Credit Year	
Phys. Ed.						Total Credit	

Date Withdrawn (Grade X) _____   Reason _____

XI
Date Entered _____   Name of School _____

COURSES	1st Qtr.	2nd Qtr.	3rd Qtr.	4th Qtr.	Av. Cr.	Attendance and Credit	Teacher
English						Days Absent / Days Tardy / Dismissed / Promoted / Dbl. Promoted / Not Promoted / Av. Year / Credit Forward / Credit Year	
Amer. History							
Phys. Ed.						Total Credit	

Date Withdrawn (Grade XI) _____   Reason _____

XII
Date Entered _____   Name of School _____

COURSES	1st Qtr.	2nd Qtr.	3rd Qtr.	4th Qtr.	Av. Cr.	Teacher
English						
Phys. Ed.						

Total Credit _____   Date Withdrawn (Grade XII) _____   Reason _____

Passing Grade D   Certification Grade B   Weeks Per Year _____   Minutes Per Period _____

Graduation Date _____   Rank in Class _____   Class Size _____

TEST DATA

NAME OF TEST	DATE GIVEN	RESULTS

_____ (Authorized Signature)   _____ (Position)

_____ (Date)

NEW BRITAIN SENIOR HIGH SCHOOL AND PULASKI SENIOR HIGH SCHOOL } ACCREDITED BY { NEW ENGLAND ASSOCIATION OF SECONDARY SCHOOLS AND COLLEGES / CONNECTICUT STATE DEPARTMENT OF EDUCATION

THIS SPACE RESERVED FOR ADHESIVE-BACKED TEST RESULTS

PUBLIC SCHOOLS — SOCIAL AND PERSONAL RECORD — NEW BRITAIN, CONNECTICUT

NAME ....
        (Last)   (First)   (Middle)

FAMILY HISTORY: (In Pencil)

Father Living? .... Mother Living? .... Lives With Both of Them? .... If Not, With Which One? ....
If Not Living With Either Parent, Lives With .... Relation, If Any? ....

Complete For Parents and/or People With Whom Pupil Is Living. Indicate Relationship. Include Mothers Maiden Name.	Name	Address (In Pencil)	City, State and Country of Birth	Language Spoken In Home

Father's Occupation	Date	Firm Name	Mother's Occupation	Date	Firm Name

Brothers and Sisters (List in Order of Age, Oldest First)

Name	Birthdate	Address (In Pencil)	Remarks

Additional Information of Significant Value For The Understanding of This Pupil

Date	Recorder	

Contacts With Special Services (Include Community Agencies and School Services)

Department	Date and Initials	Date and Initials	Date and Initials	Date and Initials	Date and Initials	Date and Initials	Date and Initials
Attendance							
Guidance							
Psychological							
Reading							
Social Work							
Speech and Hearing							
Other							
Other							
Other							

PUBLIC SCHOOLS   C I T I Z E N S H I P   NEW BRITAIN, CONNECTICUT

*TRAITS (To Be Filled in By Transferring Teacher)	Grade	Grade	Grade	Grade	Grade	Grade	Grade	Grade	Grade	Grade	Grade	Grade	Grade	Grade	Grade
Conduct															
Effort															
Initiative															
Responsibility															
Leadership															
Attitude Toward Work															
Courtesy															
Respect For Property															
Emotional Stability															
Social Maturity															

*CODE: 1. Unsatisfactory   2. Average   3. Outstanding

**SPECIAL INTERESTS, ABILITIES AND ACTIVITIES	Grade	Grade	Grade	Grade	Grade	Grade	Grade
Art							
Athletics							
Club Membership							
Club Officer							
Music—Chorus							
Band							
Orchestra							
Safety Patrol							
Honors							
National Honor Society							
Other							
Other							

**When Appropriate, Write In Activity, As: Violin, President, Football, Intramural, etc.; otherwise use check.

PUBLIC SCHOOLS HEALTH RECORD NEW BRITAIN, CONNECTICUT

NAME _____ BIRTHDATE _____ ADDRESS _____ MALE _____
  Last   First   Middle   Month Day Year   FEMALE ____

HISTORY	Date		Date		Date		Date	
Chicken Pox		Mumps		Rheumatism		Pneumonia		Cerebral Palsy		Seizures	
Measles		Diphtheria		Chorea		Tuberculosis		Nephrosis		Tonsillectomy	
German Measles		Scarlet Fever		Smallpox		Whooping Cough		Muscular Dystrophy		Operations	
Poliomyelitis		Septic Sore Throat		Typhoid		Diabetes		Other		Other	

PREVENTIVE AND CONTROL MEASURES

Smallpox Vaccination _____ Diphtheria Immunization _____ Tuberculin Test _____ Chest X-Ray _____ Other _____
Whooping Cough Immunization _____ Scarlet Fever Immunization _____ Blood Pressure _____ Polio Immunization _____ Other _____
Dental Prophylaxis and Application Sodium Fluoride: Grade 2 _____ Grade 5 _____ Grade 8 _____

School															
Grade and Age				Date				Date				Date			
Date of Examination		G.	A.		G.	A.		G.	A.		G.	A.		G.	A.
Height (in inches)															
Weight															
Nutrition															
Eyes*	*V.A. s Glasses	Both	R / L	Both	R / L	Both	R / L	Both	R / L	Both	R / L	Both	R / L	Both	R / L
	*V.A. s Glasses	Both	R / L	Both	R / L	Both	R / L	Both	R / L	Both	R / L	Both	R / L	Both	R / L
	*V.A. c Glasses	Both	R / L	Both	R / L	Both	R / L	Both	R / L	Both	R / L	Both	R / L	Both	R / L
	*V.A. c Glasses	Both	R / L	Both	R / L	Both	R / L	Both	R / L	Both	R / L	Both	R / L	Both	R / L
Other Defect															
Ears															
Teeth** (Temporary / Permanent)															
Gums															
Tonsils***															
Nose															
Glands (Cervical / Thyroid / Other (specify))															
Heart															
Lungs															
Orthopedic (Struc'l Defects / Posture / Feet)															
Nervous Sys. (specify if Epil.)															
Anemia															
Skin															
Hernia															
General Condition**															
Name of Examining Phys.															

Code For Physical Examination:
N or Blank Space = No Defect Found
U = Underweight
O = Overweight
*V.A. = Visual Acuity
s = Without Glasses
c = With Glasses
Vision = 20/20 to 20/30 is Normal. All Other Fractions indicate impaired Vision
**Good, Fair, Poor
***Tonsils
R = Removed
2 = Normal
3 = Slight
4 = Large and Diseased, Need Removing

PUBLIC SCHOOLS   HEALTH RECORD (Continued)   NEW BRITAIN, CONNECTICUT

NAME _____ Last _____ First _____ Middle _____

OFF YEAR RECORD OF HEIGHT, WEIGHT, AND EYE TEST

Grade and Age	G. A.	G. A.	G. A.	G. A.	G. A.	G. A.	G. A.	G. A.	G. A.
Date of Exam.									
Height									
Weight									
V.A. s Glasses	R / L /	R / L /	R / L /	R / L /	R / L /	R / L /	R / L /	R / L /	R / L /
V.A. s Glasses	Both /	Both /	Both /	Both /	Both /	Both /	Both /	Both /	Both /
V.A. c Glasses	R / L /	R / L /	R / L /	R / L /	R / L /	R / L /	R / L /	R / L /	R / L /
V.A. c Glasses	Both /	Both /	Both /	Both /	Both /	Both /	Both /	Both /	Both /

AUDIOMETER TEST

DATE	R L	R L	R L	R L	R L	R L	R L	R L	R L	R L
Pass Sweep Check at 15 Decibels										
* Class of Loss										
125										
250										
500										
1000										
2000										
4000										
8000										

* 1. Slight   2. Moderate   3. Severe

SUMMARY OF OBSERVATIONS OF TEACHERS AND OTHERS

DATE	NAME	

RECORD OF CONSULTATION WITH PARENTS
(Date and by whom with summary of advice)

Checklists

To obtain a fairly comprehensive check on reading attainment, the teacher may use a checklist which includes the skills stressed in the teachers' manuals for various series of basal readers.

Data concerning a child's specific reading abilities may be obtained by observing the child as he reads silently and orally. For example, the teacher can determine whether the pupil is able to note details, to follow directions, and to obtain the central thought of paragraphs in different types of materials read silently. In oral reading, too, the pupil's habits may be observed and specific needs determined.

An excellent time to gather information concerning a child's abilities is during periods of directed silent reading. At this time the teacher can observe each child's habits and can check his areas of need. Such lists yield valuable data which supplement and extend information obtained from standardized tests.

Checklists include oral reading proficiencies, silent reading abilities, study-skills, etc. A sample of a typical checklist which a fourth-grade teacher might use to appraise silent reading abilities is presented on page 388.

Informal Test

Teachers may want to devise informal tests to answer such questions as: Have the pupils achieved expected reading goals? Did I communicate concepts clearly and did the pupils grasp them? What did they learn which I did not teach and what did I attempt to teach that they did not learn? These are some of the questions teachers may wish to have answered. It is mainly by means of informal tests that such information about reading gains can be obtained.

Evaluation of students by means of informal tests is to some extent an evaluation of the teacher. If children do not do well on the teacher-designed tests, a number of hypotheses might well be questioned:

1. *Reading goals were set too high.* Sometimes a teacher has a class in which the abilities of his pupils do not compare favorably with those of previous classes. The teacher may have been aware of this fact, but may have continued to seek inappropriate goals set for other classes.

2. *The test was not well constructed.* It is not uncommon for a teacher to attempt to evaluate too many items covering too wide a range of information in a single test. It is better to sample attainments in a few areas and within a somewhat restricted range.

GRADE 4 — SILENT READING ABILITIES CHECK LIST

PUPIL _____   GROUP _____

	First Check		Second Check		Third Check
	NEEDS DIAG-NOSED	GUID-ANCE	EVALU-ATION	FUR-THER GUID-ANCE	GROWTH OB-SERVED
PHASE OF GROWTH					
A. Reading itself					
1. Amount					
2. Range					
3. Intensity					
4. Quality					
B. Reading abilities					
1. Ability to comprehend: words, phrases, sentences, paragraphs, whole selections					
2. Ability to relate materials read to past experience					
3. Ability to organize and express ideas					
4. Ability to criticize and evaluate materials read					
5. Ability to use books and library efficiently					
6. Ability to follow sequence of events or ideas					
7. Ability to compare evidence from different sources					
8. Ability to verify ideas through stated facts					
C. Related language abilities					
1. Oral expression					
2. Written expression					
D. Self-appraisal					
E. Parents' appraisal					

3. *The teaching was faulty.* Different children and different groups learn in varied ways. Although there are some general principles of learning, most learning follows specific individual patterns. The teacher who designs a test and finds that many students perform poorly on it

may well reexamine and evaluate his teaching. Is he expecting too much? Has he neglected motivation? Has he presented material too rapidly?

Interviews

The teacher of reading often finds interviews with the child's parents and other teachers of value in determining the amount and nature of a pupil's improvement. Questions such as the following have been used with success:
1. Have you noticed any improvement in the child's reading:
    (a) in the amount, the breadth, and the quality of his reading?
    (b) in the speed and accuracy with which he reads silently? orally?
2. Have you noticed any improvement in his attitudes toward his reading, especially in his gains as an independent reader?
3. Have you observed any improvement in his personal and social adjustments which may be an outgrowth of his reading:
    (a) in his play and recreational activities?
    (b) in character traits such as self-confidence, tolerance, etc.?
    (c) in ability to get along well with adults? with other children?
4. Does the child show greater interest in reading and owning books?

In addition to parent interviews the teacher may wish to arrange informal talks with his pupils, during which each pupil's interests as shown on the Interest Inventory may be discussed. (See Chapter 3, page 52; also Appendix C, page 406.) Discussions with each child will include his favorite play activities, his hobbies, his vocational ambitions, his wishes and personal problems, his attitudes toward home and school, his preferences in movies, radio, and television programs, and his reading experiences. An interest inventory offers a convenient device for obtaining significant facts which can be used in guiding the student's growth in reading.

Self-appraisal Conferences

Children are usually eager to discuss their reading progress with their teachers, and frequently show keen insight regarding their problems as well as their needs. Often children divulge information which cannot be derived in any other way. Questions such as the following have proved provocative for the pupil to consider:
1. What progress have I made in reading (as revealed by tests, reading record, etc.)?

(a) Have I gained in speed and accuracy?
  (b) Has my reading increased in amount? Has it become more varied as to type? as to content?
  (c) Have I read more books on a single subject than formerly?
2. Have I done my best? Or could I have made greater growth had I used my time to better advantage or had I made wiser choices of reading material?
3. What are my greatest needs in reading?
4. How can I best proceed in meeting those needs; that is, what should be my reading plans for next semester or next year? How should I begin to carry them out?

Informal Reading Inventories

The use of informal reading inventories has been discussed on pages 314–317 in terms of the remedial reading program. Similar techniques may be used in the developmental program. Their use is especially valuable when a child enters school late, transfers from another school, or for some reason has an incomplete cumulative folder. The teacher, wishing to determine the pupil's readiness for the work of a particular grade and to ascertain his reading strengths and weaknesses, may employ to advantage an informal inventory. The results of the inventory may be helpful, too, in determining the instructional level of any pupil.

Formal Evaluation

Standardized Tests

Many standardized tests are used in the schools today.[7] These tests have considerable value, since they have usually been given to large numbers of children and their validity and reliability have been reasonably well established. From such tests national norms are built against which a teacher may evaluate his class. Such information has value to the teacher in helping him decide on the goals for the class, as well as in enabling him to know on what levels individual and group endeavor might be initiated most profitably.

The criteria usually set forth for the selection of standard tests include: validity, reliability, objectivity, standardization, and the provision of forms.

[7] For a representative list of standardized tests, consult Table XV, pp. 303–309.

(a) *Validity*. Does the test measure that which the makers purport to measure? The teacher should examine the manuals which accompany such tests to ascertain how the tests are made and what they include. Some tests are very short and afford only crude measures of speed and comprehension; others include rate of reading. Still others are semi-diagnostic, while some are thoroughly diagnostic and test an aggregate of minute abilities associated with reading. Yet the varied tests are classified under the general heading of reading. The teacher should therefore choose the test that best suits his needs and represents his goals. Additional help may be obtained in judging the merits of various tests from Oscar Buros' *Fifth Mental Measurements Yearbook*.[8] Varied opinions and pertinent information concerning both mental and educational tests are found in the yearbook.

(b) *Reliability*. Reliability is a technical term which refers to some mechanical features of a test—actually the degree of correlation between students' scores on odd and even test items and the extent of agreement of the scores of pupils on different forms of the tests. Test manuals may be consulted to obtain this information. Relatively high correlations are recommended for group tests and very high ones for individual and diagnostic examinations.

(c) *Objectivity*. Objectivity is also a consideration in test selection. Are the tests of such a type and are directions sufficiently explicit that independent persons will obtain the same results from administering them?

(d) *Standardization*. The standardization of a test refers to the provision of age and grade norms so that pupils' scores may be readily interpreted. Norms are average scores obtained for representative samples of pupils in various age and grade groups.

(e) *Forms*. To avoid practice effects when the test is repeated, different forms of standard tests may be used. The forms contain equally difficult but different materials. In selecting a test, the teacher should check to be sure that reliability among the forms is high. Most standardized tests are available in two or more forms.

Standardized tests of silent and oral reading are helpful supplements to other information. The teacher should not attach too great significance to the results of standardized tests nor overestimate their accuracy in revealing the pupil's reading status. It is well to bear in mind that the results of such tests are only suggestive of a child's true reading status. For example, Emmett Betts found that

[8] Oscar K. Buros (editor), *The Fifth Mental Measurements Yearbook* (Highland Park, N. J.: The Gryphon Press, 1959).

not one of several standardized reading tests designed for use at the fifth-grade level was adequate for determining the achievement levels of pupils at upper or lower ends of the distribution. Although ten per cent of the class did not exhibit desirable reading behavior on first-grade materials, some of the tests graded these pupils no lower than second-, third-, or fourth-grade level. In general, standardized tests may be expected to rate those pupils from one to four grades above their manifest achievement levels. While this is not an all-out indictment of achievement tests in reading, it is a caution to those who attempt to use standardized test data as the sole criterion for appraising achievement level.[9]

Such considerations make clear that it is necessary to supplement the knowledge of a child's reading status derived from standardized tests by an estimate of his success in comprehending whole episodes or stories. Teachers are finding it practical to study the child's performance in reading from different types of reading materials *above* and *below* as well as *at* the reading level indicated by a standardized test score. In addition, understanding of each child's reading can be enhanced by examining a record of the books he has read in and out of school. In a thorough appraisal, standardized reading tests, like intelligence tests, play a part. Their significance should be recognized but not overstressed.

Another type of objective test may be employed to aid the teacher of reading. The results of intelligence tests are valuable for the classroom teacher if they are used with discrimination.

These tests are of two kinds—individual and group. Individual tests such as the *Stanford-Binet Intelligence Scale* and the *Wechsler Intelligence Scale for Children* are given by specially trained individuals. The teacher will find it valuable, when results of individual tests are unavailable, to obtain results of group intelligence tests such as the *California Test of Mental Ability* or the *Primary Mental Ability Test*. The results of such tests can readily be interpreted and may be used by the teacher to estimate roughly the pupil's potential ability. Comparison can then be made of this estimate with the pupil's attainment in reading.

School-wide Reading Surveys

Standardized reading tests are occasionally given throughout an entire school system. Clifford Bush suggests the value of such school-wide testing for both the school and the public.

[9] Emmett Albert Betts, *Foundations of Reading Instruction* (New York: American Book Company, 1957), p. 441.

Just as business and industry take an inventory, the school needs to assess its reading program thoroughly and formally to get an over-all picture of the students, the teaching, and the functioning of the curriculum. The reading survey is a formal technique for taking inventory of the current program and perhaps proposing improvements in the program. The public is critical of the schools, and individuals and groups are raising questions about current reading programs which deserve answers based on facts and professional interpretations of the facts.[10]

On the basis of the results of survey tests, an entire school system may decide to reexamine its reading programs and try to organize a more effective one for all grades. Bush suggests that survey testing is also of benefit in: "(1) providing an inventory of present practices, curriculum, and teaching, (2) providing facts to aid in answering the critics, (3) aiding the new teacher in organizing and teaching, and (4) identifying the problems and organizing the facts so that solutions can be proposed for the problem."[11]

Case Studies by Teachers

Another form of evaluation, more detailed and complex, is sometimes carried on by the classroom teacher. In almost every classroom the teacher will find some persistently poor readers whose special problems necessitate the making of somewhat detailed case studies. Actually, studies require simply an extension and intensification of methods already described as essential in understanding the needs of all pupils. Data should be obtained to reveal each pupil's physical condition, his mental status, his social and emotional maturity, his school history, and his home background. The extent of the study will be determined by the school situation as well as by the teacher's experience and competence in diagnostic work.[12]

It is the conviction of the authors of this book that the classroom teacher can readily become qualified to make case studies which will reveal the status and needs of many pupils who require individual help and encouragement to overcome their special problems. Of course, the services of well-organized clinics are needed for some cases, but it has been shown that many handicapped pupils will respond favorably to the

---

[10] Clifford L. Bush, "School Reading Surveys," *The Reading Teacher,* 15:351–355 (March, 1962).
[11] *Ibid.,* p. 352.
[12] Paul A. Witty, *Reading in Modern Education* (Boston: D. C. Heath and Company, 1949), pp. 225 ff.

help offered by the classroom teacher who has diagnosed their special needs. When case studies reveal serious defects in vision or hearing, or anomalies in learning, the pupils should be referred to competent specialists for more expert diagnosis and treatment.

No single design for making case studies can be recommended, since the training of the teacher and the circumstances associated with his particular teaching situation will determine the extent of his study; however, the accompanying outline points to some significant areas for investigation. It will be noted also that these areas are comparable to the fields of study discussed in the more general treatment of evaluation found in Chapter 13.

CASE STUDY OUTLINE

1. *Identification Data*
    Date of study, name of teacher making study, name of school
    Name, sex, age, address, and school grade of pupil
2. *Reason for Study*
    Nature of problem
3. *Home Conditions*
    Character of home
    Father's and mother's occupation
    Social and economic status of parents
    Names of brothers and sisters; their academic backgrounds and records; their attitude toward the pupil being studied
    Attitudes of parents toward the pupil's problem
    Nature and amount of reading materials in the home
    Attitude of parents toward reading
    Interview with the parents and siblings in the pupil's home
4. *Educational History*
    Present scholastic record of pupil
    Previous marks
    School history
5. *Mental Test Data*
    Results of group or individual examinations of intelligence
    Previous test results
6. *Educational Status*
    Results of standard tests and check lists disclosing strengths and weaknesses
7. *Interests and Attitudes*
    Strong interests
    Attitudes toward reading
    Results from interest inventories, anecdotal records, interviews, and observations
8. *Social and Emotional Maturity*
    Response to other pupils; to teachers

   Amount and nature of social participation
   Play activities
   Behavior disorders
   Ratings by parents and other teachers
 9. *Special Abilities or Defects*
   Results of questionnaires, observations, and reports of members of family or of friends
10. *Recommendations for Remedial Work*
   Suggestions for school; for home
   Steps in remedial program

CONCLUDING STATEMENT

The foregoing discussion has revealed clearly the need for comprehensive records to provide adequate evaluation of pupil growth in and through reading. The teacher of reading will estimate gains by reference to the following:

1. Increase in amount of reading of different kinds of materials
2. Progress shown on standardized tests
3. Success in reading materials in the different subject areas
4. Increase in ability to read critically and for varied purposes
5. Improvement in the play or recreation pattern
6. Improvement shown by the reports of parents and of other teachers concerning each pupil's reading
7. Gains reflected by the pupil's own evaluation of his status and needs

The limitations of standardized tests force the teacher to supplement formal testing by informal procedures in determining the specific needs of pupils. A variety of informal procedures have been suggested in this chapter. In essence, the success of the reading program at all levels depends on the teacher's ability to ascertain and meet the needs of pupils. The diagnosis of needs is not a simple process nor is the fulfillment of needs a task which requires only a single procedure. It is the responsibility of the teacher to use a variety of approaches such as we have suggested for studying pupil's needs and for evaluating development in and through reading.

Selected References

Austin, Mary C., Clifford Bush, and Mildred Huebner, *Reading Evaluation* (New York: The Ronald Press Company, 1961).

Austin, Mary C., Coleman Morrison, Helen J. Kenney, and Ruth R. Gutmann, *The Torchlighters: Tomorrow's Teachers of Reading* (Cambridge: Harvard University Press, 1961).

Baron, Denis, and Harold W. Bernard, *Evaluation Techniques for Classroom Teachers* (New York: McGraw-Hill Book Co., 1958).

Betts, Emmett Albert, *Foundations of Reading Instruction* (New York: American Book Company, 1957).

Dewar, John A., "When Teachers Help Plan the Curriculum," *Educational Leadership*, 19:5–7 (October, 1961).

Gans, Roma, *A Study of Critical Reading Comprehension in the Intermediate Grades* (New York: Teachers College, Columbia University, Contributions to Education No. 811, 1940).

Hall, William E., and Francis P. Robinson, "An Analytical Approach to the Study of Reading Skills," *Journal of Educational Psychology*, 36:429–442 (October, 1945).

Harris, Chester W., "Measurement of Comprehension of Literature: II. Studies of Measures of Comprehension," *School Review*, 56:332–342 (June, 1948).

Hunt, J. T., "Selecting a High School Reading Test," *High School Journal*, 39:49–52 (October, 1955).

Robinson, Helen M. (editor), *Evaluation of Reading*, Supplementary Educational Monographs no. 88 (Chicago: University of Chicago Press, 1958).

Smith, Eugene R., and Ralph W. Tyler, *Appraising and Recording Student Progress* (New York: Harper & Row, Publishers, 1942).

Thomas, R. Murray, *Judging Student Progress* (New York: David McKay Co., Inc., 1954).

Tormey, Mary K., and Walter G. Patterson, "Developmental Reading and Student Evaluation," *Journal of Developmental Reading*, 2:30–43 (Winter, 1959).

Witty, Paul A., *Reading in Modern Education* (Boston: D. C. Heath and Company, 1949).

Appendix A

SUPPLEMENTARY READING SERIES

These books are primarily designed to reinforce basal reading programs. They provide, too, for broader reading and foster independence in reading.

1. American Book Company, 55 Fifth Avenue, New York, New York 10003

    Golden Rule Series. Modern *McGuffey Readers* that emphasize morals and human relations themes. (Grades 1–6) *Open Windows, Open Doors, Open Roads, Paths to Follow, Frontiers to Explore, Widening Horizons.*

2. Benefic Press, 1900 North Narragansett, Chicago, Illinois 60639

    Animal Adventure Series. Five titles of wild animal stories based on scientific fact. (Preprimer, primer, and grade 1) *Becky, the Rabbit; Squeaky, the Squirrel; Skippy, the Skunk; Sandy, the Swallow; Pudgy, the Beaver.*

    Button Family Adventure Series. Affords practice of newly learned skills in high-interest, easy-to-read materials. (Grades 1–3) Among the twelve titles are: *The Buttons at the Zoo, The Buttons and the Pet Parade, The Buttons at the Farm, The Buttons Go Camping.*

    Cowboy Sam Series. Adult characters in high-interest stories of Western adventures. (Grades 1–3) Among the fifteen titles are: *Cowboy Sam and Dandy, Cowboy Sam and Miss Lily, Cowboy Sam and Shorty, Cowboy Sam and the Fair, Cowboy Sam and the Rustlers.*

    Dan Frontier Series. Inspiring portrayals of life in frontier days. (Grades 1–4) Among the eleven titles are: *Dan Frontier, Dan Frontier Goes Hunting, Dan Frontier Scouts with the Army, Dan Frontier Goes to Congress.*

    Easy-to-Read Books. Lively, appealing stories about a precocious parakeet. (Grade 1) *Pretty Bird, Surprise Egg, Pony Ring, Big Top, Monkey Island, Poker Dog.*

    Sailor Jack Series. Authentic information in carefully controlled vocabulary books on life in the Navy. (Reading level, grades 1–3; interest level, grades 1–6) Among the ten titles: *Sailor Jack and Homer Pots, Sailor Jack and Bluebell, Sailor Jack and the Ball Game, Sailor Jack and the Target Ship, Sailor Jack Goes North.*

Space-Age Books. Exciting, realistic accounts of how spacemen will live on their explorations. (Reading level, grades 2–3; interest level, grades 2–6) *Peter and the Unlucky Rocket, Peter and the Big Balloon, Peter and the Two-Hour Moon, Peter and the Moon Trip, Peter and the Rocket Ship.*

World of Adventures Series. Adventure stories based on expeditions to mines, to mountains, and under the sea. (Reading level, grades 2–4; interest level, grades 2–7) *Lost Uranium Mine, Hunting Grizzly Bears, Fire on the Mountain, City Beneath the Sea.*

3. The Bobbs-Merrill Company, Inc., 4300 West 62nd Street, Indianapolis, Indiana 46206

Best of Children's Literature Series. A collection of classics of children's literature. (Grades 1–6) *Sunny and Gay, Foolish and Wise, Fun All Around, Shining Hour, Time for Adventure, Beyond the Horizon.*

Childhood of Famous Americans Series. Interesting biographies of famous Americans. (Grades 4–8) Among the 122 titles are: *Abe Lincoln: Frontier Boy; Amelia Earhart: Kansas Girl; Buffalo Bill: Boy of the Plains; Davy Crockett: Young Rifleman; Dolly Madison: Quaker Girl.*

4. Children's Press, Inc., Jackson Boulevard and Racine Avenue, Chicago, Illinois 60612

Enchantment of America Books. Informational books about regions of the United States and of various states. (Reading level, grade 4; interest level, grades 4–9) Among the ten titles: *High Country—The Rocky Mountain and Plateau States; Lakes, Hills and Prairies—The Middlewestern States; Illinois; Ohio; Pacific Shores—The Pacific States.*

Indians of the Americas. The heritage of the American Indian accurately portrayed. (Reading level, grades 2–4; interest level, grades 2–6) Among the twenty-one titles: *Apaches, Cherokees, Delawares, The Hopi Indian Butterfly Dance, Seminoles.*

I Want to Be Books. Introduce children to many peoples and occupations in the world. (Reading level, grade 1; interest level, grades K–3) Among the thirty-six titles: *I Want to Be an Airplane Hostess, I Want to Be a Baker, I Want to Be a Doctor, I Want to Be a Librarian, I Want to Be a Pilot, I Want to Be a Zoo-Keeper.*

Tizz Books. Novel-length horse stories. (Reading level, grades 2–3; interest level, grades 1–4) *Tizz, Tizz and Company, Tizz Is a Cow Pony, Tizz on a Pack Trip, Tizz Plays Santa Claus, Tizz Takes a Trip.*

True Books. Books designed to create interests in children. (Reading level, grades 1–3; interest level, grades K–6) Among the sixty-two titles: *The True Book of African Animals, The True Book of Bac-*

teria, The True Book of Animals of the Sea and Shore, The True Book of Cloth, The True Book of Dinosaurs, The True Book of Knights, The True Book of Space.

5. Garrard Publishing Company, 1607 North Market Street, Champaign, Illinois 61821

    Basic Vocabulary Books. An abundance of easy-to-read practice material for an enrichment program. (Reading level, grade 2; interest level, grades 1–6) Among the sixteen titles: *Animal Stories, Circus Stories, Dog Stories, Folk Stories, Horse Stories, Irish Stories, Lion and Tiger Stories, Navaho Stories, Tepee Stories.*

    Discovery Books. Adventure stories about famous people. (Reading level, grade 3; interest level, grades 2–5) Among the thirty-one titles: *Alexander Graham Bell, Buffalo Bill, Daniel Boone, George Washington, Ulysses S. Grant, William Penn.*

    First Reading Books. Books especially designed for beginning readers. (Reading level, grade 1; interest level, grades 1–4) Among the sixteen titles: *Once There Was a Bear, Once There Was an Elephant, Once There Was a Rabbit, I Like Cats, Some Are Small, Zoo Is Home.*

    Folklore of the World Books. Folklore through glimpses of characteristic customs and native culture is opened to the reader. (Reading level, grade 3; interest level, grades 2–8) Among the eleven titles: *Stories from old China, Stories from Old Egypt, Stories from Old Russia, Stories from France, Stories from India, Stories from Italy, Stories from Spain.*

    Holiday Books. Informative books about our holidays. (Reading level, grade 3; interest level, grades 2–5) *Spring Holidays, Fourth of July, Halloween, Thanksgiving.*

    Junior Science Books. An opportunity for children to read for pleasure about nature and the world around them. (Reading level, grade 3; interest level, grades 2–5) Among the nineteen titles: *Junior Science Book of Bacteria, Junior Science Book of Heat, Junior Science Book of Big Cats, Junior Science Book of Flying.*

6. Ginn and Company, Statler Building, Back Bay Post Office Box 191, Boston, Massachusetts 02117

    Enchantment Readers. A collection of literary classics. (Grades 1–6) *Come with Us, Under the Apple Tree, Open the Gate, Ranches and Rainbows, Fun and Fancy, Down Story Roads, Along Story Trails, On Story Wings.*

7. Grosset and Dunlap, Inc., 1107 Broadway, New York, New York 10010

    Little Pepper Books. Adventures of the Little Peppers which children should enjoy. (Grades 4–8) Among the twelve titles: *Adventures of*

Joel Pepper, Five Little Peppers at School, Five Little Peppers Abroad.

We-Were-There Books. Historical events come to life through the many books of this series. (Grades 4–9) Among the thirty-five titles: *At Pearl Harbor, With Richard the Lionhearted, At the Battle of Bataan, At the Normandy Invasion, On the Oregon Trail, With Byrd at the South Pole, On the Chisholm Trail.*

8. E. M. Hale and Company, 1201 South Hastings Way, Eau Claire, Wisconsin 54702

   Through Golden Windows Series. Books centering their themes on humor, adventure, children in the world, the story of America, and science. (Reading level, grades 1–6; interest level, grades K–8) *Wide Wonderful World, Stories of Early America, Mostly Magic, Wonderful Things Happen, Good Times Together, American Backgrounds, Children Everywhere, Fun and Fantasy, Adventures Here and There, Man and his World.*

9. Harper & Row, Publishers, 49 East 33rd Street, New York, New York 10016

   American Adventure Series. Graded list of corrective readers with biographical themes. (Grades 2–6) Among the nineteen titles: *Portugee Phillips, Alec Majors, Grant Marsh—Steamboat Captain, Kit Carson, Sabre Jet Ace, Daniel Boone, John Paul Jones.*

   I Can Read Books. Controlled vocabularies for beginning readers. (Grades 1–2) *Danny and the Dinosaur, Little Bear, Little Bear's Friend, Little Runner of the Longhouse, Tell Me Some More, Tony's Birds.*

   Real People Series. A rich collection that provides a more intimate view of American history. (Grades 5–8) Among the forty-eight titles: *Columbus, De Soto, Abigail Adams, Benjamin Franklin, Rufus Putnam, Narcissa Whitman, Jane Addams, Thomas Alva Edison.*

   Wonder-Story Books. Graded collection of children's classics. (Grades 1–6) *Once Upon a Time, I Know a Story, It Happened One Day, After the Sun Sets, It Must Be Magic, They Were Brave and Bold, These Are the Tales They Tell.*

10. D. C. Heath and Company, 285 Columbus Avenue, Boston, Massachusetts 02116

    Reading Caravan. A collection of classics in children's literature. (Grades K–6) *Peppermint Fence, Sky Blue, Star Bright, Meadow Green, Peacock Lane, Silver Web, Treasure Gold.*

    Teen-Age Tales. Stories that give teen-agers highly interesting material about their problems and about adventure, sports, and science. Interest level, grades 7–12. Books A, B, and C (3rd grade reading level). Books 1–6 (5–6 grade reading level).

11. J. B. Lippincott Company, East Washington Square, Philadelphia, Pennsylvania 19105

   Time to Read Series. Graded series of literary tales. (Grades 1–6) *Happy Ranch, Bucky's Friends, Making Friends, Skipping Along, Finding Favorites, Helping Others, Sailing Ahead, Moving Forward.*

12. The Macmillan Company, 60 Fifth Avenue, New York, New York 10011

   Macmillan Reading Spectrum. Thirty children's books for each intermediate grade level. (Reading level for each grade has a range of two years below and above.) Among the ninety titles: *Six Foolish Fishermen, Pancho, Dancing Cloud, Call It Courage, Thief Island, Grimm's Fairy Tales.*

13. Charles E. Merrill Books, Inc., 1300 Alum Creek Drive, Columbus, Ohio 43216

   New Reading Skilltext Series. A graded series of texts aimed at the development of comprehension skills. (Grades 1–6) *Bibs; Nicky; Uncle Funny Bunny; Uncle Ben; Tom Trott; Pat, the Pilot.*

   Treasury of Literature Readers. A graded series of children's classics. (Grades 1–6) *Merry-Go-Round, Happiness Hill, Treat Shop, Magic Carpet, Enchanted Isles, Adventure Lands.*

14. Random House, Inc., 457 Madison Avenue, New York, New York 10022

   All About Books. A collection of books designed to broaden children's knowledge of the world about them. (Reading level, grade 4 and above; interest level, grades 4–9) Among the forty-nine titles: *All About Dinosaurs, All About Volcanoes and Earthquakes, All About Rockets and Jets, All About Great Rivers of the World, All About the Human Mind, All About Heredity, All About Maps and Map Making.*

   American Girl Library. Outstanding books of fiction and nonfiction for girls. (Reading level, grades 4–6) *The American Girl Book of Horse Stories, The American Girl Book of Pat Downing Stories, The American Girl Book of First Date Series, The American Girl Book of Teen-Age Questions.*

   Easy-to-Read Books. A wide variety of fact, fiction, humor, and childhood adventure. (Reading level, grades 3–6; interest level, grades K–6) Among the thirty-two titles: *The Snake That Went to School, No Room for a Dog, Rocks All Around Us, Katie and the Sad Noise, Your Body and How It Works, The Earth in Space, Boy in the 49th Seat.*

   Landmark Books. A series of American and world history books. (Reading level, grade 4 and above; interest level, grades 4–9) Among the one hundred and five titles: *The Landing of the Pilgrims, The*

Wright Brothers, The Panama Canal, Guadalcanal Diary, The Battle for the Atlantic, John F. Kennedy and PT–109, The Story of Submarines.

World Landmark Books. Great events and great lives of world history. (Reading level, grades 6–9; interest level, grades 6–12) Among the fifty-seven titles: *The First Men in the World, Martin Luther, Jesus of Nazareth, The Story of Atomic Energy, Winston Churchill, The War in Korea: 1950–1953.*

15. Harr Wagner Publishing Company, 609 Mission Street, San Francisco, California 94105

Deep Sea Adventure Series. Adventure stories told through a highly controlled vocabulary. (Grades 1–4) *The Sea Hunt, Treasure Under the Sea, Submarine Rescue, The Pearl Divers, Frogmen in Action.*

Jim Forest Readers. Graded stories about a forest ranger. (Reading level, grades 1–3; interest level, grades 1–6) *Jim Forest and Ranger Don, Jim Forest and the Bandits, Jim Forest and the Mystery Hunter, Jim Forest and Dead Man's Peak, Jim Forest and the Flood, Jim Forest and Lone Wolf Gulch.*

Appendix B

SUPPLEMENTARY MATERIALS FOR TEACHING READING

Part I—Films, Filmstrips, and Recordings

1. Coronet Films, Inc.
   Titles designed to aid in developing word-recognition skills, comprehension skills, and study skills. Titles include:

Fun with Speech Sounds	*Building an Outline*
Listen Well, Learn Well	*How to Prepare a Class Report*
Do Words Ever Fool You?	*Maps and Their Uses*
It's Your Library	*Maps Are Fun*
Know Your Library	*How to Read a Book*
Library Organization	*How to Study*

2. C–B Educational Films
   Pathways to Reading Series includes the following films:

Why Read?	*How to Read*
What Did You Read?	*Was It Worth Reading?*
What's in a Book?	

   Speed reading films ranging from 180 to 536 words per minute are available in a series of twelve films.
   Keys to Reading Series includes three films: *Words, Phrases and Sentences,* and *Paragraphs.*

3. E. B. F. Filmstrips
   Reading Readiness Series includes nine color filmstrips to aid oral language development.
   Filmstrip Series adapted from various Disney classics to foster interest and background for reading. Twenty-three individual series are listed:

Action Stories	*Dog Stories*
Adventure Stories	*Famous Stories Retold*
The African Lion	*Fantasy Stories*
Animal Stories	*Forests of Tropical America*
The Arctic Wilderness	*The Living Desert*
Disneyland	*Make-Believe*

Reading Readiness
Communications Skills Kit
Safety Tales
Space and the Atom
Stories of Yesterday
Story Classics

Tales of Jiminy Cricket—No. 1
Tales of Jiminy Cricket—No. 2
This is You
True-Life Adventures
The Vanishing Prairie
Wonder Tales

4. Educational Film Library Association, Inc.
   Annotated list of over 200 films (16 mm.) that can be used at the elementary and junior high school levels.

5. Educational Developmental Laboratory
   Series of thirty tapes to develop word meanings, sentences, paragraphs, and study skills. Recommended for junior high school.
   Filmstrips for visual perception and discrimination, graded from grade one to adult level.

6. Enrichment Teaching Materials
   Records and filmstrips to accompany Landmark Series.

7. Folkway Records
   A series of ten- and twelve-inch records. Among the titles are:
   "Folk Tales from West Africa"
   "The Real Story of Davy Crockett"
   "Children's Stories and Songs"

8. McGraw-Hill Text Films
   Especially designed films to develop study skills.

9. Scott, Foresman and Company
   Filmstrip series for practice in phonic skills.

10. Society for Visual Education
    Filmstrips and recordings for Animal Friends Series.
    Filmstrip series *Basic Primary Phonics* for the development of consonants, blends, and vowels.
    Filmstrip series *Graded Word Phrases* for the development of word recognition, speed of perception, and comprehension.
    Filmstrip series *Words: Their Origins, Use, and Spelling* for the development of vocabulary and spelling skills.
    Filmstrip series *Your Dictionary and How to Use It* for the development of dictionary skills.
    Filmstrip *How to Read: To Understand, to Evaluate, to Use,* designed to give insight into basic reading skills.

Part II—Children's Magazines

1. *American Girl,* Girl Scouts of the U.S.A., 830 Third Avenue, New York, New York 10022 (4–8)
2. *Boys' Life,* Boy Scouts of America, New Brunswick, New Jersey 08903 (4–8)
3. *Child Life,* Review Publishing Company, 1100 Waterway Boulevard, Indianapolis, Indiana 46207 (K–3)
4. *Current Events,* American Education Publications, Education Center, Columbus, Ohio 43216 (6–8)
5. *Current Science,* American Education Publications, Education Center, Columbus, Ohio 43216
6. *Golden Magazine,* North Road, Poughkeepsie, New York 12601.
7. *Highlights for Children,* Highlights for Children, Inc., 2300 West Fifth Avenue, Columbus, Ohio 43216
8. *Humpty Dumpty's Magazine,* The Better Reading Foundation, Inc., 52 Vanderbilt Avenue, New York, New York 10007 (K–3)
9. *Jack and Jill,* Curtis Publishing Company, Independence Square, Philadelphia, Pennsylvania 19105 (K–5)
10. *My Weekly Reader,* American Education Publications, Education Center, Columbus, Ohio 43216 (for each grade K–6)
11. *Read Magazine,* American Education Publications, Education Center, Columbus, Ohio 43216 (6–9)
12. Scholastic Magazines, Inc., 50 West 44th Street, New York, New York 10036, publishes numerous magazines for these grade levels.

Appendix C

INTEREST INVENTORIES

Part I—Inventory for Primary Grades

INTEREST INVENTORY RECORD

PUPIL REPORT OF INTERESTS AND ACTIVITIES

NAME_____ DATE OF BIRTH_____ AGE____
GRADE____ SCHOOL_____ SEX_____ DATE_____

A. PLAY AND OTHER ACTIVITIES

1. When you have an hour or two to spend as you please, what do you like best to do?_____

2. What do you usually do:
   After school?_____
   On weekends?_____

3. What game do you like best to play?_____

4. What other games do you like to play?_____

5. Do you like to make things? Yes_____ No_____
   What things have you made?_____

6. What tools or playthings do you have at home?_____

7. Is there any tool or plaything that you would like to have very much?
   Yes_____ No_____ If yes, what?_____

8. Do you have any pets? Yes_____ No_____
   If yes, what?_____

9. Do you collect things? Yes_____ No_____
   If yes, what?_____

10. Do you take lessons, such as music and dancing lessons? Yes_____ No_____
    If yes, what?_____

11. If you could have three wishes which might come true, what would they be?
    First wish_____
    Second wish_____
    Third wish_____

12. Do you ever wish you were someone else? Yes_____ No_____
    If yes, who?_____

13. Are there some things you are afraid of? Yes_____ No_____
    If yes, what are they?_____

B. TELEVISION, RADIO, AND MOVIES

14. How much time do you spend looking at TV?
    On a school day:_____hours   On a weekend:_____hours

15. What TV program do you like best?_____

16. How much time do you spend listening to the radio?
    On a school day:_____hours   On a weekend:_____hours

17. What radio program do you like best?_____

18. How often do you go to the movies?_____

19. What movie do you like best?_____

C. READING

20. Do you like to have someone read a story to you? Yes_____ No_____
    If yes, what is the best story that has been read to you? _____
    Who read it?_____

21. Do you like to have someone tell a story to you? Yes_____ No_____
    If yes, who tells the best stories to you?_____

22. Do you like to look at magazines? Yes_____ No_____
    If yes, which magazines?_____

23. Do you like to look at comic books? Yes_____ No_____
    If yes, which comic books?_____

24. Do you like to read? Yes_____ No_____
    If yes, what books or stories have you read?_____

25. What book or story do you like best?_____

26. What other books or stories do you like?_____

27. Do you have books of your own? Yes_____No_____

    If yes, about how many?_____

28. Do you go to the public library? Yes_____No_____

29. Which of the following things do you like to do best?

    a. Read books_____

    b. Listen to stories_____

    c. Go to the movies_____

    d. Listen to the radio_____

    e. Watch TV_____

    f. Play outdoors_____

Adapted from an inventory by Paul A. Witty, Robert A. Sizemore, Ann Coomer, and Paul Kinsella for use in the Northwestern University—U. S. Office of Education Interest Survey.

Part II—Inventory for Intermediate and Upper Grades

INTEREST INVENTORY RECORD

PUPIL REPORT OF INTERESTS AND ACTIVITIES

NAME_____DATE OF BIRTH_____AGE____

GRADE_____SCHOOL_____SEX_____DATE_____

This is not a test. Your answers will not be graded, but they will provide helpful information. Please answer each question carefully and as fully as possible. If you need assistance, your teacher will help you.

A. PLAY AND OTHER ACTIVITIES

1. When you have an hour or two to spend as you please, what do you like best to do?_____

2. What do you usually do:

   After school?_____

   In the evening?_____

   On weekends?_____

3. What game do you like best to play?_____

4. Do you make things? Yes_____No_____What things have you made?_____

5. What tools or playthings do you have at home?_____

6. Do you have any pets? Yes_____No_____If yes, what?_____
7. Do you collect things? Yes_____No_____If yes, what?_____
8. Do you take lessons such as music and dancing? Yes_____No_____
    If yes, what?_____
9. Do you have any hobbies? Yes_____No_____If yes, what?_____
10. Suppose you could have one wish which might come true, what would it be?
    _____
11. Are there some things you are afraid of? Yes_____No_____If yes, what are they?_____

B. Television, Radio, and Movies

12. How much time do you spend looking at TV?
    On a school day:_____hours   On a weekend:_____hours
13. What is your favorite TV program?_____
14. How much time do you spend listening to the radio?
    On a school day:_____hours   On a weekend:_____hours
15. How often do you go to the movies?_____
    Name the movie you have liked best_____

C. Reading

16. What is the best book you have ever read?_____
    Name other books you have liked:_____
17. Name some books of your own that you have at home:_____
    _____
18. Do you like to have someone read or tell a story to you? Yes_____No_____
19. Do you go to the public library? Often_____Seldom_____Never_____
20. What magazines do you read?_____
    _____
21. Do you read comic books? Yes_____No_____If yes, what are your favorite comic books?_____
22. Do you read a newspaper? Yes_____No_____If yes, which parts?_____
    _____
23. What kind of books do you like best? For example, books about animals, about pilots, about children at home, about children in other lands, or about the stars and the planets. Write the kinds of books you like best:_____
    _____

D. Vocational and Educational Interests

24. What kind of work do you want to do when you finish school?_____
    _____

25. Have you read books or stories about the kind of work you want to do? Yes_____No_____If yes, name them:_____
_____

26. Have you seen anyone on television or in the movies who does the kind of work you want to do? Yes_____No_____If yes, who?_____
_____

27. Do you plan to go to high school? Yes_____No_____To college? Yes_____No_____
   Do you want to go to college? Yes_____No_____

28. Do you like school? Yes_____No_____

29. What school subject do you like best?_____
   What school subject do you like least?_____

30. In what subject do you get your best marks?_____
   Your poorest marks?_____

Adapted from an inventory by Paul A. Witty, Robert A. Sizemore, Ann Coomer, and Paul Kinsella for use in the Northwestern University—U. S. Office of Education Interest Survey.

Appendix D

CALDECOTT AND NEWBERY MEDAL BOOKS

Part I—The Randolph Caldecott Medal Books

YEAR	TITLE	AUTHOR	ILLUSTRATOR	PUBLISHER
1938	Animals of the Bible	Dorothy P. Lathrop	author	Lippincott
1939	Mei Li	Thomas Hanforth	author	Doubleday
1940	Abraham Lincoln	Ingri D'Aulaire Edgar P. D'Aulaire	authors	Doubleday
1941	They Were Strong and Good	Robert Lawson	author	Viking
1942	Make Way for Ducklings	Robert McCloskey	author	Viking
1943	The Little House	Virginia Lee Burton	author	Houghton
1944	Many Moons	James Thurber	Louis Slobodkin	Harcourt
1945	Prayer for a Child	Rachel Field	Elizabeth Jones	Macmillan
1946	The Rooster Crows; A Book of American Rhymes and Jingles	Maud Petersham Miska Petersham	authors	Macmillan
1947	The Little Island	Golden MacDonald	Leonard Weisgard	Doubleday
1948	White Snow, Bright Snow	Alvin Tresselt	Roger Duvoisin	Lothrop
1949	The Big Snow	Berta Hader Elmer Hader	authors	Macmillan
1950	Song of the Swallows	Leo Politi	author	Scribner
1951	The Egg Tree	Katherine Milhous	author	Scribner
1952	Finders Keepers	William Lipkind	Nicolas Mordivinoff	Harcourt
1953	The Biggest Bear	Lynd Ward	author	Houghton
1954	Madeline's Rescue	Ludwig Bemelmans	author	Viking
1955	Cinderella	Marcia Brown	author	Scribner
1956	Frog Went A-Courtin'	John Langstaff	Feodor Rojankovsky	Harcourt
1957	A Tree Is Nice	Marc Simont	author	Harper
1958	Time of Wonder	Robert McCloskey	author	Viking
1959	Chanticleer and the Fox	Geoffrey Chaucer	Barbara Cooney	Crowell
1960	Nine Days to Christmas	Marie Hall Ets	author	Viking
1961	Babonshka and The Three Kings	Ruth Robbins	Nicolas Sidjakov	Parnassus
1962	Once a Mouse	Marcia Brown	Hitapadesa	Scribner
1963	These Snowy Days	Ezra Keats	author	Viking
1964	Where the Wild Things Are	Maurice Sendak	author	Harper
1965	May I Bring a Friend?	Beatrice De Regniers	Beni Montresor	Atheneum

Part II—Newbery Medal Books

YEAR	TITLE	AUTHOR	PUBLISHER
1922	The Story of Mankind	Hendrik van Loon	Liveright
1923	The Voyages of Dr. Doolittle	Hugh Lofting	Lippincott
1924	The Dark Frigate	Charles B. Hawes	Little
1925	Tales from Silver Lands	Charles Finger	Doubleday
1926	Shen of the Sea	Arthur Chrisman	Dutton
1927	Smoky, the Cowhorse	Will James	Scribner
1928	Gay-Neck: The Story of a Pigeon	Dhan Mukerji	Dutton
1929	The Trumpeter of Krakow	Eric P. Kelly	Macmillan
1930	Hitty: Her First 100 Years	Rachel Field	Macmillan
1931	The Cat Who Went to Heaven	Elizabeth Coatsworth	Macmillan
1932	Waterless Mountain	Laura Adams Armer	Longmans
1933	Young Fu of the Upper Yangtze	Elizabeth Foreman Lewis	Winston
1934	Invincible Louisa: The Story of the Author of Little Women	Cornelia Meigs	Little
1935	Dobry	Monica Shannon	Viking
1936	Caddie Woodlawn	Carol Ryrie Brink	Macmillan
1937	Roller Skates	Ruth Sawyer	Viking
1938	The White Stag	Kate Seredy	Viking
1939	Thimble Summer	Elizabeth Enright	Holt
1940	Daniel Boone	James Daugherty	Viking
1941	Call It Courage	Armstrong Sperry	Macmillan
1942	The Matchlock Gun	Walter Edmonds	Dodd
1943	Adam of the Road	Elizabeth Janet Gray	Viking
1944	Johnny Tremain	Esther Forbes	Houghton
1945	Rabbit Hill	Robert Lawson	Viking
1946	Strawberry Girl	Lois Lenski	Lippincott
1947	Miss Hickory	Carolyn Sherwin Bailey	Viking
1948	The Twenty-one Balloons	William Du Bois	Viking
1949	King of the Wind	Marguerite Henry	Rand
1950	The Door in the Wall	Marguerite De Angeli	Doubleday
1951	Amos Fortune, Free Man	Elizabeth Yates	Dutton
1952	Ginger Pye	Eleanor Estes	Harcourt
1953	Secret of the Andes	Ann Nolan Clark	Viking
1954	And Now Miguel	Joseph Krumgold	Crowell
1955	The Wheel on the School	Meindert De Jong	Harper
1956	Carry On, Mr. Bowditch	Jean Lee Latham	Houghton
1957	Miracles on Maple Hill	Virginia Sorensen	Harcourt
1958	Rifles for Watie	Harold Keith	Crowell
1959	Witch of Blackbird Pond	Elizabeth Speare	Houghton
1960	Onion John	Joseph Krumgold	Crowell
1961	Island of the Blue Dolphins	Scott Odell	Houghton
1962	Bronze Bow	Elizabeth Speare	Houghton
1963	A Wrinkle in Time	Madeleine L'Engle	Farrar
1964	It's Like This, Cat	Emily Cheney Neville	Harper
1965	Shadow of a Bull	Maia Wojciechowska	Atheneum

Index

Abilities, development of, 10; and readiness problem, 226; varying, 243–245
Abstract thinking, 115
Abstract words, 227; and meaning, 114; and illiterates, 281
Academic attainment, and televiewing, 46
Academic success, and reading, 3
Accelerated interest, 18
Accelerated pupil, 196
Acceleration, and rapid reading, 272
Acceptance, of ideas, and reading, 69
Accuracy, of fact, in books, 151, 221
Achievement, respect for, 60
Action words, 192
Activities, associated with books, 145–146; outdoor, 236; indoor, 237; and experience, 246
Adequacy, of presentation, 222
Adjustment, 82; through reading, 29, 65; bibliotherapy and, 68; and retarded reader, 283; and slow learner, 333
Adolescents, problems of, 29; interests of, 42–52; and developmental tasks, 63; and conflicts, 257
Adults, reading interest, 6, 245; selecting reading material, 119; understanding of, 234; reading instructions for, 265–288; developmental reading program for, 269–275; illiterate, 278–285
Adult reading, role of, 267–268
Advanced reading, 345
Adventure stories, 51, 237
Adventures of the Baby Fox, The, 171
Aesop's Fables, 50
Aesthetic background, 93
Affection, need for, 59
Aggression, and bibliotherapy, 68
Agnew, Donald C., 103
Aldrich, C. A., 59
Aldrich, M. M., 59
Alice Adams, 66
Alice and Jerry series, 28
All-About Books, 329
All About Famous Inventors, 235
All About Series, 231
Allen, R. V., 202, 203, 204

Alphabetizing, 191
America Grows Up, 235
America Is Born, 235
America Moves Forward, 235
American Adventure Series, The, 329
American Association for Gifted Children, 337
American classics literature, 258
American folklore, 135
American Library Association, and readability, 119; and book awards, 151
American School Achievement Tests, 303
American School Reading Readiness Test, 97
American Spelling Book, 26
America's Own Mark Twain, 138
Amos Fortune: Free Man, 66, 346
Analytic approach, and word identification, 101–102
Analytical skills, and word meaning, 192
Analytic-synthetic approach, to word identification, 101, 102
Analytic word study, 218
Analytical diagnosis, of reading disability, 300
Analytical listening, 168
Anderson, C. W., 134
Anderson, John E., 81
Anderson, Paul S., 143
Anderson, William F., Jr., 272
Andrews, Joe W., 274
Anecdotal records, 378
Animal stories, 133–134, 186
Animals, interest in, 52. *See also* Pets.
Answers, reading for, 217
Anxiety, and slow learner, 333
Apostrophe, use of, 190
Applegate, Mauree, 205
Applicatory exercises, and illiterate, 285
Appreciation, 374; reading and, 2, 10; development of, 128; of others, 129
Appreciative listening, 168
Approach, developmental, 9, 234; individualized reading, 22; individual or group, 24; functional, 29; phonics, 101; word identification,

413

101–102; direct sensory, 114; single subject integrated, 159; visual, 167; to listening, 167–168; basal reading program, 180, 181–200; Denver, 180, 202; experience chart-basal reader, 180, 181–200; linguistic, 180, 200, 206–207; to teacher reading, 200–210; language experience, 202; basic and individualized, 205; Bloomfield Barnhart, 207; skill building, 230; developmental, 234; phonic, and remedial reading, 313; to gifted pupil, 340

Approach to Individualized Reading, 205

Appy, Nellie, 65

Aranow, Miriam, 297

Arbuthnot, May Hill, 151

Are You Listening?, 170

Areas of conflict, and bibliotherapy, 68

Arithmetic, televiewing and, 46; reading in, 227; and illiterates, 282

Army Arithmetic, 280

Army Reader, 280, 282

Arrangement, sequential, 223

Art of the Story Teller, 146

Arthur Point Scale of Reading Tests, 96

Artley, A. Sterl, 160

Asheim, Lester, 268

Ashton-Warner, Sylvia, 204

Association, and experience, 163; and meaning, 192; of ideas and materials, intermediate grades, 215, 220–221; of experience and activities, 246

Association of Childhood Education, 363

Assumptions, basic, 222

Athletics, outdoor, 236; indoor, 237

Atmosphere, classroom, importance of, 54

Attention, maintaining, 77

Attention span, and New Castle Plan, 202; and slow learner, 332

Attentive listening, 168

Attitudes, improving, 55; and determining needs, 64; effect of reading on, 65; and reading, 69; and reading readiness, 83; favorable, and reading, 127; and gifted pupil, 343; teachers' 362

Audience reading, 147

Audio-visual aids, 114, 232, 260

Auditory-visual perceptions, 190

Auditory approach, to listening, 167

Auditory blending, 188

Auditory defect, and slow reader, 324

Auditory development, 84

Auditory discrimination, 91, 187; of words, 77

Auditory discrimination test, 296

Auditory factor, and retarded reader, 295

Auditory material, and reading progress, 34

Auditory perception, 187; and Denver Plan, 202

Aurex Audio-Meter, 295

Austin, Mary, 299, 357

Authenticity, of facts, 221

Autobiographies, students', and determining needs, 64

Autobiography. *See* Biography.

Averill, Esther, 53

Award books, 151

Babies Are Human Beings, 59

Background, experiential, 162; and readiness problem, 226; of slow learner, 323; of gifted pupil, 347

Background development, 160

Background information, 38

Bamman, Henry A., 83, 228, 229

Barbe, Walter B., 205

Barber, Elsie Oakes, 66

Barnhart, Clarence L., 207

Basal approach, 205

Basal materials, in reading program, 23; effective use, 196–197

Basal programs, and individualized reading, 22

Basal readers, 19, 28

Basal reading program, approach to, 180

Baseball, interest in, 43

Basic assumptions, 222

Basic Book Collection for High Schools, 259

Basic Book Collection for Junior High Schools, 259

Basic needs, and mental health, 59

Basic Sight Word Test, 303

Batchelor, Julie F., 235

Batten, T. C., 47

Battledore, 25

Baughmann, M. D., 290

Beatinest Boy, 235

Behavior, and reading, 2; effect of reading on, 65, 69–72; and bibliotherapy, 67; and reading readiness, 83; acceptable, 257; and needs, 378

Behavior patterns, and goals, 40

Bell Science Series, 55
Bemelmans, Ludwig, 344
Bendick, Jeanne, 235
Benson, Sally, 346
Berelson, Bernard, 70
Berg, Paul, 296
Best Books for Children, 66
Better Reading, 249, 317
Betts, Emmett A., 7, 8, 33, 108, 109, 310, 391, 392
Betzner, Jean, 153
Bibliography of Books for Children, 66
Bibliographies, for developmental needs, 66
Bibliotherapy, 67–69
Biography, 238–239, 257; interest in, 51; truth in, 151; reading lists, 138–139
Biological motive, and development needs, 62
Bish, Charles E., 341
Black Beauty, 237
Blair, Glenn Myers, 4, 244
Bland, Phyllis, 250, 316, 317
Blommers, Paul, 81
Bloomfield, Leonard, 207
Bloomfield-Barnhart approach, 207
Bloomster, Maurine, 104
Blue-Black Speller, The, 26
Blue Ridge Billy, 66, 137
Blumenthal, Rochelle, 352
Blumenthal, Susan Hahn, 188
Bold Journey, 55
Bolenius, Emma M., 27
Bond, Guy, 76, 86, 88, 251, 260, 291, 294, 300, 310
Bond-Clymer Factor, 290–291
Bond Silent Reading Diagnostic Test, 294
Book Bait, 259
Book lists, and developmental needs, 65–67
Book reports, 148; general, 21
Books, availability of, and reading, 6; moralistic, 26; readability of, 118–120; experiences and activities associated with, 145–149; reports, 21, 148; evaluating, 149, 150–151; difficulty, 150; content, 150; presentation, 150; physical makeup, 151; and oral reading, 172; paperbacks, 268, 359; for gifted pupil, 347; accessibility of, 366
Books, 259
Botel, Morton, 274
Boy and His Horse, A., 53

Boyd, Grace, 114
Boys of the Islands, 234
Boys' Life, 315
Bracken, Dorothy, 362
Bradshaw, Franklyn R., 70
Brain damage factor, and retarded readers, 297
Breckenridge, Marian E., 60
Brinkman, Mary Louise, 68
Brooklyn College, and adult reading, 271
Brooklyn Public Library, and adult reading, 271
Brown, Bert, 278
Brumbaugh, Florence N., 339
Bruner, Jerome Seymour, 278
Bryan, Dorothy, 54
Bryan, Fred E., 111, 112, 113
Bryan, Marguerite, 54
Buckingham, B. R., 112
Bulla, Clyde Robert, 53, 68
Bulletins, 232
Burns, Paul C., 94, 169
Buros, Oscar K., 391
Burrows, Alvina Treut, 205, 358
Burton, Dwight L., 65, 129, 130
Burton, Virginia, 54
Burton, William H., 357, 358
Bush, Clifford L., 393
Buswell & Wheeler readers, 27
Busywork, futility of, 231
Butcher, Elsa, 14
Butterfield, Marguerite, 161

Caldecott, Randolph, 152
Caldecott Medal, 151, 152
Caldecott Medal Books, list of, 411
California Phonics Survey, 303
California Reading Test, 252, 304, 317
California Test of Mental Ability, 392
California Test of Mental Maturity, 96, 251, 297
California Test norms, 244
Call It Courage, 328
Caravan Series (D. C. Heath), 231
Card catalog, 222
Carlyle, Thomas, 3
Carmichael, Leonard, 81
Carson, Louise G., 23
Case study, psychoeducational clinic, 70–72; and experience charts, 182–184; diagnosis of reading ability, 300; verbally gifted pupil, 349–353; outline, 393, 394
Caskey, Helen, 214
Cat and the Hat, The, 196

Cause-and-effect relationships, recognizing, 197
Causey, Oscar S., 296
Cavanna, Betty, 66
Central core, 54
Chall, Jeanne S., 119–120, 121, 122, 188
Chapman, Gilbert W., 171, 172
Character Formation through Books, 259
Charlotte's Web, 134
Charts, facts from, 222
Child development, psychology of, 160
Child study techniques, and interests, 40
Childhood, and developmental tasks, 62–63
Childhood Education, 196
Children, interests of, 42–52
Children's books, evaluating, 150–151
Children's Digest, 232
Children's literature, 127–157; and reading program, 127–132; and teacher, 130–132
Children's magazines, 232; sources, 405
Choral reading, 165
Chucklebait, 347
Cinderella, 132, 237
Clarity, in communications, 163; and meaning, 164; and teaching illiterates, 283
Classes, special, in reading, 248
Classification, and meaning, 192
Classroom, atmosphere, 54; ability in, wide range, 60; environment of, 90, 366
Classroom library, 21, 28, 233
Classroom observations, 369
Classroom practice, changes in, 159–161
Cleland, Donald L., 291, 301, 302, 342, 347
Cleveland, Ohio, and study of gifted students, 339
Clift, David, 266, 268
Clymer, Theodore, 191
Co-basal reading program, 28
Cobb, Lyman, 26
Cole, Charles C., Jr., 342
College education, 254; and gifted pupil, 342
College English, 110
College program, of remedial reading, 266; developmental reading, 269–275

College reading, role of, 267–268
College student, and vocational problem, 115; reading instruction for, 265–288; developmental reading program, 269–275; Negro, and reading deficiencies, 277
College texts, and reading ability, 265–266
Colloquial connotations, 193
Comic books, 255
Commission on English Curriculum, 158
Communication, reading as, 7; and language, 158–159; clarity in, 163
Communications: From Cave Writing to Television, 235
Communicative development, 9
Communicative experiences, 10
Competition, 66
Compositions, and determining needs, 64
Comprehension, 4, 374; flexibility in, 10; and reading program, 23; of words, 23; abstract words, 114, 227, 281; of ideas, 168; developing, intermediate grades, 215; and rapid reading, 272; and reading, speed tests on, 273; and slow pupil, 323
Compromise programs, 248
Conant, Margaret M., 373
Concentration, and slow learner, 332
Concept building, 30, 113; and disadvantaged pupil, 278
Concepts, and pictures, 192; building of, 30, 113; acquisition and interpretation, 115; broad, 115; development of, through books, 186; abstract, 227; broadening materials for, 230; and slow learner, 331; and gifted pupil, 338–340
Conferences, 230; and individualized reading, 22–23; pupil-teacher, 21; adult, 270; parent-teacher, 364; self-appraisal, 389
Conflicts, resolving, 69; adolescent, 257
Consistency, recognizing, 197
Consonants, audio-visual perception, 190
Construction activities, 93
Contemporary authors, 258
Content area, emotional and controversial, 226; reading in, 226–229; materials in, 231; and slow learner, 331; and reading skills, 368
Continuity, recognizing, 197
Contractions, 190

416

Controlled Reader, 272
Controversial content, in social studies field, 226
Cook, Walter W., 294
Coomer, Ann, 41, 343
Cooper, William, 269, 271, 275
Cooperative English Test: Reading Comprehension, 252
Core course, and reading program, 248–249
Corrective classes, 248
Correlation, between speed and comprehension, 273
Cotton in My Sock, 137
Creative ability, encouragement of, 203
Creative expression, 114; and language-experience approach, 202–203
Creative writing, 204–205; and determining needs, 64; poetry, 144; and oral reading, 175
Creativity, and gifted child, 341, 345
Crisis in Black and White, 209
Critical reading, 217, 221; proficiency in, 256; stress on, 267
Critical thinking, 10; and reading, 220
Crosby, Muriel, 259
Cultural groups, and language expression, 164
Culturally deprived pupil, reading program for, 275–278
Cumulative records, 369, 378
Curiosity, 235
Current Events, 232
Curriculum, criticism of, 14; core, 54; core, and reading program, 248–249; and slow learner, 330–334; and gifted pupil, 345
Custer's Last Stand, 237
Custodial personnel, cooperation with, 365

Dahl, L. A., 295
Dale, Edgar, 119, 120, 169, 170
Dallmann, Martha, 32, 79, 90, 147, 220, 292
Daniel Boone, 237
Darrow, Helen F., 205
Davis, Frederick B., 373
Davis, Helen C., 233
Davis Eells Games, 297
Davy Crockett, 237
Dawkins, John 118
Dawson, Mildred A., 83, 228, 229
De Angeli, Marguerite, 140, 234

DeBoer, John J., 32, 79, 90, 113, 147, 161, 220, 292
Dechant, Emerald V., 9, 10–11, 18, 68, 80, 215, 216, 224, 226, 227, 301
Deficient hearing, 79
De Haan, Robert F., 322, 323, 340
DeJong, Meindert, 141
Democratic ideals, development of, 129
Demonstration, 92; and illiterates, 285
Denver Approach (Plan), 180, 189, 200, 202
Des Plaines–Park Ridge Plan, 250-251
Desires, and bibliotherapy, 67
Detail, reading for, 217; remembering, 220
Detroit Adjustment Inventory, 64
Detroit First Grade Intelligence Test, 96
Deutsch, Martin, 276, 278, 322
Developing Permanent Interest in Reading, 55
Developing Your Vocabulary, 115, 256, 328, 331
Development, overall relationship of reading to, 75; listening, 171–174; and maturation, 234
Development aims, 214
Developmental approach, 9, 234
Developmental needs, 59, 234–239; fulfilling, 9; identification of, 60–65; determining, 63; and reading process, 65–71; books to meet, 65
Developmental program, 8–11; growth in reading, 76; vocabulary and concept building, 113; characteristics of, 246–251
Developmental reading, evolution of, 1–13
Developmental Reading, 206
Developmental reading program, 7–11; principles of, 9–11; continuing process, 9; flexibility in, 10; older pupils and, 243–245; at adult level, 268, 269–275
Developmental Reading Tests, 304, 325
Developmental tasks, 62, 234–239
Diagnosis, of reading ability, 300–312
Diagnostic Reading Scales, 305
Diagnostic Reading Tests, 305, 325
Diagnostic tests, and reading disability, 301
Diagrams, getting facts from, 222; interpreting, 226, 227
Diaries, and determining needs, 64
Di Carlo, Louis, 295

417

Dickinson, Emily, 346
Dictionaries, 232; use of, 217; and facts, 221; and slow learner, 331
Dietary habits, 79
Dietrich, Dorothy M., 21, 22
Difficult words, comprehension of, 114
Digraphs, audiovisual perception, 190
Diphthongs, audiovisual perception, 190
Direct sensory approach, 114
Directions, following, 216; slow learners and, 330
Disadvantaged pupil, 209; reading instruction, 275-285
Discrimination. *See* Auditory discrimination; Visual discrimination.
Discussion, and determining needs; and reading, 147
Disney, Walt, 53, 54, 196, 344
Disney Classics, 53
Docter, Robert L., 230, 231
Dr. Seuss books, 54
Dolch, Edward W., 104, 112
Dolch Basic Vocabulary, 331
Donaho, Melvin, 316
Downing, John A., 207
Drama, interest in, 51; and illiterates, 282
Dramatic play, 92
Dramatization, 148
Drawing, 93
Dresden, Katherine, 233
Dropout, 279
Duration, listening, 170
Durkin, Dolores, 77-78, 208, 209, 343
Durrell, Donald, 77, 95
Durrell Analysis of Reading Ability, 300
Durrell Diagnosis of Reading Difficulties, 325

Ear-training program, 188
Early, Margaret J., 247, 248, 249, 291, 292
Early childhood, and developmental tasks, 62
Eaton, Jeannette, 138
Edson, William H., 294
Educational Development Library, 231
Educational goals, development of, 10
Educational interests, 52
Educational opportunities, 243
Educational television, 202. *See also* Denver Approach
Educators Guide to Personalized Reading, 205

Effective reading, 2
Elementary English, 196; story telling technique, 146
Elementary School Journal, 111
Elkins, Deborah, 67
Elson-Gray Readers, 27
Emotional content, in social studies field, 226
Emotional development, 84-85; in reading readiness, 75
Emotional disturbance, 82
Emotional environment, 366-367
Emotional factor, and retarded reader, 293-294
Emotional grasp, 258
Emotional problems, and bibliotherapy, 68; and insecurity, 90
Encouragement, of slow pupil, 322
Encyclopedias, 232; use of, 217, 222
English usage, in speaking, 164
Enjoyment, and audience reading, 147
Enrichment, through reading, 2, 9; of experience, 10, 128, 186, 203, 369; and level of readiness, 92; of concepts, pictures as, 192; for gifted student, 345
Environment, and readiness, 90; and listening, 170; and retarded reader, 298; and slow learner, 323; learning, 365; physical, 366; social and emotional, 366; intellectual, 367
Escape, through reading, 129, 135
Essays, interest in, 51
Esteem needs, 61
Estes, Eleanor, 66
Ethical values, 129
Etiquette, 257
Ets, Marie Hall, 68
Evaluation, and reading skills, 10; of individualized reading program, 22; total, 83; by teacher, 83-85; of readability formulae, 121; of literature program, 149-155; of books, 150-151; of language acquisitions, 163; of reading, in content fields, 228; procedures, middle grades, 233; of growth, in reading, 260-261; in remedial reading, 315; of ability, slow learner, 325; reading material, 370; of development in reading, 373-396; essential factors, 373; scope of, 374; complexity of, 376; informal, 377; by teachers, 377; by records, 378-386; by checklist, 387; formal, 390; and standardized tests, 390; reading surveys, 392; case studies, 393

Excitement, and reading, 2
Excursions, 92
Exercise books, 216
Experience(s), through reading, 3, 69; enrichment of, 10, 128, 186, 203, 369; and readiness program, 89–94; firsthand, 114, 163–164, 228; association with books, 145–149; studying, 181; recorded on film strips, 184; and photographs, 185; and remembering, 219; association with activities, 246; and slow learners, 327, 330
Experience chart-basal reader approach, 180, 181–200
Experience charts, 93, 232; and oral reading, 172; use of, 182–184; and pre-primer, 185; and slow learner, 327
Experience Curriculum in English, 159
Experiential background, 85; in reading and speaking, 162
Experiment in Reading, An, 171
Experiments, 228
Explicit meaning, comprehension of, 324
Expression, and cultural groups, 164
Eye examination, 79
Eye movement, 94; and rapid reading, 272
Eye-sweep, 91

Facts, retention and significance, 219; verifying, 221; interpreting, 222
Faculty, and developmental problem, 246
Failure, slow learner and, 321, 333
Fairy tales, 50; by grade level, 132, 133
Family Reading and Storytelling, 127
Family relationships, and bibliotherapy, 67–68; satisfaction in, 234–235; and school, 257
Fanciful tales, 135
Fannin, Lois, 344
Fatio, Louise, 53, 134
Featherstone, William B., 324, 332
Felsen, Henry G., 66
Fenner, Phyllis R., 127, 155
Fernald, Grace M., 313
Ferrell, Frances Hunter, 345
Ferris, Donald R., 341
Ferris, Helen, 144, 260
Fiction, 237; interest in, 51; historical, 140–141

Field trips, 92, 114; and enriching experience, 203
Figurative language, 277
Figurel, J. Allen, 278, 323
Film approach, 180, 200–202
Film guide, 176
Film reader, 115
Films, 115, 260; use of, 54; and enriching experience, 203; and teaching science, 228; and listening development, 271; and slow learners, 331; sources of, 403–404
Filmstrips, 53–54, 115, 260; and literature, 130; recording experiences by, 184; and teaching reading, 200; and teaching science, 228; and teaching illiterates, 280; and slow learners, 331; sources of, 403
Finders Keepers, 54
Fingerpainting, 91
Fireman, The, 331
First Adventures in Learning Program, 209
First Book of Dogs, 54
First Book of Space Travel, 235
First Books, 238
First Under the North Pole, 235
Firsthand experiences, 114, 163–164, 228; and pre-primer, 186; and slow learner, 331
Fitzwater, James P., 115
500 Hats of Bartholomew Cubbins, 172
Flack, Marjorie, 134, 344
Flashmeter, 249, 272
Flashreader, 274
Flesch, Rudolph, 16, 119, 120, 121
Flexibility, and reading, 224
Fliegler, Louis A., 341
Folk dances, 91
Folk tales, 50, 132; by grade level, 133
Folklore, 132; by grade level, 133; and story telling, 146
Folkman, William S., 277
Football, interest in, 43
Forbes, Esther, 140
Forkner, Hamden L., 62
Forms, test, 391
Foster, Genevieve, 138
Frank, Annette, 366
Frank, Josette, 127
Frazier, Alexander, 278
Freeland, Alma, 143, 217, 239
French, John, 316
Friendly Little Jonathan, 54
Fries, Charles C., 206
Frisky the Goat, 196

419

Froe, Otis D., 277, 278
Frost, Robert, 260, 346
Frustration, and slow learner, 333
Frustration level, 310
Functional approach, 29
Functional method, and illiterates, 284
Functionally illiterate, 279, 321
Funk, Wilfred, 110

Games, interests in, 43; promote discrimination, 91; and auditory perception, 187; indoor, 236, 237
Gardner, Eric F., 295
Gates, Arthur I., 17, 19, 20, 30, 31, 103, 208, 219, 242, 275, 313
Gates Basic Reading Tests, 294, 297, 306
Gates Primary Reading Test, 306
Gates Reading Readiness Test, 88, 97
Gates word list, 331
Geisel, Theodore Seuss. *See* Seuss, Dr.
General diagnosis, of reading disability, 300
General health, 84
Generalizations, 191
Gesell, Arnold, 59
Getzels, Jacob W., 39, 40, 341
Gifted Child, The, 337
Gifted pupil, 196; reading programs for, 337–355; identifying, 338; concepts of, 338–340; and creativity, 341; and reading, 341–342; goals of, 343; and home and school, 343–344; reading progress, 345–347; grade levels, 347–348
Gilmore Oral Reading Test, 325
Gliessman, David, 272
Globes, 232
Goals, of reading program, 17; and behavior patterns, 40; word identification, 106–108; in literature program, 128–129; in language arts, 161; "expanded," 213–214; for illiterates, 284; and gifted pupil, 343; for beginners, 375; for eighth graders, 375
Goldberg, Samuel, 281
Golden Book Educational Services, 209, 210
Good Master, The, 141, 234
Good Reading for Poor Readers, 329
Grace Fernald Method, and remedial reading, 313
Grahame, Kenneth, 135
Grammatical Institute, 26

Graphs, interpreting, 222
Gray, Lillian, 226
Gray, William S., 7, 119, 120, 121, 244, 266, 345
Gray Oral Reading Paragraphs, 325
Gray Standardized Oral Reading Paragraph Test, 307
Greene, Carla, 54
Gregory, Margaret, 345
Grimm's Fairy Tales, 172
Grocery Kitten, The, 53
Grotberg, Edith, 68, 115, 256, 278, 316, 328
Group activities, interests in, 43
Group discussion, and illiterates, 282 and enriching experiences, 203; and slow learner, 332
Group instruction, 199
Group interests, 54; and remedial reading, 315
Group pattern, 257
Group tests, 82, 251; and slow learner, 325
Grouping, for instruction, 199
Growth, evaluating through reading, 260–261
Growth and development, and reading instruction, 17; and personal and social problems, 217
Guidance, of reading, 128; for high school pupils, 256; and slow learner, 322; and gifted pupil, 347
Guidance program, 255
Guiterman, Arthur, 346
Gunderson, Doris V., 278
Gunn, M. Angella, 243

Hall, Theodore, 339
Hall, William, 196
Hand to eye dominance, 296
Happy Days, 2
Happy Lion, The, 53
Harper and Row, science booklets, 231
Harris, Albert J., 81, 105, 106, 190, 293, 294, 298
Harris, Chester W., 373, 374
Harrison, Lucile, 202
Harrison-Stroud Reading Readiness Profile, 97
Harvard Reading Films, 272
Hatfield, W. Wilber, 159
Havighurst, Robert J., 62, 276, 338, 340
Health, pupils', 84, 364; teachers', 362
Hearing, 79. *See also* Auditory —.
Hearing deficiency, and retarded reader, 295

Heath, D. C., Reading for Interest Series, 28; Caravan Series, 231; Reading Roundup Series, 257
Heaton, Margaret M., 259
Heffernan, Helen, 75–76
Hegge, T. G., 313
Heidi, 55, 237
Henman-Nelson Tests of Reading Ability, 252
Henry, Marguerite, 53, 134, 344
Heroic tales, 50
Herrick, Virgil E., 173, 174
Herron, John S., 104
High frequency word list, 204
High school, reading texts for, 29; reading for interest, 30; abstract thinking and broad concepts, 115; reading instruction in, 242–263; determining pupils' needs, 251; pupil interest, 253; and gifted pupils, 348; and reading teacher, 357
High school reading list, folk and fairy tales, 133; animal stories, 134; American folklore, 135; realistic literature, 137; regional stories, 138; biography, 139; historical fiction, 140–141; other lands stories, 142; poetry, 145
High School Reading Test, 307
Highlights for Children, 91, 138, 196, 232, 327
Hildreth, Gertrude H., 160, 165, 176, 339
Hilliard, F. Pauline, 368
Historical fiction, 140–141
Hobbies, television and, 47
Hodell, Robert D., 272
Hoeber, Ethel S., 175
Hogan, Inez, 344
Hoke, Helen, 53
Hollingworth, Leta S., 338
Home, and readiness program, 92; and retarded reader, 198; and slow learner, 323; and gifted pupil, 343
Homer Price, 1, 346
Horn, Ernest A., 112
Horn Book, 196
Horn and Shields readers, 27
Hornbook, 25
Hospitality, practicing, 93
Houghton Mifflin Reading Series, 202
How to Become a Better Reader, 256, 359
How to Improve Your Reading, 256
Howell, Wallace J., 227
Howes, Virgil M., 205
Huckleberry Finn, 258

Human needs, and reading programs, 6
Humpty Dumpty, 196
Hundred Dresses, The, 66
Hunnicutt, C. W. 122
Hunt, Lyman C., Jr., 357
Hunter College Elementary School, 339
Hunter and the Forest, The, 171, 175
Hurlock, Elizabeth B., 39
Husbands, Kenneth L., 274

I Want to Be series, 54, 196
Ideas, comprehension of, 33; acceptance of, 69, 168; organizing, 169; remembering, 219; associating with materials in intermediate grades, 215, 220–221, 223; reading for, 217
Identification, with fictional characters, 235
Idiomatic English, 198
Iglehart, Robert, 340
Ilg, Frances L., 59
Illiterates, adult, 278–279; teaching, 279–285; methods and materials, 283; role of teacher, 283; functional, 279, 321
Imagery, and poetry, 143
Imagination, 181
Imaginative tales, 186
Imitation, 358
Immature readers, 113
Implicit meaning, comprehension of, 374
Independence, 60; in reading, 145
Independent reading, level of, 186
Index, locating items from, 222
Individual approach, 205
Individual interests, 54
Individual needs, and reading program, 9, 68, 258
Individualized reading, and instruction, 20–21; approaches to, 22
Individualized reading program, characteristics of, 21–24; weaknesses in, 23
Indoor activities, 236–237
Infancy, and developmental tasks, 62
Inferences, making, 169
Inflection, in oral reading, 198
Informal evaluation, 377–390
Informal reading inventories, 390
Informal tests, 387; and assessment of skills, 369
Information, from reading, 1, 2; selecting, 169; locating, 216, 221
Ingram, Christine P., 333, 334

421

Initial consonants, 189
Initial Teaching Alphabet, 189
Initial Teaching Alphabet Method, 200, 207–208
Initial Teaching Alphabet Plan, 180
Initiative, lack of, 323
Insecurity, 38, 54; and speech problems, 90; and slow learner, 333
In-service programs, 357
Insight, gaining, 69; and reading, 129
Instruction, differentiated, 10; improvement of, and individualized reading, 20; grouping for, 199
Instructional level, 33; and vocabulary, 186
Integrated approach, 158–161
Intellectual development, and reading readiness, 75
Intellectual environment, 367
Intellectual precocity, 339
Intelligence factor, and remedial reading, 297
Intelligence tests, 82, 85–86; listing of, 96. *See also* specific tests.
Interaction, of skills and habits, 180
Interest, reading for, 1; need for increased, 5–6; role of, 37–57; defined, 38; and skills, 38–39; and interests, 39–40; classroom practice and, 52–55; maintaining, 78; development of, in literature, 129, 130; and listening, 168; and oral reading, 172; fostering, through books, 186; and motivation, 238; variation in, 239; creating new, 239; lack of, 245; and high marks, 254; and mechanical devices, 274; and illiterate, 281, 284; and retarded readers, 292; and gifted pupil, 344, 345, 347
Interest areas, 42
Interest inventory, 40, 181, 253; and interviews, 64; and reading readiness, 83; and retarded reader, 292; and gifted pupils, 347; forms of, 406–410
Interests, and reading program, 30; and interest, 39; studying, 40–42, 181, 253–255; of children and adolescents, 42–52; play and recreational, 42–45; television, 45–48; radio and movies, 48–49; reading, 49–52; vocational and educational, 52; individual and group, 54; prereading, 85; satisfying, 128; stimulating and fulfilling, 146; of high school pupils, 253; group, and reme-

dial reading, 315; of slow learner, 326
Intermediate grades, reading instruction, 213–241; habits and skills, 214, 215–229; and gifted pupil, 348
Intermediate grades reading list, folk and fairy tales, 133; animal stories, 134; American folklore, 135; realistic literature, 136; regional stories, 137; biography, 139; historical fiction, 140; other lands, 142
International Reading Association, 363
Interpreting data, 222; diagrams, 226
Interviews, and interest inventories, 64; teacher-pupil, 389
Intonation, 161
Intrinsic method, and phonics, 103
Introduction to Language, 281
Iowa Every Pupil Test of Basic Skills, 307
Iowa Reading Tests, 325
Iowa Silent Reading Tests, 252, 298, 307
Iowa Tests of Educational Development, 252, 307
i.t.a., 207–208
Iverson, William J., 122

Jack and Jill, 196
Jackson, Doris C., 205
Jackson, Philip W., 341
Jacobs, Leland B., 20, 173, 174
Jenny Goes to Sea, 53
Jenny's First Party, 53
Jersild, Arthur T., 48
Jewett, Arno, 279
Joey and Patches, 68
Johnny Appleseed, 54
Johnny Tremain, 140
Johnson, George, 120
Johnson, Gerald W., 235
Johnson, Lois V., 90
Johnson, Margaret Sweet, 68
Jungblut, Ann, 77, 294, 296, 297
Junior Libraries, 196
Junior Miss, 346
Junior high school, reading instruction in, 242–263; determining pupils' needs, 251–252; and gifted pupil, 348; reading teacher, 357
Junior high school reading list; folk and fairy tales, 133; animal stories, 134; American folklore, 135; realistic literature, 137; regional stories, 138; biography, 139; historical fic-

tion, 140–141; other lands, 142; poetry, 145
Justman, Joseph, 297

Karlin, Robert, 86, 246, 247
Katy-No-Pocket, 1, 172
Kegler, Stanley B., 251, 260
Kelley-Greene Reading Comprehension Test, 252
Kerr, Margaret, 120, 121
Key, Theodore, 54, 66
Khater, Mahmand, 299
Kindergarten, readiness program, 202; teaching reading in, 208
Kingston, Albert J., 296
Kinsella, Paul, 41, 46
Kirby, Margaret, 23–24
Kircher, Clara J., 259
Kirk, Samuel A., 313
Kirk, W. D., 313
Kjelgaard, James, 134
Klausmeier, Herbert J., 233
Knief, Lotus M., 81
Knowledge, through reading, 3
Kon-Tiki, 55
Kopel, David, 7, 40, 295, 296, 314
Kottmeyer, William, 289
Kough, Jack, 323
Kress, Roy A., 290
Krippner, Stanley, 41
Krugman, Judith L., 15
Krumgold, Joseph, 235
Kuhlmann-Anderson Intelligence Test, 96

Labels, 204
LaBrant, Lou, 116
Lamoreaux, Lillian A., 182
Landmark books, 138, 235, 239, 254, 329
Language, psychology of, 160
Language arts, audience-reading correlation, 147; evaluation, 143; interrelationship, 158; change in learning theory, 159; skills and growth in, 161; and slow learner, 332
Language Arts in the Elementary School, 159
Language attainment, and televiewing, 46
Language development, 85, 158–197
Language experience approach, 202–206
Language experiences, related, and film guides, 176
Language expression, and cultural groups, 164
Language patterns, perceiving and hearing, 209
Language readiness, 89
Larrick, Nancy, 65, 82–83, 127, 129, 130
Lassie, 55
Latent meaning, comprehension of, 374
Lateral dominance factor, 196
Lathrop, Dorothy, 68, 134
Lawrence, Gertrude, 346
Lawson, Robert, 235
Lazar, Mary, 21
Learn to Study Series, 27
Learning, previous, utilizing, 169; reinforcement, and slow learners, 333
Learning efficiency, difference in, 167
Learning process, and reading, 2
Learning to Read through Experience, 202, 203, 204
Leary, Bernice E., 119, 120, 234
Lee, Dorris M., 182, 202, 203, 204
Lee-Clark Reading Readiness Test, 98
Lee-Clark Reading Test, 308
Lefevre, Carl A., 30
Left-eyedness, 296
Left-handedness, 296
Lehman, H. C., 42
Leigh, Edwin, 102
Leigh, Robert D., 34
Leisure reading, 270
Lennon, Roger T., 374
Lenski, Lois, 66, 137, 235
Let Them Write Poetry, 144
Letter-sound factor, 207
Level of thinking, 229
Lewerenz, Alfred, 120
Lewis, Helen B., 259
Librarian, and story hour, 130; and basic library skills, 199; and gifted pupil, 344; cooperation with, 365
Library, school, 6, 233; classroom, 21, 28, 232, 233; and reading program, 34; card catalog, 222; community, 232; access to, 268
Library experiences, 93
Library skills, 198
Liddle, William, 273
Life, 51, 255
Lima, Margaret, 49
Linguistic approach, 180, 200, 206–207
Linguistic maturity, 86
Linguistics, structural, 9, 116–118; and reading formulae, 121; and reading, 206; and illiterates, 281

423

Lip and throat movement, in silent reading, 197
Lipkin, William, 234
Listening, teaching, 90; and linguistics, 116; correlated with reading, 147; enhancing, 160; and vocabulary building, 162; and reading, 165–168; significance of, 165; nature, levels, and kinds of, 168; and slow learner, 327
Listening capacity test, 290, 291
Listening development, 171–174
Listening skills, development of, 169–170
Listening span, 170
Literary background, of teacher, 258
Literature, defined, 127; scope of, 128; recommended materials, 132–144; realistic, 136; grasp of, 258. *See also* Children's literature, Young people's literature.
Literature program, appraisal of, 152; goals of, 128–129; evaluating, 149–155
Little Engine That Could, The, 135
Little Fellow, 35
Little House, The, 53
Little House in the Big Woods, 235
Little Owl Stories, 196
Little Women, 55, 237
Little Wonder Books, 315
Littlest Mouse, The, 68
Loban, Walter, 278
Local resources, 365
Logical thinking, and slow learner, 330
Logs, and determining needs, 64
Longings, middle graders, 237
Look, 51, 255
Lorge, Irving, 120
Lorge-Thorndike Intelligence Test, 96
Love needs, 61
Lowenfeld, Viktor, 341

MacAllister, Mariana K., 259, 347
McCloskey, Robert, 53, 196, 346
McCracken, Glenn, 18, 201, 202
McCullough, Constance M., 44, 214, 242
McDowell, J. B., 104
McGuffey, William Holmes, 26–27
McGuffey Readers, 27
Machine teaching, 34
McKee, Paul, 190, 202, 273
McLaughlin, William J., 345
McMahan, Allan, 6
McWilliams, Earl M., 342, 347

Magazines, 254; interest in, 51; children's, 196, 232; middle-graders' choice, 238; accessibility of, 366; sources of, 405
Mailman, The, 331
Major Work Classes (Cleveland), 339
Make Way for Ducklings, 1, 53, 196
Maps, 227, 232; interpreting, 222
Marginal listening, 168
Martignoni, Marguerite, 127
Martin, Clyde I., 161
Martin, David, 175
Masefield, John, 3
Maslow, Abraham, 61, 72
Mass media, effect of, 44; influence of, 49; and reading, 52, 128; middle graders and, 235; popularity of, 254; and gifted pupil, 345
Materials, associated with ideas, intermediate grades, 215, 220–221, 223; for reading, 229–233; teacher-made, 232; instruction, 256–260
Mathematics, reading in, 227–228
Maturity, and reading, 14; and developmental tasks, 63; mental development, 80, 104, 234
Mauck, Inez L., 43
Meaning, search for, 17; and clarity, 164; development of, 192–195; clarifying, 192; extending, 192–193; reading for, 217; comprehension, 374
Measurement, of reading skills, 10
Mechanical aids, 260
Mechanical devices, and reading speed, 274
Melcher, Frederic G., 151–152
Memorization, outmoded, 160
Mencken, H. L., 2
Mental ability, and slow learner, 324–325; and tests, 296
Mental age, and phonics, 104, 189
Mental development, 84
Mental health, and basic needs, 59; reading promotes, 65; of teacher, 360
Mental maturity, 80
Mental tests, 81; and pupil needs, 251. *See also* tests by name.
Mentally advanced pupil. *See* Gifted pupil.
Mersand, Joseph, 278
Metropolitan Achievement Tests, 296, 308
Metropolitan Readiness Test, 88, 98
Michigan, University of, and reading program, 271

Middle childhood, and developmental tasks, 63
Middle grades, evaluation procedure, 233
Middle Moffat, 235
Mike Mulligan and His Steam Shovel, 135
Millay, Edna St. Vincent, 260, 348
Milne, A. A., 346
Minnich, Harvey C., 27
Mirsky, Reba P., 235
Mr. Bell Invents the Telephone, 346
Mr. T. W. Anthony Woo, 68
Moffats, The, 235
Monroe, Marion, 313
Monroe Revised Silent Reading Test, 309
Monroe-Sherman Group Diagnostic Reading Aptitude and Achievement Tests, 295
Montessori materials, 209
Mooney Check List, 64
Moralistic tone, in books, 26
More Chucklebait, 347
Morphemes, 207
Morphology, 207
Morrison, Coleman, 299, 357
Mother Goose, 50
Motivation, and reading program, 23; play and, 44; and bibliotherapy, 67; gaining insight to, 69; and reading, middle graders, 238; and reading program, 249; and illiterates, 284; and gifted child, 342
Motor development, 83, 91
Movies, 93, 255; overshadow reading, 43; interests in, 48–49; and interest inventory, 181
Murphy Durrell Diagnostic Reading Readiness Test, 98
Music, 93; readings in, 259; and gifted pupil, 349
My Weekly Reader, 196, 232, 315
Mystery stories, 51, 237
Mythology, 50

Nash, Ogden, 346
National Council of Teachers of English, 159, 363
National Society for the Study of Education, 340
Nation's Schools, The, 242
Nayder, Claribel M., 55
Needs, developmental, 234–239; recognizing, 246; determining, 251–255; of slow learner, 323–326, 327; of gifted pupil, 345; estimating, 378

Negro, culturally deprived, 276; deficiencies in reading, 277
Nelson-Denny Reading Test, 252
Neurological factor, and retarded reader, 296
New Castle Plan, 180, 200–202
New England Primer, 25, 26
New York City, readiness program, 276
Newbury, John, 152
Newbury Medal, 151, 152
Newbury Medal books, list of, 412
Newland, Ernest T., 320
News magazines, 51, 255
Newsmap, 282
Newspaper reading, 268
Newspapers, 232
Newstime, 232
Newsweek, 15, 315
Newton, Eunice Shaed, 277, 278
Nichols, Ralph G., 170
Nicholson, Alice K., 94, 95
Non-English-speaking pupils, 279, 324
Nonfiction, interest in, 51; middle-graders preference, 238; comprehension of, 273
Non-oral reading program, 18
Northwestern Psycho-Educational Clinic, 70
Northwestern University, and reading problem of undergraduates, 269
Northwestern University Interest Inventory, 40
Northwestern University–Office of Education, and interests, 48; and reading preferences, 50–51; occupational study, 52
Norvell, George W., 20, 30, 49, 56, 268

Oakland (California) study, on socio-economic levels, 44
Objectivity, in tests, 391
Observation, and determining needs, 64
Occupational preferences, 254. *See also* Vocation.
Oden, Melita, 344
Old Woman and Her Pig, The, 132
Old Yeller, 55
Olson, Willard, 80
Omission of letters, in words, 190
Onion John, 235
Open ended composition, and determining needs, 64
Opposites, 193
Oral communications, 159

Oral composition, and written, 161
Oral expression, and illiterates, 282
Oral reading, 18, 147, 171; skill development, 54; and vocabulary, 110; and linguistics, 116; and silent reading, 173, 224; developing skills in, 197–198; phrasing and inflection, 198; improving, 215; development of, 226; and illiterates, 282; standardized tests, 391
Oral tests, and slow learner, 325
Organismic age, 80
Organization, of ideas, materials, intermediate grades, 215, 223
Organized games, 43
Orthography, 207
Other lands, stories of, reading list, 141–142
Otis, Arthur S., 86
Otis Quick Scoring Mental Ability Test, 85, 96, 252
Our War, 282
Outdoor activities, middle graders, 236
Outlines, 223
Oversimplification, of linguistics problem, 117

Paintbox Summer, 66
Painter, W. I., 120
Painting, 93
Pamphlets, 232
Pancake, The, 132
Pantomime, 92
Paperbacks, 268, 359
Parent-teacher conferences, 364
Parent-teacher evaluation, of literature program, 154
Parents, role of, in reading program, 34; and vocabulary building, 163
Parent's Guide in Children's Reading, A, 127
Paresly, Kenneth M., 86
Passive Listening, 168
Passow, A., Harry, 62
Patty, W. W., 120
Peanuts the Pony, 196
Peer relationships, 367; and bibliotherapy, 67–68
Penty, Ruth C., 243, 244, 245
Perception, and phonics, 103; auditory-visual, 190; and disadvantaged pupils, 209
Perceptual ability, 94
Perceptual development, and disadvantaged pupil, 278

Periodicals, interest in, 51. *See also* Magazines, Newspapers.
Personal adjustment, 29; and bibliotherapy, 68; and reading ability, 253; and slow learner, 333
Personal development, 10
Personal experiences, of illiterates, dramatizing, 282
Personal motivation, and developmental tasks, 63
Personal problems, reading answers, 65; answering, 217; and gifted pupil, 345, 346
Personality, insight into, 129; growth in, 261; of teacher, 357
Personality problems, and retarded reader, 293
Pescosolido, John, 368
Peter Rabbit, 135
Pets, 237; interest in, 52. *See also* Animals.
Phonemes, 188, 207
Phonetic training, and social development, 111
Phonic approach, to word identification, 101; in remedial reading, 313
Phonic characters, 38
Phonic instruction, 18
Phonic study, history of, 102
Phonics, 102, 191; criticism of, 16–17; research on, 103; readiness for, 105; and vocabulary building, 162; and interdependence of listening and reading, 165; and mental age, 189; New Castle Plan, 202
Phonics instruction, 104
Photographs, and experiences, 185
Phrase recognition, 197; adult, 270
Phrasing, and oral reading, 198
Physical condition, 79
Physical development, and reading readiness, 75; of slow learner, 324
Physical environment, effect of, 59; of classroom, 366
Physical readiness, 83
Physiological needs, 61
Picture books, and pre-primers, 186; and slow learners, 327
Picture dictionaries, 204
Pictures, 232; and enrichment, 92, 192
Pierpont, John, 26
Pintner General Ability Test, 96
Pintner Intelligence Test, 297
Pitman, Sir James, 207, 208
Planning, and individualized reading, 22

Play interests, 42–45; determining, 41; range of activities, 44–45, 93; favorite, 44–45; and instruction, 44
Plays, 148, 237
Playhouse 90, 55
Pleasure, reading as, 1, 10, 129, 195
Poetry, 143–145, 237, 259, 359; interest in, 51; and oral reading, 54, 198; writing, 144; standards for, 151
Poling, Dorothy, 295
Pooley, Robert C., 117, 123, 127, 161, 164
Poor readers, 4, 113; aid to, 7; incidence of, 16; at high school level, 29, 243, 244; and remembering detail, 220; adult, 268. *See also* Retarded reader.
Potter, Beatrix, 135
Poverty, and learning ability, 322
Powell, Marvin, 86
Practice materials, 230
Prairie Schools, 239
Pratt, Fletcher, 235
Pratt, L. E., 168, 169
Preconceived ideas, and reading, 70
Prefixes, 191, 207
Prejudices, and reading, 69
Preparation, and listening, 170
Pre-primer, and vocabulary building, 30, 39; introducing, 185; supplementary, 186
Preschool children, basic needs, 59; speech training for, 105; readiness program, 202
Presentation, adequacy of, 222
Preston, Ralph C., 274, 297
Preventive program, 33
Primary grades, reading instruction, 180–212; and gifted pupil, 347
Primary grades reading list, folk and fairy tales, 133; animal stories, 134; realistic literature, 136; regional stories, 137; biography, 138; other lands, 141; poetry, 143–145
Primary Mental Ability Test, 392
Primers, and vocabulary, 30, 31
Principal ideas, reading for, 217
Printed materials, readability of, 118–120
Private Pete, 281, 282
Problem solving, reading for, 228–229
Problems, and bibliotherapy, 68; insight into, 129
Program, of individualized reading, 22
Programmed learning, 34
Progress, individual, 11

Progressive Achievement Tests, 16–17
Pronunciation, 17, 218; and phonics, 103; and oral reading, 173
Proof, finding, 221
Proof of the Pudding, 127
Protestant Tutor, The, 25
Psychological motives, and developmental needs, 62
Psychologists, and teaching, 364
Public schools, criticism of, 14
Punctuation marks, 161
Pupil-dictated charts, 163
Pupil-teacher conference, 21
Pupils, determining needs of, 251–255
Puppet shows, 92, 148
Purposes, and reading program, 17, 217; in listening skills, 169; recognizing, 246

Questionnaires, on interest, 41; and interest inventory, 181

Race, and ability, 277
Radio, overshadows reading, 43; interest in, 48–49; and interest inventory, 181; improvement of programs, 255
Random House, All About Series, 231
Rapid reading, 266; flexibility in, 224; adult, 270
Rapport, need for, 63–64
Readability, 101; improving, 119–120; concept formulae, 119–120
Readability formulae, 119; criteria of, 120, evaluation of, 121
Reader, immature, 113
Reader's Digest, 315, 329
Readers' Guide to Periodical Literature, 222
Readiness, composite of factors, 76–78; importance of, 78; enriching, 92; materials for, criticized, 94; for phonics, 105; listening, 169; and slow learner, 326. *See also* Reading readiness.
Readiness activities, by grade level, 95
Readiness books, 94
Readiness problems, background and ability, 226
Readiness program, experiences in, 89–94; in kindergarten, 202
Reading, special values, 2–4; defined, 7–8; and thinking process, 19; textbooks and, 27; voluntary, 39, 51, 145; overshadowed, 43; and socioeconomic level, 44; television a

427

stimulus, 55; continuing process, 76; and behavior, 69–72; and vocabulary development, 110; television conflicts with, 128; independence in, 145; correlation of, with listening, 147, and other languages, 160; and speaking, 162–164; and experience, 163; and writing, 174–176; independent level of, 186; purpose in, 195; for pleasure, 195; for recreation, 195; new approaches to, 200–210; linguistics and, 207; types of, 217; in content field, 226–229; and problem study, 228–229; materials and resources for, 229–233; and developmental needs, 234; special classes, 248; and interest, results, 254; for illiterates, 282; and verbally gifted, 341; advanced, 345; an individual acquisition, 356

Reading ability, range in, 4; individual, 253; variability in, 256; college and, 265; adult, improving, 268; and disadvantaged pupil, 277; slow reader, evaluating, 325; and gifted pupil, 344–345

Reading Accelerator, 249, 272, 275

Reading achievement, studies of, 15–16

Reading activities, 49–52

Reading attainment, surveys of, 14

Reading center, 366

Reading: Chaos and Cure, 17

Reading comprehension, 4

Reading Comprehensive Tests, 309

Reading consultant, 249

Reading development, evaluation of, 373–396

Reading differences, individual, 369

Reading disability, diagnosing, 300–312; standard tests, 301–302; diagnosing informally, 302, 311, 312; tests for, 303–309

Reading experiences, informal, 185; providing, 367

Reading factors, research on, 374

Reading guidance, 128

Reading Guidance, 259

Reading habits, improving, 255; intermediate grades, 214, 215–229

Reading instruction, effective, 2–7; history of, 14–36; primary grades, 180–212; intermediate grades, 213–241; junior and senior high, 242–264; college students and adults, 265–288; college assumes responsibility, 266

Reading interest, 10, need for, 5–6; and skills, 6; and pupil interests, 41; sex differences, 49, 50; middle graders, 236; developing, 245; investigating, 254; adult level, 268; and gifted pupil, 349

Reading for Interest Series, 28

Reading inventories, 390

Reading Laboratories, 28

Reading Ladders for Human Relations, 259

Reading level, 15

Reading lists, 133–144; intermediate, 133, 134, 135, 136, 137, 139, 140, 141, 145; junior high, 133, 134, 135, 137, 138, 139, 140, 141, 145; primary, 133, 134, 136, 137, 138, 141, 145; senior high, 133, 134, 135, 137, 138, 139, 140, 141, 145

Reading materials, choice of, 21; accessibility of, 366; evaluating, 370

Reading matter, types of, 258

Reading maturity, 14

Reading methods, criticisms of, 16–20

Reading period, 22

Reading preference, 49–52; tables, 50–51

Reading problems, at college level, 266, 269; specialists in, 364

Reading process, and developmental needs, 65–71

Reading proficiency, 38

Reading program, and human needs, 6; effective, 6–7; developmental, 7–8; non-oral, 18; characteristics of, 29–35; textbook and supplementary material, 32; and individual needs, 66; and children's literature, 127–132; goals, 128–129; secondary school, 129; reading lists, 132–144; balanced, 172, 368; basal approach, 180; continuity in, 213–214; establishing, 245; administering, 247–251; older pupils, 248; and reading needs, 258; college, 271; for disadvantaged, 278; gifted pupil, 343–346; strengthening, 363; planning, 365

Reading rate, 257, 359; measuring, 224; improving, 272; and slow learners, 326. See also Reading speed.

Reading Rate Controller, 275

Reading readiness, 75–100; basic concepts, 75–83; factors in, 78–83; determining, 83–88

Reading Readiness Status Score, 88–89

Reading Readiness Tests, 86–88, 97–98
Reading retardation, 4, 289
Reading Roundup Series, 257
Reading Skill Program, 21–22
Reading skills; development of, 3; improving, 4–5; and program, 31; promoting, 55; and audience reading, 147; reading for purpose, 195; in older pupils, 242; improving, 255; adult, acquiring, 270
Reading speed, and comprehension, 273; and mechanical devices, 274
Reading status, 261, studying, 251
Reading surveys, 392
Reading teacher, 356–371; defined, 356; personal assets, 357; reading by, 358; and challenge to, 359; adjustment, 360; traits of, 361; health of, 362; professional qualifications, 362–370; and experiences, 367
Reading textbook, development of, 24–29
Reading vocabulary, 162; development of, 90; in primary grades, 187
Realistic literature, 136
Reassurance, 59
Recall, 219
Recordings, 260; and literature, 130; sources of, 403–404
Records, keeping of, and individualized reading, 22. *See also* records by type.
Recreation, and reading, 10; range of activities, 44–45; and determining needs, 64; reading for, 195; vicarious, 255
Recreational interest, 42–45; determining, 41
Recreational opportunity, school and community, 255
Re-experience, 128
Reference manuals, 222
Regional stories (U.S.), 137–138
Rejection, 82; and bibliotherapy, 68
Relationship, and bibliotherapy, 67–68
Relationships, word, 193; cause-and-effect, recognizing, 197; interest and high marks, 254; family and school, 257; peer, 67–68, 366
Relevancy, factual, 221
Reliability, of tests, 391
Remedial instruction, 7
Remedial reading, 33, 289–318; and older pupils, 245; at college level,

266; specialized procedures, 313; program for, 314; in regular classroom, 317
Remember, reading to, 215, 219–220
Repetition, and slow learner, 333
Resourcefulness, 60
Resources, reading, 229–233; local, 365
Retardation, areas of, 332
Retarded readers, 37, 113, 290–312; and reading instruction, 275–285; teaching of, 279–285; identifying, 290; causes of, 291; interest factor, 292; emotional factor, 293; visual factor, 294; auditory factor, 295; lateral dominance factor, 296; brain damage factor, 297; intelligence factor, 297; home and environment factors, 298; teaching factor, 299
Rex, Buck R., Jr., 345
Rhyming test, 88
Rhythm, 259, and poetry, 143
Rhythmic expression, 91, 93
Riding the Pony Express, 68
Riessman, Frank, 275, 276
Rinsland, F. W., 112
Romances, 51
Room dividers, 366
Rosenzweig Picture Frustration Study, 293
Roswell, Florence G., 188
Rounds, Glen, 134
Rural students, abilities of, 277
Russell, David H., 17, 67, 69, 77, 78, 103, 128, 129, 147, 153, 154, 213, 217, 218, 229, 253, 328

Sabaroff, Rose, 103
Safety needs, 61
St. Louis (Missouri), pre-school program, 276
San Diego County (California), and language-experience approach, 205
San Leandro (California), television study, 46
Sandburg, Carl, 143, 260, 346
Sartain, Harry W., 22
Satisfaction, and developmental needs, 235
Saturday Evening Post, 255
Saunders, Dorothy O., 205
Sawyer, Ruth, 146
Scanning, 222
Schneyer, J. Wesley, 297
School libraries, 6, 233
School texts. *See* Textbooks.

429

Science, reading in, 228, 229
Science fiction, 51
Science Research Association, 28. *See also* SRA —
Scientific reports, 222
Scientific terminology, 228
Scoggin, Margaret, 347
Scott, Lloyd F., 46
Scott-Foresman Curriculum Foundation Series, 28
Seashore, R. H., 112
Seashore's Measures of Musical Talent, 296
Secondary school reading program, 129
Security, and reading, 37; need for, 59; promotion of, 65
Sedentary pursuits, 44; interests in, 43
Seegers, J. C., 112
Self-actualization, need for, 61
Self-appraisal, 233
Self-appraisal conferences, 154
Self-confidence, 60; and slow learner, 333
Self-insight, reading and, 65
Self-instruction devices, 34
Self-reliance, and slow learners, 333
Self-selection, and reading program, 23
Semantics, 116; and reading, 9; and illiterates, 281
Seminars, third-grade, 204
Senior high school. *See* High School.
Sensitivity, and word use, 259
Sentence meaning, 194
Sequence, recognizing, 197
Sequential arrangement, 223
Sequential development, 3
Sequential skills, development of, 230
Seredy, Kate, 141, 234
Seuss, Dr., 173, 196, 344, 346
Sex differences, 80; and reading interest, 49-50
Sexton, Elmer K., 104
Shaw, Philip B., 265, 266
Shedlock, Marie L., 146
Sheldon, William G., 248, 300
Shep, the Farm Dog, 54
Sheridan, Marion C., 345
Shertzer, Bruce, 340
Shippen, Katherine B., 346
Shirley Temple, 55
Shores, J. Harlan, 274
Shrodes, Caroline, 67, 253
Sibling rivalry, 68
Siegel, Max, 271

Sight vocabulary, 185; primary, 187
Sight words, 94
Silberman, C. E., 209, 276
Silent reading, 3, 18; and vocabulary development, 110; and linguistics, 116; and oral reading, 173; of preprimers, 185; developing skills, 197-198; lip and throat movement, 197; increasing speed, 215, 224; and illiterates, 282; standardized tests, 391
Silent reading abilities, 388
Silent Reading Diagnostic Tests, 303-309
Silent Reading Hour, 27
Silent reading test, and slow learner, 325
Simple recall, 219
Simpson, Elizabeth, 247
Single subject approach, 159
Sister Mary Nila, O.S.F., 77
Sizemore, Robert, 41, 166, 167
Skaar, Grace, 53
Skills, and effective reading, 2; and interest, 6; learning, 9; development, 10, 33; and interest, 38-39; oral reading, 54; prereading, 85; in language arts, 161; listening, 169-170; sequential introduction, 180; word analysis, 187, 189, 217-218; basic library, 198; with little utility, 191; intermediate grades, 214, 215-229; sequential, 230; building, approach to, 230; broadening, materials for, 230; reading, 245; cultivating mastery of, 246; at high school level, developing, 258; assessment of, 369; basic, identifying, 373
Skills development program, 33
Slow learner, 196, 320-336; identifying, 320; characteristics of, 322; physical development, 324; mental ability, 324; educational status, 325; interests, 326; teacher and, 326-330; needs of, 327; and curriculum, 330-334
Slum children, teaching, 209
Smith, Dora V., 158, 177
Smith, Donald E. P., 271
Smith, Henry P., 9, 10-11, 18, 68, 80, 216, 224, 226, 227, 301
Smith, Irene, 151, 152
Smith, Nila Banton, 82, 104, 299
Snellen chart, 79
Snow White, 237

430

Snyder, Alan, 274
Social adjustment, 29, 82; bibliotherapy and, 68; and reading ability, 253
Social development, 10, 84, and reading readiness, 75
Social environment, 366
Social factors, and readiness, 82
Social problems, reading for answers to, 65, 217
Social studies, reading in, 226
Social values, 235
Socially disadvantaged pupil, reading program for, 275–285
Society, and developmental tasks, 63
Socioeconomic localities, effect of, on reading, 44
Socioeconomic status, and reading skills, 4; and poor readers, 244; and ability, 277; and retarded reader, 298
Sound patterns, and poetry, 143
So'm I, 54, 66
Sounds separate, 188
Source materials, 256, selection of, 198
Spache, George D., 16, 119, 120, 206, 220, 293, 329
Speaking, and reading, 162–164; relationships with reading, 164; and English usage, 164
Speaking vocabulary, 162
Special Training Units, illiterates and, 279, 282
Special vocabularies, 111; and slow learners, 331
Specialization, by teachers, 363
Speech, 84; preschool training, 105; and language development, 158; and intonation, 161
Speech defects, and oral reading, 173
Speech development, 90
Speech problems, and insecurity, 90
Speed reading, 250; adult, 270. See also Rapid reading.
Speer, George S., 272
Spelling, and televiewing, 46; and illiterates, 282
Spelling ability, 37
Sperry, Armstrong, 328
Spiegler, Charles, 55, 322
Sports, interests in, 43; outdoors, 236; indoors, 237
SRA Developmental Reading Kits, 316
SRA Mental Ability Test, 86

SRA Primary Abilities Test, 96
SRA Primary Mental Abilities Test, 252
SRA Reading Laboratory, 256
SRA Reading Record, 326
SRA Youth Inventory, 68
Stability, need for, 59
Standardization, of tests, 391
Standardized intelligence tests, 85–86. *See also* tests by name.
Standardized inventories, and determining needs, 64
Standardized Reading Readiness Test, 86–88
Standardized tests, and evaluating growth, 261; administration and interpretation, 364; and reading difficulties, 369; evaluation, 390
Standards, for listening, 170
Stanford Achievement, 15–16
Stanford-Binet Intelligence Scale, 96, 295, 325, 392
Star Danced, A., 346
Starter Test, 316
Stauffer, Russell G., 32
Stevens, Leonard A., 170
Stimulation, and ideas, 10; and gifted child, 342
Stivers, Eugene, 340
Stolarz, Theodore, 269, 271, 275
Story hour, 130
Story presentation, 197
Story of Private Pete, The, 281, 282
Story-teller, 55
Story telling, 91, 146
Story Telling, 127
Strang, Ruth, 8, 242, 297, 362
Stratemeyer, Florence B., 62
Strawberry Girl, 1–2, 66, 137, 235
Streamline Your Reading, 317
Street Rod, 66
Strong, LaVerne, 149
Stroud, J. B., 81
Structural analysis, and vocabulary building, 162
Structural linguistics, 9, 116–118
Stuart, Jesse, 235
Success, and reading skill, 3; desire for, 257
Sucksdorff, Arne, 171, 175
Suffixes, 191, 207
Summarizing, 223, 224
Superior students, challenging, 16. *See also* Gifted pupils.
Supplementary books, and pre-primers, 186

431

Supplementary materials, for illiterates, 282, 285; sources of, 403–404
Supplementary reading material, 31, 186, 230, 231, 397–402
Survey of the Education of Gifted Children, A., 340
Survey tests, 301
Sutton, Rachel S., 77
Swenson, Esther J., 43
Syllabication, 191
Symbols, and mathematics, 228
Sympathy, 64; need for, 59
Syntax, 207
Synthetic approach, to word identification, 101, 102
Systematic instruction, 38
Systematic records, and evaluating growth, 261

Taber, Gladys, 4, 54
Table of contents, 221
Tables, interpreting, 222
Tachistoscope, 270
Tale of the Fiords, 171
Tape recorders, 232
Tarkington, Booth, 66
Tasks, specific and related, 38; development of, 128–129; developmental, 234–239
Taylor, Sidney, 235
Teacher, preparation, 19; and children's literature, 130–132; knowledge of poetry, 143; and evaluation of literature, 152; change in classroom practice, 159; developmental program, 246; attitudes of, and reading program, 248; knowledge of books, 258; and illiterate, 293; retarded reader, 299; and slow learner, 326–330; influence of, on pupil, 358; fullness of living, 359; adjusted, 360; physical health of, 362; attitudes, 362; professional advancement, 363; and reading program, 363; and special needs, 364; and environment, 365. *See also* Reading teacher.
Teacher committees, and reading programs, 248
Teacher-made materials, 232
Teacher observations, 377; forms for, 83–85
Teacher-pupil evaluation, of literature program, 152
Teacher training programs, 357
Teacher Who Helped Me Most, The, 361

Teacher's Guide to Children's Books, A., 66
Teacher's manuals, 27
Teaching Language in the Elementary Schools, 159
Teaching methods, frequency of change, 19; and reading program, 248
Techniques, word recognition, 15
Teen-age Tales, 254
Televiewing. See Television.
Television, 45–48; overshadows reading, 43, 45, 51; and socioeconomic level, 44; difference in attainment by watchers, 46; favorite programs, 47; influence of, 47; effect of, on studying, 48; conflict with reading, 128; and interest inventory, 181; and Denver Plan, 202; educational 202; middle graders and, 235; antidote for, 236; popularity of, 254; undesirable aspects, 255; improving programs, 255; and slow learners, 327
Television programs, stimulate interest, 55; offsetting threat, 56
Templeman, William Darby, 110, 111
Tennis, interest in, 43
Terman, Lewis M., 49, 338, 339, 344
Terman, Sybil, 17
Tests:
  Achievement, 16–17, 303, 304, 305, 306, 307, 308, 309
  Aptitude, 295
  Basic skills, 3
  Diagnostic reading, 303, 305, 306, 307, 309
  Educational development, 252, 307
  Intelligence, group, 82, 85, 86, 96, 251, 392; individual, 96, 325, 392
  Musical talent, 296
  Oral reading, 306, 307, 325
  Phonics, 303
  Reading readiness, 97, 98
  Silent reading, 252, 303–309
  True-false, 220
  Verbal, 293
  Whisper, 79
Textbooks, elementary, 25; readability of, 27; secondary, 29; debatable role of, 31; selection and use, 32, 119–120; repetitious, 209; in high school, 256; adult, 270
Thee, Hannah!, 140, 234
They All Want to Write, 205
They Were Strong and Good, 235
Thomas, Edith, 369

Thinking, promotion of, 10; and language experience approach, 203; wishful, 237; logical, and slow learner, 330
Thinking level, 229
Thinking process, and reading, 19
Thirty Seconds Over Tokyo, 237
Thirty-one Brothers and Sisters, 235
Thought, trends of, 169; provoking, 257
Thought units, development, 197, 216
Three Billy Goats Gruff, 132
Three Little Pigs, 132
Tidyman, Willard F., 161
Tiegs, Ernest W., 15
Tinker, Miles A., 291, 300, 310
Tom Sawyer, 258
Tomorrow's Illiterates, 14, 15
Tooze, Ruth, 127, 358, 367
Torch Lighters, The, 357
Townsend, Agatha, 86
Trabue, M. R., 159
Trace, Arthur S., Jr., 14
Traditional orthography, 207
Traxler, Arthur E., 77, 242, 289, 293, 294, 296, 297, 298
Traxler High School Reading Test, 252
Treasure for the Taking, 66, 127
Trembling Years, The, 66
Tronsburg, Josephine, 342, 347
True, M. B. C., 49
True Books, 196
True-False tests, 220
Truth, in biography, 150
Tunis, Edwin, 235
Twain, Mark, 258
Two Little Bears, 53
Tyler, Fred T., 81
Tyler, Ralph, 120
Typography, and readability, 119

Understanding, 64; reading and, 2, 3, 29; through reading, 3; of others, 129; building of, 169; and disadvantaged pupils, 209; of adults, 234; of child by child, 255; ability to, 216
Unit Study Books, 315
U.S. Army, and teaching of illiterates, 279–285; 321
Urban student, abilities of, 277
Utley, Ishmel, 320, 321
Utterances, and linguistics, 207

Valentine Cat, The, 53
Validity, 391

Values, understanding, 234
Van Allen, R., 202–204, 205
Van Buskirk, Golda, 281
Van Wagnen Reading Readiness Scales, 98
Variability, in reading formulae, 121
Veatch, Jeannette, 117, 118
Verbal direction and slow learners, 330
Verbal expression, and reading readiness, 83
Verbal factor, 374
Verification, of facts, 221
Verse pattern, 259
Vicarious experience, 128
Vincent, H. Lee, 60
Vision, 79
Visual acuity, 79
Visual aids, 92; and illiterates, 280, 284
Visual approach, to listening, 167
Visual defects, and slow learner, 324
Visual development, 84
Visual discrimination, 79, 91, 94; of words, 77
Visual factor, and retarded reader, 294
Visual material, and reading progress, 34
Visual perception, 188–189; and Denver Plan, 202
Vocabulary, pre-primers and primers, 39; and silent and oral reading, 110; special, 111; and relation to I.Q., 111; size, 111; at high school and college levels, 115; speaking, 162; and instructional level, 186; primary grade, 187; in social studies, 226, in science, 228
Vocabulary building, 27, 30, 90; 111, 113, 217; and word recognition, 101-126; and listening, 162; reading and speaking, 162–163; primary grades, 187; and superior student, 256; adult, 270; and disadvantaged pupil, 278; slow learner, 330–331
Vocabulary building exercises, 110
Vocabulary control, 31
Vocabulary notebook, 228
Vocation, and reading skills, 3; and gifted student, 346
Vocational interest, 52
Vocational preference, 53; middle grades, 238
Voluntary reading, 39, 51, 145
Vowel sounds, audio-visual perception, 190

433

Wagner, Eva Bond, 76, 80
Waite, William H., 4
Walcutt, Charles C., 14, 15, 17
Walker, Elinor, 259
Walt Disney Story Books, 196
Walter, Nina W., 144
Waples, Douglas, 70
Ward, Edward G., 27
Ward, Lynd, 344
Watch the Puppy Grow, 196
Watts, A. F., 190
Way of the Story Teller, The, 146
Webster, Noah, 26, 102
Wechsler Bellevue Intelligence Scales, 295
Wechsler Intelligence Scale for Children, 96, 325, 392
Wechsler Verbal Scale, 293
Westerns, interest in, 51
Westover, Frederick L., 272
What Ivan Knows That Johnny Doesn't, 14
Wheel on the School, 141
Whipple, Gertrude, 113
Wheeler, Lester R., 295, 296
Wheeler, Opal, 349
Wheeler, Viola D., 295, 296
Whisper test, 79
White, E. B., 134
Whole word approach, 101
Wiese, M. Bernice, 131, 132
Wilder, Laura Ingalls, 235
Will and Nicholas readers, 54
Wilson, Frank T., 339
Wilt, Miriam E., 165
Wind in the Willows, 135
Wishes, and bibliotherapy, 67
Wishful thinking, middle graders, 237
Wittich, Walter Arno, 233
Witty, Paul A., 7, 12, 37, 38, 41, 42, 46, 47, 65, 70, 81, 88, 95, 113, 115, 116, 129, 146, 150, 161, 173, 175, 181, 216, 225, 236, 242, 254, 255, 266, 275, 281, 292, 293, 294, 295, 296, 314, 328, 337, 338, 340, 343, 352, 360, 361, 393
———— and Blumenthal, Rochelle, 352
———— and Coomer, Ann, 343
———— and Fitzwater, James P., 115
———— and Goldberg, Samuel, 281
———— and Grotberg, Edith, 115; 256, 328
———— and Kopel, David, 40, 295, 296, 314
———— and LaBrant, Lou, 116
———— and Kinsella, Paul, 46
———— and Martin, William, 175

———— and Sizemore, Robert A., 166, 167
————, Stolarz, Theodore and Cooper, William, 269, 271, 275
———— and Van Buskirk, Golda, 281
Witty-Kopel Child Diagnostic Study Record, 40
Witty-Kopel Interest Inventory, 314
Wood, Roger I., 271
Word analysis, history of, 102
Word analysis program, 189
Word analysis skills, 187, 189, 217–218
Word analysis techniques, and vocal development, 111
Word attack, and reading program, 23
Word Card Matching, 88
Word comprehension, 33
Word discrimination, 77
Word endings, 190
Word identification, 33, 101–102; goals, planned sequence, 106–108; and skills taught, 191
Word interpretation, 101, 109–117
Word lists, 111, 204; and illiterate, 280
Word mastery, 204
Word matching, 88
Word meanings, at primary level, 114; developing, 192
Word patterns, and poetry, 143
Word perception, 168
Word recognition, 15, 216; and vocabulary development, 101–126; promoting, 188
Word reinforcement, through books, 186
Word relationships, 193
Word repetition, and vocabulary building, 30
Word study, fostering, 187
Words, relationships of, 192–193; structure of, 207; abstract, comprehending, 114, 227; understanding and analyzing, 217; sensitivity to, 259
Work habits, 84
Workbooks, 19, 228; and experience, 163
World Almanac, The, 232
World Landmark publications, 138
World Landmark Series, 329
Worry, and bibliotherapy, 67
Wrightstone, J. Wayne, 15
Writing, skill in, 91; and language development, 158; and reading, 174–176; and illiterates, 282

Writing ability, 204
Written composition, and oral, 161

Yates, Elizabeth, 66, 346
Yearling, The, 55
Ylla, 53
Yoakum, Gerald, 120
Young America, 315

Young People (book list), 259
Young people's literature, 127–157
Your Child's Reading Today, 127
Your Job in the Army, 282
Your Reading, A Book List for Junior High Schools, 259

Zinkin, Vivian, 289